From Napoleon to the Second International

A. J. P. TAYLOR

From Napoleon to the Second International
Essays on Nineteenth-Century Europe

* * *

EDITED WITH AN INTRODUCTION

BY CHRIS WRIGLEY

ALLEN LANE
THE PENGUIN PRESS

ALLEN LANE
THE PENGUIN PRESS

Published by the Penguin Group
Penguin Books Ltd, 27 Wrights Lane, London w8 5 tz, England
Penguin Books USA Inc., 375 Hudson Street, New York, New York 10014, USA
Penguin Books Australia Ltd, Ringwood, Victoria, Australia
Penguin Books Canada Ltd, 10 Alcorn Avenue, Toronto, Ontario, Canada m4v 3b2
Penguin Books (NZ) Ltd, 182–190 Wairau Road, Auckland 10, New Zealand

Penguin Books Ltd, Registered Offices: Harmondsworth, Middlesex, England

First American edition published in 1994 by Viking Penguin, a division of Penguin Books USA Inc.
1 3 5 7 9 10 8 6 4 2

Copyright © Eva Taylor, 1993
All rights reserved

A CIP catalogue record for this book is available from the British Library

ISBN 0–7139–9113–5

Printed in England by Clays Ltd, St Ives plc
Set in Monophoto Baskerville

Contents

Introduction

Alan John Percivale Taylor (25 March 1906–7 September 1990) was a historian who commanded both a wide popular audience and the respect of his peers. From the end of the Second World War he combined a prolific output of historical studies with substantial journalistic writing and broadcasting. He became a leading radio and television personality soon after the war and remained so for some four decades.

Alan Taylor's historical writing was distinctive, both in its style and in the nature of the mind it revealed. He took great care in the presentation of his work, employing paradoxes and epigrams to make his reader reconsider the topic under discussion. He delighted in challenging received opinions, whether of the Right or of the Left. For Taylor, nothing historical should be taken for granted and no orthodoxy was sacrosanct. 'The problem of the historian,' he wrote in 1949 when reviewing a dull academic tome, 'is to write a book which shall be both accurate and interesting; the problem is not solved by writing a book that is accurate.' He may not have established a Taylor school of history but he did teach a generation of able younger historians to challenge received opinions and to consider carefully the stylistic presentation of their findings.

In terms of his own aims and objectives, Alan Taylor was successful as a writer of history. He admired the great stylists of previous centuries from Edward Gibbon and Thomas Babington Macaulay to Thomas Carlyle and Sir Walter Scott, and was not displeased when he was dubbed the modern Macaulay. Indeed as early as 1936 he reflected:

Macaulay claimed that his *History* had ousted the latest novel from the ladies' dressing table; no living historian, except Macaulay's nephew, Professor [G M] Trevelyan, can boast as much. The most important works of history often seem to the general reader dull and technical, while the popular successes usually merit the censure of the historian. It is no easy task to be both interesting and accurate.

Throughout his career he aimed to write work which attained a high scholarly standard yet which would sell to a wider body of readers than most academic historians reach. More than that, he hoped that his work would be distinctive: in Taylor's view this was the key to lasting fame as a historian. Thus in 1953 he rhetorically enquired:

What is it that such individual authors as, say, Sir Lewis Namier, E H Carr and Hugh Trevor-Roper have in common? Great scholarship, of course; but also literary mastery and clear personal convictions. A work of history, like any other book that is good, must bear its author's stamp. The reader should feel that no one else could have written this particular book in this particular way.

Alan Taylor's distinctiveness as a historian owed much to his own background. He was proud to be a northern radical of dissenting stock. He extolled a radical tradition which ran through John Wilkes, Charles James Fox, Richard Cobden, John Bright and others down to Michael Foot. One might add: and to Alan Taylor. Of Charles James Fox, the subject of an essay in this volume, he commented in a radio broadcast at the time of the 150th anniversary of Fox's death: 'Charles Fox became a saint for all who love liberty.' Historically quite probably true, but when such points were put by Taylor they carried his mark of approval. When invited to give the prestigious Ford Lectures at Oxford in 1956, he turned for his subject to those who had rejected, root and branch, Britain's established foreign policy. Thereafter he deemed the resulting book, *The Trouble Makers: Dissent over Foreign Policy 1792–1939* (London, Hamish Hamilton, 1957), to be his 'favourite brainchild'. A little earlier, in 1952, at the time of the tercentenary of the Society of Friends, he wrote to BBC Radio: 'I could offer John Bright. I am, with G N Clark, the only historian of Quaker training (and Clark is ashamed of it), and a school-fellow of Bright; so for once I'm qualified!'

*   *   *

Taylor's schooling was indeed Quaker – but his family background was Nonconformist, not Quaker. His father, Percy Lees Taylor, was the eldest partner in a family-owned Manchester-based cotton cloth exporting firm. According to Alan his father had earned the then large sum of £5,000 or more each year from 1898 until he sold his share of the business in 1920 at the peak of the post-war boom.

Alan Taylor's Quaker schooling at Bootham, York, between 1919 and 1924 was a major formative influence. (He was sent there, rather than to Rugby, because his parents did not approve of boys being required to join the Officers' Training Corps. His mother, a strong-willed woman of decidedly left-wing views, had warmly applauded the stance of her brother, Harry Thompson, as a conscientious objector during the First World War.) At Bootham Taylor continued to develop his intellectual abilities and found a new solitary pursuit, studying church architecture. He had been a precocious child, reading at an early age and exhibiting the Taylor and Thompson families' trait of being great arguers, over both current affairs and more philosophic matters. At Bootham he was encouraged in his studies and allowed to shine in discussions and debates. Though religious faith fell away from him there, he benefited in a secular way from the discussions and from the periods of silence of Society of Friends' meetings. His writing shows a tendency both to personify people or groups somewhat in the manner of *The Pilgrim's Progress* (a book he often read in his youth), and to deliver moral judgements. Bootham also encouraged his interest in John Bright, an interest represented by two essays in this volume.

However, until his marriage to his first wife Margaret Adams in 1931, it was Taylor's home life that exerted the most formative influence. He was close to his father and appears to have struggled hard to win the approval of his mother through skill in argument and intellectual ability. As an only child (an older sister had died of meningitis when only eighteen months old), he had been a much looked-after and spoiled boy. Both parents had moved from radicalism before the First World War to socialism after it. Leading Labour movement figures – Arthur Henderson, George Lansbury and Harry Pollitt among them – visited the Taylor household in the 1920s. Percy Taylor, despite being a retired wealthy man living partly on capital, had joined a general union and represented it on Preston Trades Council, a path later followed by his son, who in the mid-1930s gained experience in public speaking on Manchester Trades Council platforms. Alan was also influenced by his mother's close friend Henry Sara, a founder member of the Communist Party of Great Britain, who introduced him to various Marxist classics and to the communist press. Thus he was raised in a well-to-do but radical environment, being encouraged to read and to think for himself, and becoming a rather solitary and self-centred youth.

After narrowly failing to win a scholarship to Balliol, he was awarded one at Oriel. When he arrived in Oxford in October 1924 he brought with him not only a northern accent and a proud, secular Nonconformity but also radical political views. He had joined the Independent Labour Party at fifteen and in the summer of 1925 he joined the small contingent of university students in the Communist Party of Great Britain. This was partly due to the influence of Henry Sara, but was also probably a case of him putting his money where his mouth was. He was never afraid to draw attention to himself by shocking the more conventional with his views, and at Oriel the undergraduates were notably conventional.

For all this, he was a studious undergraduate who avoided most sports, other than rowing, and the Oxford Union. He continued to be an avid reader, to view old churches and to talk late into the night with a small circle of friends. Otherwise his world still revolved round his family. In 1925, after visiting the

Lake District (a favourite holiday location of the Taylor family),
he travelled round Russia with his mother and Henry Sara. In
his autobiography he recalled that, on seeing the mummified
Lenin, 'I decided then that he was a good man, an opinion I
have not changed.' During the General Strike of 1926 he
returned home to Preston and drove a car on behalf of the
local strike committee. In 1927 he graduated with first class
honours in History. He later affected surprise at this. Yet he had
read very widely and could apply his argumentative and original
mind well to essay questions.

   Alan Taylor's progress to professional historian has an element
of an older style about it; a little of the gentleman scholar. At
Oxford his parents had provided him with the then very rare
undergraduate luxury of a Rover sports car. After graduating they
provided him with an expensive six-room flat beside Hampstead
Heath, complete with housekeeper, while he worked as an articled
clerk (with a partnership arrangement) in his uncle Harry
Thompson's solicitors' practice. He had no taste for legal work,
however, even in a firm which specialized in representing the
Labour movement. He preferred to read, watch films or go to the
theatre, and after six months he returned to Oxford, where he
worked unsuccessfully on a prize essay on the foreign policy of
the parliamentary radicals of the 1830s and 1840s – a topic which
he later revised as part of *The Trouble Makers*. At the suggestion of
H W C Davis, then Regius Professor, he wrote to Professor A F
Pribram of Vienna to enquire if he would supervise research which
linked the British parliamentary and Viennese radicals in the
period before the 1848 revolutions. After visiting Pribram in
Vienna, he began research in the autumn of 1928.

   Alan Taylor's parents ensured that, by student standards, he
had a very comfortable time in Vienna. As well as wisely
spending money on private German lessons, he could afford to
eat out, learn to ride and skate, and regularly attend the opera
and concerts. In his second year in Vienna, by which time he
had won a Rockefeller Research Fellowship, he held a season
ticket for the Vienna Philharmonic Orchestra. In the 1920s

there can have been few who could have afforded to live in some comfort in central Vienna while conducting research in the state archive for two years.

Like most postgraduates, Taylor defined his own research area, doing so within Pribram's broad suggestion of Anglo-Austrian relations, 1848–1866. In the tradition of many Oxbridge gentleman scholars he never submitted his work for a higher degree, much to the chagrin of the authorities at Manchester University when he worked there. He did publish a book, *The Italian Problem in European Diplomacy 1847–1849* (Manchester University Press, 1934), and a substantial essay, 'European Mediation and the Agreement of Villafranca, 1859' (*English Historical Review*, 1936), largely based on this work. He also took the opportunity while in Vienna to work through the best German-language historical works. This provided a valuable grounding for his later work on the Habsburg Monarchy and German history as well as improving his grasp of the language. Alfred Pribram successfully recommended Taylor for his first academic job, at Manchester University from October 1930.

* * *

For the first three decades of Alan Taylor's academic career as a historian his subject matter was Europe between the French Revolution and the outbreak of war in 1939, with particular emphasis on the period 1848 to 1918, on Austria-Hungary and Germany, and on European international relations. This is partly reflected in his essays '1848', 'Bismarck and Europe' and, more generally, the 'Men of 1862'.

This choice of direction was encouraged not only by his research in Vienna and by his teaching commitments at Manchester (and from autumn 1938 at Oxford) but also by his background. His home life had been cosmopolitan in outlook, with reading and discussion greatly encouraged and with visitors such as Henry Sara extending the scope beyond British radicalism. He had travelled with his mother and Henry Sara on the

Continent, notably to Germany and Russia. At Oxford, while he had taken the reign of Richard II as his special subject, he had greatly enjoyed studying the French Revolution and the upheavals of 1848. His interest in European history had been stimulated by having had 'Sligger' (L Francis Fortescue) Urquhart of Balliol as his tutor for a year, Urquhart having much personal and family knowledge of nineteenth-century Europe. (He was later similarly stimulated by the first-hand knowledge of Lewis Namier, Michael Karolyi and Lord Beaverbrook.)

Alan Taylor's work on European history was very traditional in some major respects. Diplomatic history was very much in vogue as historians of many countries tried to explain why war had occurred in the summer of 1914. Indeed his own supervisor, Pribram, had changed his research field from Oliver Cromwell to the origins of the Great War. Taylor's early publications at Manchester University were based on his archival research in Vienna plus further primary work in London and Paris. Thereafter he came to rely heavily on published foreign policy documents, making careful use of a set of the fifty-four volumes of *Die grosse Politik* which he had bought from a German Jewish refugee in 1933. In writing his diplomatic history masterpiece, *The Struggle for Mastery in Europe 1848–1918* (Oxford University Press, 1954), he made a virtue of not adding some archival research to his extensive use of printed documents. Similarly, his short biography *Bismarck* (London, Hamish Hamilton, 1955) was written without consulting Bismarck's surviving records. The dangers of relying too heavily on printed diplomatic documents became apparent in *The Origins of the Second World War* (London, Hamish Hamilton, 1961), when the Nazi state's foreign policy was segregated from its domestic policy even though the two were dynamically linked. Moreover, although by his own admission *The Struggle for Mastery in Europe* dealt with 'the last age when Europe was the centre of the world', in *The Origins* his coverage remained Eurocentric, the book ending with the outbreak of war in western Europe and a brief mention that Russia and the USA were to enter the war in 1941.

Reliance on published diplomatic documents may well have contributed to him overemphasizing the importance of Britain and France during this period.

Much of Taylor's work was a study of High Politics: of emperors and premiers, rarely of politics in the regions or at grass-roots level. He often appears to have had an ambivalent attitude to men of power. Sometimes he was clearly fascinated by them – men such as Bismarck, Lloyd George and Lenin – and was much taken with the more agreeable of those whom he knew – Michael Karolyi, Max Beaverbrook, Eduard Beneš and Jan Masaryk. Yet in his role of sturdy Nonconformist he cocked a snook at the powerful and delighted in praising Cobbett (as in these essays), 'Captain Swing', the Chartists and more generally his 'Trouble Makers' over British foreign policy. He also varied his position as to the role of Great People (or, in his work, Great Men) in history. Thus in a 1950 radio broadcast on 'How History Should Be Written' he commented: 'I would say Napoleon, Bismarck, Lenin are the three who pulled our modern history almost out of step.' As this volume bears witness, he paid such figures much attention. Yet at other times he depicted Bismarck, the Kaiser and Hitler as responders to the events or forces of their times. Thus in *Bismarck* Alan Taylor observed: 'He always lived in the moment and responded to its challenge.' In *The Origins of the Second World War* he somewhat provocatively stated: 'Human blunders . . . usually do more to shape history than human wickedness. At any rate this is a rival dogma which is worth developing, if only as an academic exercise.'

And develop it he did. It became almost an 'accident prone' view of history (to quote his intellectual autobiography which opens this collection). In this view great men brilliantly improvise according to circumstances or, where things go wrong, humans are the victims of fate. This could be considered a fatalistic or even pessimistic view akin to much in Thomas Hardy's writings or to Shakespeare's tragic figure King Lear. Perhaps this part of his approach to the role of major individuals

in history owed something to the last vestiges of his youthful
Marxism. By making Hitler and the others opportunists he
avoided making any claim that a solitary individual could
determine a nation's fate. There was also a degree of economic
determinism behind his European history. German diplomacy,
whether under Bismarck, the Kaiser or Hitler, was likely to follow
certain courses. For, in his view, if the other powers permitted it,
Germany would inevitably dominate Europe because of its
geographic, demographic and economic advantages.

What made Taylor's European work outstanding, then, was
not the novelty of its topic or its approach. It was more his ability
to take reasonably well-known areas and make the reader see
them differently. He was fascinated by history and engaged in his
own debate with the past, unwilling to accept standard views
without challenge. In writing essays and books he applied his
intellect and his powers as a great arguer to the study of history.
From the 1940s he developed his ability to write a sustained
critique of the received wisdom on a subject, presenting it in a
lucid and sparkling style. He summed up this in his comment that
he possessed a 'ruthless intellect, criticizing everything, never
satisfied, always forcing up the standards of academic truth and
artistic achievement'. Books such as *The Course of German History*
(London, Hamish Hamilton, 1945) and *Bismarck* are extended
essays in which Taylor pushed his themes to volume length.

Alan Taylor turned increasingly towards British history from
the mid-1950s. In June 1956, after *The Struggle for Mastery in
Europe* and *Bismarck* had been published, he commented to his
publisher: 'At the moment I feel that I have used up my stock
of intellectual capital and must accumulate for a bit before
writing more. But if I saw the perfect biographical subject, I
would seize it.' He turned down suggestions to write on Charles
James Fox, Metternich, Sir Charles Dilke, the Kaiser and
Adam von Trott. Instead he worked on *The Origins of the Second
World War* and eagerly accepted an opportunity to write the
1914–1945 volume in the *Oxford History of England*. In preparing
for *English History 1914–1945* (Oxford University Press, 1965) he

took to reviewing more books on British history, not only on the twentieth century but also on earlier periods.

His move towards British history was further encouraged by the stormy reception given to his *Origins of the Second World War*. In spite of his very critical comments on Germany in *The Course of German History* and his own record in the late 1930s as an anti-appeaser, he was deemed by some critics to be an apologist for Hitler as his revisionist account suggested that there was much more involved in the outbreak of war in Europe in September 1939 than Hitler's misdeeds. Indeed he suggested that Hitler had not followed long-laid plans but had been an opportunist, responding to circumstances. Taylor had been suggesting some of the revisionist themes of the book even as the Second World War was ending. He felt his views had been confirmed with the publication of various diplomatic documents after the war. When reviewing Lewis Namier's *Diplomatic Prelude* (London, Macmillan, 1948) on the diplomacy before the outbreak of war, he wrote: 'You can find in Namier the more humdrum truth, discreditable no doubt to both sides in the negotiations – not discreditable from wickedness or sinister intention [but] discreditable from short-sightedness, vanity and ignorance.'

In the aftermath of the furore over *The Origins of the Second World War* Alan Taylor was not offered another, better post or renewal of his special lectureship at Oxford University when it ran out in 1963. He remained a Fellow of Magdalen College until he reached retirement age (whereupon he was elected an Honorary Fellow). He continued to give occasional lectures at Oxford, but his regular income from lecturing there had ended. He became more London based, going on to write the official biography of his friend Lord Beaverbrook and becoming the Honorary Director of the Beaverbrook Library from its opening in 1967 until its closure in 1975. These tasks took him back to research on primary documents and to working on both twentieth-century British history and the Second World War.

*   *   *

Alan Taylor's activities as a major radio, television and newspaper personality are thought by some to have detracted from
his standing as a historian. Yet, by making him one of the best-
known major academic historians, these activities helped to
communicate history to wider audiences.

Initially his opportunities arose from being the right person in
the right place. He was the bright young Modern History
lecturer at Manchester University at a time when the *Manchester
Guardian* was firmly centred on Manchester. He began writing
book reviews for that newspaper when his Professor, Lewis
Namier, had tired of writing them quickly and regularly. From
this opening he later successfully lobbied to write historical
essays to mark anniversaries (several of which are in this
volume). During the Second World War he was still teaching in
Oxford and so was available to give talks in southern England
on current affairs, especially on his specialist area of central
Europe. With so many rivals absent he had a golden opportunity
to make a name for himself on the radio and in the press. By
1942 he was providing broadcasts for BBC Radio and by
March 1944 he was writing leaders for the *Manchester Guardian*.
Before the end of the Second World War he was well entrenched
with BBC Radio as a commentator on foreign affairs and as a
fiery controversialist in discussion programmes.

As well as to his abilities and to the fact that he was available
when others were away on war service, Alan Taylor's success in
the media also owed something to his willingness to push himself;
for example, in early 1945, when discussing a possible
programme on current affairs, he urged a producer: 'Boost me
to the Brains Trust again – they obviously don't love me, but it
is such easy money.' The Alan Taylor of the 1940s combined
radical individualism and a striking ability to argue with brazen
self-assurance.

When BBC Television decided to broadcast a regular discussion programme, following US models, Alan Taylor became
one of its regular team of four. This programme, *In the News*,
made Robert Boothby, W J Brown, Michael Foot and Taylor

household names. Later, after their appearances were rationed as a result of political pressure, the four transferred to the infant commercial television and continued their weekly arguments in a programme entitled *Free Speech*. Taylor's fame as a television personality directly led to him becoming a weekly columnist in the popular press, successively for the *Sunday Pictorial*, the *Daily Herald* and the *Sunday Express*.

He also tried to take advantage of his radio and television current affairs contacts to broadcast history lectures. As early as February 1944 he was asking to give a radio broadcast to mark the fortieth anniversary of the Anglo-French Entente. In 1947 he did give two history broadcasts (one, on Lord John Russell, is reprinted in this volume) and in the following year he gave more, plus several book reviews. Thereafter he succeeded in interesting BBC Radio in broadcasting his major public lectures, including 'John Bright and the Crimean War' (which is reprinted here) as well as his 1956 Ford Lectures (subsequently published as *The Trouble Makers*). He also continued to give occasional radio talks on some of his favourite topics such as Charles James Fox, Metternich, Macaulay and Carlyle.

Independent television gave Alan Taylor the opportunity to deliver lectures to a mass audience. The first ITV series, in August 1957, was on events in Russia forty years earlier. These three Russian Revolution lectures were followed by another series, entitled 'When Europe was the Centre of the World', which dealt mostly with the period 1789 to 1914. For the latter series, broadcast at six p.m. on Mondays, Associated Television Ltd gave viewing figures of 750,000. In publishing the Russian lectures, ATV stated that in the summer of 1957 it had 'set Mr A J P Taylor the challenge of inviting him to deliver the first series of lectures in television, entirely unscripted and without recourse to film or other visual aids. Mr Taylor accepted the challenge and by the turn of the year he had delivered the first twelve half-hour lectures.'

Alan Taylor's ability to give half-hour television lectures from memory, with no visual aids and ending exactly on time, became legendary. It was, in fact, his norm. He had established an excellent reputation as a lecturer at Oxford, in part due to his capacity to lecture without notes, a skill also possessed by Alfred Pribram, whom Taylor probably chose to emulate. For television he carefully thought out his main points and memorized two or three different endings which he would use according to the time available.

As well as giving six series of lectures on ITV (between 1957 and 1967), Taylor gave five series on BBC and one on Channel 4. The BBC lectures were more substantial and were published at the time in *The Listener*. The later series of 1976, 1977, 1978 and 1983 each formed the basis of an illustrated book. The first series, 'The Twenties', broadcast in 1962, was something of a trial run for his *English History 1914–1945* and so was not reprinted. 'The Men of 1862', a series broadcast in 1963, has never before been reprinted. The lectures dealt mostly with major figures about whom he had written before, providing his updated opinions on them. In terms of delivery, he was then at the height of his powers, his fascination with his subjects making compelling viewing. Even so, on rare occasions his legendary sense of timing was not always quite right. He ended the lecture on Louis Napoleon with abbreviated comments:

In 1873 Napoleon III became an exile in England, hoped to come back, was operated upon so that he could sit upon a horse again, died under the surgeon's knife

before calmly delivering his final sentence:

At his funeral, the only Frenchman who came over from France to be with him was a trade unionist.

In the case of the Francis Joseph lecture all went well until he reached his concluding section, when he appears to have become agitated as he saw his time running out, jumbling his sentences quite badly.* But this was rare.

---

* This passage has been unjumbled, and other minor changes made to the lectures such as A J P Taylor might have introduced if he had included 'The Men of 1862' in a book.

Alan Taylor's enthusiasm for writing for the popular press and for his television and radio work cost him academic promotion in Oxford during the 1950s. Indeed it was the issue over which he broke off relations with his old mentor Lewis Namier, Taylor arguing that as a historian his powers of communication were strengthened by his forays into journalism. Taylor had learnt much from Namier about writing contemporary history in an easy to understand style, not to mention a great deal about the history of central Europe. When reviewing Namier's *Diplomatic Prelude* he had observed: 'The first aim of the journalist is to interest; of the historian to instruct − of course the good journalist and the good historian try to do both.'

But Taylor was a historian first and foremost. He was eager to communicate his enthusiasm for the past, whether by the printed, broadcast or spoken word. When reflecting in 1950 on how history should be written, he observed that 'a lot of historians forget that one purpose . . . of writing a book is that someone should read it'. He wrote his books with an eye to their having both wide and lasting appeal.

As a historian Alan Taylor was committed to discovering the truth about the past. The value that he found in the subject is well expressed in these comments he made in 1950:

History is the one way in which you can experience at second hand all kinds of varieties of human behaviour, and after all the greatest problem in life is to understand how other people behave, and this is what history enables us to do . . . It makes the reader and to a certain extent the historian aware of a fuller, much wider life than somebody could possibly have merely by his own private experience.

*　　*　　*

Alan Taylor was a skilled writer of short essays and long book reviews. He often combined in them his argumentative, questioning turn of mind, his feel for history and his sparkling style. He could always spot the telling anecdote, and learnt from Namier to open with something striking wherever possible. This is well illustrated here, not least by the memorable, but not especially apposite, opening of 'Tory History'.

He gathered together five collections of essays, all published in London by Hamish Hamilton: *From Napoleon to Stalin* (1950), *Rumours of Wars* (1952), *Englishmen and Others* (1956), *Politics in Wartime* (1964) and *Politicians, Socialism and Historians* (1980). From the first three of these were later drawn a one-volume selection published in the United States: *From Napoleon to Lenin* (New York, Harper and Row, 1966) and also the Penguin selection *Europe: Grandeur and Decline* (1967). He drew from the first four (and added a further five hitherto uncollected pieces) for the second Penguin selection, *Essays in English History* (1976). The present volume contains the best from Alan Taylor's five original collections, but also adds many pieces (just over half) which have not been reprinted before. The new essays stand comparison with those from the earlier volumes. Where Alan Taylor had written well on a topic on several occasions (such as Louis Napoleon or Lord Salisbury) it made sense here to print a fresh essay rather than one that has appeared two or three times before.

This book presents Alan Taylor on major topics of nineteenth-century European history (including Britain). It begins with his intellectual autobiography and some of his reflective pieces on writing history. It concludes with a selection of his writings on the history of places he knew and loved: Vienna, York, Manchester and the Lancashire resorts.

Alan Taylor's essays have the qualities of some of the best types of lectures. They arouse interest in their subject and make the reader want to find out more. They were not intended to be potted factual notes – there are plenty of reference works or textbooks for that. For the older reader, they may have the equivalent quality of a glass of old port after an excellent meal.

Accident Prone, or What Happened Next

Previously published in the Journal of Modern History, *March 1977.*

*   *   *

The *Journal of Modern History* occasionally devotes an entire number to a non-American historian. First came the prestigious French historian Braudel. Then the editor hit on me as a representative English historian which I fear I am not. The editor asked how I had become a historian, what were my aims and standards, what difficulties I had encountered. I had never considered these questions previously. The result came out as an essay in intellectual autobiography.

> A Galician priest was explaining to a peasant what miracles were.
> 'If I fell from that church tower and landed unhurt, what would you call it?'
> 'An accident.'
> 'And if I fell again and was unhurt?'
> 'Another accident.'
> 'And if I did it a third time?'
> 'A habit.'
>
> [A story told me by Lewis Namier]

In my version of history, I am told, everything happens by accident. This, though not I think true of my books, has applied in my own life time and again. Or perhaps such a steady record of accidents implies some kind of predestination. It never crossed my mind, when young, that I might become a professional historian. I did not seek my various careers – historian, journalist, television star. They sought me. I did not even devise the subjects of my books. All, with one exception, were suggested to me by others. Ironically the one exception, *The Origins of the*

Second World War, brought more trouble on my head than all my other books put together, trouble that I did not foresee or intend to provoke. There must be a moral here.

Certainly I loved history as far back as I can remember. I cannot explain this. It seems to me natural, just like loving music or the Lake District mountains. The first book I read, at the age of four, was *Pilgrim's Progress* – in its way a great historical work. Later I read all the historical novels I could lay my hands on: Harrison Ainsworth, Kingsley, Bulwer Lytton, G A Henty, the drabber and more factual the better. I could not take historical novels with real characters in them. That, I suppose, is why I never read Scott, greatest of historical novelists, until I was adult. Later I read indiscriminately works of histori- cal narration. It seemed obvious to me that the historian's prime duty was to answer my childish question: 'What hap- pened next?' It seems almost as obvious to me now. The book that pleased me most was H G Wells's *Outline of History*, read as it came out in its original fortnightly parts – not that I accepted Wells's version of events moving inevitably toward a World State. This passion for history is still with me. Every book that arrives on my desk for review excites me, and the prospect of myself writing a book on a good theme excites me still more.

I was always a 'loner', a solitary only child, out of step in all sorts of ways, rarely influenced by others and learning by the painful process of trial and error. I was born and grew up in Lancashire, which marked me off from the predominant, non-industrial culture of southern England. When I first went to Oxford, I was astonished to find a town not dominated by mill chimneys and with few mean streets. I came of radical, dissent- ing stock on both sides. A collateral ancestor of my father's was killed at Peterloo. My maternal great-grandfather voted for Orator Hunt at the Preston by-election in 1830 and received one of the medals struck in honour of 'the free and independent voters of Preston'. My father was a Lloyd George radical before the First World War. After it, when most of his fellow cotton merchants went Right, he went Left. He joined the Independent

Labour Party. In due course he became a Labour representative on Preston town council and was a member of the local strike committee during the General Strike of 1926.

I was always on good terms with my father and went along with his socialism. I am told this is an abnormal relationship psychologically, making one uncombative and lacking in self-confidence. I cannot say that it had any such effect in my case. On the contrary it made me more confident to have a secure family background. It is a curious thing to be a hereditary dissenter. On the one hand, you reject established views – religious in earlier times, political and social in our own. On the other, you have no inner conflict in doing so. Indeed you would have a conflict only if you accepted them. On a committee I usually put forward subversive ideas and at the same time insist that the existing rules must be rigorously observed until they are changed. Something the same applies to my books. The framework is strictly conventional – old-fashioned history, as one reviewer recently called it. But the ideas stuffed into the framework do not conform to accepted views. This is, I suppose, why my books annoy some people – I am a traitor within the gates.

My education increased my separation from the traditional stream of English culture. I went first to a Quaker preparatory school and then to Bootham, a Quaker public school at York. At both I experienced the physical hardships which were then the distinctive mark of English education. In other ways, my schools were different. The Society of Friends is certainly a community, but one resolutely out of step with the larger one. In spirit and outlook I am closer to the Friends than to any other body, except that they believe in God and I do not. Theirs is of course a special sort of God. What they really believe in is That of God in every man, a belief I share. This has given another firm point in my life, or rather two: I am no better than anyone else, and no one else is better than me. These rules of thumb have carried me a long way.

I did not acquire much understanding of history at either of my schools. At my preparatory school I learned the dates of the kings and queens of England, went on to the dates of the kings of France and the Holy Roman Emperors, and was hesitating whether to do the sultans of Turkey or the popes of Rome next when I left the school. At Bootham I read innumerable textbooks and, when my history master challenged me to read a long book, went right through Gibbon in a fortnight. But my history was still no more than an undiscriminating appetite. Understanding came in a different way. I collected Gothic churches and abbeys, spending far more time on this than on my schoolwork. This was the first field that brought the past alive to me. I carried a tape measure and a set square and produced ground plans of impeccable accuracy, with the various styles picked out in colour. But being unable to draw freehand, I could never produce elevations. There is a parallel here with my books. They provide ground plans and the reader has to put in the elevations.

I had no doubt what I wanted to do when I left school: simply to go on with what I loved, history, though with no idea of what this would lead to or how to turn it to any practical use. Oxford was my first encounter with traditional England, and very surprising it was. For instance, though I had measured and described countless churches, I had never reflected on what they were for. I had never attended a service of the Church of England and was astonished when I first entered the college chapel. I soon cried off attendance as an atheist. The dean said to me: 'Do come and talk to me about your doubts.' I answered: 'I have none.' Oxford's reaction to the General Strike also took me unawares. Most of the undergraduates went off as strike-breakers. I went back to Lancashire and drove a car for my father's strike committee.

Most of my time at Oxford was spent on medieval history, then a flourishing subject. The older views were being knocked about, which had a certain charm. Otherwise not much of it interested me except for the Peasants' Revolt. As to modern history, when we reached the Glorious Revolution, my tutor said to me: 'You know all the rest from your work at school, so we do not need to do any more.' I picked up my knowledge of modern history, such as it was, mainly from the works of Sir John Marriott, a historian now no doubt forgotten. I suspect that I am the Marriott *de nos jours*, except that he was very much on the Right and I am very much on the Left. I cultivated the revolutions of 1848 after reading Marx's *Eighteenth Brumaire of Louis Napoleon*, the book of his – apart of course from the *Communist Manifesto* – that I most admired. I also conceived a great admiration for Sorel's *Europe and the French Revolution*, more for its style than its content, and for many years tried to emulate his epigrammatic style, as readers of *The Course of German History* can see for themselves.

I did not go to any lectures except those of Sir Charles Oman and that only because Sir Charles, being very old, was a period piece. I never saw an original document or received any guidance in historical method. I was unaware of the existence of the Stubbs Society, the select society which promising historians are invited to join, or of the Ford Lectures, the most prestigious lectures in the English-speaking world. Now that I come to think of it, I did not have as a friend a single undergraduate who was reading history. My own friends were either literary, such as Norman Cameron the poet and J I M Stewart, later famous as a detective-story writer, or merely young men who like me were enjoying themselves.

I called myself a Marxist from the time I became a socialist. But, reading more history at Oxford, I began to feel that Marxism did not work. Consider the famous sentence in the *Communist Manifesto*: 'The history of all hitherto recorded society is the history of class struggles.' Very impressive but not true. Perhaps all history ought to have been the history of class struggles, but things did not work out that way. There have been long periods of class collaboration and many struggles that were not about class at all. I suppose my mind is too anarchic to be fitted into any system of thought. Like Johnson's friend Edwards, I, too, have tried to be a Marxist but common sense kept breaking in.

One day a friend said to me: 'Why do you not join the Communist Party?' Offhand I could think of no ready answer and on these inadequate grounds became a member of the party for a couple of years. My experiences in the General Strike showed me that the Communist Party played no significant part in the working-class movement, and my disillusionment was complete when Trotsky was expelled from the Russian party and then from Russia. Not that I understood the rights and wrongs of the dispute if it had any. I simply thought that a party which expelled a man of such gifts, merely because he disagreed with the accepted line, was not for me. I quietly lapsed and so escaped the soul torments over communism that racked so many British and American intellectuals during the 1930s.

In 1927 I got a first in my history finals. This surprised me. I had thought that perhaps I was clever-clever, but certainly not that I was history-clever. Perhaps clever-clever is enough in the History School at Oxford. However, it did not concern me. I wanted to escape the ivory towers of Oxford and go into what I imagined was 'real life'. Six months in a law office taught me my mistake. I drifted back to Oxford, at a loss what to do. Someone, I think Davis, the Regius Professor, suggested that I should go to Vienna and work under Pribram, who was reputed to be an authority on Oliver Cromwell. This seemed as good a way as any of learning German, quite apart from the fact that Vienna was highly esteemed in socialist circles. So off I went and lived in Vienna for two years.

I found that Pribram had lost interest in Cromwell and had now moved on to the origins of the First World War. This was no good to me who knew no history after the Congress of Berlin. Pribram charitably suggested that I should work on Anglo-Austrian relations between 1848 and 1860 and I duly settled down in the Staatsarchiv. I received no instruction how to conduct research. I was not even warned to put down the number of the document I was copying, which caused me a great deal of unnecessary work later. I knew none of the techniques of diplomatic history. I just dived in at the deep end. Imperceptibly I found a better subject: not Anglo-Austrian relations in the void, but the diplomacy of the North Italian question during the revolution of 1848. I gradually trained myself to be a diplomatic historian and was quite competent in this modest art by the time I went on to work in the British and French archives. I suppose I ought to have worked in the Italian archives as well, but of course it was out of the question for me to go to Italy in Mussolini's time.

Though I was now doing historical research, I was far from certain that I should become a professional historian. I had no patron or supervisor in England. I did not enrol as a student at Vienna university and, though I had many social meetings with Pribram, never received any guidance from him after his initial suggestion. I vaguely foresaw that, with my newly acquired command of German, I might become a foreign correspondent. Even more wildly, I took serious steps to become an inspector of ancient monuments, a post for which, apart from my knowledge of Gothic architecture, I was totally unqualified. However, events decided for me in their usual way.

In the spring of 1930 Pribram went to Oxford and delivered the Ford Lectures. One night he sat next to Ernest Jacob at dinner. Jacob had just become head of the history department at Manchester. The professor and lecturer in modern European history had both left, and Jacob was without anyone to teach the subject in the coming academic year. He asked whether Pribram knew of anyone. Pribram, perhaps grateful for the help I had given him in translating his Ford Lectures into English, mentioned me. The next morning Jacob sent me a telegram offering me the job of lecturer. And that is how I became committed to history.

I had hardly been aware until that moment that there was a university in Manchester, and my main feeling was pleasure at going home to Lancashire. In fact the Manchester History School was at that time the most distinguished in Great Britain. The department was very small: three professors, one reader,

and four lecturers in all. It never occurred to us that we might
have a duty to society. Our sole task, we thought, was to train
historians. No professor of modern history had yet been appointed. Hence, in my first year at Manchester I did the work
of both professor and lecturer, another case of diving in at the
deep end.

I had to cover all European history from 1494 to 1914 and
knew none of it except for the French Revolution and patches of
the nineteenth century until the Congress of Berlin. I bought a
set of old-fashioned textbooks (Rivington blue) and compiled
notes for ninety-six lectures. For the period before the First
World War I used the 'revisionist' books that were then in
favour and produced an impeccably pro-German account. After
delivering my lectures once, I decided that it would be tedious
to give the same lectures year after year. I threw away my notes
and thereafter lectured without notes as I have done ever since.
I do not know whether I taught my enormous classes anything.
But I taught myself history, literally on my feet. I also taught
myself to address mass audiences without a tremor. This has
often worried me. Most orators are desperately nervous before
they speak – Lloyd George's shirt was always wet through. I
have never trembled before either an audience or the television
cameras.

When I had been at Manchester a year, Namier arrived as
professor of modern history. It is sometimes said that I was his
pupil. This is not so. I was already an established lecturer when
Namier came and, if anything, he was my pupil, not I his. At least
I tried to teach him how Manchester University worked, in which
I was unsuccessful. Namier was at this time wholly taken up with
English politics in the early reign of George III, a subject that did
not concern me. Of course I was fascinated by his stories, but I
did not share his outlook and was indeed 'the friendly critic', as he
called me, who accused him of taking the mind out of history. It is
strange that this great man, who deplored the influence of
political ideas, should have repeatedly jeopardized his career for
the sake of Zionism, a political idea if ever there were one.

My views of European history were reached independently of Namier, though we broadly agreed on most things. He had not kept up with the most recent work on the subject and occasionally I was in the happy position of telling him something instead of listening. Also our methods were different. He was a painstaking and laborious scholar. I often relied on intuition. I once made some point in a review. Namier asked me: 'How did you know that? I worked on the topic for three weeks before I found it.' I said I felt it must be so. He replied: 'Ah, you have green fingers. I have not.' Some may say that I have relied on my green fingers too much. I think I have relied on them too little. For instance I felt from the first day that van der Lubbe set fire to the Reichstag all alone. But I hesitated to champion this view against the weight of received opinion until Tobias vindicated it some thirty years afterwards.

If I had a teacher at Manchester and indeed afterwards, it was A P Wadsworth, not Namier. Wadsworth was deputy editor and then editor of the *Manchester Guardian* and also an economic historian of great distinction. He set me to writing leader-page articles on anniversaries of famous men or events and later on the interwar diplomatic documents as they came out. Wadsworth was a hard taskmaster. He constantly said to me: 'An article in the *Guardian* is no good unless people read it on the way to work.' I followed his instruction. My guiding principle, in my writings as in my lectures, has always been: 'Give the customer what he wants' – which does not of course mean 'what he would like to hear'. I worried about my style as much as about my scholarship. In my opinion a work of history misfires unless readers get the same pleasure from it that they do from a novel. My models were Bunyan, Cobbett and Shaw, though I would not claim to reach their standard. I suspect that those who are shocked by my views would be less perturbed if I wrapped them up in the prolixity usual in historical writing.

I also learned a good deal at Manchester from contemporary events and my own political activities. I advocated resistance to Hitler from the moment he came to power. But I also thought

that the National government were more likely to support
Hitler against Russia than to go against him and therefore I
opposed rearmament until we got a change of government. In
1935 I opposed support for the League of Nations by the
existing government as a fraud, which it turned out to be, and
remember one splendid meeting with the entire audience,
composed half of communists and half of members of the League
of Nations Union, vociferously against me. With the reoccupa-
tion of the Rhineland, I decided that we must rearm even under
the National government and was convinced that if we took a
firm line with Hitler there would be no war. I was one of the
few people outside London who addressed meetings against
appeasement at the time of Munich, and very rough they were.
I have not changed the views I held then.

Though I often dabbled in politics I never devoted myself to
them or sought a political career. Once when I applied for an
appointment at Oxford which I did not get, the president of the
college concerned said to me sternly: 'I hear you have strong
political views.' I said: 'Oh no, President. Extreme views weakly
held.' This has remained my position. But, growing up in a
political household and myself involved in politics on the fringe,
I automatically assumed that politics expressed the activities of
'man in society', as the theme of history has rightly been called.
All other forms of history – economic history, social history,
psychological history, above all sociology – seem to me history
with the history left out. And when I am told quite erroneously
that my form of history is merely a record of events, I can only
reply that so are all other forms. A ship sailing from Venice to
Constantinople is as much an event as a general election or an
army marching to battle. It all depends on what you make of
them.

Namier affected me in one practical way. He thought we
ought to have a special subject on pre-war diplomacy and,
being too busy to do this himself, shoved it on to me. I forgot all
my previous views, and started again from scratch, reading *Die
grosse Politik* and then the British and French documents from

cover to cover. When I had finished, I no longer thought that Germany was the innocent victim of Entente diplomacy. I was not even sure that the First World War happened by accident. My new absorption with pre-war diplomacy attracted the attention of E L Woodward, who was almost alone at Oxford in promoting its study, and in 1938 he helped me to get a fellowship at Magdalen, which I have held happily ever since.

My first real books which I wrote soon after moving to Oxford again came to me by chance. Harold Macmillan wanted a short history of the Habsburg Monarchy in its later days. Namier was again too busy and again I took it on. Then during the war PWE (Political Warfare Executive) wanted a chapter on the Weimar Republic for a handbook they were preparing. I wrote it. However, PWE found my chapter not sufficiently enthusiastic about German democracy and therefore too depressing for their handbook. Denis Brogan said: 'Why not turn it into a book?' I took his advice and wrote *The Course of German History*. Of course both books were affected by the war, but not more, I think, than it affects me still. Since the war centred on Germany, I had to explain why the Germans got where they did. With *The Habsburg Monarchy*, I learned a great deal from central European refugees: Hubert Ripka, the predestined successor of Beneš, though he never stepped into his inheritance; Michael Karolyi, who became one of my dearest friends; and the Slovenes with whom I worked toward the end of the war in an attempt to get Trieste for Yugoslavia.

I have often been called a narrative historian, a title of which I am not ashamed. After all, the distinguishing mark of history is that events happen in order of time. How else can you present them? But these two books of mine are not really narrative; they are explanation. They try to answer the question, how did it happen? How did the Habsburg Monarchy decline and go to pieces? How did Germany remain a militaristic power, less democratic than either England or France? The customer wanted explanations; I tried to provide them. Actually I was less affected by the war than I ought to have been. I should have seen that the Habsburg Monarchy disintegrated because of defeat in the war and for no other reason. However I am still reasonably content with *The Habsburg Monarchy*. I saw German history from outside – partly as an Englishman, partly as an Austrian – and I would not claim that there is anything original in *The Course of German History*. But at least I had read Eckhart Kehr, which most English historians at that time had not.

The war affected me in other ways. It gave me a warning, which I did not always heed, against trying to learn from history. In 1940 I was convinced that the Germans would not invade England. I was right but for entirely the wrong reason. I thought that, on the analogy of Bonaparte in 1798, the Germans would make ostensible preparations to invade England and in fact invade the Middle East. The analogy was false: Hitler never had any offensive plans in the Middle East and did not invade England simply because his forces were not strong enough to do so. Later during the war I gave innumerable talks on the war and current affairs which enabled me to see the war in some sort of historical perspective. Indeed looking back I remember much more of my lectures and interpretations than of what was actually happening.

The Oxford History School, however, stopped in 1939, as it still does, and there was no academic use for my knowledge of the Second World War. I went back to my study of diplomatic history before 1914 and was wondering what use to make of this when I had another stroke of luck. Deakin and Bullock launched the *Oxford History of Modern Europe*. There were to be volumes on the general history of the principal nation states and in addition three on diplomatic history. I gladly undertook the middle one of these, extending from the revolutions of 1848 to the coming of Lenin and Woodrow Wilson in 1918. Thus accident had intervened again. By definition I was strictly confined to diplomatic history which suited me very well.

This was the first book I thought about before I wrote it. I should have no difficulty, except hard work, over the diplomatic details. But what about '*les forces profondes*', as Renouvin has called them? I had difficulty, as Renouvin had, in reconciling them with the play of accident that determines the day-to-day course of events. For instance a war between the two Germanic powers and the rest was very likely in the early years of the twentieth century. But the actual war that broke out in August 1914 would not have occurred as it did if Archduke Franz Ferdinand had not gone to Sarajevo on June 28 or even if his chauffeur had not taken a wrong turning. I suppose something the same is true of all history. *Les forces profondes* are there all right if you cover a century in a single essay, as Namier did in that wonderful essay 'From Vienna to Versailles'. But when you look at details, individual men affect even the greatest events. No doubt France would have been diminished somehow in the later nineteenth century, but she would have declined differently without Napoleon III. No doubt Germany would have become greater in any case, but the way in which she became great was determined by Bismarck. The historian, I think, just has to accept life and put up with it.

I tried to strike a balance by drawing the general outline of these seventy years in a long introduction and then putting in the details as the Pre-Raphaelites used to do with their pictures. Maybe I did not get the balance right. When I think back to *The Struggle for Mastery in Europe*, it seems to me a fascinating recital of diplomatic episodes, each chapter suited to appear as an article in a learned journal and adding up to an unreadable book. However when I open the book again I do not see how it could have been done otherwise and there is far more in it about *les forces profondes* than I had remembered. The book established my reputation as a scholar, at any rate in some circles, and is the only one of my books to be translated into Russian. Of course the Russians paid me only in blocked roubles and it exasperates me to see copies of the Russian translation on the shelves of university libraries whenever I go to eastern Europe. Incidentally the Russian translator changed my sentence 'Wilson was as much a Utopian as Lenin' to 'Wilson was a Utopian.'

The Struggle for Mastery in Europe, though I did not know it, was virtually my farewell to nineteenth-century Europe and, in a sense, to diplomatic history also. I followed it up by a biography of Bismarck, written on the initiative of an American publisher, but the interest in it for me was not the political history, which I was now writing for the third time, but Bismarck the man. For once I tried to be a psychologist. I did not get very far. I found that Bismarck, too, got on well with his father and, according to all the rules, should have been timid and unaggressive. I decided that psychology did not provide much help to historians and that men have the disposition they are born with – a conclusion reinforced later when I wrote the life of Beaverbrook. Apart from that I fell mildly in love with Bismarck. Every historian, I think, should write one biography, if only to learn how different it is from writing history. Men become more important than events, as I suppose they should be. I prefer writing history all the same.

And now an extraordinary thing happened to me, the most extraordinary indeed that happened in my life. One evening I received an invitation to deliver the Ford Lectures at Oxford. I knew great historians gave the Ford Lectures. My friend Richard Pares had given them, and so had my colleague Bruce McFarlane. But me – the industrious hack, compiling records of events? Besides, the Ford Lectures were on English history, and I still thought of myself as a historian of Europe. I wandered out into the night, encountered Alan Bullock, and told him my plight. He said: 'You have always opposed British foreign policy. Now tell us about the men who opposed it in the past.' I was intoxicated with delight: a wonderful subject that no one had thought of before. The outcome was *The Trouble Makers*, by far my favourite brainchild and the one I hope to be remembered by. I suppose it should be classed as history of ideas. For me, the ideas, the men, and the excitement of presenting them were all mixed up. *The Trouble Makers* was not all praise. Michael Foot called it: 'The book in which you stabbed all your friends in the back' – a complaint he repeated about my political arguments when we used to appear together on television. All the same the Trouble Makers are my heroes so far as I have ever found any.

1956 was altogether a wonderful year. I delivered the Ford Lectures. I was elected to the British Academy, according to Galbraith on the strength of my bibliography in *The Struggle for Mastery in Europe*. It was the year of the Suez crisis when I thought that the Boer War had come again and that we faced a long period of unpopularity, persecution and perhaps imprisonment. This was another error in trying to learn from history: the miserable British government could not even sin properly and called off their aggression within a week. Most of all, 1956 was the year I met Beaverbrook. The occasion for this was characteristic. He had just published *Men and Power*. In it he told how Lloyd George, when imposing convoy on the reluctant admirals, descended on the Admiralty 'and seated himself in the First Lord's chair'. I was pretty sure that there had not been a meeting of the Admiralty Board that day. I wrote asking Beaverbrook for his evidence. He invited me to lunch and said: 'I'm sure it happened' and, when I pressed him again, 'I'll ask Churchill,' which of course he never did. Years later I found that he had inserted the story on the proof in order to liven things up.

However it did not matter. I was bewitched by this master of political narrative and by the historical zest that inspired a man nearly eighty. Beaverbrook, apart from delighting me, switched my attention to English history. Another pull towards it came in a more orthodox way. One afternoon I went for a walk with G N Clark, the editor of the *Oxford History of England*. He said casually: 'I must do something about a final volume in the *Oxford History of England*, to pick up in 1914 where Ensor leaves off. Ensor was planning to do it and now he is dead. Perhaps I'll have a try at it myself.' I said: 'What about me?' and with that I was in – not only my next book, but many years of my life determined. Yet it would never have happened if G N Clark and I had not gone for a walk in Wytham Woods that autumn afternoon.

I was starting this time much more from scratch. I had never taught twentieth-century English history and had not kept up with the work on it systematically. I had reviewed most of the principal memoirs and other books as they came out. But mostly my knowledge was a matter of memory – an unreliable source. However I began to read very hard. The subject had at any rate the advantage that most of the books on it were in English and the even greater advantage that they were nearly all in the London Library. No more reading German; no more going to the British Museum. These two things were almost reward enough in themselves.

I had hardly settled down when I had to break off. Distractions made a hole in my life for two years and more. It was my turn to serve as vice-president of Magdalen College just when it cele-brated its quincentenary and as vice-president I had to organize it all. This was very enjoyable and, for a historian, very interest-ing. But it took up much of my time: arranging dinners and parties, commissioning a fireworks display, even attending a service at the tomb of our founder, William of Waynflete, in Winchester Cathedral. I left a note of my mistakes for my successor in 2058. He will learn from it how to make new ones.

A greater distraction was the call of duty when the Campaign for Nuclear Disarmament started. This was the only public cause to which I devoted myself wholeheartedly and, I think, the one worthy thing I have done in my life. I became one of the national speakers and for two years or so toured in more halls than either Bright or Gladstone did, if only because some of the halls were not built in their time. With *The Trouble Makers* fresh in my mind, I tried to achieve the same effect. Where my colleagues appealed to emotion, I relied on hard argument to show the folly as well as the wickedness of nuclear weapons. My model was Cobden – 'I know the Blue Books as well as the noble Lord does.' My best evening came at Birmingham Town Hall where I spoke precisely a hundred years after Bright delivered there his great speech on British foreign policy – 'a gigantic system of out-relief for the British aristocracy'.

The campaign was very instructive for me as a historian. Mass meetings are intoxicating for both audience and speaker. You imagine you have really achieved something when you get four thousand people on their feet with enthusiasm, and I suppose much the same is true of a successful speech in the House of Commons. This was a warning to me that politicians cannot be wholly sane. Nor were we in the great days of the campaign. We genuinely believed when we started that the whole world would be impressed if Great Britain renounced nuclear weapons and would follow our moral lead. In this way CND was a last splutter of imperial pride. The Cuba missile crisis taught us better. No one cared in the slightest whether we had nuclear weapons or not, which was of course a strong argument for abandoning them. The Cuba crisis virtually killed CND, and I have never involved myself in politics since.

Though I was too busy to do much serious research during this turmoil, I needed to write something – 'always scribble, scribble, scribble! Eh! Mr Gibbon?' I had been studying the background to the Second World War ever since the material began to come out and now could go straight ahead. This is how I came to write *The Origins of the Second World War*, the only subject I thought of myself. The title was of course wrong, as I realized when I came to write the last sentence. What happened in September 1939 was a minor episode in the Second World War, not the world war itself, which began either much earlier (April 1932) or much later (December 1941). But at this time my mind was still centred on Europe. The views expressed in the book followed logically on those I had developed in *The Course of German History*. They have now become the current orthodoxy. Indeed with Fritz Fischer and his school claiming that German statesmen actually designed the First World War and were, if anything, more extreme than Hitler, I find myself trailing far behind. However I do not intend to fight again the controversies that the book provoked. I had tried to write history in detachment; my critics were concerned to express their emotions. I will only add that, when criticizing an author,

I have never descended to personal abuse. I cannot say the same about my critics.

When I returned to *English History 1914–1945*, I was not a free agent. I came at the end of a long-established series and had to conform to its pattern, putting in biographical footnotes and lists of cabinet ministers. I read all the preceding fourteen volumes in the series, though, to be honest, I managed to get right through only five of them. They troubled me. Where was the story line? Most of the books seemed to me collections of independent essays. I decided to write in the form of a continuous narrative. There was some sleight of hand about this. Continuous narrative works when you are confined to a single theme, such as the origins of a war. It is harder, indeed almost impossible, when you have to handle every aspect of national life. So I used a narrative framework and slipped in what I called 'occasional pauses for refreshment'. I maintained the solemn tone of the previous writers, pontificating about writers as though I were qualified to judge them. Somehow the book did not come out all that solemn in the end.

There were other problems. For instance, what was 'England'? All the previous writers had used England, Great Britain, the United Kingdom, and even the British Empire as synonymous terms, as they were when the series had been launched thirty years before. Now with the Scotch roaring at my back, I could not do this and yet could not write the history of twentieth-century England in isolation. This is a problem not encountered by historians of other European countries except perhaps the Germans, who, I notice, often manage to write the history of Germany without mentioning Austria. I did my best with a compromise that worked out all right.

More seriously, what England was I writing about? Again my predecessors had not worried about this and had written the history of the English upper classes. I wanted to write the history of the English people. But even in the twentieth century the English people had little history except at moments of crisis, though I do not know whether this made them happy. I kept slithering into the old fashion of writing about the 'in' classes and then pulled myself up every now and then. I must have done better than I expected. At any rate Max Beloff called me a populist historian, which was exactly what I wanted to be.

I wrote all my earlier works virtually without consulting anybody. *English History 1914–1945* went through the mill. G N Clark was a model editor, often querying what I wrote and then accepting it when I said it was necessary. My greatest aid came from Ken Tite, my colleague who was politics tutor at Magdalen. He should have been an outstanding political historian himself, but he was a sick man who died comparatively young without writing a book. Ken read my draft and wrote some forty pages of foolscap comments on it. I absorbed his points, and he then wrote fifteen more pages. My book was certainly chewed over, and I record with a full heart my gratitude to Ken Tite. Beaverbrook provided some of the anecdotes, not all of them reliable. More than this he gave me a firm conviction that English history was an exciting subject. Indeed on one occasion he inspired me to go on when my spirits flagged and I was inclined to break off.

There is not much to add to this record. I spent five years writing a life of Beaverbrook. This was a labour of love and does not illustrate any theory of history or biography. Beaverbrook lived a long time and managed to combine six different sorts of careers, so the book came out much longer than he would have liked. He himself came out a greater man than I had expected, but that was his doing, not mine. At any rate I wrote the book with my heart as well as with my head.

I even tried my hand at cultural history. Geoffrey Barraclough conscripted me to contribute to a series on the history of civilization he was editing. I tried to find out what 'civilization' meant and received many dusty answers. I decided that it meant the predominating patterns of life at any given time and, as war and economic problems predominated in the first half of the twentieth century, *From Sarajevo to Potsdam* came out political after all. My short histories of the two world wars – both

suggested by a publisher – gave me greater pleasure. Without
design they are curiously, and I think appropriately, different in
tone. *The First World War* appears as a muddle from beginning
to end. Shortly after it was published, I went to Joan Little-
wood's show *Oh! What a Lovely War* and found the entire cast
reading my book, delighted to have their version confirmed by
a serious, or fairly serious, historian. *The Second World War* has a
much firmer construction. It is, I think, the first account that
binds the two wars, German and Japanese, into a single coherent
pattern. I regard the book as being, in relatively short compass,
the best demonstration of my way of writing history. Perhaps
this is only because it is the most recent book I have written.

The difficulties I have encountered in writing history have
been practical and technical. The greatest difficulty is time. You
have to read a great deal, chase evidence all over the place, and
make copious notes many of which you cannot lay hands on
when you need them. I have of course never used a research
assistant. No individual history can be written with one. As a
writer my first model was Albert Sorel, and *The Course of German
History* is peppered with epigrams that seek to imitate his. *The
Habsburg Monarchy* often echoes the style of *The Thirties* by
Malcolm Muggeridge which I happened to be reading at the
time. Since then my style has been my own. It has however
changed with my writing instruments. With a pen you write
words. With a typewriter you write sentences. With an electric
typewriter, which I use now, you write paragraphs. In military
terms: bow and arrow, musket, machine gun. I try to keep up a
continuous fire.

No Oxford Chair of History has come my way, though there
were plenty around in my time. This was no doubt accidental,
with perhaps a tinge of disapproval for either me or recent
history. I was glad to escape the administrative duties that fall
to a professor. My only regret is that professors tend to grab
most of the research students, and I could have done with more.
This has been a loss for me and perhaps for some research
students.

My emancipation from teaching was completed in 1963, when the History Faculty Board terminated my university lectureship for reasons that are still obscure to me. Magdalen College gave me a research fellowship, and University College, London, made me a special lecturer, which gave me just enough lecturing to keep my hand in. When I had passed the retiring age for university lecturers I began lecturing again at Oxford just to show what it had missed. For this the Faculty Board paid me £40 a year. For the most part I make my living from journalism and television. Even so, I do not suppose anyone would dispute my claim to be a professional historian.

The other great difficulty is material. History, unlike poetry or fiction, does not write itself. For recent times, which I have always stuck to, there seems only too much material, and yet new evidence is constantly coming out. Often I have had to change my ground while writing a book or, still worse, after it has been written. When I finished *English History 1914–1945* in July 1964, the fifty-year rule was in force and not a single classified British paper was available. Now the British archives are open, I suspect a little selectively, until 1945. I fear that my next task is to write the whole book all over again. If I do, it will work out differently. In the early 1960s I was still writing under the impact of the Second World War which was the most inspiring time in our history. Now I regard the state and still more the future of my country more gloomily. Indeed I often wonder whether it is worthwhile writing history at all. The record, I think, is nearly over. However history is fun to write and, I hope, fun to read. That to my mind is its justification.

On a more serious level, I believe that history enables us to understand the past better, no more and no less. This is a matter of detached curiosity, and there can be no nobler exercise of the human mind. I have never supposed, as many earlier historians did, that men can learn any useful lessons from history, political or otherwise. Of course you can learn certain obvious commonplaces, such as that all men die or that one day the deterrent, whatever it may be, will fail to deter. Apart from this, history is an art just like painting or architecture and is designed like them to give intellectual and artistic pleasure.

I have never been troubled by the dogmas of others about what history should be or how it should be written. Most of this is sales talk by academics anxious to justify their existence. My view is that they should get on with writing books in their way and I will get on with writing them in mine. I have always been conscious of the artificiality of history. We sort human beings into national or class categories, when in reality each one of them is unique. Bernard Shaw was delighted to learn from an oculist that only one man in a thousand has completely 'normal' vision. Who has ever known a typical working man or even a typical university professor? When I sit on the beach at Brighton, I am surrounded by the masses, but I do not number myself among them and no doubt each one of the others would make the same exception for himself.

Some historians understand science and technology. Some understand philosophy. I know how a newspaper office works, which makes me sceptical about studies of public opinion. I know what to do in a television studio and can talk straight to camera for twenty-five minutes, twenty-seven seconds, which allows for the commercial break. Even in my more adventurous days, I kept almost entirely to Europe. I have been to almost every European country, including Soviet Russia in the happy days of NEP (New Economic Policy). Outside Europe I went once to Morocco and once to New Brunswick. On the latter occasion I looked across the bay from St Andrews to Maine, so I can say I have seen the United States or at any rate one of them. Nowadays I stick mainly to England and recently kept my sense of history alive by walking the 150 miles of Offa's Dike.

I am English by birth and preference and, I suppose, in character. This has no relevance to my work as a historian. Seeley – or was it Freeman? – said: 'History is past politics.' If this means that history should be used as a political weapon, I am not of Seeley's (or Freeman's) opinion. When I write, I have no loyalty except to historical truth as I see it and care no more about British achievements or mistakes than about any others. I was deeply concerned in the General Strike, the Second World War, and the Campaign for Nuclear Disarmament. But this does not weigh with me when I treat them historically. I think that the English people of the twentieth century were a fine people and deserved better leaders than on the whole they got. This is, if anything, the moral of *English History 1914–1945*, but I left the reader to find it out for himself. At any rate national loyalty or even disloyalty has never been among my difficulties as a historian.

Dr Johnson said, 'Great abilities are not requisite for an Historian; for in historical composition, all the greatest powers of the human mind are quiescent. He has facts ready to his hand; so there is no exercise of invention. Imagination is not required in any high degree; only about as much as is used in the lower kinds of poetry. Some penetration, accuracy, and colouring will fit a man for the task, if he can give the application which is necessary.' That is about right, though the historian needs more invention than Johnson supposed. I am short on imagination and have never managed to write a line of poetry or a paragraph of fiction. Penetration is, I hope, another name for green fingers. Every historian tries to be accurate, though none succeeds as fully as he would like to. Style is colouring and something more: it sets its stamp on the whole work. As Johnson says, application is the main thing. Writing history is like W C Fields juggling. It looks easy until you try to do it.

The Historian as a Biographer

Previously published in Wiener Beiträge zur Geschichte der Neuzeit, *1979.*

*　　*　　*

A contribution to a volume of essays on History and Biography, written at the invitation of my old friend, Friedrich Engel-Janosi, who, alas, died before he could read my completed piece.

Inside every historian there lies concealed a biographer struggling to get out. In his own work the historian faces an endless task. He arbitrarily abstracts some small stretch from the seamless web of history, knowing full well that his theme existed before the moment when his book begins and will go on after the moment when his book finishes. The biographer is more fortunate: the limits of his subject are defined for him in advance. His book will begin with the subject's birth, perhaps with some prelude of family background, and will end with the subject's death, again perhaps with an epilogue on the subject's legacy, political, financial or personal.

The historian looks at this good fortune with envy. How happy he would be to enjoy the same advantages. No more need to search for a theme; no more worrying over what to put in and what to leave out; no more hesitation over the interpretation to set on events. Everything is clear before him. The theme is set; the sources are available. All he has to do is to sit down and write. Surely the historian's training in his own craft will enable him to write a biography without difficulty. He knows how to judge evidence and where to find it.

Biography is only a particular form of history or so the historian thinks. Both historian and biographer rely primarily on written records. The biographer may get more guidance from portraits and sculpture than the historian usually does. On the other hand the historian gets more guidance from public buildings such as cathedrals and castles, to say nothing of houses of parliament. The biographer even more than the historian writes a narrative where events move in order of time. If history is essentially story – indeed the two words are the same in many languages other than English – biography is certainly a story also.

On second thoughts the historian becomes less confident. Every historian treats some aspect of man in society. It may be political man, economic man, military man, aesthetic man, but always man in society. Society comes first. The historian seeks for what is common in men, not what distinguishes one man from another. The individual is a great problem for the historian. He knows from his own experience that every man is unique. No historian for instance would admit that he is exactly like any other historian in character or achievement. Every face is different; every handwriting is different; every character is different. Nevertheless the individual has to be subordinated to the grand central design. Men have to be placed in arbitrary categories – epoch, class, nation, creed. One man has to represent the medieval monk or the colonial explorer; another, the merchant banker or the Jacobin revolutionary.

Of course the historian knows that these types are fictions. The men of the Middle Ages for instance were unaware that they were living in the middle of anything. The class-conscious proletarian is a rare phenomenon, often, as in the case of Marx, drawn from another class. Revolutionary France is often held up as the outstanding example of modern nationalism. Yet an 1850 inquiry showed that the majority of the inhabitants of France did not know that they were French. However, the historian cannot get on without these fictions and indeed soon forgets that he invented them. It is not surprising that historians have often been the ringleaders of national or class movements. Nationalism did not begin in the peasant villages; it began in academic lecture rooms.

Nowadays the historian professes to be less enslaved by national or class loyalties. In other ways the problem of how to treat the individual becomes increasingly difficult. There was a time when historians wrote mainly about the few figures at the top – the Great Man theory of history as it has been called. The fate of the Roman Empire was determined by the shape of Cleopatra's nose. Kings and queens, popes and chief ministers crowded the historian's pages. History was a series of biographies, loosely strung together in a framework of general events. Gibbon, perhaps the greatest of English historians, has some splendid passages on the development of the Christian religion. But most of his narrative is a succession of emperors and gives the impression that their individual failings did more than crushing taxation or the barbarian invasions to bring about the empire's fall. Ranke is generally supposed to have inaugurated a more scientific and less personal version of history. Careful reading shows that his pages often contain brilliant passages of individual characterization, especially when the individual presented happens to be a ruler of Prussia. On a humbler level, as a boy I learnt the dates of the kings and queens of England and thought when I had done so that I knew the whole of English history.

The historian is no longer allowed to lapse into biography in this way. Now he must present 'the profound forces' of history. Movements, not men, are his theme. He must write about public opinion or imperialism, not about an individual editor or the founder of a colony. Indeed under pressure from the dominant school of French historians he is now ashamed to write at all about events, which have become as unfashionable as the individual. The biographer is no longer an ally or a writer to be envied. He has become a deplorable example any historian would do well to avoid. The conscientious historian turned biographer has to grasp that the two tasks are fundamentally different despite their apparent similarities. To write a successful biography the historian must learn a new trade.

Often the historian fails to carry through a complete

transformation. Given his training and background, he is unlikely to choose an artist or a literary figure as his subject and this cuts him off from a rich field of biography. Boswell's *Life of Johnson* is undoubtedly the greatest biography in the English language but its greatness does not lie in the occasional light it sheds on British politics in the eighteenth century. The historian inevitably chooses some public man: a statesman, a soldier or a political writer, someone in fact who will be an example of man in society. All the same the emphasis is changed: the individual comes first and society second.

I learnt this when I wrote my life of Bismarck. He occupied the centre of the stage and seemed to create events even when he claimed only to take advantage of them. I was back with the Great Man theory of history. Bismarck created the German Reich. He set his stamp on German society and, after designing three wars, gave Europe a long period of peace. This is not how historians now see German history. Railways and the factories of the Ruhr, not Bismarck, united Germany; the strength of the Junkers, not Bismarck, shaped German society; and the unconscious workings of the balance of power, not Bismarck, gave Europe first wars and then peace. However, I consoled myself with the thought that even historians who most pride themselves on being up to date lapse into the Great Man theory, as when they treat Hitler personally as the cause of the Second World War.

However, it is not enough for the historian to write history disguised as biography. If he is to be a thoroughgoing biographer he must forget about events and treat his subject as an individual human being. This raises the terrible shadow of psychology. Until recently this was a subject neglected by nearly all historians and indeed by many biographers. Of course the historian was aware from his experience of others if not of himself that no man was entirely sane and rational. But he assumed that men were rational when they were going about their own business, whether it were diplomacy or running a factory. Now we are told by psychologists and particularly by the followers of Freud that the important thing is the workings of our subject's unconscious mind.

This is all very well when the psychologist or perhaps even the historian has personal contacts with a living man. Even the most uninstructed of us can form some sort of impression, noting whether our subject is bad-tempered, vain or sympathetic. The psychologist goes much deeper: he conducts prolonged interviews which he calls psychoanalysis. I have my doubts about the results achieved by these interviews. In particular I doubt whether a technique perhaps applicable to the mentally unbalanced has much relevance to those who behave in a reasonably normal way. But this is a heresy I will not pursue.

But how do you interview a dead man? The answer is: you guess. The psychologist takes concepts that he has derived from living subjects and imposes them on the dead ones. The results are far from satisfactory. The psychoanalytic biography of Woodrow Wilson by Sigmund Freud and W C Bullitt was one of the most preposterous works ever written and revealed more about the psychopathology of the two authors than of the American president. Hitler has been a favourite subject for psychologists. I read one such work recently where Hitler's character was explained by the fact that at the age of three he saw his father and mother having sexual intercourse. The proof of this was that, even if he did not see them, he had the psychology of one who had and therefore must have seen them. If this sounds like nonsense, I can only plead that it represents my view of psychoanalysis as a biographical weapon.

However, the biographer must employ psychology in less extreme ways. In practical terms psychology for the biographer means two things: family background and sex. Family background sounds easy. Every man, it seems, either loves his mother and is jealous of his father or loves his father and finds his mother tiresome. The first relationship is apparently the more usual and even the more natural. Its results are said to be admirable. The subject develops a strong character by fighting with his father and at the same time a tenderness by loving his mother. The second relationship is abnormal. The subject has never fought and therefore remains an immature, unassertive character who also fails to establish any stable relationship with a woman.

In the two biographies I have attempted – one on Bismarck and the other on Lord Beaverbrook – I found this did not work out. Bismarck admired his slow, heavy father and disliked his mother, from whom he got his brains. He should therefore have been weak and unassertive. On the contrary he became the most powerful figure of his age. He was combative on every issue great and small, fighting with everyone from the King of Prussia to his local tax inspector. He had a happy married life and was not above sentimental love affairs, which included the daughter of an English duke and the wife of a Russian ambassador. All men feared him though he could be winning enough when he wished to be. Bismarck did not confirm the psychologist's rule.

With Beaverbrook I approached the problem the other way round. I described his character to a psychologist. Beaverbrook had a zest for power. He enjoyed making money and was captivating to women. He had also an inner uncertainty and a craving for affection which he often mistakenly thought money would win him. The psychologist answered without hesitation, 'He must have been a neglected only child.' In fact he was nothing of the kind. He was the fifth child in a family of eleven. His brothers and sisters assured me that their family life was uniformly happy and that Beaverbrook was an exception only in that he preferred to be a 'loner' – in his own words, 'a cat that walked by itself'. I decided that men have the disposition they are born with, not a helpful doctrine. Henceforward I left psychology alone.

Sex cannot be put aside so lightly. For one thing readers expect it. A biography is of little interest to them unless its subject has a glamorous love life. Sex may be important with literary figures. The Dark Lady of the Sonnets apparently mattered for Shakespeare though I think his gifts as a dramatist are to be taken more seriously. The relations of Dickens with Ellen Ternan provide an interesting gloss on his later novels but these novels read just as well without any knowledge of Ellen Ternan. Perhaps it is enlightening to learn that some novelist is homosexual, as happens often enough nowadays, but this is not what makes his novels memorable.

When we come to the political or other public figures that the historian turned biographer has to handle, their sex life has little relevance except for purposes of entertainment. Was Palmerston's foreign policy determined by the fact that he had a number of children by another man's wife? The relationship may have helped him to get the post of foreign secretary originally. Thereafter it does not seem to have mattered any more than if he had been married in the ordinary way. Did the longstanding friendship of Franz Joseph with Frau Schratt affect the constitutional history or the foreign policy of the Habsburg Monarchy? The platonic love that Bismarck had for Kathy Orloff makes a touching story but it did not even provide him with an excuse for meeting Napoleon III at Biarritz. Gladstone said at the end of his life that he had known eleven prime ministers and that seven of them were adulterers. No one, I think, could distinguish the adulterers from the chaste by examining their political activities. Lloyd George had many love affairs; Churchill had none. This had no influence on their respective careers except that Churchill claimed to have had more time for public affairs because he did not run after women.

Of course even the most political biographer finds interest in the more obvious features of his subject's character. It is useful to know how the subject handled other men; whether he was hard-working or lazy; what were his gifts as a public speaker and so on. One topic neglected by most biographers is what their subject ate and drank. Bismarck ate far too much for most of his life. He drank countless bottles of champagne and brandy and smoked fourteen Havana cigars a day. Churchill also drank a great deal and lit a great many cigars though he did not keep them alight for long. Were these two great men in a constant haze of alcohol and tobacco? It does not seem so from the clarity of their speeches or state papers. Stalin is said to have drunk plain water when he appeared to be drinking vodka. I doubt whether this was the secret of his power.

The historian turned biographer has no difficulty when he is merely recording his subject's career. But for a biography this is not enough. The author must also depict the subject's character, writing as though he understood what was going on in his subject's mind. Novelists find this easy. They have created the character; therefore they know everything about him. The professional biographer behaves in much the same way. He claims to know what his subject was thinking as well as what his subject was doing. He writes confidently of his subject's aims even when they were not revealed at the time. He often provides us with a vivid picture of the subject's thoughts. As a result each biographer presents an entirely different version, based more on conjecture than on evidence, and there are as many Napoleons and Hitlers as there are biographers.

The conscientious historian is at first distressed by this. He is accustomed to set down only the things for which he has evidence. Now he is required to use his imagination, not a quality with which historians are well endowed. But there is no escape from it. The historian has to recognize that biography is a literary art, much nearer to fiction or poetry than it is to serious history. However much the historian is concerned to record his subject's public acts, his essential task as a biographer is to present a single human being with all the contradictions that this involves.

Inevitably the writer of a biography becomes committed to his subject for good or bad. Some biographers come to dislike their subject and write what is commonly known as a debunking book. These books are often highly entertaining and a useful contribution to knowledge, as witness for instance that once-popular book, *Eminent Victorians* by Lytton Strachey. Most biographers, including myself, go the other way. They fall mildly in love with their subject and interpret everything in a favourable way. My admiration for Bismarck already existed before I wrote my biography of him but it may well have run away with me. With Beaverbrook I already had a deep personal affection which no doubt showed in my biography, some reviewers thought too much so. The best the historian can do when he grows attached to his subject is to keep this feeling within bounds. Even the most admirable man is all the better for a few black spots.

There are more technical problems involved in writing a man's biography. The greatest is the problem of documents. Most great men left large archives and the historian is anxious to publish copious extracts from them. If he publishes too many, he runs the risk of obscuring the subject's character. Nineteenth-century writers were fond of that composite form, Life and Letters – half a biography and half a collection of documents. The result was usually almost unreadable. With Bismarck I had little difficulty. I relied entirely on the printed sources which gave his letters and state papers and could safely refer the reader to these for further details. With Beaverbrook it was the other way round. I worked mostly from the manuscript collection of his letters and often, I am afraid, printed letters because they were amusing or eccentric rather than because they added to historical knowledge.

There is a further danger. Very often the biographer has had a predecessor; the subject himself. Many great men have been prolific writers; some have been brilliant writers. The greatest contemporary example is Winston Churchill whose version of both world wars has been indelibly stamped on the minds of most English readers. At one time historians treated Churchill's books as an impeccable source. Now we are gradually coming to realize that they are one-sided and often unreliable in their reproduction of documents. I had much the same problem with both my subjects. No one who has read *Gedanken und Erinnerungen* is likely to escape its influence. Now we know that Bismarck wrote or rather dictated it in extreme old age, often without consulting the contemporary documents, and that he was more concerned to depreciate Wilhelm II than to provide an impartial account for future generations. Beaverbrook was easier. He never aimed at supreme power despite what some of his critics have said. He was an observer who witnessed with interest and amusement the struggle of others for power. As a result his two books, *Politicians and the War* and *Men and Power*, are among the most entertaining and brilliant works of memoirs ever written. All the same he was not above twisting his record of events in order to come out more creditably than he deserved.

Autobiographies by the great men are often explosive tools to be used by the biographer with caution. But the lack of an autobiography is worse. It is unlikely that either Stalin or F D Roosevelt would have written autobiographies with much literary sparkle. But surely they would have told us something. As it is both men remain, what Sukhanov called Stalin in 1917, 'a grey blur'.

I have a word of counsel for any historian who is puzzled as to how to assess an autobiography: he should write one himself. He will find that however resolutely he tries to tell the truth the narrative gets out of control. Little successes are magnified and failures passed over unless of course they are blown up into monstrous grievances. Memory becomes selective. Often you remember what you ought to have done rather than what you did. Also your actions make more sense than they did at the time. In retrospect everything can be explained, usually to your own credit. Moreover when you write of friends or colleagues you see them as they are now, not as they were once. The best that can be said for a historian as autobiographer is that he knows he is cheating whereas the great men did not.

What applies to autobiographies applies also to anecdotes. Here the biographer has to be critical in two fields. He has to be critical about the subject. He has also to be critical about the source of the anecdote. Those who have climbed to success on the backs of great men are not likely to remember with much detachment. Alternatively the anecdotist will write with resentment against the humiliations and disappointments he had to endure. Having set down these difficulties I realize that they are much like what the historian has to face when he is working in his own field. First we have to find sources; then we have to criticize them. We are equipped to do both. After all, our training makes us more critical than other people. Hence there is a good case for historians writing biographies even if they have less imagination than the professionals.

The relationship between history and biography must also be considered the other way round. Not what contribution can the historian make as a biographer, but what use can biography be for the historian? The first answer is simple: historians have to use biographies whether they would or no. Though I do not know the statistics, I surmise that more biographies are published than serious works of history. They are our essential sources from ancient times to the present day. We accumulate pictures of individuals in the hope that they will merge into a general pattern. Not long ago Sir Lewis Namier and others set out to compile brief biographies of members of parliament. This, Namier claimed, would constitute a history of parliament. I asked him whether this history should not rather be sought in parliamentary debates and the resolutions or bills which a parliament passed. Namier brushed me aside. History, he insisted, was to be found in the biographies of innumerable ordinary men.

I was not convinced. However much we question the Great Man theory of history, the course of events is shaped by the leaders as much as by the followers. Historians treat one aspect of this process; biographies treat another. Historians are usually more cautious and hesitant in their judgements, at any rate nowadays. Biographers provide a more vivid, but not necessarily a truer version. In the last resort their ways part. The biographer builds up his individual subject until society is almost forgotten. The historian controls his interest in the individual and imposes the needs of society. The historian is perhaps too sceptical about Freud. The biographer neglects Marx who has provided essential instruments for historians. Where would historians be without the concept of class struggles and class characteristics?

Both historians and biographers use fictions, intellectual devices to produce an illusion of reality. The biographer relies on the fiction that he can recapture a man's character by literary skill and imagination. The historian welds individuals into a composite picture to which their individual existences are subordinated. The greatest achievements have been made by mixing biography and history together. This, too, is a literary art and hard to accomplish.

Fiction in History

This first appeared in The Times Literary Supplement *on 23 March 1973, with a companion, 'History in Fiction', by Mary Renault, a writer of historical novels.*

*   *   *

In most European languages 'story' and 'history' are the same word: *histoire* in French, *Geschichte* in German. *Quelle histoire* or *Was für eine Geschichte* does not mean 'What admirable history A J P Taylor writes' (even if he does) but 'What a far-fetched yarn.' It would save much trouble if we had the same coincidence of words in English. Then perhaps we should not be ashamed to admit that history is at bottom simply a form of story-telling. Historians nowadays have higher aims. They analyse past societies, generalize about human nature, or seek to draw morals about political or economic behaviour that will provide lessons for the present. Some of them even claim to foretell the future. These are admirable ambitions which have produced work of high quality. But there is no escaping the fact that the original task of the historian is to answer the child's question: 'What happened next?'

The past, or more precisely the past of literate mankind, is our raw material. In this past events succeed each other in order of time. This awareness of time came quite late in man's consciousness. Some civilizations do not have it. Early Indian chroniclers put in anecdotes higgledy-piggledy without caring which happened first. No true history can be written on this basis. We cannot change the order of time unless of course we or our sources have made a mistake, which is by no means unknown. We cannot have the events other than they are. Some historians like to play at the game 'If it had happened otherwise'.

This only goes to show that they would be better employed writing romantic novels where dreams come true.

History is not just a catalogue of events put in the right order like a railway timetable. History is a version of events. Between the events and the historian there is a constant interplay. The historian tries to impose on events some kind of rational pattern: how they happened and even why they happened. No historian starts with a blank mind as a jury is supposed to do. He does not go to documents or archives with a childlike innocence of mind and wait patiently until they dictate conclusions to him. Quite the contrary.

His picture, his version of events, is formed before he begins to write or even to research. I am told that scientists do much the same. They conduct experiments to confirm their ideas. They do not sit open-mouthed until an idea falls into it. Similarly the historian is after details to thicken up his picture and make it look intellectually convincing. Usually he finds them. Sometimes the opposite happens. He comes across events that upset his preconceived picture. The picture changes under his hand often without his realizing that it is doing so.

This happened with me when I wrote a book about the origins of the Second World War. I set out with the firm conviction, inherited from my pre-war years, that Hitler planned it all. I discovered, or thought I discovered, that Hitler, though no doubt resolved to make Germany a world power, had no clear-cut plan how to do it and moved forward with the changing situation. Some critics were shocked by this and attributed to me all kinds of wickedness – apologizing for Hitler or justifying the later appeasement of Soviet Russia. I had no such aims. My historian's conscience simply carried me in an unexpected direction. I do not think any historian is worth his salt who has not had a similar experience.

Are we then to say that there is nothing to choose between the different versions of events produced by historians? It sometimes looks like it. Pieter Geyl whiled away his years in a German concentration camp by analysing the views of French

historians on Napoleon: *for* and *against*. In this country singing
the praises of the Industrial Revolution or displaying its brutalities has itself become a major industry. Certainly these are very
different versions, but they remain versions of events, and the
historian who cheats on his events will be beyond the pale even
if his version happens to be a welcome one. Take a photograph
of the west front of York Minster if the scaffolding is now down.
Take another of the interior. You will have different versions
but both of York Minster. Slip in a photograph of Lincoln
Cathedral, and you are cheating.

When a historian is working on his subject, the events or
statistical data or whatever he is using change under his hand
all the time and his ideas about these events change with them.
He upgrades some of the evidence and downgrades other parts
according to the changes of his outlook. Sometimes, I am afraid,
he exaggerates the importance of a piece of evidence because it
fits in well with what he is trying to say.

Sometimes he puts an unwelcome piece of evidence at the
bottom of the pile. But, if he is any good, the omitted piece nags
at him. He pulls it out and confesses: 'Oh dear, I was wrong.'
Recently some younger scholars disproved my interpretation of
Lloyd George's Mansion House speech at the time of the Agadir
crisis. I was just ordering a very smart suit of sackcloth and ashes
when another young scholar demonstrated that I was not all that
wrong after all. Now I do not know where I stand. However I
cannot say I was altogether pleased when one bit of my interpretation, or rather a guess, slipped into a television play on
Lloyd George.

Certainly we guess. We are writing to shape into a version a
tangle of events that was not designed as a pattern. 'Ceaselessly
explain' was Lenin's motto and is also mine. Guessing is the only
way of explaining when solid evidence runs out. There are
gradations of guessing. Consider a general conducting a battle.
If we know from his later dispatch or from what others recorded
at the time, we say: 'He saw the enemy advancing.' If we
can deduce what he saw from studying the map or ourselves

reconnoitring the battlefield, we say: 'He must have seen the enemy advancing.' If we can only deduce what he saw from his subsequent actions, then we say: 'Probably he saw the enemy advancing.' If he behaved like a complete idiot, as generals often do, we fall back on what we know of his character or previous actions. This is the way we explain Gamelin's total failure to do anything about the German breakthrough at Sedan in May 1940. One day evidence may provide a different explanation. Perhaps Gamelin had a heart attack. Perhaps his staff concealed the news of the breakthrough from him. Then our version will change. All the time we are tied to the events though the connection sometimes becomes remote. We never actually invent, though we sometimes practise sleight of hand. History, just like historical fiction, is an exercise in creative imagination, though in our case the exercise is restrained by the limits of our knowledge. One essential ingredient we learnt from a writer of historical novels: the past is different from the present. This is quite a recent discovery. Until the beginning of the nineteenth century historians did not know it, though they sometimes appreciated it unconsciously. Machiavelli, for instance, wrote his *Discourses* in the belief that the political affairs of ancient Rome provided useful guidance for the Italian republics of his time. For that matter, the Greats school at Oxford assumed that the study of ancient history and philosophy was perfect equipment for the administrators of the Indian Empire. I do not think that even Gibbon, despite his superlative gift of narration, regarded the Romans as different from himself. He thought that Commodus was another version of Louis XV, though with less usual tastes, just as eighteenth-century statesmen did not feel it incongruous that their statues should be draped in togas.

True history began with Sir Walter Scott. He felt himself backwards into time. He did not always succeed. *Ivanhoe* is not a convincing picture of the Middle Ages: it is simply lay figures in fancy dress. But *Old Mortality* is a convincing picture of the later seventeenth century. It is the cloak from which we are all cut. That the past is different from the present is a hard doctrine.

Though we try to operate it, we never wholly succeed. The historian who now looks at the English Revolution or Great Rebellion of the seventeenth century cannot help seeing in it a form of class war. So no doubt it was. But when I am told that Bunyan voiced the outlook of independent artisans, I cannot altogether forget that what he attached importance to was being a Baptist.

There is another difficulty that comes from our dealing with events that succeed each other in time. Maitland, to my mind the greatest of English historians, formulated it: 'It is very difficult to remember that events now in the past were once far in the future.' We know what is going to happen. The characters of our history did not.

Hitler maybe knew that he was going to aim at world power, and also knew incidentally that he had a pretty thin chance of getting it. But did Napoleon know that there would be a Napoleonic Empire of Europe? Did F D Roosevelt foresee that under his direction the United States would become the greatest power in the world? Cromwell made a boast of not knowing where he was going. Others often claim to know and end up somewhere quite different. The historian uses his mixture of information and creative imagination to sort out what was in men's minds: not attributing conscious design unless there is some evidence for it and yet admitting its existence sometimes all the same.

In spite of our virtuous resolves, we often stray from history into fiction. We never actually invent, though the temptation to do so is often great. Beaverbrook, a historian whom I greatly admired, played tricks that the more scrupulous would shrink from. Here is an example. In 1917 Lloyd George was having difficulties with Sir William Robertson, the CIGS (Chief of the Imperial General Staff). F E Smith was consulted. Beaverbrook records: 'He recommended an immediate reorganization of the high offices in the military command at the War Office.' That accords with the evidence. It is a drab statement. So Beaverbrook inserted on the proof: '"Sack him now," said F E in effect.'

The last two words, I suppose, just make the sentence allow-able, but it was sailing very near the wind. A professional historian would not risk it. Certainly we speculate. We produce explanations that seem reasonable to us rather than being provided by the evidence. But we draw a clear line and warn the reader what we are doing.

Our fiction comes in quite another way and is all the more dangerous for being usually unconscious. We take the characters of the past too seriously. Most of our evidence until fairly recent times is about the thin top layer of society – kings, nobles, ministers and high clerics. They may be a poor lot but they are all we have, and we blow them up beyond their deserts. Experi-ence teaches that hereditary succession is not a good way of producing ability. Yet we go on treating kings as though they possessed the sort of ability shown by men who had to fight their way to the top. Of course we acknowledge bad kings, according to the immortal phrase of Sellar and Yeatman, but we also find good kings and even great kings.

My late colleague Bruce McFarlane described Henry V as 'the greatest man that ever ruled England'. Great, say, compared with Churchill, let alone Cromwell? I do not believe it. I doubt whether he was much improvement on Ramsay MacDonald. Looking around the crowned heads who have bestrewn the European stage over the centuries, I cannot see any other than Frederick the Great as a man of more than common abilities, and even his abilities were on the thin side.

Of course many kings conducted the affairs of state in a reasonably competent way just as the wealthy man who inherits a great industrial undertaking makes a tolerable chairman of the board. But we cannot be content with that. We manufacture heroes simply because they occupy great positions. We forget that most of these heroes were mainly concerned to show off and enjoy themselves – hunting, running after mistresses, building palaces, collecting works of art, or merely eating and drinking. If they carry this too far, we rebuke our heroes for neglecting what we regard as their true historical duty of ruling.

In my opinion, most great men of the past were only there for the beer – the wealth, prestige and grandeur that went with power. What blinds us to this is the occupational disease of the historian: assuming, when we think back into the past, that we too will be in the top drawer. We shall be jesting with Queen Elizabeth I, building our own palace to rival Blenheim or running a faro bank with Charles Fox. My grandfather was a weaver, so I am less liable to this delusion. If I went back, I should more likely be working eighteen hours a day at a hand-loom or dying of starvation in a ditch.

Of course historians no longer neglect the common people as they did in the days when G M Trevelyan defined social history as 'history with the politics left out'. Now they are interested in how people lived and what made society work. Indeed 'political historian' has almost become a term of reproach. We of this despised class also try to bring in the people and, I fear, often slip into fiction when we do so. We invent national sentiments and attribute to past generations a conscious community of ideas that may exist nowadays. There is perhaps just enough evidence for us to say that in August 1914 the peoples of the major European countries were enthusiastic for war. Looking at that sentence again, I begin to doubt. Are we taking too seriously cheering crowds in the capital cities? Is it not possible that they would have cheered just as vociferously an announcement that peace had been preserved?

In earlier times national sentiment is surely a fiction, though perhaps a necessary one. Were the ordinary people of England running over with eagerness to destroy the French Revolution? The governing classes did not think so. They believed that they were sitting on a Jacobin volcano. Take another example. Dr Johnson, a good judge though a Tory, said that if the people had been polled in 1714 the Old Pretender would have been restored. The riotous mobs at the time of Sacheverell's impeachment suggest that he was right. Did the common people really rejoice at Henry V's conquest of France? And what did they think of William the Conqueror's victory at Hastings? When did they even learn of it? Not until months, perhaps not even until years, afterwards. It is easy to forget that people once did not have newspapers, let alone television.

Such are the myths with which we try to give the historical record some sort of rational shape. Our work looks duller and less dramatic than the work of avowed fiction. So it is in appearance, with its scrabbling over sources, its footnotes, and its hesitations. But our material is often more dramatic than anything a historical novelist would dare to invent. Real life outdoes imagination. When Laurence Sterne wanted to put his father into a book, he had to make two of him; Walter Shandy and Uncle Toby. The real man was too much. No one would have believed it. No political novel has ever had a story as dramatic as the fall of Parnell. For that we go not to a novelist but to a modest work by F S L Lyons.

I recently saw a television play about Hitler in the bunker. Stuffed figures, dressed as German generals, delivered remarks taken from the sources. Bormann displayed an anonymity which would, it was said, enable him to vanish into thin air. But where was Hitler – the demonic character who carried a world into war and commanded the unquestioning allegiance of the vast majority of Germans to his last day? He had shrunk to a crazy neurotic, which of course he was as well. But we can find him again in the acknowledged masterpiece by Hugh Trevor-Roper, which leaves fiction far behind.

Marx was fond of quoting Heraclitus: *panta rei*, all things move. This is the one truth we seek to recapture when we write history. We know that our version, being set into words, is itself false. We are trying to stop something that never stays still. Once written, our version too will move. It will be challenged and revised. It will take on appearances that we did not expect. We are content to repeat the words with which Geyl finished his book on Napoleon: 'History is an argument without end.'

Tory History

Firstly published in the New Statesman *on 6 May 1950 as a review of Keith Feiling's* A History of England *(London, Macmillan, 1950)*.

*   *   *

'Good people, I am the Protestant whore!' So Nell Gwynn quietened a mob which had taken her for one of her Roman Catholic colleagues. Professor Feiling is a writer with too many idiosyncrasies to be so simply docketed. Still, when a man writes a massive history of England, he challenges comparison with Trevelyan, with J R Green, even, his publishers think, with Macaulay. Compared with these Feiling is the Tory historian. Yet this is an elusive category. The Whig interpretation of history is easy to define; all our political thinking rests on it. It is the story of English liberty, founded by Magna Carta, consolidated by the Glorious Revolution, expanded by the great Reform Bill, and reaching its highest achievement with the Labour government. In the words of Ramsay MacDonald, 'Up and up and up and on and on and on.' It is the doctrine of history as progress: men always getting wiser and more tolerant; houses more comfortable, food more plentiful; new laws always better than old laws; new ideas always better than old ideas; new wives, I suppose, always better than old wives (this last much practised by the Whig aristocracy).

Liberty ought to be a revolutionary doctrine, the creed of a minority; in England it has become traditional, respectable, universally accepted. This is a result of the Glorious Revolution. True Toryism perished in 1688 or, at any rate, with the Hanoverian succession. What sense had 'Church and King' in the age of latitudinarian bishops and German princes? For that matter, even in the twentieth century the Tories, despite their loyal phrases, were responsible for the only real subversion of modern times, the Ulster rebellion of 1914. If Toryism means anything, it rejects the sovereignty of parliament and the doctrine of the Social Contract, which underlay the revolution of 1688. In practice, as Macaulay observed, Toryism amounts to no more than defending Whig achievements of a previous generation. In the world of ideas, the Tories have had to make do with unprincipled adventurers, like Bolingbroke and Disraeli, or to borrow from the other side. Burke, whom Feiling calls 'the largest mind ever given to politics in our island' and 'the inspiration of a second party of Tories', was a corrupt Whig hack. A century later, the Tories learnt their imperialism from the renegade radical, Chamberlain. It would be unfair to blame Toryism for being short of ideas. Ideas are an affair of the mind, and Toryism distrusts the mind in politics. In essence, Toryism rests on doubt in human nature; it distrusts improvement, clings to traditional institutions, prefers the past to the future. It is a sentiment rather than a principle. Feiling carries this sentiment so far that he can even include Oliver Cromwell in it.

Though reason may be a good guide in politics, it is inadequate for the writing of history, and the very qualities which make Tories detestable as politicians should make them good historians. After all a historian should start by appreciating the past. It is true that Gibbon, the greatest of our historians, had nothing but contempt for his chosen subject; this merely shows that genius can disregard all rules. In lesser men Whig rationalism produces what has been well called 'the linotype school of history'; in which everyone behaves according to rule, the mysteries of human behaviour vanish and everything moves relentlessly towards infinite improvement – or to infinite disaster. Mr Feiling writes with a greater understanding of human affairs. He does not pretend to know the answer to every problem in the universe. In his book events remain, as they are, blurred and confused; it is like listening to a story told entirely in echoes. When we read the narrative of a cocksure historian, we tend to forget that the historian can never speak with first-hand authority; he can only piece together the accounts of others. A novelist creates his characters and therefore knows their every motive and action; Feiling never forgets that he did not create the English people. Very often he puts his narrative in the form of hearsay. 'We hear of Saxon invaders on the south coast'; 'there are reports of great acts of cruelty'. The effect is of news arriving late and contradictory to a remote country house, where a slow-witted squire is trying to make sense of events in the short intervals between hunting and fishing. It needs a writer of supreme skill, far from slow-witted, to create this impression, so much nearer to life than our neat explanations.

Toryism starts with the squire, the lesser landowner. Everyone knows that. Feiling emphasizes again and again the permanent elements in rural society. He recognizes, as few Whig historians have done, the importance of local government; indeed even parliament bulks largest in his eyes as a gathering of country gentry. The traditional 'liberties of England' rested on law and custom, not on rational dogma, and the man who maintained them, as in Poland or Hungary, was the country squire. He maintained them no doubt for his own profit and advantage, a point which Feiling is inclined to slide over; still England would not be a free country without him. The unique feature of our history is that the conservative defender of liberty had to take other classes into partnership and finally indeed found himself in the position of a tolerated minority. Feiling says rightly: 'in ages when everywhere in Europe public liberties were being quenched, English law defended freedom', but he also admits that this 'venerable common law' was by the end of the eighteenth century wholly unfit to deal with a new age.

Would these changes come by violence or by agreement? This was the great question of the early nineteenth century. As we know, they came by agreement or, at any rate, by constitutional process. This is usually regarded as the greatest triumph of the Whig spirit. The new Toryism may claim almost as much credit – meaning by this an attitude of mind rather than either the practical common sense of Peel or the flashy trivialities of Disraeli. Though Tory government of the early nineteenth century needed the votes of country squires, it did not represent their outlook nor was it run by them. The squires got the Corn Laws; in return they voted for a government of administrators and soldiers, the former 'King's friends'. This is a point which Feiling does not make explicit, but it conditions all the later part of his work. If by Liberalism is meant all those who try to apply reason to politics, and who enter politics in order to improve things, then it is not only Tory landowners who are on the other side. Conservatism becomes the party also of those who are in politics simply to make things work: to promote, no doubt, their own careers, but to promote them by public service. In a splendid Tory phrase, Feiling quotes the East India Company as declaring on its extinction that the Crown had inherited 'such a body of civil and military officers as the world has never seen before'. Toryism is no longer a creed merely for the man in the country; it becomes the creed also for the man in the office. Further, when the enterprising capitalist ceases to be adventurous and becomes also a man in the office, Toryism becomes his creed too. Of course this knocks the remaining romance out of Toryism. As Feiling says regretfully of Peel, 'he was cold or deaf to some high sentiments in Tory tradition, whether religious passion or the vision of paternal government'.

Thus what may be called the Tory interpretation of history has no longer much to do with high-flown loyalty to the Crown or devotion to the Church of England: it is not even the exaltation of traditional institutions. The Tory spirit in history is shown by an emphasis on administration, by getting ideas out of history and putting humdrum personal motives and office routine in. Until reading Feiling's book I had thought that the opposite to Whig history was history as it really worked. I now see for the first time that when you take ideas out of history you put Toryism in. When Tout emphasized the administrative history of Edward II against Stubbs's search for the growth of the British constitution, he was not being a better historian than

Stubbs; he was being a Tory historian. When Namier emptied Hanoverian Whiggism of principle and analysed the personal or family motives which took men into politics, he was not being a better historian than Macaulay; he was being a Tory historian. When Sir Charles Webster admired Palmerston for the efficient way in which he organized the Foreign Office instead of for the great liberal principles which he tried to apply, he, too, was unwittingly opening the gates to the Tory interpretation of history. In fact, as Sir William Harcourt might so wittily have said: 'We are all Tories nowadays.'

History is no doubt best conducted, like the British constitution, on the principle that Whig plus Tory equals eternal truth. This principle works only so long as it is clear that Toryism is only half the truth, just as Conservatives are only a substantial minority of the nation despite the Union Jack on their platforms and their masquerade as the national party. Tory history becomes dangerous only when it is presented as impartial history. Feiling, for instance, appears extremely fair and detached until you look at his treatment of the radicals. Try him on Wat Tyler, on the Levellers, on the Chartists, and you discover a point at which his English sympathies break down. It is revealing that the only spiteful remark in the book is about Major Cartwright, first advocate of universal suffrage. Characteristic also is the judgement that Tom Paine 'had not a rudiment of English feeling, nor was he a thinker', this of the author of *The Rights of Man*, the best statement of democratic belief in any language. The administrator sees the reformer and the agitator as disturbing elements, upsetting office routine and putting forward impractical ideas based on a Utopian faith in human reason.

It was no doubt inevitable that Tory history should gradually take the place of a Whig interpretation which had become traditional and formal. More than this, our whole educational system is now directed to turning out administrators, and these administrators want history with passion left out and machinery put in. Above all, Whig history was the work of an age which believed in progress. For Feiling, British greatness ended in 1918. The rest was 'aftermath', redeemed only by Neville Chamberlain. This is history written in the spirit of a Roman of the late empire. The administrator still sits at his desk, the army officer still drills his men; but the wall is crumbling, the barbarians are breaking in, nostalgia has taken the place of hope. Yet even nostalgia is a human sentiment. If we survive at all, both Trevelyan and Feiling will be outmoded. What we must expect is history that will be neither Whig nor Tory, but Byzantine.

The Thing

First published in The Twentieth Century, *October 1957.*

* * *

A contribution to a symposium, 'Is there a Power Elite?' I wish I had thought of the opening by Philip Toynbee, the following contributor; 'Who governs Britain? The governing *class*, surely.'

Lord Attlee, on some wartime journey, was reading a life of Sir Robert Walpole. He looked across at his companion, a high civil servant, and reflected: 'I wonder who really ran the country in those days?' An apocryphal story no doubt like most stories about Lord Attlee, but a reasonable speculation. In every society Lenin's rule applies: 'Who whom?' Some men give orders; the rest obey them. In a truly democratic society the rulers would be chosen by lot for short stretches. Failing that we should at least postulate that every citizen have an equal chance of reaching the top if he wants to get there. This does not apply in any known community, not even in Switzerland, the country that comes nearest to democracy. Everywhere the potential ruler has to pass some test other than ambition and ability. It may be birth, money, class, colour, religion, even (as in old China) capacity to pass examinations. But some test there will be. The minority that emerges will constitute the power élite from whom the actual rulers are chosen. What we call democracy is merely a system by which the members of this power élite receive an occasional popular endorsement.

The requirements for entering the British power élite are fairly well known. You must be white in colour; male; wear collar and tie and a dark suit; and able to spend most of your life indoors sitting down. You must also be able to dictate reasonably grammatical English. Oratory – once highly regarded – is no longer required. Anyone capable of reading from typescript can go to the highest place. These are the bare essentials. The right parents are a considerable asset. It is still best to come from 'the nobility and gentry', though it is probably a mistake to be the eldest son of a peer. Parents from the professional class are good, particularly if they pay surtax. Rich businessmen, oddly, not at all good. If you are so foolish as to be born into the industrial working class, then you must get out of it by winning a scholarship to a grammar school or, failing this, by becoming either a trade union official or a WEA tutor. If you are born of an agricultural labourer, you should give up at the start. The right education helps. It is of little moment what you learn, though Latin is still probably the most useful subject and any form of science a handicap; the important thing is where you learn. Eton remains by far the best bet; Winchester runs it close in the Labour Party. Otherwise prefer a first-rate grammar school to a minor public school and run away to sea rather than go to a secondary modern. Oxford and Cambridge are so obvious a requirement as hardly to need mention. Any other university can be valued only for the instruction it provides. As to accomplishments, it is no longer necessary to ride a horse, shoot, fish, or even play bridge. In fact, the less accomplished you are outside your work the better. And even at work it is wiser to seem devoted rather than clever. Otherwise you are in danger of becoming a 'character', and this is hard to live down.

The picture drawn here differs little from that of the power élite in Washington or Moscow. Religion, however, provides a distinguishing mark. I use the word to mean morality and rules of conduct, not acceptance or denial of any theological dogma. You may choose anything from Roman Catholicism in its English version to 'humanism' – that is, unassertive atheism. But it must be broadly within the tradition of liberal Christianity. Fundamentalism, aggressive atheism and of course

adherence to any non-Christian religion other than Judaism,
exclude. In other words, the members of the British power élite
observe the standards created by the nineteenth-century public
schools. Once upon a time you could have found the mainspring
of British public life by assembling the leading headmasters,
some bishops (themselves former headmasters) and the Master
of Balliol. Now the position is more complicated. By no means
all our rulers have been to public schools, and even public
schoolboys take much of their instruction from without the
school walls. Our guardians of tradition are self-appointed; our
high priests for the most part unfrocked. Nevertheless they exist
and they give English life its unique flavour.

It has lately become the fashion to call them 'the Establishment'. Henry Fairlie is said to have started this, though I have
also seen it attributed to myself. I regret the idea, whoever had
it. The very word, so plummy, so ponderous, so respectable,
tempts us to acknowledge the moral superiority of 'the Establishment'. It conjures up benign, upholstered figures, calm, steady,
reliable. They would never pass a dud cheque or cheat at cards.
Not intellectually dazzling perhaps, but patient, understanding,
and tolerant – above all tolerant. Anyone who challenges them
is disarmed by the quizzical, superior smile and the enquiry:
'Well, my little man, what is it now?' It was a great blunder to
take the Establishment at its own valuation. We ought to have
revived Cobbett's name: THE THING. That suggests much better
the complacency, the incompetence and the selfishness which lie
behind the façade. THE THING exists for the sake of its members,
not for ours. They look comfortable because they are comfortable. They are upholstered because they are well fed. Their air
of moral superiority is really an assumption that someone else
will always cook their dinner – and a good dinner at that.

Yet in one way the word 'Establishment' has its uses. It
emphasizes the historical foundation of THE THING, a foundation
still essential despite being obscured by later buildings. The
basis of the Establishment is quite simply the Church of England
as by law established. I doubt whether anyone with an Anglican

background can become a true radical. George Lansbury came nearest to it. Yet there was always a subtle dividing line between him and the rebels round him. Gladstone tried hard, but he could never rid himself of the belief that a duke or a bishop had more political sense than Cobden or John Stuart Mill. The rule still applies in the Labour Party. Its leaders with an Anglican education seek radical ideas, but they lack radical instincts. Time and again they end up on the Right without ever meaning to do so. Religious dissent is the only safe background for a radical, but militant dissent has long been on the decline until now the remnants of the Free Churches regard themselves as a junior branch of the Establishment. THE THING is more secure than it was fifty years ago. It runs into difficulties from its own mistakes, not from any aggressive and conscious challenge.

On paper things have changed since the classical constitution of the eighteenth century. In reality they are much the same. THE THING still assumes that it should receive all the plums and it gets them. For instance, every college at Oxford and Cambridge still has an Anglican chapel maintained from college endowments, though they claim to be members of a national university. Bishops still pontificate on every conceivable subject from nuclear fission to the private lives of unbelievers. The Test Act, though repealed, is still wondrously effective. We note with surprise when a judge is a Roman Catholic or a cabinet minister has been divorced. Why should it not be surprising the other way round?

THE THING has always boasted that it is not exclusive. This is true. Accept its standards, conform to its pattern, and you reap a rich reward. Incompetent in everything else, THE THING has a wonderful aptitude for seeing that there are enough plums to go round. Just as the British Empire was wasting away, the nationalized industries came along to restore the balance. There has been no such manna of jobbery since the palmy days of Sir Robert Walpole. You need not even conform to the rules so long as you pay lip-service to them. A nineteenth-century Duke of Devonshire, who lived openly with a woman not his wife, enjoyed the unique distinction of having been offered the premiership by each political party in turn. And Stanley Baldwin did not jib at the idea that a king of England should keep a mistress.

But try to disregard THE THING. Tolerance and good behaviour vanish at once. Lloyd George is the supreme illustration. He was beyond question the greatest political genius of his time, incomparable alike in peace and in war. He had every quality except conformity. THE THING turned to him in the desperate circumstances of 1916. Once the crisis was past, it hunted him from power. Between the wars all the energies of THE THING were devoted to keeping Lloyd George out. No wonder there was nothing left over to deal with such problems as unemployment or Hitler.

Is THE THING any use? None at all except for its members. Most people lead industrious decent lives without the moral guidance of the Archbishop of Canterbury. Those who wish to read books or listen to music do so without seeking the blessing of Sir Ian Jacob. It would be a great improvement in every way if we got rid of THE THING. The country would be more alert, more receptive to new ideas, more capable of holding its own in the world. THE THING is on the surface a system of holding its own in the world. THE THING is on the surface a system of public morals. Underneath it is a system of public plunder. Its true purpose was revealed by a poster which the Chamberlain government rashly displayed early in the war:

> *Your* COURAGE, *Your* CHEERFULNESS, *Your* RESOLUTION WILL
> BRING US VICTORY

There was once, I suppose, some sense in THE THING. In former times the mass of people had to live in hardship and want. There was luxury enough only for a few; and THE THING was a reasonable device for ladling the luxury around. Now life is improving for everybody. Why should the members of THE THING get more of the proceeds than others? Already in the United States a university professor is paid less than a skilled worker in an automobile works. Economics will succeed where dissent failed. The time is coming when the average reader of the *Daily Mirror* will get more than the average reader of *The Times*. Who will care then if the readers of *The Times* go on imagining that they are the Top People?

British Pamphleteers

This essay was published in 1951 as the Introduction to A J P Taylor and Reginald Reynolds, British Pamphleteers, *Volume 2:* From the French Revolution to the Nineteen-Thirties *(London, Allan Wingate). Reginald Reynolds made the selection of twenty-one pamphlets or parts of pamphlets as he had done for the first volume. Then George Orwell had provided the Introduction. In the second volume the Acknowledgements included the unusual note :*

The complete disagreement between the views expressed by Mr Taylor in his Introduction and Mr Reynolds in his notes to the individual pamphlets will be obvious. It needs no apology and is, indeed, appropriate to a volume dealing with controversial literature. But it should be emphasized that neither writer is in any way responsible for the opinions of his collaborator.

The most striking clash of views was over Saunders Lewis's pamphlet 'Why We Burnt the Bombing School'. While Reynolds sympathetically recounted the action of Saunders Lewis and two other 'respected citizens' at Penros, Alan Taylor's comments on the loss of Lewis's job were insensitive. Taylor was not to feel so lightly about the loss of his own special lectureship at Oxford University when his unorthodox views led to it not being renewed in 1963. The other pamphlets which Alan Taylor mentions in this essay were Edward Carpenter's 'Non-Governmental Society', Joseph Pease's 'On Slavery and its Remedy', Charles Kingsley's 'Cheap Clothes and Nasty', Lord Brougham's 'A Letter to Isaac Tomkins, Gent.', Sydney Smith's 'Ballot', William Hone's 'The Late John Wilkes' Catechism', H N Brailsford's 'The Origins of the Great War' and Thomas Carlyle's 'Occasional Discourse on the Nigger Question'. Reynolds deemed this last to be an outstanding 'specimen of venomous hatred against people the writer had never met, whose only crime was their unwillingness to work themselves to death in order to provide wealth and luxury for others' − a view which Taylor, who loathed racism,

*might have been expected to endorse. Instead Alan Taylor chose to con-
firm his television reputation as a great and unpredictable controversialist
and, throughout this essay, one who clearly enjoyed attacking the comfortable assumptions of his own radical and nonconformist background.
This habit of mind, of challenging received opinions of all kinds, was
at the root of his appeal as a revisionist historian. The essay is also
notable for the strong anti-communist line that he took for some years
after 1948.*

* * *

The subject of this anthology is British pamphleteers, not British
pamphlets. Its aim is to display some remarkable individuals, not
to illustrate the development of a particular literary form. Or
perhaps it would be truer to say that the pamphlet becomes
literature only when it is written by a remarkable individual. The
ordinary pamphlet does not merit resurrection. It is designed to
be read quickly and to be thrown away. Like the bee, it can only
sting once. Yet anyone who recollects the Labour movement in
its missionary days thirty or forty years ago must look back with
some nostalgia to the 'literature' stall where pamphlets by Lenin,
Blatchford, Daniel De Leon, Walton Newbold, and the secretary
of the Vegetarian Society were indiscriminately displayed. 'Don't
forget the literature, comrades!' was the last, the parting cry of
the chairman; it took the place of the Blessing at more orthodox
gatherings. Now the chairman's voice is silent (unless he is
presiding over the board of a nationalized industry); and the
'literature' is forgotten. Nowhere in the world is there a complete
collection of the stuff; no one anywhere will ever read it through.
Something has survived! the best of it reprinted here. It has
survived, by virtue of its literary excellence; preserved, as it
were, from destruction by the strong spirits of individualism
which soak through these pages. It is agreeable to reflect how
enraged the authors of these pamphlets would be if they were
ever to know that one day people would read them merely
for fun.

Individualism is the essence of the successful pamphlet. It is the most immediate and the most personal of all literary forms; the Hyde Park of the written word. The writer of a pamphlet has a single idea to express and is in a hurry to express it; usually he thinks in terms of addressing a single reader. A pamphlet is argument or it is nothing; and it is not surprising that so many pamphlets are written in the form of dialogue – failing a more satisfactory opponent the pamphleteer has to argue with himself. Even if the pamphlet is written as straight prose, it still proceeds in terms of personal intimacy; and the reader usually finds himself addressed in the second person. You can feel the pamphleteer reaching out of the pages, buttonholing you, prodding home his points with aggressive forefinger. Sometimes you are made to feel foolish; sometimes your vanity is flattered (though the writer clearly despises you all the time); one way or another you are never allowed to forget that you are being argued at. You can be pretty sure when you pick up a pamphlet that at the end you will be expected to agree with something or to protest against something or, most usual of all, to send a subscription. It is, I suppose, true that the first pamphlets were in the nature of reprinted sermons; and the pamphlet has always retained something of the atmosphere of the pulpit, with its mixture of intimacy and exhortation.

All this, and much more, was said by George Orwell in his introduction to the first volume of British pamphleteers. Here we are concerned with something more limited: the pamphleteers of the nineteenth and early twentieth centuries. It would be hard to say whether they are better or worse than their predecessors; it is certain that they are different. Though they say more daring things, they say it in more commonplace language; though they are more individualistic, they have less to be individual about. What has happened to them is that they have won; and the moment of their victory is the French Revolution, which quite rightly marks the division between our first volume and our second. Until the time of the French Revolution, the individual who was out of step knew that he was threatened; that he had to keep up the attack in order to hold his own at all. Defoe might enter the pay of William III; and Swift might accept a deanery from Queen Anne. They still belonged to a secret conspiracy, the sect of those who thought for themselves. Samuel Johnson, despite his supposedly orthodox views, was the last of the old school. No one can read Johnson, even when he was justifying Lord North's treatment of America, without realizing that here was a man fighting desperately against great odds to hold his own. When Johnson gets a pension from George III, we are not so much shocked as surprised – staggered indeed at the incongruity. No one would be surprised if Carlyle got a pension from Queen Victoria; indeed it would be curious if he did not. All the authors in this book are individualists for whom rebellion has paid big dividends. If they had remained respectable and conformist, no one would ever have heard of them; and their bank balances would have been very much smaller. I observe from Mr Reynolds' note that the author of the last pamphlet in this book lost his post as a lecturer at Swansea University College after the action which he describes. This does not prove that individual opinions are dangerous; it only proves that the Welsh are intolerant – more backward than the English, in fact, which it was the argument of the pamphlet to refute. If Mr Saunders Lewis achieved the independent Wales of his dreams, he would undoubtedly be flung into prison, if not burnt alive. As it is, his martyrdom (thanks to English protection) has been gentle in the extreme; after all no one can regard the position of a lecturer at Swansea University College as something of which one is deprived with regret.

It is worth considering why individualism did the trick at the time of the French Revolution, and what the trick is that it has done. The secret I believe to be this. The earlier pamphleteers praised by George Orwell, though individualistic, did not extol individualism as a good in itself; they extolled it for the rewards it would bring. The Protestant, however extreme, did not say: 'It is desirable that every single person should have a religion different from that of everyone else.' He said : 'The judgement of the individual will lead him to a religion which will be finer, purer, truer – which will be, in fact, remarkably like mine.' The Protestants of the seventeenth century used to puzzle a good deal what they should do if the individual's judgement led him to believe in the Devil, or even in no religion at all. The 'inner light' was recognized as an admirable illumination only so long as my voltage was the same as yours. Even now Quakers who take to drink or divorce or even to an enthusiasm for the Mass are not easily accommodated within the Society of Friends. The French Revolution changed all that. Liberty was demanded for its own sake, not for what it would produce. This is really the only argument by which liberty can be justified. It is humbug, for instance, to suppose that scientists produce better results if they are allowed to ramble over the universe on their own than if they are organized in high-grade concentration camps. Both Russian and American scientists are chained by the leg, the one to the secret police, the other to their dollar-balances; but they are doing very well as scientists all the same. They can keep up the bidding indefinitely until between them they bring civilized life to an end. The English scientist, in comparison, is quite a harmless creature.

The argument is just as true of literature, thought, or the arts. Spain produced great art at the height of the Inquisition; French civilization flourished under the absolutism of Louis XIV; Mozart and Beethoven managed to compose great music under the dead hand of the Habsburgs. Freedom is not justified of its fruits. Why should it be? It is justified of itself. This was the great achievement of the French Revolution. It launched the irresistible doctrine of human rights. The established order does very well so long as it can keep up an air of superiority and can make rebels appear tiresome, insignificant people. Even the greatest rebels were weighed down by their fault. For instance, it never occurred to Milton or to any of his contemporaries that Satan was the hero of his poem; to us it is so obvious as hardly to be worth saying. The English rebels of the seventeenth century had to devise all sorts of imaginary crimes in order to justify their execution of Charles I. By the nineteenth century a rebel could propose as a matter of course his admirable objective 'to strangle the last king with the bowels of the last priest'. And once he had coined the phrase he did not need to put his precept into action – no kings were in fact strangled in Europe in the nineteenth century or even executed. A tsar was assassinated in Russia; that only proves its remoteness from Europe. After the French Revolution the bottom fell out of the Establishment. It had to go over to the defensive, and a very half-hearted defensive at that. France, for instance, became divided into the party of movement and the party of resistance; a very revealing distinction. Who would be against movement for its own sake? Genuine conservatism disappeared. What has called itself conservatism in the last hundred years has merely consisted in putting a brake on 'the march of progress'; at best conservatism has defended the liberal achievements of the previous generation.

It is very nice to feel yourself on the winning side; and the individual has been very much on the winning side for the last century and a half in our European civilization. John Stuart Mill or Victor Hugo or Mazzini said daring things; but nothing could stop them becoming the most respected citizens of their countries. In our own day Bernard Shaw spent an inordinately long lifetime trying to shock public opinion on every conceivable subject. He left the largest fortune of any contemporary writer; and his tasteless suburban house has become a national shrine. George Orwell, who wrote the admirable introduction to the first volume of this work, wanted to be a rebel all his life; when he died, tragically young, he was a best-seller in two continents. Long ago David really marched out to challenge Goliath. Nowadays Goliath welcomes David to the field; picks up the pebbles for him; and then falls down flat before the sling is discharged. Talk about 'dare to be a Daniel; dare to stand alone!' It is impossible to be alone, if you are a Daniel. The lion's den is close crammed; except, of course, for the lion. He is out hunting food for the Daniels.

Agreeable as is the life of a Daniel under such circumstances, it has its disadvantages. The Daniels of today are no more conformist in spirit than their predecessors; it is the age which has conformed to them. The desire to be out of step remains; and the agility of foot required for this becomes greater. It is difficult to be both advanced and unpopular in an age which has seen such oddities as the voluntary recognition by this country of the Irish and Indian republics; a Labour government with a large majority; the hanging of the principal Nazi leaders; Bertrand Russell an OM and the principal sage of British broadcasting. As a result the adventurous individual has to get increasingly odd and queer in his views. You can see the process at work in this volume – the chase for eccentricity getting ever more difficult, as the rewards for eccentricity mount ever higher. One solution of this problem, the most paradoxical of all, is to astonish everyone by remaining upright instead of standing on your head. This is why our gayest and most irresponsible characters are to be found writing leaders for respectable Conservative papers or producing novels in favour of the Roman Catholic Church. Mr Betjeman, most daring of all, actually patronizes the Church of England. This is a good line, and has been spotted as such by acute intellects for some time. It is curious that even Mr Reynolds has been taken in by it. He is himself something of a connoisseur in the individual and daring; yet when it comes to the really adventurous pamphlets in this volume, he is shocked by them and dismisses them as nonsense. Though, for my part, I do not care much for Carlyle's style, I find his pamphlet on 'the Nigger Question' a thousand times more sensible than Edward Carpenter's soft-headed ramblings. Carpenter, it seems to me, was individualism at its worst. He really thought that if he let his beard grow, wore homespun tweeds, lived on grated carrots and preached (though without much practice) free love, he became a remarkable man. No one can share this belief who has tried to struggle through his prose.

Now Carlyle was a remarkable man, though in many ways a detestable one. With Scottish clarity and cynicism he realized, almost the first, that the game of straight individualism was played out; and so turned himself into the champion of intolerance, despotism, and obscurantism. All the same he was too great a man not to be sensible occasionally; and his pamphlet here stands like an oasis of profundity among the sands of the Quaker Pease and the muscular curate Kingsley. It needed penetration as well as daring to understand, in the age of individualism and emancipation, that little would be achieved for the negroes of the West Indies merely by abolishing slavery; the history of the West Indies in the hundred odd years since then has proved Carlyle right and the abolitionists wrong. Or rather the abolitionists were too high-minded even to be wrong; though they detested slavery, they did not care for the slaves, and, once slavery was abolished, they were indifferent to what happened afterwards. Mr Reynolds, I suspect, dislikes Carlyle's pamphlet from its relevance to our own day. Carlyle's 'Quashee' is no longer confined to a few West Indian islands; and, much as our hearts glow at the destruction of the British Raj, they will glow less as the vast Indian continent gradually sinks back into the anarchy and violence from which it was preserved by a century and a half of British rule.

Take another example from this volume. Brougham on reform is all very well; and it brought him a good life into the bargain. But is Sydney Smith on the ballot, or rather against it, such rubbish as Mr Reynolds makes out? Would Hitler have succeeded without the ballot-box? At least it did nothing to stop him. Probably Sydney Smith attached too much importance to the ballot; probably Gresham's Law will operate in politics and the bad defeat the good with the ballot or without. But at least Sydney Smith did not think that everything would be perfect if only we had a system of universal suffrage, combined with secret voting. The fresh air of common sense blows through his admirable prose. Or again, William Hone on George IV is highly entertaining; it was well worth doing at the time. But who now cares for George IV's infidelities, or even for those of Queen Caroline? On the other hand, George IV was the only

king of England who did anything to make his capital beautiful;
and, looking at the work of John Nash which George IV inspired,
there can be no two answers to the question – which king of
England did most good and deserves to be remembered with
most gratitude? It was the elderly lecher, once a figure of fun,
now a king without a rival.

It is the nature of pamphlets to provoke disagreement. Mr
Reynolds and I seem to have managed between us to have
disagreed with every one of them. Our pleasure in them is no
whit the less. But every man has his boiling point, the moment
at which eccentricity ceases to be funny or even engaging and
becomes merely malicious and irresponsible. I have, I fear,
sometimes provoked this reaction in others; and therefore it is
deserved that it should be here provoked in me. For my
conscience would be offended were I not to make it clear, in all
seriousness, that – to my mind – Mr Brailsford's pamphlet on
the origins of World War One is an example of British
complacency at its worst, as well as being bad history. It is easy
to understand how British pamphleteers, with a century and a
half of wrongheadedness behind them, were tempted to keep
out of step even when their country became involved in war
with Germany. This was admirable so long as their criticism
was confined to the reputation of their own rulers. After all the
government which trod down the Easter rebellion in Ireland
was not the most perfect champion of Belgian independence.
Still, this independence was being championed; and even the
most contrary hesitated to argue that Belgium would be better
off under German rule (though Mr Brailsford seems to have
done his best in a pamphlet not reprinted here). Instead British
complacency took it out on the Serbs. How enlightened and
how daring to argue that the Serbs were really much better off
under Austrian rule, representing 'an older and maturer civilization'! How challenging (though untrue) to state that the Serbs
in Austria-Hungary had home rule! It is not surprising that
most of the leading members of the Union of Democratic
Control, which sponsored this pamphlet, ended up as cabinet

ministers. To use a phrase of Johnson's in another connection, this British cleverness at the expense of others is mighty offensive. Mr Brailsford has often criticized British imperialism in India; more recently he has criticized American imperialism in Korea. But when it comes to German–Austrian imperialism in the Balkans, he can only find it 'alien, but relatively civilized'. It is one thing to say: 'the government of my country is always wrong'. It is quite another to say: 'the enemies of my country are always right'. It is more likely that all governments are pretty bad, and that our government, exposed as it is to the constant harrying of the eccentrics, is rather better than the others. At any rate, it is certain that no one who values intellectual freedom would choose any other country to live in.

There are, of course, some limitations on that complacent judgement. It may be true, as George Orwell suggested in his introduction, that the expression of unpopular or unusual views is becoming more difficult. I should doubt it; though I would admit that unpopular or unusual views are becoming more difficult to find. On the other hand, the practice of intellectual freedom may sink into a game and one which no one takes seriously; even this introduction may have given some excuse for doing so. In fact I care for intellectual freedom very deeply; and can think of nothing else which can make existence tolerable. The danger is not that we should abuse it; but rather that it should seem irrelevant. The greatest error of the nineteenth century, of which we are reaping the fruits, was to try to make out that freedom was good for something – usually that it would make you better off. If you had democracy and national self-determination, it was suggested that you would have more to eat. When this did not happen, the intellectuals at once began to cry out: What is the good of freedom if it does not fill your belly? The answer is simple: You are still free. I wish that Mr Reynolds had found room for a Chartist pamphlet or two, in order to remind us that not only educated and relatively well-to-do men cared for freedom. The Chartists were the one truly independent working-class movement in our history; yet they cared as much for freedom as though they had been journalists, dons, or lawyers all their lives. It was middle-class writers, from Marx onwards, who told the workers that they wanted more food and better houses, not more freedom. It was the middle-class Trotsky, and the country-gentleman Lenin, who told the Russian workers that they would not mind losing their new freedom if they got communism instead; and now it is the former theological student Stalin who tells them that they don't mind losing their freedom even if they don't get communism. William Morris said: 'No one is good enough to be another man's master.' And I'd add: 'No one is good enough to take away another man's freedom.'

That brings us to the spook in the cupboard at any discussion of intellectual freedom – the spook at which, incidentally, George Orwell took fright towards the end of his life. The most monstrous tyranny is on the march, and not only in countries which have never known freedom; it seeks to capture the minds of the most enlightened Europeans, and often does so. In face of communism, dare we risk intellectual freedom any more? Ought we not instead to organize anti-communism and merely call it a Congress of Intellectual Liberty (as the communists call their war propaganda World Peace)? There are reasons to be frightened. For a hundred and fifty years authority, as I remarked earlier, has been on the defensive. It has had to apologize for itself; it has even had to pretend that really it was on the side of freedom, though of course in an orderly fashion. Communism is the first serious counter-offensive by the forces of authority and tyranny. Instead of apologizing it claims that oppression is actually better. It either waves freedom aside as unimportant or else makes out that it does not exist. The temptation to drop every trivial difference in face of communism is very strong; there has been no peril like it since the days of militant Islam.

All the same, it is a temptation to be shunned. So far as communism depends simply on material power, it can be resisted only by superior power; no one in his senses would dispute that proposition. But communism is not solely a movement of power;

it is much more a disease of the mind, a perversion of the liberal world. Though you cannot argue people out of communism, you can shake their faith in it by the general atmosphere of argument which it is still possible to breathe in the western world. I hope we shall never see anti-communist pamphlets; and, if we do, they are not likely to merit a place in an anthology. But every pamphlet which expresses an individual opinion forcibly is, in its way, a stroke against the march of uniformity. A great deal of humbug is talked about 'the British way of life', as though it were synonymous with respectability and good taste. The British way of life, at its best, has meant a great deal that was disreputable, irresponsible, and explosive; in fact the outstanding merit of the British way of life is that there is no British way of life. There is solely the practice of intellectual freedom, which is common to all humanity. The only way to defend freedom is to assert it; and no one has asserted it better than the British pamphleteers of the last century and a half. He who cares for freedom will do well to remember the chairman's cry: 'Don't forget the literature, comrades!' Hence this volume is presented not only as a collection of literature in the stricter sense. It is presented also as a display of freedom, and a justification for it.

Napoleon

Alan Taylor's initial interests in modern history both as a student and then as a lecturer at Manchester University were the French Revolution of 1789 and its aftermath and the revolutions of 1848. When Lewis Namier, the Professor of Modern History at Manchester, tired of hurriedly reviewing books for the Manchester Guardian, *he passed a biography of Robespierre to Alan Taylor. This set him off on a long career of reviewing for nationally read newspapers. Between his review of Reginald S Ward's* Maximilian Robespierre *(London, Macmillan, 1934) and his departure to take up a post at Oxford University in the autumn of 1938, Alan Taylor reviewed a further twenty books on the French Revolution and Napoleonic era.*

With Alan Taylor, substantial reviewing in an area of history was usually a precursor of writing a major book. The main exception was French Revolutionary and Napoleonic history. However, when he was seventy-three he gave television lectures on 1789 and 1848 as part of his series 'Revolution'. When these were published as Revolutions and Revolutionaries *(London, Hamish Hamilton, 1980) he began his Preface: 'This volume represents a return to my first love.'*

The first essay – 'On Himself' – was published in the New Statesman *on 25 September 1948 as a review of* Napoleon's Memoirs, *edited by Somerset de Chair (London, Faber, 1948). Taylor's review aroused George Bernard Shaw to write a lengthy letter to the journal in which he accused Alan Taylor, like H G Wells in his* Outline of History, *of failing to understand Napoleon: 'People who believe that a nobody such as Mr Taylor has described could have achieved Napoleon's fame can believe anything.' Taylor's reply to Shaw included:*

The real catastrophe was for the French people to have fallen into the hands of a genius. Without Napoleon there would have been no Napoleonic Empire; all the same, without Napoleon, France would probably have kept her natural frontiers and remained the greatest power in Europe. As it was, Napoleon started France on her way downhill.

Napoleon's Memoirs *nevertheless attracted readers. Indeed in 1993 it was available with many illustrations as* Napoleon on Napoleon: An Autobiography of the Emperor, *edited by Somerset de Chair (London, Cassell, 1993).*

Alan Taylor was as severe elsewhere on Napoleon. In 1958 in a review of an anthology of contemporary views of the Emperor, he wrote: 'All this bragging and strutting ... now seem to be poor stuff.' In 1961 he observed of a collection of Napoleon's letters and documents: 'Napoleon's letters seem to me plumb boring ... His letters are full of lies ... His emotions are all sham.'

The second of the two essays here – 'The Verdict of History' – appeared in the New Statesman *on 26 February 1949 as a review of Pieter Geyl's* Napoleon: For and Against *(London, Cape, 1949). Taylor greatly admired Geyl (1887–1966) both as a person and as a historian. In his autobiography he recalled that when first teaching at Manchester University he had read Geyl on the revolt of The Netherlands: 'Geyl in particular pleased me by his view, already unconsciously mine, that most things in history happen by accident.' After Geyl's death Taylor gave a memorial address to the Flemish Society of Antwerp.*

*　　*　　*

On Himself

A life of Napoleon written by himself! The appeal seems irresistible. Mr de Chair, the editor, describes it as 'the voice of the giant himself'. The conversation of giants, then, must be very dull. The proclamations and bulletins of Napoleon show him to have been a propagandist of genius; so, too, was Goebbels. Yet the memoirs of the one are as dreary as the diaries of the other. In fact, the memoirs of Napoleon – undoubtedly a genuine product of his mind – convinced me that the Goebbels diaries were genuine; if Napoleon could write as boringly as this,

Goebbels could also. Both works are, of course, full of lies; that was to be expected. It is the drabness, the fatuity, the common-placeness of mind, that are surprising. What, for instance, could be more idiotic than Napoleon's explanation of polygamy in his chapter on Egypt? It occurs, he says, in countries inhabited by men of several colours and 'is the only means of preventing them persecuting each other', since every man can have a black wife, a white one, a copper-coloured one 'and one of some other colour'. He proceeds to recommend it in the French colonies as the solution of the colour question, so that every man can have 'one white, one black, and one Mulatto wife, at the same time'.

Napoleon knew well that he was not a brilliant author; and he protected himself by speaking contemptuously of writers, as he did of his other enemies. Just as he described the English as 'men who were continually at table, almost always intoxicated, and of uncommunicative disposition', so he dismissed writers as men of no practical sense.

He was not concerned to compete with those detestable ideologues; he had no interest at all in creating a work of art – his life in action had been creation enough. His reminiscences were written, or rather dictated, for effect. They were to launch a legend, the legend of Divine Caesar. Cold and aloof like a marble statue in classical robes, they are without personality; and it was a great error of judgement by Mr de Chair to substitute the first person singular for 'Napoleon', 'the emperor', 'the general' of the original text. For Napoleon's statue is not vocal even after the fashion of the statue in *Don Giovanni*; and the essential purpose of these writings is in their remoteness from life. Napoleon the man was finished; Napoleon the institution had to be perpetuated.

It is not surprising therefore that the only section of memoirs which Napoleon completed and finally polished is the part dealing with the campaign of Waterloo. A defeat of such finality needs a good deal of explaining away. Napoleon had an excuse in Grouchy's failure to come up with Blücher on 18 June; and he repeats this excuse again and again. But he is pulled up by an uneasy sense that the real failure lay in the faulty orders which Grouchy received from his supreme commander; and Napoleon swings off on the other tack that Waterloo was an indecisive battle, the effect of which could have been undone by a further campaign. This line, too, has its dangers; for the failure to continue the war could be explained only by the war-weariness of the French. This was not an argument with which to appeal to posterity. The only way out is to assert that his strategy was throughout correct and that Wellington and Blücher committed 'every conceivable mistake'. Thus Napoleon persuaded himself that he had in fact won the battle of Waterloo and his memoirs end with an expression of sympathy for the people of London 'when they learnt of the catastrophe which had befallen their army'.

The main section of the record, which runs from the siege of Toulon to the battle of Marengo, lacks the finish of the Waterloo narrative. Napoleon dictated these chapters haphazard to two amanuenses; and the two rivals kept their work separate when they published it after Napoleon's death. Mr de Chair has sorted out the two sources and pruned away the asides with which Napoleon relieved the tedium. In this story of his early success Napoleon had less to explain away; all the same he never missed a chance to heighten the emphasis on the unique character and achievement of 'the emperor'. Thus Paoli, the Corsican patriot, 'used frequently to say of the young artillery officer [myself], "He is a man for a Plutarch's biography."' With this unlikely anecdote Napoleon blots out the story of his equivocal behaviour in Corsican affairs. Entertaining, too, in their way are the passages on naval warfare, in which Napoleon proves that it is much easier to win battles at sea than on land; Trafalgar is successfully rubbed out of existence. But for the most part the principles of Plutarch are observed all too seriously. There are accounts of Italy and Egypt which could have been taken from any gazetteer; even the military narrative lacks spirit. This served Napoleon's purpose. 'The general' remained without a rival figure; and Napoleon could conclude with an account of Marengo which conceals that he had lost the battle and slides, almost without mention, over Desaix who had come to Bonaparte's rescue. It is a fitting end to a narrative which is unreliable from beginning to end.

Can Napoleon have supposed that this dull and lying record would really secure his fame? This puzzle is the only point of interest raised by this book. Some part of the explanation may be found in the decline of his faculties. The only exciting passages are the quotations from the proclamations which Bonaparte wrote as the young general of the army of Italy; these still ring with life, and their author could not have written dully however hard he tried. Success corrupts; and Napoleon had achieved success without parallel in modern history. The spare, beautiful artillery officer had become fat and coarse; and his mind became coarse at the same time. Besides, Napoleon had expected everyone to sacrifice himself for the empire; and the first sacrifice had been his own personality. The young Bonaparte had been vital, though no doubt unattractive; Napoleon had squeezed the life out of him. Flashes of personality persisted, even at St Helena. These make Napoleon interesting to history; they did not interest Napoleon himself. He was concerned only with his public performance. Stendhal found the key to Napoleon, when he described Julien Sorel, after his first night with Mme de Rênal, asking himself: 'Ai-je bien joué mon rôle?' Sorel, like Napoleon, was dominated by ambition; he lacked inner life and so fails to hold the reader's sympathy or even attention. Napoleon's was a more complicated case. He had begun as a romantic figure in the spirit of Rousseau; he ended as an abstraction from Plutarch. To use the clumsy contemporary phrase, this destruction of Napoleon by himself was the last triumph of the classical over the romantic. The essence of the romantic movement was the elevation of individual sentiment and of individual character; yet Napoleon, with a more remarkable character than any, was ashamed of possessing it and returned to a classical worship of the external world.

The explanation of this outmoded artificiality is simple; and Napoleon himself hints at it in the early pages of his memoirs. He could have been genuine – 'romantic' – only as a Corsican patriot; once he deserted his natural cause, he could only play parts and to do this he had to crush out his individuality. Sometimes, as when he played at being a French patriot or even a French emperor, the part came off; at others, as when he played at being a Muslim in Egypt or wished to play at being the liberator-general after Waterloo, the pretence was too blatant. But, for a man who claimed to possess a sense of reality, Napoleon's judgement was strangely unreliable from start to finish. The eighteenth Brumaire was as wild an adventure as the Hundred Days; in neither case did Napoleon have any clear idea what he was doing – he was simply 'playing his role'. For that matter Marengo was as much a gamble as Waterloo. It implanted in Napoleon the belief that he had truly mastered the external world; this gave him the necessary self-confidence for his career, though it ultimately brought him to disaster. Traditional ideas and traditional institutions had lost their force. Losing faith in God, men sought a human saviour. The first of these human gods was Napoleon; and the condition of his fame was the confident readiness to attempt the impossible. Napoleon believed in himself; he continued to believe even when reality had shattered the basis of this belief, and he supposed that others would believe too. Hence he even believed that readers could be found for his memoirs.

All the same, despite Napoleon, a human being is buried in these writings. Napoleon no doubt thought that he was building a monument to his future fame. Most of the time, in reality, he was fighting his battles over again simply for the pleasure of it; and this time without risk of failure. No reader can be persuaded that the catalogue of divisions and the description of obscure skirmishes serve any literary purpose. Napoleon had ceased to think of the reader. He had escaped from the unpleasant reality of St Helena and was manoeuvring imaginary armies. There once more he could exercise the devotion to detail and the implacable demands for speed that had been the secret of his success (though also of his failure). Bending over the map of Lombardy, he could once more forget that Josephine had been unfaithful to him immediately after marriage (and he expected the reader to forget it too). In fact, if only he exerted his will strongly enough, he might again master the external world: St Helena would disappear and Lombardy, or Paris under the Consulate, become once more reality. It was this belief in the human will, at any rate his own, that made Napoleon the representative and culmination of the French Revolution.

The essence of the revolution was belief in man. Once you believe that man is naturally good, you must believe, too, that he can do anything. Napoleon certainly held this belief about himself. And no doubt man can do anything, if he goes the right way about it. The right way, as the events of the last century and a half have shown, is the way of science: the improvement of technique. The men of the French Revolution, and Napoleon with them, supposed that they could master the world by will alone. Hence the Napoleonic armies, for example, marched faster than other armies simply by the compelling force of Napoleon's command; modern armies move faster by train or aeroplane. Napoleon killed his secretaries by overwork; with the dictaphone and the typewriter they would have survived quite easily. Napoleon was following the wrong course; the further his will carried him, the greater was bound to be his final catastrophe. He supposed that events could be made; in the end events took their revenge on him. There was no essential difference between Napoleon in victory and in defeat (hence his own bewilderment at Waterloo): he always asked the impossible, and sometimes it was granted him. This is the real basis of the Napoleonic legend (as it will be for the legend of Hitler). Napoleon is the hero of all those who resent reality, of all those who will not trouble to master 'the art of the possible'. Napoleon is the supreme example of the human being who became more than life-size; and those who admire Napoleon are really flattering the human being in themselves. Yet what did this wonderful human being end in? A querulous sick man on a sub-tropical island dictating a drab and meaningless record to while away the time. The memoirs of Napoleon suggest that there is something to be said for not thinking that you are God.

The Verdict of History

Events are well enough in their way; what historians write about them is much better. Who really cares about the later Roman emperors, about Dutch William, or even about Pericles? These survive by grace of Gibbon, Macaulay, and Thucydides. The greatest figure of modern times made himself such by providing a myth which would provide endless fascination for historians. Napoleon knew the secret of survival: *quel roman que ma vie!* His own literary gifts were those of an amateur – characteristic of one who carried that second-rate tear-jerker, *The Sorrows of Werther*, in his hip-pocket; the Napoleonic legend would never have taken hold had it depended on Napoleon's own writings. Napoleon's great stroke was to provide raw material for works of genius, so that French historians wrote about Napoleon inevitably, as every Greek playwright interpreted the story of the Trojan wars. Of course there is always a certain amount to be discovered about Napoleon, as no doubt matter of archaeological interest can be found by grubbing in the ruins of Troy. But the profundities of the human spirit are to be found in what men have made of the legend, not in the archives and the rubble. The career of Napoleon is the greatest of modern legends.

This fact, once noticed, seems obvious and inescapable; and it is surprising that no one has had the idea long ago of discussing what French writers have made of Napoleon. To discover the obvious which no one else has thought of is the speciality of Professor Geyl, one of the great historical minds of our time. It would be unfair to say that he demolishes the reputations of the great French historians; though he exposes their flaws, there remains, in his words, 'what life and energy, what creative power, what ingenuity, imagination and daring!' These words are a reminder of peculiar value for the English reader. Every continental student of history, even if he be a German, knows that the French are the greatest practitioners of the art. English historians have never recovered from the fraud put over on us by Acton (or perhaps Carlyle) and still suppose that serious history – scientific history as it is called – was perfected in Germany. But what tawdry stuff the German historians are compared to the stars of Professor Geyl's book – and how long-winded!

Professor Geyl gives a plain analysis of what French historians from the Restoration to the present day have written about Napoleon. He starts with Chateaubriand and ends with Georges Lefebvre. Each writer is summarized with the painstaking detachment with which a newspaper correspondent gives a summary of the foreign press. There are no graces of style, no novelty in the point of view; the general effect is humdrum, almost dull. It is like listening to a conversation where tones are never raised, where there is never a flicker of emphasis nor even, one supposes, of interest. As the conversation proceeds, it gradually becomes clear that Professor Geyl, far from being the club bore, declines to raise his voice simply because he is discussing the most profound topics of human experience. It is rare enough to find a work of history which is interesting, let alone exciting. This book is vastly more, an infinite consolation to the professional historian: it shows that history is a subject which can provoke thought. For my part, I would rather have written Professor Geyl's book than invented existentialism or the new fashion in academic philosophy – what is it called? The subject, at any rate, which now spends its time debating whether it was once correct to describe itself as logical positivism. Professor Geyl's book enables the historian to look the philosopher in the face without cringing for quite a week.

His book teaches one, in the first place, a great deal about Napoleon. French historians have found in Napoleon infinite variety; and all of it was there. It is impossible to read this catalogue of their judgements without realizing that Napoleon really was a most extraordinary man, probably the most extraordinary figure that has ever appeared in the world of politics. Sorel saw him as the man who devoted his life to the defence of the natural frontiers; Bourgeois as the man who lived only for the creation of a great empire of the Middle East; Driault as the restorer of the Roman Empire in Europe, the greatest of the Caesars; Vandal even discovered in him the pacifier of the world – no wonder he spoke of 'the ultimate justice and grandeur of his aim'. The same variety and the same vastness are revealed in the descriptions of Napoleon's work as a civilian ruler – the heir of the revolution, the restorer of order, the architect of the Code Napoleon, the founder of the French Empire, the protector of the Catholic Church. All these things happened in Napoleon's time; yet the cumulative effect of them is not to increase admiration for Napoleon, rather to rouse doubts.

Here Professor Geyl, as it were, turns the tables on Napoleon: for his book, despite its cool tone and its scholarship, is an anti-Napoleonic tract, the most formidable ever composed. He has given the legend a good showing in order to show that it is a legend, that it overreaches itself by its very absurdity. He quotes the rhetoric of Thiers, the brilliance of Vandal, the sophistication of Sorel; then brings them to earth with a gentle query – the murder of the Duke of Enghien? the breach of the Treaty of Amiens? the oppression and exploitation of Europe? the stifling of French Liberalism? Above all, the lies, the intrigues, the dishonesty? Professor Geyl has no doubt of his own verdict:

He was a conqueror with whom it was impossible to live; who could not help turning an ally into a vassal or at least interpreting the relationship to his own exclusive advantage; who decorated his lust of conquest with the fine-sounding phrases of progress and civilization; and who at last, in the name of the whole of Europe, which was to look to him for order and peace, presumed to brand England as the universal disturber and enemy.

This is not, however, only the verdict of a dispassionate Dutch observer. The historians of the legend do not exhaust French writings on Napoleon. Indeed, all Professor Geyl's criticism of the admirers of Napoleon is based on the work of French scholars; and his analysis of the two attitudes, *for* and *against*, is a splendid contribution to the study of French ideas. The cleavage is, in the first place, political. In England admiration for Napoleon has often (perhaps usually) been found on the 'Left' – a line running from Lady Holland to Hilaire Belloc and (dare I say it?) Bernard Shaw. What English admirers of Napoleon have in common is simple: they are all 'agin the government' and, since Napoleon was also against the British government, they suppose that he was on their side. In France, however, the 'establishment' has been on the Left, especially in the time of the Third Republic; and Napoleon has been the hero of the conservatives. They did not need to pretend that Napoleon cared for liberty: they were delighted that he had destroyed it and wished to follow his example. They echoed the phrase of Barrès: 'Napoleon, Teacher of Energy', and praised, perhaps exaggerated, those qualities which made Napoleon the precursor of fascism. Moreover, unlike English writers, they did not conceal that Napoleon was the enemy of England, not merely of the British government; for, since England represented the principles of liberty, of constitutional government, and of agreement between the nations, she was their enemy also. This tradition, though strong, was the school of a minority in France. French writers who cared for liberty, who opposed militarism, had no illusions about Napoleon and exposed the errors of those who had. French liberals in the nineteenth century, and socialists in the twentieth, stood unanimously for 'the other France' which repudiated Napoleon with his gospel of energy and violence.

The cleavage *for* and *against*, as well as being political, is also professional; this is a point of peculiar interest fully worked out by Professor Geyl. The men of letters, with the exception of Taine, have been for Napoleon, and Taine was only against Napoleon because he recognized in Napoleon himself; the men of learning have been against him. The men of letters have often been distinguished scholars, as Vandal and Sorel were; but, in the last resort, they were concerned to produce an effect, to write a work of literary genius. It is a very different Napoleon who appears in the school textbooks. Indeed one is almost driven to postulate the general rule: the better written a book, the more unreliable as history. But there is more in it than that. Tocqueville said of Napoleon: 'He was as great as a man can be without morality'; and the truth is that all men of letters, that is all who care for good writing, are, in this sense, immoral. They will always subordinate reality to effects and facts to phrases. Paine's judgement on Burke will serve for every French writer on Napoleon whose works one reads for pleasure: 'He pities the plumage but forgets the dying bird.' Nothing is stranger than the delusion of our time that men of letters are, by nature, champions of political, or even of intellectual, liberty. If Professor Geyl's book is not evidence enough to the contrary, consider the famous writers who made the pilgrimage to Mussolini. Of course, scientists are even worse – but then one hardly expects political sense from them. It was only when reading Professor Geyl's book that I realized that professors of history, at any rate in France, are so much better. Their record of integrity has been almost unbroken. Even in the Second Empire the committee of scholars, employed to publish the correspondence of Napoleon I, was too resolutely honest to please Napoleon III; it had to be replaced in 1864 by a committee of literary men (including Sainte-Beuve) which set out to publish only what Napoleon 'would have made available to the public if he had wished to display himself and his system to posterity'. Still, the achievement of the French professional historians cannot necessarily be counted to the general credit of the trade. What German historian stood out against the cult of Bismarck, at any rate until Bismarck had failed? And what chance is there that any German historian will stand out against the coming cult of Hitler? As for English historians, they have hardly escaped from the Anglican sycophancy which marked the universities until the beginning of this century. Chaplains of the pirate ship, they have extolled the British Empire as persistently as the French men of letters extolled the empire of Napoleon. The French professors represented a general 'university' culture which hardly exists outside France. As Professor Geyl says:

The scholarliness of their method . . . disciplines their mental attitude. But it would be foolish to overlook the fact that these authors came to Napoleon with their own, with different, *a priori* ideas, that they measure him against standards of spiritual freedom, of culture, of humanity, of social progress, that politically they are as a rule of the Left. With some of them anti-clericalism is predominant, with others liberalism, or socialism.

What a wonderful country of which these things can be said of university professors!

The last quotation is a reminder that Geyl's book, as well as being a book about Napoleon and about French historians, is about clerical values (using the word in Benda's sense). Geyl concludes his praise of the professional historian, Georges Lefebvre, in whom he finds the most convincing version of Napoleon, with criticism: 'I should like to see the eternal postulates of respect for the human personality, of the feeling for spiritual freedom, of lofty idealism, of truthfulness, taken into account when the final reckoning is made.' This is a startling evocation of the shade of Acton; and it leaves me wondering whether the virtues of a historian and those of a 'clerk' are the same after all.

Charles James Fox

First published in the Manchester Guardian *on 13 September 1956. Written for the 150th anniversary of Fox's death, this was the last piece commissioned from Alan Taylor by A P Wadsworth, editor of the* Manchester Guardian, *who died soon afterwards.*

*   *   *

On 13 September 1806 Charles James Fox died in the Palladian villa of the Duke of Devonshire at Chiswick. His last words echoed the royal ancestor whom he rivalled in charm: 'It don't signify, my dearest, dearest Liz.' Charles Fox was a legend even in his lifetime. No public man has been so loved by his associates. He was the first statesman, incidentally, to be universally addressed by his Christian name. His picture in the National Portrait Gallery conveys something of his unique fascination – a flushed stout man, sitting on a stile in disarray amid the delights of nature; a welcome contrast indeed to the formal figures who surround him on the walls. Many historians have seen in Fox a charmer and nothing more; a blundering tactician greedy for power; an irresponsible declaimer who drove himself and his followers from one disaster to another.

The picture has a touch of truth. Fox had an incurable love for members of the great Whig families. There was something absurd in a champion of the people who set up a ministry composed predominantly of dukes and marquises. His private life did not show the austere morality that the British public expects from its leaders. Other Whigs, including his father, made fortunes from the service of the state; Charles Fox lost an even vaster fortune on the racecourse and at the gambling tables. His father, Lord Holland, brought him up on the doctrine: 'The young are always right; the old are always wrong.' Everyone knows the story of Lord Holland's remark when Charles smashed a gold watch: 'If you must, you must.' On the same principle Lord Holland provided £300,000 to pay his son's more pressing debts. Charles himself tried to meet this same need by running a faro bank at Brooks's – a bank which he continued to run even when he was secretary of state for foreign affairs.

When all else had failed, his aristocratic friends had a whip-round and provided him with £3,000 a year. 'How will he take it?' one of them asked anxiously. Another gave the correct reply: 'Quarterly, I suppose.' Gambling, drinking and late hours did not exhaust his vices. He had a number of natural children, all of whom he adored. He lived with Mrs Armitstead, 'dearest Liz', for nearly twenty years before he married her – she had grown rich by living previously with other men. Then he kept his marriage secret so that he might continue to flaunt the immorality that he was no longer practising. If there was only his love of nature and the classics to set off against all this, we should say that he was a curious character, an amusing period piece, no more; certainly not worth commemoration.

But there is a great deal more. For one thing, Fox invented the modern British constitution – invented, that is, the two-party system and the doctrine that the Crown must accept as prime minister the political leader favoured by a majority of the House of Commons. Earlier politicians had in fact 'opposed', but they wrapped up their opposition as patriotic advice or took shelter under the patronage of the heir apparent. Fox criticized whatever was done by the government of the day and claimed on every issue that he could have done better; he was the first leader of a formed and avowed Opposition. Again, earlier politicians had forced their unwelcome services on the king, but always with loyal apologies and in the belief that the favour of the Crown would bring with it support from the House of Commons, not the other way round. Fox, with a gambler's extremism, resolved to win or lose all. He regarded George III as Satan and held that the Crown should be reduced to a cipher. 'The Crown is endowed with no faculty whatever of a private nature.'

Charles Fox lost in his lifetime, but he won the future. In the words of Richard Pares: 'George III undoubtedly beat Charles Fox in 1784, and trampled on his ghost in 1807; but our politicians act, today, on Charles Fox's constitutional principles.' It was evidence of Fox's triumph when Victoria had to accept Gladstone as prime minister in spite of her violent protest, and even more striking evidence when George V sent for Ramsay MacDonald in 1924 with no protest at all. We are supposed to owe the British constitution to the wisdom of our ancestors. It would be truer to say that in its present form it sprang fully grown from Charles Fox's personal hostility to George III. The 'Whig interpretation of history' is a horse from the same stable. Fox asserted, quite wrongly, that his view of the constitution had flourished ever since the Glorious Revolution. His Whig friends echoed this belief, and historians followed suit until they were put right in our own day by Sir Lewis Namier.

This political doctrine makes Fox interesting, important, even great; it does not make him admirable. What gave him a unique place in English history was his championing of liberty, both individual and national. He was a long time coming to it. In his early days he had a wrongheaded enthusiasm for the House of Commons – even defending its right to expel and disqualify Wilkes. The revolt of the American colonies taught him that there were more important things than legal niceties or the struggle for political power. Fox was among the first to advocate the complete independence of America, and he staked his political career on this cause until it was won. The impeachment of Warren Hastings, which he shared with Burke, took him a stage further. However doubtful the detailed charges, that case established the principle that the British Empire was something more than an empire of exploitation.

Fox's finest hour came with the war against the French Revolution. All calculation of personal advantage was swept aside. Fox could have been a leading war minister. He, not Pitt, would have been 'the pilot who weathered the storm'. Fox never considered this course for a moment. He was convinced that the war was unnecessary and morally wrong. Almost alone among Englishmen of the governing class, he recognized the principle of liberty in France in spite of the violence of the Terror and was convinced that Great Britain was fighting on the side of tyranny. He broke with his closest friends and for five years argued against the war almost single-handed. There is no more glorious story in our history. Sixty years later Richard Cobden, contemplating a similar course of action himself, wrote of Fox:

It is impossible to read the speeches of Fox at this time without feeling one's heart yearn with admiration and gratitude for the bold and resolute manner in which he opposed the war, never yielding and never repining, under the most discouraging defeats. The annals of Parliament do not record a nobler struggle in a nobler cause.

Here again Fox lost the present and won the future. He saw his supporters in the House shrink from fifty to twenty; he was struck off the Privy Council for toasting 'Our Sovereign Lord, the People'; police spies were set on him, and Pitt considered sending him to the Tower. But posterity has confirmed his judgement on this war for despotism, and in the nineteenth century British policy welcomed the liberal revolutions which Pitt had tried to suppress. The spirit of Fox prevails whenever England stands on the side of freedom. The independence of Ireland and India are his memorials, and those who now champion the peoples of Africa are only the latest who belong to 'the party of Mr Fox'.

Talleyrand's Cut

First published in the New York Review of Books, *on 13 June 1974*

* * *

A review of *Talleyrand: The Art of Survival* by Jean Orieux, translated by Patricia Wolf (Knopf, New York).

Talleyrand once asked a lady friend: 'What do you think posterity's opinion of me will be?' She replied: 'That you set out to stir up controversy about yourself.' Staring at her in amazement, he said: 'You are right, you are absolutely right. I want people to go on for centuries debating what I was like, what I believed, what I stood for.' This only shows that a man will go to any lengths in order to impress the woman he happens to be pursuing. For there is no mystery about Talleyrand except that created by writers who wish to turn an honest penny. He liked women; he liked money; he liked an easy comfortable life. To his misfortune he was caught in the storm of the French Revolution. He waited for it to blow over and sometimes tried to help on the process. He said many things that were esteemed witty at the time. His career was unusual even in a revolutionary epoch. But a great man? A statesman? It is hard to believe it.

M. Orieux, however, has no doubts. His book is in the worst style of French writing – rhapsodical, disorderly, overblown, more a cheap romantic novel than a work of history. Perhaps it is tolerable in French; it is unreadable in English. M. Orieux is given to addressing his characters. Here is an early example. Talleyrand's foot was injured at birth. His mother thought this disqualified him from becoming head of the family and turned him into a priest, remarking, 'My son is well adjusted to his new profession.' On which M. Orieux breaks out:

What profession? Buttoning a cassock over one's ordinary dress and playing choirboy is not a profession, Madam, it is a travesty ... You did an astonishing thing, Madam: without knowing it, you turned your rejected son into the most illustrious member of your race ... Measured against a mother's initial betrayal, all subsequent betrayals were insignificant.

At any rate Talleyrand became a bishop, duly collecting the rewards in money and women which this brought. In 1789 he went with the revolution, perhaps from conviction. When his acts provoked the disapproval of the pope, he wrote to a friend: 'You know about my excommunication. Come cheer me up and dine with me. As no one will offer me fire or water, we will have to make do tonight with cold meat and iced wine.' Comment by M. Orieux: 'O flippant statement if there ever was one.' M. Orieux also remarks:

His critics never mention that one major failing of his, far more serious than his love of gambling, women and money: a flabby will that brought his worst instincts into play. Napoleon forgave all his faults except his alarming pliability – and he knew the man he was dealing with.

If Talleyrand had not been pliable, he would have been guillotined during the French Revolution and no one would have heard of him. As it was, he celebrated an open-air mass on the anniversary of the taking of the Bastille and whispered, as he clambered on to the platform: 'Don't make me laugh.' He left France before the Terror, first for England and then for the United States, where he ran some successful land speculation. His favourite American word, he said, was 'sweetener', and, when later he squeezed £50,000 out of American negotiators, remarked that since the Americans had invented such an appropriate word they must know how to use it.

Talleyrand returned to France under the Directory when the worst days of the revolution were over. He made love to Mme de Staël, and she thrust him on the Directors. When asked who she was, he replied: 'An intriguer, to such a degree that I am here in the foreign ministry because of her.' And in answer to a further question whether she was a good friend: 'Friend? She would toss her friends in the river in order to fish them out.' Being without a carriage, he drove to meet the Directors in Mme de Staël's and, as he did so, muttered under his breath that he would make 'une fortune immense, une immense fortune'.

So he did. Probably no foreign minister has ever made so much money while in office or continued his activities over so long a time. He was paid by everybody – by Napoleon, by German princes, by Tsar Alexander I, by the British government. His foreign policy, so far as he had one, was often directed to the best interests of France, but he saw no reason why he should not be paid for promoting them. With this fortune he acquired a great landed estate and the vast château of Valençay. He was also a compulsive gambler, running through millions of francs.

Napoleon Bonaparte was the decisive figure in Talleyrand's life. Talleyrand helped Bonaparte up the ladder, served him as emperor, and then engineered his overthrow. Even after this he wrote: 'I loved Napoleon. I became personally attached to him despite his faults; at the start of his career I felt drawn to him by the irresistible magnetism exerted by all great geniuses.' It was Talleyrand who encouraged Bonaparte's expedition to Egypt. M. Orieux accepts Talleyrand's explanation that the expedition was intended to 'turn official thoughts and acts away from revolutionary Europe' – an unlikely proposition. The Egyptian expedition was a quick alternative to the invasion of England which had proved impossible.

A transaction just before Bonaparte left was characteristic of both men. Bonaparte was short of money, and Talleyrand lent him 100,000 francs. On his return Bonaparte repaid the money and asked: 'Why did you lend it to me? I have often wondered about it and could never understand your motive.' Talleyrand replied: 'I had no motive; you were young and made such a vital, intense impression on me that I wanted to help you without any ulterior purpose.' To which Bonaparte remarked: 'In that case you acted deceitfully.'

Talleyrand's great days came when he was Napoleon's foreign minister – great at any rate from the point of view of making money. He began well. When Napoleon asked him how he had made so much money, he replied: 'Oh, that's simple. I bought bonds on the seventeenth Brumaire and sold them three days later.' Seventeenth Brumaire was the day before Bonaparte seized power. Thereafter Napoleon used to say: 'His great ancestry makes up for everything.' There was little skill or originality in Talleyrand's policy: he did what he was told and pocketed his percentage. Napoleon summed up his qualifications: 'Sophistication, first-hand knowledge of the courts of Europe, a shrewd tongue that says just enough and no more, an inscrutable countenance that never changes, and finally a great name.' In later years Talleyrand made out that he had always opposed Napoleon's pursuit of conquest. He did so only when it began to go wrong.

Even then his opposition was confined to private mutterings. The idea that he contributed to Napoleon's overthrow is pure myth, partly manufactured by himself and partly by Metternich, who was another character of the same kind. In 1809 Metternich reported from Paris that Talleyrand and Fouché were preparing to resist Napoleon. They 'are firmly resolved to seize the opportunity if the opportunity arises, lacking courage to provoke it'. The opportunity never arose. Talleyrand and Fouché contributed to Napoleon's overthrow only in the sense that the so-called German Resistance contributed to Hitler's. Napoleon ruined himself by his limitless ambitions; his overthrow stemmed from the Russian Army. When all was over Talleyrand stepped on to the scene and headed the French Provisional government. He said with some excusable exaggeration: 'The only conspiring I have ever done was when I had the majority of France as an accomplice and was seeking hand in hand with her the salvation of my country.'

Talleyrand did not long remain in power. The restored King

Louis XVIII no doubt disliked him. M. Orieux remarks that he was not Cardinal Richelieu or even Mazarin. He lacked strength of character and needed a master. Also he was lazy: alert in a crisis and off on pleasure the next day. Talleyrand made some stir at the Congress of Vienna, though circumstances made this easy, when all the victorious powers except Prussia wanted to keep France active in the balance of power. After this he departed to a profitable retirement until the French revolution of 1830 when he became French ambassador in London and secured the independence of Belgium. His last negotiation was a prolonged bargaining whereby he made his peace with the Church a few hours before he died. When he received extreme unction he held out his clenched fists instead of his palms and said: 'Do not forget that I am a bishop.' He had received episcopal unction on 16 January 1789. Much had happened since then including the secularization of church lands on Talleyrand's initiative and his own marriage. However the Church was ready to welcome the belatedly repentant sinner.

Considerable ingenuity is needed to deduce any significant principles of foreign policy from Talleyrand's career. He was an adroit and unscrupulous negotiator. He never conducted a negotiation without financial profit for himself. He distrusted the arrogance of power and did not regret the loss of Napoleon's conquests. If pressed to define what he believed in he would have answered with his favourite refrain: 'Une fortune immense, une immense fortune.'

Talleyrand had unparalleled success with women despite his lameness and clumsy figure. He shared Mme de Flahaut with Gouverneur Morris, the American minister in Paris, and of course with her husband. Their son, the comte de Flahaut, following his father's fashion, had a son by Queen Hortense, Napoleon's stepdaughter, and their offspring, the duc de Morny, was able to boast: 'I am the great-grandson of a king, grandson of a bishop, son of a queen, and half-brother of an emperor.' Morny's daughter married a marquis of Lansdowne, and their son became the British foreign secretary who created the Entente

Cordiale – altogether a distinguished record for Talleyrand's descendants. When Talleyrand became foreign minister he ousted his predecessor from the marriage bed as well as from office. The outcome of this was Eugène Delacroix, the great romantic painter, whose career Talleyrand followed with paternal solicitude.

Talleyrand's last mistress was his niece by marriage, Dorothy, whose mother the duchess of Courland was also his mistress whenever she could afford the time to come to France. Yet even his lovemaking was pursued with indifference. He was a voluptuary, not a seducer, and Mme de Flahaut complained that, though *suaviter in modo,* he lacked *fortiter in re.* Talleyrand would probably have accepted this as a flattering verdict. He never did anything with energy or conviction except of course when he laid his hands on money. If indifference, lack of principle and self-interest are the essential qualities for diplomacy, Talleyrand was perhaps a model diplomat after all.

Metternich

Alan Taylor had studied the final part of Metternich's period of power when he had been a postgraduate student in Vienna in 1928–30. After his 1955 biography of Bismarck had proved successful and he had declared a willingness to write another short biography, his publisher in 1958 suggested Metternich as a suitable subject. Taylor, then turning more towards British history, replied to Hamish Hamilton:

Metternich is worked out. And for that matter so am I. My intellectual capital needs replenishing . . .

This essay appeared in the New Statesman, *9 January 1954, as a review of Constantin de Grunwald's biography,* Metternich *(London, Falcon, 1953). The essay deflates Metternich who, in the early years of the Cold War, was finding favour among conservatives.*

*   *   *

Men live after their own deaths in the minds of others. Samuel Butler thought that this was the only form of immortality. For most men it is a wasting asset. Memories fade; causes change. Who now cares what Gladstone said in 1868? Occasionally the historian acts as a resurrection-man. He discovers that some forgotten figure was the real saviour of his country or maker of empire. Our nineteenth-century prime ministers, for instance, are being pushed aside; and their fame is being usurped by civil servants, hitherto obscure. There is another, and more lasting, way to survival. The historical figure is turned into a symbol. The man becomes a myth; and, though his real deeds are forgotten, he is mobilized in defence of some cause which might have surprised him. The founders of the great religions have all enjoyed this fate. Millions of men repeat their names, while knowing nothing of the details of their lives. The carpenter's son

of Galilee blesses the grandeurs of the papacy; and the tyranny
of the Politburo is carried out in the name of a crabbed German
scholar.

Metternich knew this success, even in his lifetime. His name
was the symbol of resistance to the revolution – abused by the
radicals, praised, though more rarely, by conservatives. His fall
in 1848 was the decisive sign that 'the springtime of peoples'
had begun. Soon he was being treated as the great opponent of
German unity, his immortality turned to ridicule by Treitschke,
only his interminable 'five metaphors' remembered. Every
textbook of history rejoiced that 'the system of Metternich' had
been overthrown; and the most humble politician assumed that
any future settlement would improve on the work of the
Congress of Vienna. The peace-making of Versailles began the
disillusionment. Metternich crept back into favour as the
exponent of a less idealistic diplomacy. The balance of power
seemed a more sensible and a more effective principle than the
League of Nations. But Metternich had to wait for his full
restoration until the present Cold War of creeds. He has re-
emerged as 'the rock of order', and every renegade liberal in
America discovers an admiration for this desiccated aristocrat.
Metternich is again to fight the Jacobins, but this time with the
big battalions on his side. Nationalism is frowned on; and
Western Union is to replace 'the mouldering edifice' of the
Habsburg Monarchy, which Metternich lamented that he had
spent his life in propping up.

The new saint of conservatism is a long way from the Metternich of history. He was a very silly man. This is revealed even
in the flattering portrait by Lawrence. Vain and complacent,
with fatuous good looks, his first thought in a crisis was to see
whether his skin-tight breeches fitted perfectly and the Order of
the Golden Fleece was hanging rightly. Even his love-affairs –
and he had many – were calculated for their political effect. He
sought influence on Napoleon through the Queen of Naples and
learnt the secrets of Russia from Countess Lieven. It must have
been disturbing when he whispered political gossip in bed. He

never made a clever remark. His thoughts, like those of most conservatives, were banal and obvious. 'Things must get worse before they get better'; 'after war Europe needs peace'; 'everyone has his allotted place in society'. Most men could do better than this when shaving. As he grew older, he grew more sententious. His deafness gave him an irresistible hold over his visitors. Bismarck wisely slept during his discourse and so won the old man's favour. There are those whom we would recall from the dead. Metternich is not among them. Even Mr Viereck and Professor Morgenthau would blench if he appeared on their doorstep, his empty sentences already phrased.

He was good at his job, though it was not so difficult a job as is often supposed. His job was diplomacy, and in particular, to maintain the greatness of the house of Habsburg. He was spared the greatest difficulty of the diplomat, which is to convince his own employer. The Emperor Francis gave Metternich a free run so long as Austria was kept out of war; and even the Austrian generals counted on being beaten. He liked to present himself in later life as the symbol of resistance. In reality he had been the greatest of appeasers. His first stroke was 'the Austrian marriage', by which he hoped to buy off Napoleon with an Austrian archduchess. Far from being the enemy of Napoleon, Metternich was the most anxious of allied statesmen to compromise with him. He hesitated to enter the last coalition; strove for an agreed peace; and regretted Napoleon's downfall. He justified his policy by fear of Russia; it was pointless, he argued, to overthrow one tyrant of Europe if another took his place. The truth is that he wanted others to do the fighting for him. Besides, he supposed that a plump archduchess would turn Napoleon into a harmless, almost legitimate monarch and that the man who had grown great through the revolution would now tame it. It made the delusion no less absurd that Napoleon sometimes shared it.

Metternich did not invent the balance of power, nor do much to develop it. The Great Powers of Europe existed without his assistance; and his only initiative at the Congress of Vienna was to project an unnecessary war over Poland – a war which others had too much sense to fight. In international affairs, too, he offered a series of platitudes. 'All I ask is a moral understanding between the five Great Powers. I ask that they take no important step, without a previous joint understanding.' Even the United Nations would work if Metternich's request were granted. But what if the Great Powers disagreed? Metternich offered only lamentations and reproaches. He abused Canning for putting British interests first; yet was ready to wreck his conservative partnership with Russia for the sake of Austrian interests in the Balkans. In the usual way of statesmen who rule over a decaying empire, he urged others to preserve the Austrian monarchy for their own good. He invented an Austrian 'mission' and assured his foreign visitors how unwillingly he had added Lombardy to the empire in 1815. It is, of course, rare for upholders of empire ever to admit that they get advantage or profit from it. And as Metternich went from one palace to another or pocketed the rewards which other sovereigns as well as his own showered upon him, the cares of office were no doubt the only thought in his mind.

He played some diplomatic problems competently, though Palmerston, his contemporary, did better with less fuss. The two shared the credit for a peaceful outcome to the eastern crisis of 1840. But ten years earlier Metternich might have muddled the Belgian alarm into a war, if it had not been for Palmerston's firm handling. Again, Metternich put years of wasted effort into attempts at intervening in the Spanish civil wars. His most original move in Austrian policy was to concentrate her strength on Italy. Though himself a German from the Rhineland, he encouraged Austria's withdrawal from Germany. He did not assert her supremacy in the German confederation nor even grudge Prussia her private score of the Zollverein. Yet he was too much a man of western Europe to be content with the Balkans as compensation. For him Asia began at the road eastwards from Vienna. Italy alone seemed worthy to be the Habsburg prize. And Metternich taught the doctrine – quite erroneous, as it turned out – that the Habsburg Monarchy could remain great only so long as it continued to dominate in Italy. All his diplomatic combinations centred on the Italian provinces. Yet he knew both that the Italians hated Austrian rule and that France would not tolerate it indefinitely.

This double threat was in itself an attraction to him. It was always his aim 'to fight the revolution on the field of international politics'. He had no faith in principles or ideas despite his theoretical posturing. Though he claimed to be a disciple of Burke, he doubted whether historical institutions would hold against radical ideas. In any case, there were no historical institutions in central Europe except for the Hungarian parliament; and this Metternich never managed to control. The kings and emperors were almost as new as Napoleon, who had indeed created many of them. The Habsburgs had laid their hands on the historic states of Hungary and Bohemia; and Poland, the greatest historic state of all, had been eaten up by Metternich and his two conservative partners of the Holy Alliance. If tradition was useless, concession was dangerous. Metternich never wearied of explaining that moderate liberalism inevitably opened the door to extreme radicalism – a judgement repeatedly belied by events. Indeed, he argued in a perverse way that extreme radicalism, being less concealed, was somehow less alarming, even less destructive, than moderate reform.

His only answer to either liberalism or radicalism was, in fact, repression. If people were not allowed to think for themselves, they would be satisfied with material prosperity – and even this could be neglected. Since he had no genuine conservative ideas himself, he denied that radical ideas were genuine; and solemnly maintained that discontent everywhere was the result of 'a conspiracy'. When Confalonieri, the Italian patriot, was brought as a political prisoner to Vienna, Metternich wrangled with him for hours in the hope that 'the conspiracy' would at last be revealed. His view of radicalism was exactly that of Senator McCarthy. The good conservative must look under the bed every night. One day he will find a radical lurking there. A conspiracy needs a centre; and Metternich found it in Paris, as his present admirers find it in Moscow. How much easier to forget men's political grievances and to raise the cry of foreign war. But Metternich had more sense than those who now tread in his footsteps. Though he advocated a conservative crusade against France and 'the revolution', he proposed that it should be fought by others. Austria did her duty to civilization by existing; it was for others to keep her going. He said in old age: 'Error has never approached my spirit.' And certainly he never made the error of getting into the front line if he could avoid it. In this way at least he set an example to us all.

Metternich and His 'System' for Europe

This essay was broadcast on BBC Radio on 21 July 1959 as 'Two Centenaries: Metternich and Solferino' and subsequently published in The Listener *on 30 July 1959.*

*　　*　　*

In 1822, just before the opening of the Congress of Verona, the Russian ambassador suddenly died. Metternich is supposed to have said: 'I wonder why he did that.' An old story, probably made up years later as a parody of Metternich's habit of finding a hidden significance in every event. At any rate there is no need to search for the significance in Metternich's own death on 11 June 1859. The significance hits one in the eye. The battle of Solferino was fought a fortnight later. The Austrian Army was defeated by the combined forces of France and Sardinia. Austrian supremacy in Italy was ended, and the age of Metternich ended with it.

Solferino was not much of a battle except for the terrible casualties. It was a brutal slogging match. Neither side showed any gift of leadership or strategical insight. All the same, it was a decisive battle; the first lasting success of European nationalism. National Italy and, more remotely, national Germany were born on the field of Solferino. More distantly still, all the national states of east-central Europe can trace their victory back to the same day. The ill-directed armies, lurching clumsily against each other, symbolized the clash of two great principles: the conservative tradition of dynastic rights on the one side, revolutionary nationalism on the other. No wonder that Metternich withdrew from the scene. He and his Europe died together.

As a matter of fact, Metternich dated his own death rather

earlier. 'Yes, we are all dead,' he said to his wife on 13 March 1848, when he came home after resigning as Austrian chancellor under the pressure of street rioting. The revolutions of 1848 were all directed against 'the Metternich system' – against the social system which he was supposed to represent; against the international settlement made at the Congress of Vienna; and against the conservative principles which Metternich enunciated at such length. In March 1848 he supposed that the revolution had triumphed. He went into exile – at Brighton oddly enough, though that is symbolic, too. In fact the revolutions were defeated. The old order had another ten years of existence, though hardly of life. Metternich himself got back to Vienna: a neglected ghost to whom nobody listened.

The Italian war of 1859 saw the next round in the struggle and a more decisive one. This time the national cause triumphed for good. But in a different way from 1848. Then men had believed that the idealist cause would triumph of its own weight. 'Italy will do it herself.' And not only Italy – Poland, Germany, Hungary, radicalism, democracy, socialism: they were all supposed to be irresistible; and they were all defeated. Solferino was not a bit like that. It was won by conventional, disciplined armies in an old-fashioned way, and the war was brought about by old-style secret diplomacy – the successors of Metternich were outwitted by his own methods. Though conservatism was defeated at Solferino, radicalism was defeated too. This set the pattern for the future. All the great radical hopes of 1848 were achieved within a couple of generations. But they were achieved in a hardheaded cynical way, and by the time they arrived they had lost their glamour. Though there were celebrations of a rather modest sort on the field of Solferino in 1959, no one said, as Charles Fox said of the fall of the Bastille: 'How much the greatest event since the beginning of the world – and how much the best.'

Metternich's system has gone. There are national states all over Europe. Men contemplate this outcome gloomily. They even regret that they did not take Metternich's advice and leave things alone. Indeed it is the fashion now among historians to go wandering about the past regretting what has happened. I do not share this contemporary taste. It is equally little the task of the historian to be forever rejoicing in what happened, or to keep pointing out – as Macaulay did – that events were on the move, faster and faster, to that most perfect of times: the present. The great thing about the past is that it has happened – very fortunately for historians. It is hard enough to find out about it without trying to alter it. Least of all can we put it back. So-called restorations simply create new systems and institutions with the old names. This is how it worked out with the great Restoration which followed the defeat of Napoleon. Even the Austrian empire of 1815 was markedly different – in structure, spirit, geographic shape – from the anonymous empire which had stumbled into war with the French Revolution in 1792. It was this remade empire that Metternich spent his life defending, and which we now see through a romantic haze.

Even the haze of time is a romantic illusion. The Austrian Empire is supposed to have been extremely old. Strictly speaking, it was quite new. The title, Emperor of Austria, was invented only in 1804, to have something to set off against Napoleon's own invention, Emperor of the French. As for the Austrian Empire, as distinct from the emperor, I am not sure that it ever existed at all. It was an idea, not a state; or, on a more prosaic level, a convenient name for the territorial possessions, shifting and scattered, of the house of Habsburg.

Other dynasties managed to associate themselves, more or less, with some sort of national consciousness long before the age of nationalism. The house of Habsburg remained purely a family concern. It is often called 'international', but this is the wrong word. International implies cooperation between nations or at any rate between nationalities. The house of Habsburg did not want nations and nationalities to cooperate; it did not want them to exist. The Austrian Empire was not international; it was 'non-national', as indeed it was negative in everything. From start to finish the Habsburg Monarchy could be defined only in terms of what it was not. In the sixteenth century it was not Turkish. Later on, it was not aggressive – a slightly sham claim this one. At the end, it was not German. It had many fine mottoes and maxims. Its real spirit was expressed by the lines of Hilaire Belloc:

> Always keep a-hold of Nurse
> For fear of finding something worse

or, for that matter, something better.

It was this negative character that suited Metternich, and led him to serve the house of Habsburg for a lifetime. At least, this is the more charitable interpretation of his conduct: the public face, as it were, with which historians credit statesmen. As a matter of fact, he served the house of Habsburg because he made a fortune out of it: turned from a count into a prince, acquired castles and palaces, lined his pockets. Certainly Metternich and the Habsburg Monarchy were well in tune. It had always been negative; he was the great 'No-man'. One can make a long list of the changes he did not like, from the French Revolution to the change of date on New Year's Day. But what did he like except economic amelioration for his own benefit? He claimed to like railways, but this was only to move troops about better for purposes of resistance. In old age he used to sit at his desk, consoling himself with the murmur 'I have been a rock of order.'

This was largely pretence: deception of others and still more of himself. Metternich was no rock. He was obstinate, but soft, always trying to talk difficulties out of existence. He made his name as the man who organized Europe for the overthrow of Napoleon. But he had not intended to do it. What he wanted was to turn Napoleon – the conqueror and tyrant of Europe – into a gentle, bumbling family man, devoted to his silly Habsburg wife. The Habsburg Monarchy was much the same – resisting in the last ditch, not the first. It had to save Europe from Mohammedanism in the sixteenth century when the Turks actually reached the gates of Vienna. But it undertook the task unwillingly; more than a century and a half passed before it liberated Hungary; and even this had to be provoked by another Turkish siege of Vienna.

So, too, in the nineteenth century, after the defeat of Napoleon, Metternich deliberately did not reclaim the Austrian Netherlands and the old Habsburg lands on the Rhine. Others could have the honour and the burden of meeting the next wave of French aggression. The Habsburg emperor refused also to restore the Holy Roman Empire in Germany, leaving the German princes to resist nationalism. On the other hand, the Habsburg Monarchy, under Metternich's guidance, pushed itself into Italy more assertively than before. This is a puzzle, a contradiction. Metternich did not like trouble if it could be avoided. Yet in Italy the Habsburg Monarchy acquired new territories; distributed guarantees to the princes; and deliberately marked itself out as the target for nationalism.

I doubt whether there is a rational explanation for this policy. The Italian peninsula was a power vacuum after the fall of Napoleon, and the Habsburg Monarchy got sucked into it. The Great Powers have always felt the glamour of Italy, and statesmen have attached more strategic importance to it than it had in reality, from Charles VIII of France in 1494 to Winston Churchill in 1943. Metternich made the same miscalculation. Besides, he believed that Italy was more favourable ground on which to conduct the struggle against revolutionary ideas. In Germany, he had little faith in the princes; he recognized the strength of German nationalism, and felt its appeal himself. Italian nationalism was an ideal, pure abstraction. There had never been any kind of Italian national state before the time of Napoleon, and even his Kingdom of Italy was a sham. Italy was, in Metternich's well-known phrase, a geographic expression, without even a unity of language – what we nowadays call 'Italian' used to be called 'Tuscan'. The Italian states had a glorious historical record. Venice, Florence, and the papacy were already flourishing when most of the contemporary Great

Powers had not been heard of. The conflict between tradition and abstract ideal was sharpest and clearest in Italy. It was the best field of conflict for Metternich to choose if he were determined to fight at all. Italy became the parade-ground both of his policy and of the Habsburg Army.

A man who conducts the foreign policy of a Great Power for almost forty years cannot concentrate all the time on a single problem; and Italian affairs were often obscured by Poland, Spain, the Eastern question, Belgium, and even at one moment by Switzerland. Nevertheless Italy always occupied the central position in Metternich's calculations. Italy was to demonstrate his own skill. It was to convince everyone that the Habsburg Monarchy was 'a European necessity'. Instead it worked the other way round. It was Italy which first created the moral discredit of the Habsburg Monarchy. Think of the English poets denouncing Metternich and Austria – Byron, Landor, Swinburne, the Brownings; it was experience in Italy which moved them. Think of Gladstone exclaiming: 'There is not an instance – there is not a spot upon the whole map where you can lay your finger and say, "There Austria did good!"' The spot where in fact he laid his finger was Naples – a kingdom which was kept in existence by Austrian protection.

Elsewhere in Europe others shared the blame for oppression: Russia, for instance, shared it in Poland, and indeed deserved the greater share. In Italy the Habsburg Empire oppressed alone. Austrian rule in Italy appeared as one of the two big moral blots on nineteenth-century Europe – Turkish rule in the Balkans was the other. It was Italy which turned the Austrian Empire into a second 'sick man'. The moral defeat went further. Even after Italy had been liberated and united, the moral smear remained; and when the nationalities of the Austrian Empire voiced their claims during the First World War, they soon found sympathetic hearers. Englishmen and Americans had grown up believing that Austria once oppressed the Italians; therefore they readily believed that she was now oppressing the

Czechs, Romanians, and south Slavs. It was Austrian rule in Italy that launched her on the path of disintegration.

The Austrian defeat in Italy was a European defeat, not simply a defeat by Italian nationalism. This is what Solferino symbolizes. And this is why Italians rejoiced less over the anniversary of the success at Solferino than they did over the centenary of the unsuccessful revolutions of 1848. In 1848 the Habsburg Monarchy had contended against the Italian revolution without interference from foreign powers. The British government advised the Habsburgs to give up their Italian possessions – in its usual generous way with other people's property. The French republicans sympathized with Italian nationalism, but not to the extent of going to war. The Austrian Army fought alone, and won alone. Afterwards things changed. Austrian rule, now based on martial law, was in fact more oppressive than it had been before. The other powers wearied of 'the Italian question'. Once they had perhaps agreed that Austrian rule in Italy was a European necessity. Now they came to feel that the European necessity was to get Austria out of Italy, and all the Great Powers welcomed Austria's defeat in 1859.

There was another factor on which Italian historians have recently laid much stress. The movements of 1848 had relied solely on the national ideal; and this appealed only to the intellectual middle class. After 1848 Mazzini went on preaching nationalism, but others thought that they must add social appeals if they were to win the masses: land reform for the peasants; social reform for the workers in the towns. There was no longer the old choice between acquiescence and revolution. The question for Italians was now: Which sort of revolution? A great radical revolution on the French scale of 1789, or a respectable revolution with moderate methods and foreign allies? Cavour, prime minister of Sardinia, chose the second course. From the moment he came to power in 1852 he regarded it as his task to expel the Austrians without shaking the social foundations. He, not Metternich – or rather Metternich's successors – was now the true conservative.

The Italian war of 1859 was made by diplomacy, not by popular enthusiasm. The revolution was there, but it came from without: Napoleon III, himself a revolutionary, turned respectable, or at any rate turned emperor. The Austrian Army was defeated, not morally overwhelmed. Solferino was not the end of the story, only the beginning. Garibaldi, the great radical, won Sicily and Naples by radical methods in 1860. But Cavour was too strong for him. Garibaldi abandoned the social revolution for the sake of Italian unity. Not much more than twenty years later, Italy became the ally of the Habsburg Monarchy. More ironical still, in the nineteen-thirties, after the dissolution of the Austrian Empire, Dollfuss and Schuschnigg – the last Austrian statesmen who claimed to be the heirs of Metternich – were kept going by Mussolini's protection. Now, strangely enough, all the Great Powers are agreed that Austria is a European necessity. It is about the only thing on which they are agreed. And they are agreed upon it because the Austrian Empire, the empire of Metternich, has ceased to exist. He is dead all right.

Cobbett

Cobbett was one of Alan Taylor's favourite historical figures. He wrote the first of these essays – 'Voice of the Many' – for the Guardian *of 9 March 1962 to mark the 200th anniversary of Cobbett's birth. However, at this time his contract for the* Sunday Express *barred him from writing other than book reviews for other newspapers. Hence, as Alan Taylor recalled in his autobiography:*

A fortnight later I had a note from Junor [the editor of the *Sunday Express*]: 'A reader in the South of France complains that you published an article on William Cobbett which ought to have appeared in the *Sunday Express*.' This was the kind of prank Beaverbrook liked to play on his friends. I wisely decided not to reply – my case was in fact indefensible.

In his essay Alan Taylor emphasizes Cobbett's hostility to THE THING. *In an earlier essay on Cobbett, published in 1953, Taylor had written that 'in no other European country is the Establishment so clearly defined and so complacently secure' – and in the course of the essay he used 'the Establishment' nine times in all. Later he claimed that he, not Henry Fairlie, had used the term first.*

The second essay is the last that he wrote on Cobbett, appearing in the Observer *on 18 April 1982 as a review of George Spater's* William Cobbett: The Poor Man's Friend *(Cambridge, Cambridge University Press, 1982).*

*   *   *

Voice of the Many

William Cobbett was born on 9 March 1762. This was according to the old reckoning by which the year ended on 25 March. On our system he was born in 1763. It makes no odds. Whether born in 1762 or 1763, Cobbett strides across the centuries, red-faced, unshakably assertive in his opinions and prejudices – a great writer, a remarkable personality, and, beyond question, the greatest of English radicals. Cobbett was more than a man of the people. He was the people, the voice of the many. His powers of work were extraordinary. His energy never relaxed. For more than thirty years he brought out the *Political Register* almost single-handed. He wrote it all – political articles, disquisitions on finance, horticultural instruction, advice on housekeeping, surveys of the countryside. At the same time, he ran a farm, a seed-merchant's business, and a bookshop. He toured the country, making political speeches and collecting subscriptions for his *Register*.

He lived abstemiously. He rose at five; breakfasted on an apple and a few nuts; and often went through the day on a glass of milk. Once, when over sixty, he attended a farmers' meeting, where someone proposed that William Cobbett be put out of the room. 'I rose,' Cobbett writes, 'to show what manner of man they had to put out.' The motion was not proceeded with. No one will manage to put Cobbett out of English history, though many have tried.

Cobbett made himself to a unique extent. His father was a failed farmer, turned innkeeper at Farnham. Someone presumably taught Cobbett to read. No one taught him to write. His earliest fragments show his incomparable style in all its simplicity and power: direct statements; calculated iteration; devastating climax. No man has used the English language to greater effect. His writings remain the perfect model both for those who seek to persuade and for those who wish to denounce. Every great journalist, from Blatchford to Cassandra, follows Cobbett's example. Cobbett was nearly forty before he emerged from obscurity. As a young man he joined the army, served in New Brunswick, and rose to be a sergeant-major. He discovered that one of the officers was making off with regimental funds. He sought justice and it was denied him. This experience shaped his life. Not only did he leave the army; he drew two conclusions which henceforth formed his political philosophy. He concluded first that all of superior rank had their hands in the till; secondly that this would be ended only when the 'other ranks' gained control. The analysis was crude. No doubt there were some honest officers even in the old British Army, and some honest politicians even in British society. Still, it is a fair generalization of most public life. The few rob the many; acquire power, and then use it for their own profit and glory. Bunyan had called this arrangement Vanity Fair. Cobbett called it THE THING. He was its greatest enemy, the most relentless, and the most telling.

He imagined at first that he would find allies. He started the *Political Register* in cooperation with dissident Whigs. When these proved to be much like other politicians, he turned to the radicals, whom he had earlier denounced in his usual sweeping way. He backed Burdett at the famous Westminster election; sat on committees with Francis Place; shared public platforms with Orator Hunt. These associations did not last. Though Cobbett had admirers and assistants, he could never collaborate. The dogmatic conviction that he was right implied that all others, however radical, were wrong. Cobbett's great days came in the hard years after the Napoleonic War, and particularly after the return to gold currency in 1819. We tend to think of Cobbett as primarily an advocate of parliamentary reform, differing from more moderate reformers in demanding universal suffrage. This is a misunderstanding. Parliamentary reform was a more or less casual conclusion to Cobbett's analysis of society; and he was more taken up with what was wrong than with how it could be put right.

Cobbett held the common view that things had been better in 'the good old days'. He believed that the population had once been much greater, and of course more prosperous, than it was in his time; and demonstrated this by calculating how many people the village churches would have held if packed to the door. The census figures showed that the population was increasing; Cobbett rejected these figures as another fraud by THE THING. What had happened to the old prosperity when every labourer had bacon and beer for breakfast? Some radicals blamed it on the Norman Conquest. Cobbett did not go farther back than the Reformation. His *History of the Protestant Reformation*, though still reprinted as a Roman Catholic tract, is poorly regarded by historians. Still, it remarked on the previously neglected fact that families, now pious and respectable, grew rich on the spoils of the monasteries. Usually Cobbett was content to blame the Napoleonic War. This had increased the taxes. Even worse, it had increased the funds and the national debt. Fundholders and stockjobbers were taking over from the old landed gentry. Cobbett pointed out, quite correctly, that the debt had been incurred in depreciated paper money. Hence the crushing burden imposed by deflation and the return to gold. This became his obsession. His *Paper against Gold* is his most sustained political piece. When he entered the House of Commons after the Reform Bill, his one independent act was to move the impeachment of Peel for promoting the return to gold in 1819. His own programme was simple: repudiation of the national debt except for smallholders; drastic reduction of the army and military establishments; ending of all sinecure appointments in the Civil Service – and he did not think that there were any appointments which were not sinecures. This programme achieved great popularity among the farmers and lesser gentry in the years 1821 to 1823. This was Cobbett's finest hour: riding round the countryside to rouse his followers, and describing what he saw and did for readers of the *Political Register*.

The hardship and discontent died away in the middle of the decade. England was saved by the new industries. Cobbett hardly knew them, and disliked what he knew. He became less prominent as a leader: contested Preston, unsuccessfully, in 1826, and was returned, ironically for smoky Oldham, in 1833. He failed to repudiate the national debt; failed to shake the gold currency; failed to prevent the new Poor Law, against which he fought his last campaign. There was little to show at his death in 1835 except his incomparable writings and a great name. Yet he still stands, unchallenged and alone: the English people grown articulate.

Though there have been other great radicals, all have yielded just a little bit. Flattery has caught some; money has worked with others; honours have proved irresistible. Even John Bright became a privy counsellor. Cobbett alone did not go one inch towards the other side. He remained cantankerous, troublesome, persistent; at the end still contemptuous of the Crown, the Church, the governing classes, and their hangers-on. He knew what public life was for: to enable the officers to get their hands in the till. He told the truth about the system even though he failed to change it. THE THING is still with us; and Cobbett is still there, defying it. He was a shining example to the other ranks.

The People's Champion

William Cobbett wrote as his epitaph: 'He was a friend of Liberty, his power he derived from the spirit of freedom, and his exertions were directed to the benevolent purpose of bettering the condition of England.' When he died one newspaper described him as 'one of the greatest men whom England has ever produced' and *The Times* (usually described by Cobbett as 'the bloody old *Times*') wrote: 'Take this self-taught peasant for all in all, he was perhaps a more extraordinary Englishman than any other of his time.' Some of Cobbett's books are still in print; one, *Rural Rides*, in generous numbers. Without doubt he was a great writer, a champion of liberty and of the poor.

Cobbett ran over with wise advice: to the young, to farmers, to statesmen, to clergymen, in fact to almost everyone. There was one exception: he rarely took the advice he distributed so generously to others. He could never live within his income. When he took a house at Botley, he immediately rented four farms to go with it. When he later set up a seedsman's shop in Kensington (now an Underground station) he hired a hundred labourers to cultivate the surrounding fields. When he published a bestseller, *Cottage Economy*, he priced it so low that every copy increased the drain on his pocket. He mortgaged his land; he contracted loans that he could not repay; well-wishers repeatedly had to take the hat round. When rebuked for not following his own advice he replied, 'Very true; but then, I should not have been *the man I am*: observe that. To be careful of money; to sue and be sued; to squabble about shillings and pennies: these are wholly incompatible with the pursuit of great public objects.'

Here are the two themes of William Cobbett's life. On the one hand, the champion of the poor and defenceless: protesting against the harsh treatment of the poor and against the flogging of English militiamen by Hanoverian mercenaries, for which latter act he was sent to Newgate for two years. He was the campaigner against the government policy of inflation during the Napoleonic War. He denounced the corrupt electoral system and did more than any other single man to carry through the great Reform Act of 1832. Incidentally he began the publication of *Parliamentary Debates*, subsequently called *Hansard*.

On the other hand he never launched on a project without predicting its success and always ended in a tangle of loans. He quarrelled with his best friends and patrons. Towards the end of his life he quarrelled with his beloved wife. He quarrelled with his children and he died alone except for one loyal adherent. He was among other things a barrack-room lawyer. When serving as a sergeant-major in Canada he detected fraud among officers, charged them with it when he returned to England, and had to bolt for the United States.

There he campaigned against Dr Rush, the most distinguished American medical man of the day, was heavily amerced for libel, and had to bolt again, this time back to England – it was some consolation that Washington, Rush's patient, died on the day the libel verdict was announced. He opposed the war against France, he supported the war against France; he supported the war against the United States, he opposed it. Each time he was right, or so he claimed. His life makes a wonderful story, full of inspiration and gallantry, at the same time full of fun. No sooner is Cobbett irremediably down than he is up again, almost until his last moment when, already unconscious, he waved a hand in farewell and died without a gasp.

G D H Cole published a substantial life of Cobbett some sixty years ago, and also acquired a great stock of Cobbett material which he passed on to Nuffield College. American enthusiasts have also unearthed further material including an account of Cobbett's quarrel with his wife and family in his last days. On the basis of this material George Spater has now written a new life of Cobbett. An American lawyer who became chairman and chief executive officer of American Airlines, he is an unusual figure to become a devoted Cobbett biographer. Despite this, or perhaps because of it, his book is a complete success. Every admirer of Cobbett must read it.

Statistics are the great thing nowadays. Here are some statistics from Spater about Cobbett. His total output was more than twenty million words, all still readable. His writings on America alone make up twelve substantial volumes. *The Times* wrote somewhat ungrammatically, 'Cobbett was by far the most voluminous writer that has lived for centuries' – and all done with a quill pen. *Cottage Economy* sold 100,000 copies in its first ten years. *Advice to Young Men, and, incidentally, to Young Women* has sold well throughout the twentieth century. *A History of the Protestant Reformation* sold 700,000 copies during Cobbett's lifetime. No wonder Cobbett wrote: 'When I am asked what books a young man or young woman ought to read, I always answer: Let him or her read all the books that I have written.'

A couple of statistics about Cobbett's lecture tours when advocating the Reform Bill are also memorable. In early 1830 Cobbett toured Lancashire and Yorkshire. He travelled nearly 700 miles and in fifty-three days he had made twenty-seven speeches for a total of some sixty-one hours. In late 1831 he stumped the Midlands. He travelled 980-odd miles. 'I stood upon my legs, speaking, upwards of 130 hours; that is to say, more than five days and five nights.'

The best story comes at the end. Cobbett was elected to the first reformed parliament. When the House met he was one of the first to arrive. Having taken the oath he sat down on the Treasury bench in the place usually occupied by the Leader of the House, in this case Lord Althorp, who when he arrived modestly took his place next to Cobbett. And quite right, too. Cobbett was truly the People's William. He would be my hero if I ever had one.

Castlereagh

This essay was published as 'Laying a Troubled Ghost' in the Observer *on 6 September 1981, as a review of Wendy Hinde's* Castlereagh *(London, Collins, 1981).*

* * *

Robert Stewart, Viscount Castlereagh and for a short time before his death Marquis of Londonderry, was a controversial figure during his lifetime and has continued to provoke argument ever since. The radicals of the day regarded him as the champion of every tyrannical act from the suppression of the Irish rebellion in 1798 to the massacre of Peterloo in 1819. Even in governmental circles, as Spencer Perceval remarked, he had 'a great want of popularity'.

Later historians will have none of this. He now appears as a foreign secretary of the first rank, sustaining the grand alliance against Napoleon and using the Congress of Vienna to make the wisest and most successful settlement of a great European war, a settlement far superior to that of the conference of Paris in 1919, let alone the meeting at Potsdam in 1945. No one has surpassed him in diplomatic skill except perhaps Metternich and even he, according to Castlereagh, 'had an inordinate taste for spies and police . . . which put their employer much oftener on the *wrong*, than the *right* scent'.

Wendy Hinde is the right biographer to reconcile these conflicting views. Her favourite word is 'amiable' – a word she applies to such different characters as Addington, Dundas, Spencer Perceval and Sir Harry Burrard. She certainly merits the description and indeed her attitude towards Castlereagh is touched even with affection which I should have thought impossible. She has a firm grasp of the politics of the time, both domestic and foreign. She writes clearly with impeccable scholarship. Though I still regard Castlereagh as a dull fellow I found him a little less dull after reading Ms Hinde's book.

Castlereagh had repeated runs of bad luck. As chief secretary at the time of the Irish rebellion he had to shoulder responsibility for the brutality of its suppression which in fact he repeatedly tried to restrain. In 1800 he carried the Act of Union through the Irish parliament by a mixture of coercion and corruption. This was not his fault. Corruption was the only instrument to use in a parliament that had been ineradicably corrupt throughout its life. Against this may be set a mark of great merit. Castlereagh was a clear-cut advocate of Catholic emancipation who also urged the endowment of the Catholic Church in Ireland. He could not be blamed for the fact that these proposals threatened to deprive George III of his somewhat limited wits.

Castlereagh had bad luck in British politics also. As secretary for war he bore the blame for the ineffective strategy which at first miscarried against Napoleon's domination of Europe. His nonsensical project of an expedition to aid the king of Sweden was less foolish than the projected Allied expedition to aid Finland in 1940. Castlereagh was denied credit for the campaign in the Spanish peninsula only because he had moved from the War Department to the Foreign Office before Wellington had carried the campaign to its triumphant conclusion.

Still more unfortunately, Castlereagh was one of the few cabinet ministers in the House of Commons and served as Leader of the House throughout the years of unrest that followed the Napoleonic Wars. No doubt Castlereagh accepted Sidmouth's Six Acts without demur and shared the general approval in government circles for the blundering Manchester magistrates at St Peter's Fields. But these things were not really his affair. It is also clear from his contribution to debates that he had not the slightest understanding of the economic and financial questions involved. He would have done better to hand these affairs over to Sir Robert Peel. Shelley, judging from afar, said that Murder had a face like Castlereagh's. This is not confirmed by Lawrence's portrait of Castlereagh reproduced on the dust cover of Ms Hinde's book.

Castlereagh's true reputation rests on his foreign policy, where he showed gifts of the highest quality. The office of foreign secretary was only thirty years old when Castlereagh accepted it and he was the first to develop a foreign policy that was specifically his own, independent of prime minister or cabinet. Castlereagh can claim to have launched the Concert of Europe, which brought a longer peace to Europe than any new-fangled organization has done. He did better than any of his successors in being on good terms with the ruler of Russia. Castlereagh also laid down the principle of non-intervention in the internal affairs of other countries which has been or should have been the foundation of British foreign policy ever since. This is a very impressive record and all done without any flings of rhetoric.

In 1822 Castlereagh killed himself, the only cabinet minister, I think, ever to do so. What drove this cool, restrained man to such an act? Was it the recent death of his father whom he much loved? Was he blackmailed for homosexual activities which he had really committed or for which he was framed? Or was it merely a mental and physical collapse brought on by overwork? It is useless to speculate. I surmise that he lacked some vital spark, a lack which kept him cool in crisis and left him at a loss when the dreary round of business overcame him. In some ways he remains a great statesman and deserves the admirable biography that Ms Hinde has devoted to him.

Wellington : Silly Soldier Man?

This essay was published in the Observer *on 5 November 1972 as a review of Elizabeth Longford's* Wellington: Pillar of State *(London, Weidenfeld and Nicolson, 1972). Taylor had earlier praised its companion volume,* Wellington: The Year of the Sword *(London, Weidenfeld and Nicolson, 1969), in the* Observer *of 16 November 1969.*

*   *   *

Retired generals should keep clear of politics, as may be seen from the warning examples of, say, Hindenburg, Pétain and Sir Henry Wilson. Compared with these and other silly soldiermen turned politicians, the Duke of Wellington did very well when he entered British politics after Waterloo. To some extent he was not retired though he never saw active service again. He commanded the Allied Armies in France until 1818 and would have been recalled as Allied Commander-in-Chief if a European war had broken out in 1840. He took command in what was expected to be a civil war during the great Chartist demonstration of 1848. He remained British Commander-in-Chief, with some interruption, until his death in 1852 – a persistence that is usually held not to have benefited the British Army.

Nevertheless Wellington was more politician than soldier in the remaining thirty-seven years of his life after Waterloo. It was a matter of great curiosity what Lady Longford would make of him. The first volume of her biography provided its own material so long as Wellington was waging campaigns in India, the Peninsula, or at Waterloo. But could Lady Longford sustain the interest when Wellington was bumbling along in politics and attaining only the eminence of being described by a distinguished historian as 'the worst British prime minister of the nineteenth century'?

The answer is that Elizabeth Longford has surpassed herself. This volume is the best she has ever written, and that is saying a great deal. Of course she is still a bit in love with Wellington. She is soft on his follies, whether in politics or with women. She exaggerates his importance. It is hard to believe that he was really the Pillar of State, the man who more than any other ensured the peaceful course of British domestic history during the nineteenth century. But every biographer is entitled to exaggerate the importance of his subject. What matters is that the book is scholarly, well written and above all offers lavish helpings of fun.

Much of the fun was deliberately provided by Wellington himself. He had a characteristic Anglo-Irish showmanship that almost put him in the same class as Bernard Shaw. When asked whether he was not pleased by the enthusiastic crowds after Waterloo, he replied: 'Not in the least: if I had failed, they would have shot me.' He disliked being greeted by his soldiers: 'I hate that cheering. If once you allow soldiers to express an opinion, they may, on some other occasion, hiss instead of cheer.' He took a perverse pleasure at his unpopularity during the Reform Bill crisis. He installed iron shutters after Apsley House had been attacked and thereafter, if a crowd began cheering him, was apt to raise his hat ironically and point towards the shutters.

In war Wellington was distinguished by his caution. In politics and in his private life he rushed his fences, committing himself irrevocably to one line of action and then doing the opposite. He said in 1828:

There is no person in this House whose feelings are more decided than mine with regard to the subject of the Roman Catholic claims; and until I see a great change in that quarter, I certainly shall oppose it.

In 1829 he carried Catholic Emancipation. The next year he declared that the system of representation was perfect – 'the nature of man is incapable of reaching such *excellence* at once' – and announced his opposition to parliamentary reform:

I am not only not prepared to bring forward any measure of this nature, but I will at once declare that ... I shall always feel it my duty to resist such measures when proposed by others.

He told Croker in 1831 concerning the Reform Bill: 'I certainly will never enter the House of Lords from the time that it passes.' Little more than twelve months later he ensured the passage of the Bill through the House of Lords, and when Croker, following the Duke's precept, refused to stand for the reformed parliament, Wellington replied:

My dear Croker,
   I have received your letter.
   I am very sorry that you do not intend again to serve in Parliament.
   I cannot conceive for what reason.

Lady Longford holds that Wellington, being unhappily married to a sweet but scatty wife, sought consolation in the society of smart, clever women. That, she suggests, was all. But she is honest enough now and then to hint the contrary. There is one superb episode that ranks high in the annals of comedy. Anna Maria Jenkins, a young religious enthusiast who was also very attractive, resolved to save the Duke's soul. He called on her. She began to read the Bible: 'Ye *MUST* be born again.' Suddenly the Duke roared out: 'Oh, *how* I *love* you! *how* I *love* you! This must be for life! This must be for life! ... Do you feel sufficiently for me to be with me a whole life?' When Anna Maria modestly declined his proposition the Duke escaped by the manoeuvre of making out that she, not he, wanted to get married: 'What would be said, if I, a man of seventy years of age, nearly, were to take in marriage a lady young enough to be my granddaughter?' Thereafter Miss Jenkins continued to pursue his soul. Wellington soon wearied of pursuing her body.

Another suitor was Angela Burdett-Coutts, the immensely rich daughter of Sir Francis Burdett. In 1847, when she was thirty-two and he was seventy-seven, she actually proposed to him. He replied:

You are Young, my Dearest! You have before you the Prospect of at least another twenty years of enjoyment of Happiness in Life. I entreat you again, in this way, not to throw yourself away upon a Man old enough to be your Grandfather, who, however strong, Hearty and Healthy at present, must and will certainly in time feel the consequences and Infirmities of Age.

Baroness Burdett-Coutts lived to be ninety-two, making at sixty-seven a happy marriage with a man less than half her age. The Duke of Wellington certainly had some odd acquaintances.

In one matter the historian must lament the Duke's activities. He was a great destroyer of royal papers. He destroyed all the correspondence between Mrs FitzHerbert and George, Prince of Wales, and between Prince George and Princess Caroline. He also destroyed all the papers that revealed who was the father of Thomas Garth, son of Princess Sophia. One fragment of the story has survived: 'An accusation by a Sister that Her Own Brother had more than once attempted to violate her Person.' The brother is of course the Duke of Cumberland, a man credited with many other wicked acts. Lady Longford thinks that the phraseology exonerates him: 'Cumberland was said to have "attempted" rather than achieved his object.' Like Anna Maria Jenkins, Lady Longford is a bit on the innocent side.

Sir Robert Peel

These essays were reviews of Norman Gash's standard two-volume life of Peel. Alan Taylor warmed to the work with the second volume. Originally he deemed the first volume to be 'a crushing monument of dullness'. 'Orange Peel' appeared in the Observer *on 7 May 1961, reviewing* Mr Secretary Peel *(London, Longmans, 1961), and 'The Cotton Spinner's Son' in the* New Statesman *on 15 September 1972, reviewing* Sir Robert Peel *(London, Longmans, 1972).*

*   *   *

Orange Peel

Between the wars streamlined biographies were in fashion. Eminent statesmen were dug up from the ponderous Lives which enshrined them; their personalities were displayed, and their public labours passed over briefly. The fashion has changed. Historians have become the new resurrection men, providing revised versions of the standard Lives rather than cutting them down to the size of a novel. Dr Plumb is doing this for Walpole. There is a new Life of Disraeli, and a new Asquith. Now Norman Gash presents two substantial volumes on Sir Robert Peel.

There is good excuse for this. Peel was in the first rank of nineteenth-century statesmen. He carried Catholic emancipation; he repealed the Corn Laws; he created the modern Conservative Party on the ruins of old Toryism. Yet, strangely enough, his Life has never been written. The three volumes by C S Parker, though a valuable source, are simply a collection of letters, with little attempt at narration, and Parker's editing leaves much to be desired. Peel's papers have long been in the British Museum, waiting for a biographer, and Gash has used them thoroughly. His book, in the conventional phrase, fills a long-felt gap. It takes its place at once as a standard work on nineteenth-century British history.

Gash writes competently. His scholarship is careful and exhaustive. His clear narrative rests firmly on the sources and is sound in its interpretation. Nevertheless his book is somewhat dull. Peel himself is partly to blame. Though a sensitive and perhaps an interesting nature lay behind his cold exterior, he took care not to reveal it. He wrote few letters of a personal kind and destroyed those which he did. He was content to survive only as a 'public man' and there is not much fun in that. Moreover, history is one thing, and biography another. Most historians are not greatly interested in human nature or, if they are, do not know how to reveal it. Gash is no exception. None of his figures comes alive. He has a historian's zest for detail and spares the reader nothing.

The first volume deals with Peel's life only to 1830. During this time he was chief secretary for Ireland and home secretary. The book tells us a great deal about Irish conditions and about Peel's reform of the criminal law. It dissects the personal intrigues and manoeuvres within the Tory Party. It displays the relations between Crown and cabinet in the last years before the great Reform Bill. These things are interesting; some of them are important. But it is really excessive that we should have to read nearly 700 pages in order to learn about them. Every historian is reluctant to throw away even the tiniest scrap of information about the past. But even historians should bear in mind the great principle of economy of effort, both for themselves and, still more, for the reader. Gash has disregarded it.

It is not as though there were any great mystery about Peel or his policy. By inclination he was simply a first-rate administrator with a tidy mind, the sort of man who in a slightly later period would have gone into the Civil Service. He had no desire to change things nor any belief that change would do good. He said: 'We are told that we cannot stop where we are; I answer that we are more likely to stop where we are, than we shall if we advance to the point to which we are invited.' When he became member for Oxford, he accepted the principle that his views would never change. One of his supporters wrote to him: 'It is change and versatility in any way which will at any time injure the reputation of the member for the University in the University itself.' Hence Peel never met trouble half-way. He waited until the trouble came and then succumbed to it.

Catholic emancipation was the great example. Peel was for many years the outstanding spokesman of the 'Protestant' cause, always ready to jump into the breach. Emancipation, he argued, would destroy the historic constitution; it would threaten the security of the established Church; it would not satisfy the Irish. Faced with rebellion in Ireland, he turned round, jettisoned his previous arguments, and announced that emancipation was the only way to keep Ireland quiet. Both sets of arguments made sense but not in the mouth of the same person. Yet Peel was impatient, too, with those who changed their minds before he did.

Peel had almost every gift of statesmanship except foresight, and here he set the pattern for Conservatism to the present day. When our rulers announce that they will never do this or that and then do it, we recognize that the spirit of Peel is still with us. Daniel O'Connell was the first to benefit from Peel's policy or lack of it; Jomo Kenyatta, at present, the last and there are sure to be others. Peel charted the course for British Conservatism: 'no concessions – except to threats'. Even concessions thus extracted are better than none at all. But it is strange that Peel and his followers never appreciated that telling men they will get concessions only if they make trouble is hardly the best recipe for a quiet life.

The Cotton Spinner's Son

'I will not be the Peel of my party.' Thus Balfour, leader of the Unionist Party, in 1910. At first sight a curious remark. Balfour had been a singularly ineffective leader and was destined to be unshipped by his own followers the year after he made the remark. His record as prime minister was distinguished only by an Education Act that was in a minor way a betrayal of what his followers believed in. Against this, Peel's record as leader and prime minister was perhaps the greatest that any modern British statesman has to show. He gave England an unarmed police force under civilian control; a fiscal and financial system that lasted for nearly a hundred years; a political system freed from religious monopoly; and above all free trade. In 1848, thanks to Peel, England experienced only the Chartist picnic on Kennington Common when nearly every European country was gripped by revolution. Yet it was all in vain. On two occasions – Catholic emancipation and the repeal of the Corn Laws – he put nation before party. His name became a byword among politicians and has remained so to the present day.

Of course most leaders have trouble with their party, particularly when they are in office. Every leader has then to water down the principles that he previously professed. Conservative prime ministers are harassed from the Right, Liberal and Labour prime ministers from the Left. Again, nearly every leader practises the doctrine that David Low attributed to Baldwin: 'If I hadn't told you I wouldn't bring you here, you wouldn't have come.' Disraeli led the aristocratic Conservatives to household suffrage. Asquith led the pacific Liberals into the Great War. Macmillan led the imperialist Conservatives into discarding the British Empire. Even splitting the party, as Peel did in 1846, has been repeated. Gladstone split the Liberals over home rule; MacDonald split Labour by forming the National government in 1931. In both these cases the impact was less. Gladstone retained the allegiance of the majority of Liberals. MacDonald took so few followers with him that the unity of the Labour Party was not affected. Peel held a third of his followers, including all the able administrators – enough to cripple the Conservative Party and not enough to start a party of their own. This was not the worst. Peel's real offence was to disregard almost without warning principles which his supporters cherished and to which he himself had professed unquestioning devotion.

It was not that Peel was a casual or incompetent party leader. His construction of a modern Conservative Party from the Tory fragments shattered by the passing of the great Reform Bill was an incomparable achievement which brought its reward. The general election of 1841 was the first occasion in British history when a party, as distinct from a conglomeration of groups, won a clear majority, and the feat was not repeated until after the second Reform Act of 1867. As prime minister, Peel dominated his cabinet and seemed to dominate his party. In those great days he was the only British statesman, apart from the aged Duke of Wellington, of clear national stature. Whence then the catastrophe? Was it all an accident or were there in Peel hidden weaknesses?

These are topics which those interested in political history, from Bagehot to Crossman, have often debated. Norman Gash makes a contribution of unique importance in this, the first serious biography of Peel. The first volume which brought Peel to 1830, though eminently sound, was, I thought, on the dull side. The second volume however is a wonderful book, as good a political biography as has appeared for many years past. It contains no surprises. As Gash remarks, the memoirs which Peel wrote after leaving office 'still stand as an authentic record of the events with which they are concerned'. Gash has added a great deal more from the various sources which he uses with unobtrusive skill. His presentation never allows the ample details to obscure the march of events. Gash has matured into a beautiful biographer. Occasionally, being a Conservative himself, he takes the rhetoric of the time a little too seriously, and this may make the less engaged reader giggle. Thus he writes of the attempt to reform the Irish corporations:

The reform in the abstract was unexceptionable. The practical effect, however, would be to install Catholics in power in nearly every Irish borough. It raised therefore the constant dilemma which dogged all

Irish politics: how to apply rational and acceptable reforms to Irish institutions without destroying the Protestant ascendancy.

How indeed?

Gash's book is strictly political biography, just as the biography of a general should be about war. Some prime ministers, perhaps most great ones, have been interesting in themselves. They were eccentrics in either character or behaviour. Gladstone appeared extraordinary, for good or ill, to everyone who met him. Disraeli was odd in the highest degree. Palmerston was a law unto himself. Lloyd George was like no one who had ever been. Even Baldwin was decidedly rum. But unless Peel had been prime minister, and a great one, there would have been little to say about him. He was a faithful husband. Gladstone said that he had known eleven prime ministers and that seven of them were adulterers. Peel was certainly one of the virtuous four. He was very rich – Gash computes his income at £40,000 a year or more. He was also very generous, giving inconspicuous assistance to writers and artists. He collected pictures, sticking to the Dutch, Flemish and English schools then in vogue. When tempted towards the Italian primitives by Prince Albert, he replied: 'I think we should not collect curiosities.' Gash gives some examples of his lighter remarks. They are all right, acceptable enough at the dinner table. But any man with a turn for conversation could have done as well.

The effect is very different as soon as politics enter in. Peel had a mastery of performance that has rarely been equalled. Disraeli described him as the greatest parliamentarian that ever lived, though the remark was not meant as a compliment. Peel was conscious of his gifts. Shortly after becoming prime minister for the first time (in 1834), he wrote:

I do not hesitate to say that I feel that I can do more than any other man can who means his reforms to work practically, and who respects, and wishes to preserve, the British Constitution.

The Bank Charter Act of 1844 is a good example of Peel's art. Without any specialist knowledge of banking, he picked up from bankers a grasp so clear that the system he devised lasted for nearly a century. Bagehot's famous diagnosis of ordinary ideas and extraordinary abilities was unfair. It was rather that Peel carried practical ideas to an extraordinary level.

Peel grew up in politics as the servant of the Crown and, though he used party as an instrument for gaining power, never reconciled himself to the fact that as the party leader he must be to some extent its servant. After his fall in 1846 he rejoiced at his 'freedom from the base servitude to which a minister must submit who is content to sacrifice the interests of a great empire to those of a party'. Gash is content to make the contrast between national statesman and party leader without going further. Peel is presented as a great administrator impatient with party considerations much as present-day civil servants are impatient with their political masters. In this view Peel was a forerunner of Hankey or Warren Fisher.

There was surely a more positive reason for the cleavage between Peel and his party. He was consciously leading his followers where they did not want to go, pushing them into the nineteenth century and industrial England. Gash points out that in the general election of 1841, though the Conservatives were still 'primarily the party of England and above all of the English counties', there could have been no Conservative victory without the forty-four Conservative MPs returned for the larger boroughs. Peel's aim was to create an alliance between landowners and capitalists, to make in a sense a single nation of all those with a stake in the country. Bismarck, who avowedly modelled himself on Peel, had the same aim when he pushed the Prussian Junkers into accepting national middle-class Germany. And Bismarck, like Peel, got precious little thanks from the class that he preserved.

There was a further factor that made Peel's offence the more heinous, a factor that Gash does not perhaps sufficiently develop. Bismarck caused the Junkers much trouble, but no one could deny that he himself was a Junker and stuffed with Junker prejudices. Peel was to outward appearance a Tory – upper-class education, a great landowner and much given to cracking up Tory beliefs, such as the Protestant ascendancy or the Corn Laws. But his Toryism was only skin deep. Consider for instance the Church of England, the institution that Tory squires loved above all else. Here is Peel's definition of it:

That is the Established Church of England to which the King must conform – whose chief ministers have a right to seats in the House of Lords – which has an unalienable claim to ecclesiastical property.

In fact a mere property-owning organization like any city company. Once the Catholics were emancipated, Peel hoped that their priests too would be endowed – then presumably there would be nothing to choose between the two Churches in his eyes.

Similarly over the Corn Laws he never seems to have grasped that they symbolized the traditional social superiority of the landed classes. He said in 1845:

I am afraid of other interests getting damaged in this struggle about the Corn Laws: already the system of promotion in the Army, the Game Laws, the Church are getting attacked with the aid of the League.

A felicitous list indeed: the Game Laws and the purchase of commissions put on the same level as the established Church – all privileges of the landed classes and all, in Peel's eyes, increasingly indefensible. Peel let slip the truth about himself in 1835 when he boasted 'that the King had sent for the son of a cotton-spinner to Rome, in order to make him Prime Minister of England'. Maybe he never realized how much his origins removed him emotionally from historic Toryism. Though he resided in a great mansion at Drayton, he still belonged spiritually to Oswaldtwistle. In his later years the cotton-spinner's son predominated more and more. When he first avowed his loss of faith in the Corn Laws, he defined his real belief:

We must make this country a cheap country for living, and thus induce parties to remain and settle here, enable them to consume more by having more to spend.

It is not surprising that when Peel resigned he said that the main credit for the repeal of the Corn Laws should go to Cobden. Peel was not out-argued by Cobden. He was not even converted by Cobden. He discovered to his surprise that he had really agreed with Cobden all along. The cotton-spinner's son returned to his true allegiance.

Macaulay

Paperback editions of Macaulay's Essays *(1843) and his* History of England *from the Accession of James II, 4 volumes (1855–61) provided Alan Taylor with the occasions to return to one of his favourite topics – Thomas Babington Macaulay (1800–1859). Macaulay appealed because of his style, his support for progressive causes and his success in taking history to a very large reading public. Indeed Alan Taylor on several occasions quoted with approval Macaulay's claim that his* History of England *had ousted the latest novel from ladies' dressing tables. He was not displeased when reviewers suggested that he was the modern Macaulay.*

Hugh Trevor-Roper's selection from Macaulay's History of England *encouraged Taylor to read again Macaulay's full work. In December 1980 he commented:*

I had expected the style to be rather old-fashioned, almost Gibbonian. Not at all. There are more single-verb sentences one after another than I should ever dare to attempt. Macaulay invented the Bren-gun style long before I did and used it far more ruthlessly. Another thing I had forgotten were the allusions to contemporary events which I should not venture on: wise words on Catholic emancipation, a penetrating analysis of the Irish question and a correct demonstration that Torbay was a pleasanter place in the 19th century than it had been when William the Deliverer landed there. The essays are a different matter: mostly reviews, hastily written and overemphatic, as I dare say mine are. (*An Old Man's Diary*, London, Hamish Hamilton, 1984, p. 10)

The first essay appeared in the Observer *on 16 May 1965, reviewing* Macaulay's Essays, *selected and introduced by Hugh Trevor-Roper (London, Fontana, 1965). The second was published in the* Observer *on 29 July 1979, reviewing* Lord Macaulay: The History of England, *edited and abridged with an Introduction by Hugh Trevor-Roper (Harmondsworth, Penguin, 1979).*

*   *   *

The Man Who was Always Right

There can be no denying that Macaulay was a very good writer. Start off on any page, in the middle of a paragraph, and it is impossible not to read on. Macaulay's style is like tank warfare, as defined by Guderian: mobility, velocity, momentum, and the flash of deadly fire. One element, postulated by Captain Liddell Hart, is lacking. Instead of 'indirect approach', Macaulay went straight for the enemy, meaning by that the author of the book which he was ostensibly reviewing or some historical character whom he had resolved to denounce. Macaulay never guarded his flank or relied on surprise. He was confident that he would sweep all before him by an immediate onslaught and, to judge by his success with generations of readers, he always did.

In a longer view, his faults grow more obvious. He disappoints on re-reading. His emphasis becomes wearisome. His certainty provokes doubts. We begin to discover merits in the characters whom he most condemns. With every new assertion, Macaulay seems smaller instead of more commanding, until in the end he appears as a rather absurd little figure – so confident that he knew the answer to everything and really a cork on the surface of events.

Macaulay had one great quality which is essential for the historian. He was excited by the past. He lacked other qualities which are equally essential. He had no real sympathy for the past, which he judged always by the standards of the present. And he never suspended judgement. His researches, and they were considerable, were undertaken in order to confirm conclusions at which he had already arrived, not to modify them. Imagination boggles at the thought of Macaulay's encountering some piece of evidence which really shook his established picture. Fortunately he did not have this experience. The study of history is often said to make men wiser, more cautious, and more restrained. It did not have these effects on Macaulay. As he began, so he remained.

It is perhaps a little unfair to judge Macaulay from his *Essays*, brilliant though these are. The best of Macaulay is in his *History of England*, however plausibly Professor Trevor-Roper may argue that Macaulay's writings are all of a piece. This is not because the *History* was written later – some of the *Essays* are quite late also. It is a difference of scale and purpose. The *History* gave Macaulay room to expand and even to relax. The *Essays*, despite their length, were too tight for him. Their metallic noise is often beyond endurance. Moreover, in the *Essays*, Macaulay was showing off. His superior wisdom and his encyclopaedic knowledge were forever on display. In the *History*, Macaulay was less demonstrative and less combative. He even forgot occasionally to fight the Tories.

Macaulay was at his best in the *Essays* on historical subjects and at his worst in controversy. He chose easy game. Poor Southey was not much good as a social philosopher. All the same, he saw the evils of the industrial system where Macaulay saw none, and he stumbled on a Keynesian view of the merits of public spending, which seemed to Macaulay merely ridiculous.

Again, Gladstone was no doubt absurd when he defended the privileges of the established Church without actually proposing to persecute dissenters. But Macaulay, like many others then and since, would have used exactly the same arguments if 'Christianity' had been substituted for 'the Church of England'. Macaulay was in favour of past changes and against new ones, as Chesterton pointed out when he contrasted Macaulay's speeches for the Reform Bill and his speech against the Chartists. So now, those who benefit from the accomplishment of the Charter denounce the heirs of the Chartists themselves.

One passage neatly illustrates the qualities which made Macaulay more preposterous than any on whom he poured scorn. It begins: 'The history of England is emphatically the history of progress,' and goes on to contrast the England of the twelfth century with that of the nineteenth:

In the course of seven centuries the wretched and degraded race have become the greatest and most highly civilised people that ever the world saw ... have carried the science of healing, the means of locomotion and correspondence, every mechanical art, every manufacture, every thing that promotes the convenience of life to a perfection which our ancestors would have thought magical ... have speculated with exquisite subtlety on the operations of the human mind, have been the acknowledged leaders of the human race in the career of political improvement.

The truth is that Macaulay never had an original thought in his life. He reflected, in glittering words, what was in the minds of complacent contemporaries. He did not try to outrun his age. His opinions on literature were as narrow as those on life. For instance, he remarks of Johnson: 'The reputation of those writings, which he probably expected to be immortal, is every day fading.' Yet who now would trade *The Lives of the Poets* for Macaulay's *Essays* or even for his *History? The Lives of the Poets* is at any rate, of all the books of the past, the one I would most wish to have written.

The professional reviewer especially must look at Macaulay with critical disapproval. All these essays were produced ostensibly as book reviews. Yet none of them discusses the author or editor unless it is to condemn him. Few editors and fewer readers would stomach this nowadays. The reviewer's duty is to tell potential readers what the book is about, not to show off.

No doubt some of the writers who provided Macaulay with a peg did not deserve much attention. But what about Ranke, the greatest historian of his age, perhaps of any age? Surely Macaulay should display to the reader something of Ranke's quality, of his merits and achievements. Not at all. When Macaulay is presented with Ranke's *History of the Popes*, the book gets two sentences: 'An excellent book excellently translated ... written in an admirable spirit, equally remote from levity and bigotry, serious and earnest, yet tolerant and impartial.' Then off Macaulay goes on forty pages of rather commonplace generalities about the ups and downs of the

Roman Church. Macaulay would not survive long as a book reviewer nowadays.

Yet there remains the brilliance and vigour, history at its most glamorous. The reader may come out bruised and certainly no wiser. But he has certainly been for an exciting ride. In addition, there is an introductory essay by Professor Trevor-Roper, of which one may say, without exaggeration, that it might have been written by Macaulay himself.

Leviathan of History

When Macaulay visited the zoo soon after the appearance of the first two volumes of his *History*, one young lady was heard to exclaim to another, 'Is that Mr Macaulay? Never mind the hippopotamus.'

Macaulay was too agile to be a hippopotamus but he was certainly a leviathan of history. His early run of historical essays was prodigious. He intended to write the history of England from the Glorious Revolution to the Great Reform Bill and covered only the reign of William III before he died. Even the surviving four volumes are more than life size.

Macaulay had many faults. He was not profound. He was grossly unfair to such different characters as John Churchill and William Penn. He had a complacent preference for the present over the past and his enthusiasm reached its height when he contemplated Torquay. Despite his famous third chapter, depicting English society in 1685, his consuming interest was in aristocratic politics and a present-day sociologist would shake his head at the way in which Macaulay composed his picture.

But he had also many virtues. He was immensely learned, able to draw illustrations from the time of ancient Rome to the latest event of the day before. He was one of the first modern historians to use original sources. He had learnt from Sir Walter Scott that the present was different from the past though he did not always observe his own rule. Above all Macaulay was a great writer. The casual reader who picks up a volume of Macaulay's *History* will be taken prisoner and unable to rest until he has finished the volume or preferably all four of them.

Perhaps I am hopeful. The fashion has turned against long books. There are some who can still surmount James Joyce's *Ulysses* or even the interminable volumes of Marcel Proust. Few read Gibbon from beginning to end and even fewer, I fear, the four volumes of Macaulay. This neglect is, I think, lamentably mistaken. Macaulay may be superficial. He may be out of date. But in my opinion he remains the most readable of all historians. Macaulay offers every literary virtue from drama to comedy. His pictures of the bucolic squire and the impoverished cleric are unrivalled despite the critical scrutiny they have suffered from later writers. If his characters were often neither as heroic nor as wicked as he presented them, they ought to have been.

How shall we lure readers back to Macaulay? Hugh Trevor-Roper has provided a gallant answer by cutting the *History* down from four substantial volumes to one paperback. Here indeed are some of the finest passages and the most irresistible. But of course the result is a series of isolated delights, not Macaulay's *History*. Macaulay was a supreme master of narrative and his book is narrative history from beginning to end with some entertaining interruptions. Without this continuity the majesty of the *History* is lost.

However we have a consolation in return. Hugh Trevor-Roper has provided an introduction of over thirty pages, in which he displays his own incomparable gifts as a writer of historical essays. There has never been a finer presentation of Macaulay or a wiser analysis of his achievements – and of his failings. I am not always in agreement with the Regius Professor. There is rather too much psycho-history, ranging from Macaulay's uneasy relations with his father to his unusual relations with his sisters.

Trevor-Roper is inclined to depreciate the Whig interpretation of history. I still see its merits. After all, our political forerunners stumbled on a system of government the least imperfect that has been known. We still benefit from their inheritance. We still enjoy ordered liberty. The authority of the state is still limited though not as much as it should be. Macaulay erred, I think, when he added to the Whig interpretation the great delusion of his age, which was until the other day the great delusion of ours: belief in limitless progress and in the possibility, indeed the inevitability, of limitless improvement, both moral and material. Nevertheless we should remain grateful to the Glorious Revolution and to him whom Macaulay called with some hyperbole William the Deliverer.

I am grateful to Trevor-Roper for bringing readers back to Macaulay. Above all I am grateful to Macaulay. After some hesitation I am prepared to adapt Johnson's phrase about *Paradise Lost* and to say of Macaulay's work that it is not the greatest of histories only because it is not the first.

Carlyle

Thomas Carlyle (1795–1881) was another of Alan Taylor's favourite subjects. He frequently spoke warmly of Carlyle's The French Revolution, *a book which he had first read when he was eighteen. Earlier at school he had read* Heroes and Hero-Worship *and* Oliver Cromwell. *Taylor enjoyed Carlyle's style, but often not his views.*

The first of these essays was published in the New Statesman *on 18 April 1953, as a review occasioned by G M Trevelyan's* Carlyle: An Anthology *(London, Longmans, 1953). 'Carlyle Warts and All' was published in the* Observer *on 23 September 1979 as a review of Froude's Life of Carlyle, abridged and edited by John Clubbe (London, John Murray, 1979).*

*   *   *

Trevelyan's *Carlyle*

Carlyle was married to a clever woman. This alone keeps his name before us. We read her letters to him, and his to her. We debate in more or less cautious terms the great question – was he impotent? It is all of little moment. Carlyle's private life will not keep him going. There is only one question that matters – was he a great writer? Our first reaction, based on reading long ago and half-forgotten, is to reply: No, he was detestable as a writer, and trivial as a thinker. G M Trevelyan invites us to look at Carlyle again. His slim anthology offers a collection of personal fragments and one piece of sustained historical narrative, dealing with the September massacres in 1792. The selection makes its point. It drives us back to read Carlyle's own works on a grander scale; and, once we are absorbed in them, there is no mistake about the verdict. Carlyle was a writer of the greatest magnitude. His genius was unique.

Carlyle has a unique quality, which he did not understand himself and which his contemporaries failed to appreciate. He was the first great writer of English prose to spring from the people. This does not mean that he admired the people or got on with them. Like D H Lawrence, his twentieth-century equivalent, he despised the class to which he belonged and ran after Lady Ashburton even more assiduously than D H Lawrence cultivated Lady Ottoline Morrell. Yet there was no escaping his origin or his character. Though he called Christianity 'Hebrew Old Clothes' and railed against 'the multitudinous *canaille*', he remained a Scots Calvinist with a stonemason for his father. Carlyle taught himself. His ideas, his values, even his style, were original in the most literal sense. They sprang from his own efforts, and owed nothing to traditional culture. His style is like nothing else in English. Carlyle acquired it by translating Goethe; and his writing is, in fact, German put into English word for word. If put back into German, it appears simple and unaffected. It sheds an odd light on the two languages that Goethe, the most classical of German writers, should have inspired the most uncouth writer of English. Carlyle did not learn ideas from Goethe as well as style. His ideas are those of a man of the people who has suddenly become supremely articulate – if only in Anglo-German; ideas still spluttering and half-formed, ideas of revolt and rejection with nothing constructive to follow, but rooted in humanity, not in class-feeling or good taste.

Carlyle sensed the masses, as no other writer has ever done; he expressed their outlook, against his own conscious convictions. He was shaped in the turbulent years when the masses of England straightened their backs and shook off respect, the great age of the Chartists. Carlyle had all the Chartist hatred of privilege, their contempt for the 'grouse-shooting aristocracy'. He knew what was at stake in 'the Condition-of-England question'. His *French Revolution* was a prophecy – all the more powerful for being unconscious – of what might come in England. But when Chartism really stirred, Carlyle backed away. He should have been the greatest of the Chartists. Instead, he went sour – a terrifying warning to every disillusioned radical who turns Tory. Was it intellectual arrogance, snobbery, fear, that set him against the people? Betrayal is too common to need any explanation; but few have paid so high a penalty for it. Emerson once asked an anti-slavery agitator in prison: 'Friend, why art thou here?' The other replied: 'Why art thou not here?' The same question rang through Carlyle's mind. Why was he not there? All his later writings sprang from the goad of this question. To escape self-reproach, he had to reproach all the world.

After all, what is there left to believe in if you cease to believe in your own people? Carlyle early discovered the way out which is now almost universal with the lost rebels of our own time: authoritarianism in politics and religion. Too Calvinist to turn Roman Catholic, he set up as a self-made Jehovah, thundering out more violent commandments every day. He defended slavery and preached the worship of Force. He ran round the world looking for a hero and found some odd ones. He called Bismarck 'a magnanimous, noble and deep-seeing Man'; and wanted Sir Garnet Wolseley to shut up the House of Commons, sword in hand. He wasted years of his life trying to make a hero out of Frederick II of Prussia – as perverse a task as could ever be attempted. He anticipated every trick of the twentieth-century demagogue – prejudice against Negroes and Jews, admiration of the Germans. The abolitionists were 'rabid Nigger-Philanthropists'; Heine 'a slimy and greasy Jew'. The 'hopefulest public fact' in his time was that 'noble, patient, deep, pious and solid Germany' had become queen of the Continent instead of 'vaporing, vainglorious, gesticulating, quarrelsome, restless and oversensitive France'. His cure for all ills was that the masses should acknowledge the hero and then slave for him. The Victorians, themselves full of doubt, enjoyed his reproaches and imagined that his strenuous exhortations had a message concealed in them somewhere. Even Huxley supposed that he had learnt from Carlyle to work harder. We recognize the symptoms more easily. Like most people who set out to order the lives of others, Carlyle had the mark of Cain on him. His later writings are neither prophecy nor political thought; they are material for an anthology of nonsense, though not even funny.

Carlyle is saved from oblivion by the greatness of his betrayal. In his impetuous course towards embittered nihilism, he showed what he might have done had he kept his loyalty. He expressed the spontaneous outlook of the masses before he turned against them. In *Past and Present* he called English history to the aid of radicalism against the tyranny of wealth and economic law. This was not perhaps good history – if we are to admire anyone in the Middle Ages, let it be John Ball rather than a wealthy abbot; but it was a translation of popular nostalgia for a lost Utopia into something coherent and effective. Again, when he was already hell-bent on the search for a hero, he found one almost deserving hero-worship. Carlyle and Cromwell had much in common, though not in their origin: the same battle with words, the more powerful for being sometimes unsuccessful; the same baffled search for a better way; and, at heart, the same regret for the causes they had abandoned. Carlyle's picture of Cromwell was designed as an attack on radicalism and democracy; its effect, most unwelcome to him, was to rehabilitate Cromwell as a popular hero. The only practical outcome that Carlyle's writings ever had was to begin the change of feeling which later enabled Cromwell to have a statue outside Westminster Hall as the champion of democracy. It is hard to know whether this would have been more distasteful to Cromwell or to Carlyle.

Carlyle's *Cromwell* is enough to keep his name alive. But the best things in it are by Cromwell, not by Carlyle. In *The French Revolution* there is no fault or weakness at all; it is a book without a peer. Though Carlyle worked hard before he wrote it, he did not keep up even with the scholarship of his own time; and he has been outmoded still more by all that has been done since. Darwin was no doubt right when he said: 'As far as I could judge, I never met a man with a mind so ill adapted for scientific research.' Instead Carlyle brought to the French Revolution a gift which no other has ever done: a prophetic sense, which enabled him to feel the revolution and all that happened in it. He may have meant to write a warning against democracy and the reign of the Sansculottes; he may have intended to discover a hero who would master the *canaille*. All this was swept aside by the torrent of events. *The French Revolution* is a history without a hero; or rather, the hero is the people of France. Carlyle did his best, first for Mirabeau, then for Danton. But both appear great only when they are expressing the popular will. Once out of touch with it, they fade away, interest emptied from them. And, on the other side, Carlyle did his worst for Robespierre, the man who continued to personify the revolution where others failed. Yet in this he did not falsify history. It was the great tragedy of the revolution that Robespierre, its supreme exponent, lacked personality. No Lenin he, we might say in Carlyle's own style.

Lacking a hero, Carlyle had to fall back for once on the inspiration of the masses. No other book has ever so created the atmosphere of revolution; enabled us to understand what it was like; indeed, to relive it. Carlyle had no gift for historical movement; he never described how one situation developed into another. His book is a prolonged and violent storm. There is darkness, broken only by heavy thunder. Then the lightning flash of genius, in which every detail stands out to remain vivid in the memory for ever. And after it, new darkness, until broken by another vivid flash. It is no joke to ride through the greatest storm in history. Carlyle alone sensed what happened in these years. The revolution was not a product of political theorizing or even of economic discontent. The bottom had dropped out of the world; and the masses were thrust on their own resources. It was a master-stroke to begin with the affair of the Diamond Necklace; to depict the rotten feebleness of the old order, which had lost all capacity to govern and all faith in itself. When tradition is shaken, the theorists come into their own. They were easy game for Carlyle, as for many writers since. But he never lost sight of the masses, stirring behind the scenes and shaping the outcome. The climax of his book is the overthrow of the monarchy and the September massacres that followed. The world began anew in September 1792, as the revolutionaries knew when they called it 'Year One'. Carlyle knew it too; all his genius had carried him higher and higher to this point. But from that moment he faltered. He had too much sense to idealize the Girondins; yet when the Jacobins took power and began to shape a new order, he saw only Terror. It was, in fact, a Terror to which he himself succumbed. This was the turning-point of his life. He had damned the Old World; he would not face the New. A last splutter of pride and common sense kept him from worshipping Napoleon; but he soon found other and even less deserving heroes. It is Carlyle's triumph that we say, when reading *The French Revolution*: 'How much the greatest event since the beginning of the world.' It is his failure that we do not add: 'And how much the best.'

Carlyle Warts and All

Froude's Life of Carlyle ranks high among English biographies: the equal of Lockhart's Scott or Trevelyan's Macaulay, though not, I think a rival to Boswell's Johnson. However highly esteemed, it is rarely read: its four large volumes are really too much. Professor Clubbe has done a great service by cutting out most of the letters and reducing the work to three-eighths of the original. Even so we are left with 650 pages of text and fifty of notes. Professor Clubbe has not been content to abridge. He also comments lavishly, facing head-on the controversies that the biography provoked.

For Froude's book is not set in the usual hagiographical pattern. Froude, though a devoted disciple of Carlyle's was far from blind to his hero's failings. Given a completely free hand by Carlyle, he used his freedom to the full. Froude brought out Carlyle's impatience, his solitary broodings and his hostility to the spirit of the age. Above all Froude discussed frankly Carlyle's relations with his wife. They were deplorable. Jane Welsh Carlyle was a tender spirit, reared in a comfortable home and unused to hardship. Carlyle turned her into a domestic drudge with rarely a word of thanks.

Jane warned him before marriage: 'though I *love* you, I am not *in love with you*'. Carlyle ignored the warning and insisted on marriage. Whether their sexual relations were ever consummated is a question that cannot be resolved. (Clubbe, judging from their letters, thinks they were.) It was more important that Carlyle did not behave like a loving husband. Jane said towards the end of her life, 'I married for ambition. Carlyle has exceeded all that my wildest hopes ever imagined of him – and I am miserable.' And on a more prosaic note, she felt, she said, as if she was 'keeper in a madhouse'. 'If Carlyle wakes once in a night, he will complain for a week. I wake thirty times every night, but that is nothing.'

Like many writers, Carlyle was solitary when in creative mood and bad-tempered when he was not. He would walk or ride alone for hours, returning only to demand that his meal was ready and his home well kept. Despite his contempt for the upper classes, he did not disdain visits to aristocratic households when success came to him. For some years his greatest resource was in Lady Ashburton, his Gloriana. Jane was sometimes included for these visits. Lady Ashburton and Carlyle travelled in an elegant saloon coach while Jane was consigned, like any domestic servant, to an ordinary first-class carriage. Maybe many Victorian husbands behaved in this way but Carlyle professed to be someone different. After Jane's death he paraded bitter remorse and as a gesture of atonement gave all the material to Froude. The other Victorian husbands were shocked at Froude's frankness, not at Carlyle's behaviour.

There was a great deal more to Carlyle than an ill-assorted marriage. Conventional Christianity was in decay, as Froude knew from personal experience. Carlyle supplied an alternative creed which he preached with all the fervour of an Old Testament prophet. Most of this seems tawdry stuff now: injunctions that every man must obey the laws of God and warnings of what would happen if these warnings were disregarded. But how do we know what are the laws of God? Carlyle's God was an indefinable force which somehow pushed the universe along. His laws, it would seem, had been revealed to Carlyle and no one else. Alternatively God's laws were revealed by the results of men's actions. If their enterprises prospered, they were acting in accord with God's laws. God, it appeared, was another name for success. Contemporary society was doomed by its materialism and its worship of democracy – 'counting Judas Iscariot and Paul of Tarsus equal at the polling station', as Carlyle described it. Salvation lay in rule by the noblest and best – to be nominated by God or, God failing, by Carlyle.

Carlyle understood the hardships and grievances of the poor, none better. His pamphlet on Chartism outdid Marx's writings in its social analysis. Thereafter Carlyle was carried away by his search for a hero, beginning with Cromwell and ending with Frederick II. Bismarck was 'a magnanimous, noble and deep-seeing Man'. The last in the array was Sir Garnet Wolseley, to whom Carlyle said of the House of Commons, 'Lock the door of yonder place, and turn the six hundred talking asses all out about their business.' Poor Sir Garnet did not receive even the accolade of success.

Carlyle's works of history were a by-product of his prophesying – warnings in *The French Revolution*, discoveries of heroes later. But they are what preserves his fame. Carlyle's views may be wrongheaded, his scholarship may be imperfect. He was a great historian all the same, perhaps the greatest who has set out to recapture the spirit of the past. In my opinion *The French Revolution* is much the best, the most powerful of all his works, as Froude describes it, and the only one which has the character of a work of art. The *Letters and Speeches of Oliver Cromwell* revolutionized the subject and the Cromwell over whom historians still dispute stems from Carlyle's interpretation. Froude has some wise words about Carlyle's character as a historian:

This was Carlyle's special gift – to bring dead things and dead people actually back to life; to make the past once more the present, and to show us men and women playing their parts on the mortal stage as real flesh-and-blood human creatures, with every feature which he ascribes to them authenticated, not the most trifling incident invented, and yet as a result with figures as completely alive as Shakespeare's own.

To put it less grandiloquently, Carlyle was the greatest of all historical novelists. He deserves to be remembered by *The French Revolution* rather than for his failings as a husband, though these, too, are quite interesting.

Lord John Russell: The Last Great Whig

This was broadcast in a series on British Prime Ministers on the Third Programme of BBC Radio on 7 March 1947 and published under the title 'The Last Great Whig' in The Listener *on 20 March 1947. The whole series received much adverse criticism. Alan Taylor defended his two lectures (Lord Salisbury in addition to Lord John Russell) by commenting:*

I had hoped . . . that my talk succeeded in starting people off thinking about the subject, and my aim, in which I apparently did not succeed, was to stimulate by new thought not merely by provocation.

He added that 'Russell was meant to be a study of the transition from Whiggism to Liberalism.'

* * *

Lord John Russell as prime minister, leading and inspiring a government, was not a success. Indeed, his government of 1846 to 1852 was the ruin of the Whig Party: it never composed a government again, and his government of 1865 to 1866, which might be described as the first Liberal government, was very nearly the ruin of the Liberal Party also. He was certainly not a great leader: he was not 'outsize' – I do not mean in stature, though he was tiny, I mean in character. He was not more than life-size as really great political figures are – Gladstone, for instance. He spoke aridly, with a dry pedantic voice, and made no effort to win the affection of his followers. He was the first prime minister not to take direct personal responsibility for the public finances, and the finances of his government (it was their worst feature) were always rickety – like those of a spendthrift Whig peer. He was too sensitive, too, to be a successful politician, so upset by the criticisms of his diplomatic muddles during the Crimean War that he had to take to buying land as a distraction. He had too much pride to get on with his fellows: pride of the house of Russell, of being a son of the sixth Duke of Bedford, pride also at having a better intellect and a better education than most politicians. Still, these are both things worth being proud of, and they are the things which give Russell his place in history.

His life spanned the change from aristocratic to middle-class England, from the England of broad acres to the England of factory chimneys. Russell was the man of the transition, the link between the old order and the new, belonging to the old order by birth, carried over to the new order by his ideas. He was the last great Whig; he became the first Liberal. Russell, more than any other single man, created the Victorian compromise; he made the England that we know, or knew rather, the England that is vanishing before our eyes.

The unique thing in our political history is the way that we have been able to carry through great changes without violent revolution, going fast enough (just) to satisfy rising social classes without driving the possessing classes into open resistance. Someone has just ascertained that a third of the members of the present House of Commons are the sons of manual labourers; a little more than a hundred years ago five members of parliament out of six were landowners – that is the measure of our revolution. The symbol of that revolution was the reform of parliament in 1832. The Reform Bill does not look much in itself: the vote was still limited to quite a small electorate, and the House of Commons remained much as it had been before – in fact, for some years, there were rather more aristocrats and landowners in it. But the Reform Bill was a promise, a guarantee that the constitution would not be treated as something rigid and fixed for ever but as a set of habits which would change as public opinion changed. The Reform Bill was not intended to prepare the way for democracy; indeed, its purpose was to win over the prosperous middle classes to the side of the governing order and so bar the way against democracy, the rule of the people. Russell, its principal architect, defended it for years as a final settlement and opposed, for instance, the radical demands of the Chartists. All the same, it was the vital and decisive concession which set the pattern for the political changes which have followed. Russell himself, in 1866, at the end of his political life, started the discussions for the second Reform Bill, which granted household suffrage in the towns – and so accepted the principle of democracy.

I have called Russell the principal architect of the Reform Bill. That is true in the sense that, although a junior minister without a seat in the cabinet, he was one of the three who drafted the original Bill in 1831 and also in the sense that he was chosen to introduce the Bill into the House of Commons. It is true in a deeper sense that Russell, more than any other, represented the willingness of the great Whig families to surrender their position of privilege in the state. No, that is wrong: they thought that the more they surrendered of their legal privileges the more their claim to political pre-eminence would be recognized. Russell himself never forgot that he was a member of one of the greatest ducal families and, I dare say, ranked the house of Russell higher than most royalty. When, as a young man, he visited Napoleon on the island of Elba, they discussed these topics in order of their importance: the political influence of the Duke of Bedford; the allowance which the Duke paid to his son; and third, the condition of France and Italy. Despite his own intellectual ability, he never supposed that ability was a qualification for office – look at the colleagues he chose for his government in 1846. Long after the Reform Bill, Russell never imagined that high office would cease to be a monopoly of the Russells and Cavendishes and Stanleys, the 'Venetian oligarchy' which Disraeli wrongly supposed to have existed in the eighteenth century, but which really existed in the early reign of Victoria.

All the same, and this was his redeeming quality, Russell believed in liberty. No doubt he regarded this, too, as a sort of family property. He never forgot that Lord William Russell, who was the founder of the family greatness and whose life he wrote, had died on the scaffold for conspiring against Charles II; for the sake of this ancestor, Russell, too, had to be on the side of radicals and rebels. The ideas of the Glorious Revolution of 1688 were still to Russell living ideas, and the guiding idea of 1688 was certainly liberty. Liberty meant then – and often still meant to Russell – the liberty of the property owner to do what he liked with his property, but it had been justified by appealing to the will of the people and therefore when a popular cause arose, Russell, despite his whiggish narrowness, had to come down on the popular side. Russell took the lead in turning the Whigs into political reformers. The results of these reforms, as we see them today, would often have surprised him. But if you ask why there are still dukes, why there is still a House of Lords and why we still listen, sometimes with respect and always with patience, to the opinions of members of the house of Russell, the answer is: Lord John Russell and his devotion, in his own phrase, to 'the cause of civil and religious liberty all over the world'.

Russell led the Whigs in their conversion to reform; he was not, though, the only reformer among the Whigs. In a different sphere of public affairs he took the lead more on his own: he was, I think, the link between the governing classes and the new economic idea of individualism, of *laissez-faire*. Two tremendous changes took place in England in Russell's lifetime. One was the political change. The other was a change in economic outlook, which cleared the way for the fabulous prosperity of this country later in the nineteenth century: the change from the traditional pattern of life in which every man had his allotted place in society:

> The rich man in his castle
> The poor man at his gate
> He made them high and lowly
> And ordered their estate,

a society in which even the poorest had some sort of assured existence, the change from this to the view that men were 'hands', that their labour was a commodity, the price of which (like any other commodity) should be determined by the law of supply and demand. This was the great revolutionary discovery of the early nineteenth century: that there were so-called natural economic laws (actually extremely unnatural) and that the only job of government was to get out of the way and let these laws work. Everything, even human beings, had to be subordinated to the 'price mechanism', that terrible Moloch to which old-fashioned economists still bow down. We do not care for the 'law of the market' now that it has become the 'American way of life'; it looks too much like the law of the jungle. But in its day it was a tremendous instrument of progress. In fact, as a result of it, human productivity increased more in a century than in all the rest of recorded history.

It is easy to trace the growth of these new ideas in writers and thinkers, not so easy to see how they were translated into practice. It was a bigger question than merely free trade – the part of the change which Peel came to understand. It was the transformation of the whole of social life. Russell was the only member of the ruling classes, the only man in really high office, who understood what Bentham and the economists were driving at. He had been educated: instead of going to Cambridge, where he might have learnt a little mathematics (and that would have done his finances, private and public, no harm), or to Oxford, where he could have learnt only theology and classics, the two most useless studies known to man – instead he went to Edinburgh and learnt economics and political theory.

Later in life he was a friend of Nassau Senior, the leading orthodox economist of the day, and swallowed his doctrines open-mouthed, as recently our rulers tried to keep up with every flash of Keynes's nimble brain. Therefore it was no accident that Russell introduced the new Poor Law in 1834, the most revolutionary economic measure of the early nineteenth century. The new Poor Law swept away the old principle of the right to work or maintenance, the idea that society had some responsibility for its members; it substituted the idea that men must be driven to work by hunger – the basic idea without which capitalism will not work. We are trying to work capitalism without it now; hence all our present troubles. The new Poor Law and all that it implied – treating human beings as individuals who must struggle for themselves or else succumb – all this was Russell's work. He showed this in his attitude to the Irish famine of 1846, which took place when he was prime minister. Russell was a tender-hearted man and was made wretched by the thought of all the suffering of the Irish, but he set his face against any measure of relief which would interfere with the workings of natural economic law. He was the man who translated the theories of the economists into practice.

Russell himself would have added other claims to fame. He attached great importance to his fight for religious freedom, by which he meant, to put it crudely, keeping the churches in their place, a very subordinate place. His own religion was a vague benevolent Deism and he had no patience with deep religious feelings. He made a famous reply to a dean of Hereford who had scruples against electing as bishop someone whom Russell had nominated: 'Dear Sir, I have received your letter in which you inform me of your intention to break the law.' The most popular act of his life was not the Reform Bill, but the Ecclesiastical Titles Bill of 1851, which forbade Roman Catholic bishops to take territorial titles of places in England – an odd way of defending religious liberty. Even odder, the last public act of this soldier of liberty was to congratulate Bismarck on his campaign against the Roman Catholic Church in Germany. In fact Russell was a Protestant, in the sense of being hostile to the Church of Rome, but not a Christian; a combination formerly common, though now, I think, extinct.

Russell was proud, too, of his record as foreign secretary between 1859 and 1865, when Palmerston was prime minister. He had objected to Palmerston's wildness, when he had been prime minister and Palmerston foreign secretary. Curiously enough, Russell was much wilder when the roles were reversed. Russell's stock-in-trade as foreign secretary was the hectoring lecturing dispatch, when he told foreign rulers the awful things that would happen to them if they did not follow the British constitutional pattern. He lectured the Tsar on how to govern Poland; he lectured the emperor of Austria on the way to treat Hungary; he lectured Bismarck for daring to attack Denmark; he lectured the United States for having a civil war; he lectured the whole of Europe on the virtues of Italian nationalism. In fact he started the tradition that it is part of the duty of a British foreign secretary to tell other countries how to run their affairs. Russell never followed up his lectures with any kind of action; he thought it would be quite enough to threaten tsars and emperors with his displeasure, the displeasure of a member of the house of Russell. He only succeeded in bringing the name of Great Britain into contempt. Still, if only these rulers had listened, Russell, in his pedantic way, had something to tell them: this country had hit on the secret of making great social and political changes without revolution, and it was Russell who had shown how the trick was done.

Genocide

First published in the New Statesman on 23 November 1962 as a review of The Great Hunger by Cecil Woodham-Smith (London, Hamish, Hamilton, 1962).

*   *   *

When British forces entered the so-called 'convalescent camp' at Belsen in 1945, they found a scene of indescribable horror: the wasted bodies of 50,000 human beings who had died from starvation and disease. Kramer, 'the beast of Belsen', and his assistants were hanged for this atrocious crime. Only a century before, all Ireland was a Belsen. Nearly two million Irish people died of starvation and fever within five years; another million fled, carrying disease to Liverpool and the New World.

The story can be told in general terms, presenting the famine as a natural catastrophe like an earthquake. The population of Ireland had greatly increased in the preceding years – why, no one knows. Most of the people depended almost exclusively on the potato. In 1845 potato blight arrived, apparently from America. It was a fungus that rotted first the plants and then the potatoes in the clamps. A run of wet summers helped the spread of the blight. The potato harvest failed four years running. The Irish peasants had no reserves to fall back on. Many of their landlords were harsh; some almost as impoverished as their peasants – though it is not recorded that any landlord died of starvation. It all happened because it had to happen.

This is how historians usually treat the past. We explain, and with that our duty is finished. The dead are dead. They have become so many figures in a notebook. But they were once human beings, and other human beings sent them to their death. The blight was 'natural'; the failure of the potato crop was 'natural'. After that, men played a part. There was food available to save the Irish people from starvation. It was denied them. Nor did Ireland stand alone. Ireland was at this time part of the United Kingdom, the wealthiest country in the world. The British government had insisted on undertaking responsibility for Ireland. When crisis arose, they ran away from it. The men in Whitehall were usually of humane disposition and the bearers of honoured names: Lord John Russell; Sir Charles Wood, later first Viscount Halifax; Sir Charles Trevelyan. These men, too, were in a sense victims. They were gripped by the most horrible, and perhaps the most universal, of human maladies: the belief that principles and doctrines are more important than lives. They imagined that rules, invented by economists, were as 'natural' as the potato blight. Trevelyan, who did most to determine events, always wanted to leave Ireland to 'the operation of natural causes'. He refused to recognize that only the gigantic operation of an artificial cause – the exertion of British power – prevented the Irish people from adopting the natural remedy and eating the food which was available for them. Like most members of the comfortable classes of all times, he regarded the police and the law courts as natural phenomena.

Mrs Woodham-Smith in her most admirable and thorough book writes: 'The 1840s must not be judged by the standards of today.' Of course she is right, even though she goes on to judge, and to condemn, the British government. Russell, Wood and Trevelyan were highly conscientious men, and their consciences never reproached them. Nor are the standards of today much to rely on. The British rulers of the 1840s were no worse than those who later sent millions of men to their deaths in two world wars; no worse than those who now plan to blow all mankind to pieces for the sake of some principle or other. But they were also no better. Though they killed only two million Irish people, this was not for want of trying. Jowett once said:

I have always felt a certain horror of political economists since I heard one of them say that the famine in Ireland would not kill more than a million people, and that would scarcely be enough to do much good.

The successors of these economists are the same in spirit. They preach the virtue of a little healthy unemployment, and do not rely on the whip of starvation only because it has been taken from their hands. If the particular crime committed in Ireland a century ago could not happen now, it is not because present-day statesmen are an improvement on their predecessors. It is because the common conscience of mankind no longer allows statesmen to live up to their principles.

Here was the peculiar tragedy of the Irish famine. The common conscience failed to work, or at least did not work effectively. It is easy to understand how Trevelyan and the rest thought that they were doing their duty. They were handling human beings as ciphers on a bit of paper. They looked up the answers in a textbook of economics without ever once setting eyes on the living skeletons of the Irish people. They invented a distinction between those who were starving because of the potato blight and those starving from normal distress. They excused the Irish for being hit by the blight once. They condemned them for persisting in planting potatoes after blight appeared – as though the Irish could do anything else. Most of all, these enlightened men feared that the whole social structure would topple down if men and women were once given food which they could not pay for.

Not all Englishmen were enlightened in this way. This was already the England of good works, the England which emancipated the slaves and ended child labour, the England that repealed the Corn Laws and brought sanitation to the towns. The public conscience was in many ways more sensitive, quicker to respond, than it is now. It responded over Ireland, though not enough. The British government did much when it was in the hands of Sir Robert Peel. They contributed the stupendous sum of eight million pounds to meet the first disaster of 1845, set up relief organizations and provided public works on a scale never attempted before. Peel's fall from office in 1846 was an additional disaster for Ireland. He was never one to confess impotence, and he might have been powerful enough to override even the principles of Sir Charles Trevelyan.

Official and private individuals in Ireland did all that men could do. Doctors died of fever. Administrators drove themselves to death and often provided relief out of their own pockets. Trevelyan complained that his Commissariat officers could 'bear anything but the ceaseless misery of the children'. The British Relief Association raised large sums, including £2,000 from Queen Victoria. The Society of Friends had a record of spotless honour, as it often does when men are suffering. Quakers contributed money, ran their own system of relief, sacrificed their lives. All these efforts touched only the edge of the famine. Everything combined against the Irish people. Ignorance played a large part. Even capable Irish administrators did not grasp that there were no harbours on the west coast which could discharge cargoes of food. No enterprising newspaper correspondent described the horrors in Ireland for the English press as Russell was to describe the lesser horrors in the Crimea nine years later. Nearly all Englishmen regarded Ireland as an inferior version of England, inhabited by lazier and less efficient people. The Irish administrators themselves were bewildered that the problems of Ireland could not be somehow solved by the well-tried methods of the poor rate, boards of guardians and the workhouse test. In many districts there was no one to pay the poor rate or to sit on the board of guardians: most of the Irish would have regarded an English workhouse as a haven of luxury.

The ignorance was often wilful. Men make out that a problem does not exist when they do not know how to solve it. So it has been in all English dealings with Ireland. Again, the famine went on so long. English people, and even the British government, were ready to do something for one hard season. They were exasperated out of their pity when the blight reappeared year after year. How were they to understand that the blight, hitherto unknown, would settle permanently in the soil and flourish every wet summer? It was easy to slip into the belief that the blight was the fault of the Irish themselves. They were a feckless people; the blight was worse in Ireland than in England; the self-righteous conclusion was obvious. English antagonism was not turned only against the Irish poor. Though the landlords are often supposed to have represented a common Anglo-Irish interest, Englishmen and their government were as hostile to Irish landlords as to Irish peasants. At the height of the famine the full system of the English Poor Law was extended to Ireland. This was quite as much to make life unpleasant for the landlords as to benefit the starving. The Irish landlords were 'very much like slave holders with white slaves . . . they had done nothing but sit down and howl for English money'. Lord John Russell doubted whether 'taken as a whole the exertions of property for the relief of distress have been what they ought to have been'. The starving tenants could not pay their rent. Yet landlords were told to relieve them out of the rents which they could not pay. Some landlords were still prosperous. A few contributed honourably. Most did their duty by keeping up a sumptuous estate, which is what landlords are for.

The Irish people were driven off their land. They were starved, degraded, treated worse than animals. They lamented, they suffered, they died. Yet they made hardly an attempt at resistance. This is perhaps the most dreadful part of the story – a people allowing themselves to be murdered. Mrs Woodham-Smith suggests that the Irish were physically too weak to resist, that famine only gave a final push to their perpetual course of misery and want. Surely it was more than that. Centuries of English tyranny had destroyed Irish will and Irish confidence. O'Connell told the House of Commons in his last speech: 'Ireland is in your hands, in your power. If you do not save her, she cannot save herself.' The few political leaders in Ireland themselves accepted the economic doctrines of their conquerors.

They demanded Repeal of the Union, not a reform of the landed system, and Repeal was the cause which brought Smith O'Brien to the widow McCormack's cabbage patch in his attempt at rebellion in 1848. This provided a farcical note at the end of the tragic story.

Yet not quite the end, which was more farcical still. The English governing class ran true to form. They had killed two million Irish people. They abused the Irish for disliking this. Lord John Russell said in 1848: 'We have subscribed, worked, visited, clothed, for the Irish, millions of money, years of debate, etc., etc., etc. The only return is rebellion and calumny.'

Lastly, as a gesture of forgiveness no doubt by the British government for the crimes which they had committed in Ireland, royalty was trundled out. Queen Victoria and Prince Albert visited Ireland. They were received everywhere with great enthusiasm.

The famine did not end in Ireland. It was repeated year after year, sometimes in milder form. Natural causes did their work. The Society of Friends alone saw the condition of Ireland in its true light. In 1849 they refused to act any longer as a relief agency. Only the government, they wrote, 'could carry out the measures necessary in many districts to save the lives of the people'. 'The condition of our country has not improved in spite of the great exertions made by charitable bodies.' It could not be improved until the land system of Ireland was reformed, which was a matter for legislation, not philanthropy. The British government ignored the Quakers' advice. Nothing was done for Ireland until an embittered and more resolute generation of Irishmen acted for themselves.

1848

Alan Taylor was delighted to return to the topic of 1848, part of his original period of research, in its centenary year. In the spring he went to Paris for the French government's congress on the revolutions of 1848. He provided reports of its proceedings for BBC Radio and for the Manchester Guardian, *drawing the moral that 'European civilization will be ruined if it is "saved" by either Russia or America.' Also, at Oxford, he heard his old mentor Lewis Namier give his views on the German problem in 1848 (a subject largely ignored at the Paris congress) as the 1948 Waynflete Lectures.*

These essays were published as feature articles in the Manchester Guardian *on 1 January, 24 February, 13 March and 2 June 1948.*

*   *   *

Year of Revolution

'We are making together the sublimest of poems.' Lamartine embodied the revolutions of 1848 in speech and in deed; and his grandiose phrase was echoed by every radical in the revolutionary year. Heaven on earth seemed nearer in 1848 than at any other moment in modern history. Eighteen forty-eight was the link between the centuries: it carried to the highest point the eighteenth-century belief in the perfectibility of man, yet, all unexpectedly, launched the social and national conflicts which ravage Europe a century later. Socialism and nationalism, as mass forces, were both the product of 1848. The revolutions determined the character of every country in Europe (except Belgium) from the Pyrenees to the frontiers of the Russian and Turkish empires; and these countries have since shown common characteristics not shared by England, Russia, the Balkans, or Scandinavia. Politically speaking, a 'European' is an heir of 1848.

The moment of the revolution was determined by the financial crisis of 1846 and by bad harvests in 1846 and 1847. These caused food riots in the towns and sharpened the longstanding grievances of the peasants in eastern Germany and in the Austrian Empire. Economic discontent gave force to revolts; only the moral upheaval turned these into a revolution. Eighteen forty-eight was the victory of the 'ideologues', as Napoleon had contemptuously named them. Respect for traditional beliefs and forms of government had broken down; as a German poet wrote, 'Monarchy is dead, though monarchs still live.' Even the rulers had lost faith in themselves. The king of Prussia received the revolutionary poet Herwegh in order to bow 'before a worthy opponent', and Metternich denounced 'the rotten edifice' which it was his duty to uphold.

The revolutions repudiated 'throne and altar'; equally they repudiated existing state frontiers and the treaty settlement of the Congress of Vienna. After forty years of peace and stability men were bored: they wished to translate into real life the poetry of Victor Hugo and the music of Berlioz. Most of the radical leaders were between thirty-five and forty years of age; they represented the generation which had caught only the echoes of the Napoleonic Empire and which wished to hear again through Europe the thunder of the guns – though this time on the barricades. The barricades, built in every city in Europe and often erected even when there was no fighting, were the symbol of 1848. The ideologues had evoked the masses for sixty years; in 1848 the masses at last took their call.

The ideas of 1848 were the ideas of the French Revolution, applied now without doubt or reserve. The men of 1789 had been concerned with freedom from arbitrary government and equality before the law; though they used democratic phrases they restricted 'the people' to the property-owning middle class – even Robespierre only brought in the skilled artisan and petty shopkeeper. The men of 1848 had infinite faith in 'the people', whom they identified with themselves; and every little radical club spoke for 'the nation', as, say, the British Communist Party speaks for the British 'working class'. The liberals, prizing the rights of 1789, saw these endangered by the intrusion of the masses and were thus driven on to the side of the counter-revolution; indeed, in most of Europe, the defeat of the revolution was achieved by liberals, to their own subsequent ruin. In the enmity between liberal and radical, too, 1848 created a political pattern peculiar to the continent of Europe.

Though the masses certainly broke on to the political stage, they did not fill the humble parts which had been allotted to them by the ideologues. The urban movements were revolts against hard conditions of life and work; caused not by the Industrial Revolution but by its absence. They were 'Luddite' in character, seeking to destroy the new machines (especially seeking to destroy the railways which were being built by British capital and labour in western Europe). With the general increase of population, towns were growing; these, as yet, lacked the cheap goods of mass production which make urban life tolerable. The less industry, the more revolution. Belgium, the only industrialized country in Europe, escaped revolution; Italy, with no modern industry, had seven.

Marx, prophesying revolution for the rest of his life, was in fact foretelling the revolution of 1848 which he had experienced as a young man; but he drew the wrong conclusion. Far from industrial development producing revolution, it was a protection against it; a century later the most advanced industrial countries are the least in danger from communism. The urban masses of 1848 had no socialist programme; they demanded 'the right to work', the programme of Napoleon III and, subsequently, of Hitler. Their 'social republic' was not social democracy; it was a longing for the days of mercantilism. Still, 'the right to work' challenged 'the rights of property', which had been the essential revolutionary condition for the middle class; it was the claim by the disinherited of the great revolution that they, too, had rights, and so announced the class struggle between capitalists and proletarians.

Social conflict broke the unity of 'the people' within the

nation; national conflicts broke the unity of 'the people' throughout Europe. The French Revolution had preached nationalism; it meant by this only the right of existing nations to succeed to the inheritance of their kings. The revolution of 1848 aspired to destroy existing states and to create new ones in accordance with the national principle. This doctrine was destructive of existing monarchies; it menaced also the preponderance of France, the existing Great Power. The 'historic nations', Italy, Hungary, and Poland, announced their claims in 1848; they were overshadowed by Germany, where the revolutionary idea reached its highest point. The German movement was at once the most romantic and the most radical; and 1848 ushered in 'the German century', which has left Europe torn in pieces.

The 'historic nations' all had a past, a literature and an intellectual class; their appearance was expected. The surprise of 1848 was the appearance of the 'unhistoric nations', the submerged Slav peoples of east-central Europe. Emancipation of the peasants brought to life nations without aristocrats or burghers – their only spokesmen the educated sons of peasants – and therefore at one bound most under the leadership of ideologues. The historic nations, challenging the traditional order of Europe, were themselves challenged by the unhistoric nations. Slovenes and Croats disputed the historic claims of national Italy; Slovenes, Croats, Serbs and Romanians (not a Slav people, but with similar social conditions) repudiated Great Hungary; the Czechs questioned German predominance in Bohemia; the Poles fought in both camps – they resisted the claims of the Germans in Posnania, yet to the east their own 'historic' claims were challenged by the Little Russians or Ukrainians. In the words of Professor Namier: 'With 1848 starts the Great European War of every nation against its neighbours.' Metternich's Europe, in spite of its dullness, lasted more than a generation; the Europe of Lamartine never came into existence.

The sovereignty of the people was the cardinal doctrine of 1848; all frontiers were to be redrawn and all political institu-

tions remade in its name. Hence the great practical expression
of 1848 was direct universal suffrage, practised for the first time:
the people were not to be limited in their sovereignty, nor was
the power of the people to be weakened by any intermediary.
France set the example for the political events of the following
hundred years. The sovereign people were offered the 'ideologues';
they chose Louis Napoleon. Proudhon, a democrat without illusions, drew the lesson: 'Universal suffrage is counter-revolution.'
This lesson was applied by Bismarck and, later, by Hitler and
Mussolini. Hitler, incorporating the General Will of the German
people, united nationalism and socialism and redrew the map of
Europe according to the German principles of 1848. Like the
German radicals of 1848, Hitler ran against the rock of Slav
resistance; and the Slav peoples were the residuary legatees of
1848.

The French Revolution

24 February 1848 was the last day of Great France, the last day
of the France which had overshadowed the rest of Europe and
had called the tune in political ideas. It was the last time when
France sneezed and the rest of Europe caught a cold; henceforth
France caught colds from others, as in the recent malady of
Vichy. In 1848 the radicals of all Europe still looked to Paris, as
the communists now look to Moscow. Paris was the mother of
revolutions; but in 1848 her progeny got out of control. Though
there had been previous outbreaks in Galicia and in Sicily the
revolution in Paris gave the signal for the real storm, and the
street fighting which overthrew Louis Philippe brought down,
too, Metternich and the absolute monarchy in Prussia. Yet the
revolutions which swept Europe did not remain under the spell
of French ideas; still less did they restore French hegemony in
Europe, as the French radicals had expected. Instead the French
began to realize that the victory of the national principle, which
they had launched, far from restoring Napoleon's domination of

Europe, would destroy French security and would bring France under the threatening shadow of a Germany more powerful than herself.

Once a revolution is successful the revolutionaries become conservative in their turn. This is the key to French history in the 150 years since the Great Revolution. In 1789 the rights of man were subversive of the existing order and had to be fought for; later they became the existing order and had to be defended, until today the adherents of the rights of man are the most conservative element in European politics. The transition from one attitude to the other took place in France between February and June 1848; on both occasions the radicals fought – but on different sides of the barricades. The revolution of 24 February had no deep-seated cause; as Proudhon said, it was made 'without an idea'. The demand for an extension of the franchise, which was its excuse, could have been met without a revolution; indeed, Louis Philippe had already granted it before his fall. But peaceful reform would have seemed a drab outcome, unworthy of the traditions of revolutionary France. The revolution was, in fact, its own object; the emotional experience provided the satisfaction of a religious conversion. A radical journalist expressed this: 'My hopes are in an act of providence, in a religious transformation to regenerate society.' The revolutionaries repeated the attitudes of 1789, as in 1939 the French tried, in vain, to recapture the inspiration of 1914. Tocqueville, sitting in the Chamber when it was invaded by the mob, was puzzled that he felt no fear; suddenly he realized that he was watching men striking postures which they had seen in an old print, not a spontaneous revolution – it is difficult to be frightened of a musket which was loaded sixty years before and has become a theatrical prop.

The radicals established a Provisional government; this was hard put to it to find a programme. Lamartine describes the members of the Provisional government sitting round and racking their heads in vain for some great symbolical act which should make the revolution worth while. He solved the problem by proposing the abolition of the death penalty; within four months it was restored for political offences and applied wholesale to those who had won the battle of February for the Provisional government. Though the radicals proclaimed the sovereignty of the people, they feared it in practice. They had no agrarian programme with which to win the allegiance of the peasants, who made up the majority of the population. The revolution of 1789 gave the peasants their land, free of feudal duties; the revolution of 1848 compelled the peasants to pay their debts and increased the taxation on land. For the radicals of 1848 tried to combine revolution and a stable currency; not surprisingly, the peasants preferred Louis Napoleon, distinguished by his debts as well as by his great name. The radicals knew that universal suffrage would go against them; yet they insisted on perishing from their own principles. Lamartine declared: 'The people must be left free to make mistakes.' This mistake was the Second Empire.

Before 1848 the radicals had thought little of internal affairs. Their greatest grievance had been against the humiliation of the Congress of Vienna, and they expected to escape from their problems by renewing the glories of revolutionary war. Lamartine reserved his highest rhetoric for the circular dispatch in which he declared that France no longer recognized the treaties of 1815. Still, though France wished to see these treaties disappear, she would not herself make the effort to destroy them. Besides, on reflection it was not in the interests of France to replace the weak states across the Alps and the Rhine by a united Italy and a united Germany; and – in spite of past lip-service to the idea – even radical Frenchmen saw the defeat of Italian and German nationalism with some relief. The army originally prepared to go to the assistance of revolutionary Italy went off in 1849 to restore the pope. There could be no such practical arguments against aiding Poland, and war for Poland was the slogan with which the extreme radicals, Blanqui and Barbès, attempted to overthrow the Provisional government on 15 May. In 1848, as in 1939, France could aid Poland only by resuming the mastery of Europe which Napoleon had won and then lost; the task was already beyond her. Hence the defeat of Blanqui and his associates marked the turning-point in France's position in the world, as well as being the crisis of the revolution.

Still, behind the revolutionary echoes a true revolution existed. This was the movement of the town working classes, especially in Paris. The Great Revolution had found no place for them; rather it had established an alliance of peasants and bourgeoisie against them. Now to the traditional rights of man they claimed to add 'the right to work'. This demand sprang from handicraft workers, threatened by the machine, not from factory workers, enslaved to it. In England at the same time the workers, more mature, were demanding the right to work less. 'The right to work' was a demand for recognition rather than an economic programme; it was rejected by all those who had profited by the Great Revolution. The result was the June Days, the most formidable slave-war of modern times. The workers of Paris fought without leaders and without hope against a united front of nobles, middle class, and peasants. Reactionaries and radicals, estranged since the execution of Louis XVI, were reconciled over the bodies of the Parisian workers. The June Days showed that radicalism would not satisfy the working class; they became, and remained, an alien body in the French Republic. The radicals of 1848 had tried to be a 'third force'; instead the June Days drove France into the arms of Napoleon. A hundred years later, the shadow of the June Days, and of its sequel, still lies across French political life.

Vienna and Berlin

On 13 March 1848, revolution reached Vienna: Metternich was driven from power after thirty-nine years of office. The Vienna revolution was the central event of 1848, as significant as the fall of the Bastille in 1789. The Bastille was an antiquated fortress, virtually without a garrison; Metternich a feeble old man without supporters. Yet both symbolized the old order and brought it down with them. Monarchical authority over 'subjects' lost its divine sanction on 14 July 1789; dynastic right over peoples lost its hold on 13 March 1848. The Rights of Man triumphed in the streets of Paris; the rights of nations in the streets of Vienna. It was the end of government based on tradition. Henceforth peoples could be ruled only by consent – or by force. European history of the following hundred years recounts the oscillations between these two methods.

Though the Habsburg dynasty maintained a precarious existence in 1848 (and indeed for another seventy years) the fall of Metternich ended its independent position. Previously it had stood above the peoples; thereafter it manoeuvred between them. The Vienna revolution was the cardinal date in the history of both national Hungary and national Italy; it was a victory for Kossuth and Mazzini. National Italy sought only separation from central Europe (a separation never fully achieved from the days of the Triple Alliance to the Axis or the present). National Hungary hoped to remain a great state without the Habsburgs, or rather to substitute the Magyar landowners for the dynasty as the ruling authority in central Europe. This aim was subsequently realized, though in association with the dynasty, in the period of dualism (1867–1918); in the end it brought 'thousand-year-old' Hungary to ruin.

Once the dynasty lost its traditional appeal, Central Europe needed some other principle of association. The Slav peoples (who were in the majority) would not accept German and Magyar hegemony which was offered them as an alternative. Against this they raised the demand for their own national freedom and thus prepared the way for the national states of 1918. Still, they wished also for association; and the few far-sighted Habsburg ministers, after Metternich's fall, saw that the empire could be saved only by invoking the peasant masses against the disruptive liberalism and nationalism of the middle classes. This was the significance of the emancipation of the peasants on 7 September 1848, the enduring achievement of the Austrian revolution. Aristocrats and liberals alike accused the Habsburg ministers of 'communism'. A century later the same programme is being operated, though by the heirs of the Romanovs, not of the Habsburgs.

Still, the Vienna revolution found its greatest immediate impact in Germany. National Germany, too, was born in the streets of Vienna. If Hungary and Italy were to shake off the Habsburgs the remaining Austrian dominions could also follow the national principle: the way seemed open for Greater Germany. This faced the Hohenzollerns, the only other real power in Germany, with a problem of existence. If they resisted German nationalism they would be swept aside; if they went with it they would be submerged. Frederick William IV, astute though neurotic, avoided the dilemma and, with unconscious genius, stumbled on the programme of Little Germany. The revolution of 18 March 1848, in Berlin, though a victory for liberalism, did not break Hohenzollern power; the army remained confident and intact. Frederick William IV granted a constitution with a semblance of goodwill; this was his bid for German leadership. He announced: 'Prussia merges into Germany.' The phrase was fraudulent. Prussia continued to exist with an independent strength; the German liberals were invited to accept Berlin as the capital of Germany, solely in virtue of Frederick William's word. The revolutions in Vienna and Berlin offered to Germany alternative solutions. The Vienna revolution aspired to a Greater Germany, based on radical violence, which would embrace all Germans and extend German supremacy throughout south-eastern Europe. The Berlin revolution was the first announcement of a more limited Germany, based on an alliance of moderate liberalism and Prussian military strength, and which would repudiate the German inheritance in the south-east. Berlin anticipated Bismarck, and Vienna Hitler.

In 1848 neither programme won unreserved acceptance. National Germany rejected both Vienna and Berlin, the two seats of power; it looked to Frankfurt, symbol of unification by consent. The greatest event in the history of German liberalism was the meeting of the National Assembly at Frankfurt on 18 May 1848. The Frankfurt parliament hoped to give Germany freedom and unity; but above these it rated power (*Macht*). When German claims were challenged in Bohemia and in Posen, German liberals forgot the Rights of Man and invoked the right of the stronger; they expected the Austrian and Prussian armies to provide the strength which they themselves did not possess. They applauded the Habsburg victory in Prague over the Czechs and sought to use Prussian power against the Poles. In November the Frankfurt liberals even welcomed the victory of Frederick William IV over the Prussian parliament, which they regarded as an impudent rival.

These victories did not help liberal Germany; it became the next victim of the power which it worshipped. In April 1849, delegates from Frankfurt went humbly to Berlin to offer the Imperial Crown to Frederick William IV: liberal Germany was willing to merge into Prussia. The offer was rejected by Frederick William IV, and the Frankfurt parliament was soon after dispersed by Prussian soldiers. Nevertheless Bismarck took up the offer, on terms still more favourable to Prussia, twenty years later.

Two great negatives were the legacy of the German revolutions of 1848. Dynastic power could not survive unless it took on a national colouring; on the other hand the Germans could not maintain the hegemony over Poles and Czechs on which the liberals most of all insisted unless they compromised with the possessors of power. This compromise is still sought by the Germans a century later; equally the foreign powers who have replaced the dynasties compete for the favour of German nationalism.

March 13 will not be celebrated this year in Germany; it is the symbol of Greater Germany and so of Hitler's vanished empire. The Russians have decreed 18 March as Germany's 'day of freedom': like Frederick William IV they hope to pass off a spurious revolution as the real thing and, succeeding the Hohenzollerns as rulers in Berlin, announce that Prussia merges into Germany. As in the days of Bismarck, Little Germany is the best outcome for the Russians – a protection at once against Greater German power and against the West. The Western powers follow in the footsteps of the liberals of 1848 to Frankfurt; they, too, will find themselves embarrassed by frontier disputes with Poland and by the agitation of Germans from Bohemia. Disappointment awaits those who seek national Germany at Frankfurt; as in 1848, Frankfurt is the symbol of the Germany of the idea, peaceful, liberal, contented – and non-existent.

The Slav Congress

The Slav Congress which met in Prague on 2 June 1848 was the least expected event in the year of revolutions. The Slav peoples of central Europe had not been allowed for in radical calculations. Engels wrote of the Czechs and Croats (he was unaware even of the existence of the Slovaks): 'The natural and inevitable fate of these dying nations was to allow the process of dissolution and absorption by their stronger neighbours [Germany and Hungary] to complete itself.' Exception was made only for the Poles, as a historic nation, not as Slavs; the German radicals proposed to push Poland against Russia and then to jettison her later (the reverse of Russia's Polish policy a century later). Since Bohemia had been included in the Holy Roman Empire, it was assumed that it would become part of the new national Germany, and distinguished Bohemians were invited to join the preliminary meetings at Frankfurt. Palacký, the first historian of Bohemia and the recreator of Czech national consciousness, refused the invitation; he repudiated allegiance to Germany – 'I am a Bohemian of Slav race' – and looked instead to the Habsburg dynasty as the protector of the Slav peoples from German tyranny. 'If the Austrian Empire did not exist, it would have to be created in the interest of Europe and of humanity.' This famous sentence launched the programme of Austroslavism, the idea of maintaining a modest national existence under the wing of the most clerical and traditional dynasty in Europe.

In 1848 the dynasty seemed too shaken to act as the sole bond of union between different peoples, and those who feared incorporation in Greater Germany sought some more popular alternative. They thought to have found it in their Slav race. This was more than crude racialism: it assumed that all peoples with a Slav language had a common cultural background. In reality most Slav peoples outside Russia had been submerged by the culture of their conquerors, German, Hungarian, or even Turkish; hence the importance of ethnography in the Slav movement – the evidence for a common Slav 'folk' had to be found in the designs on peasant costume or pottery. The Slav Congress was intended as a gesture against the German National Assembly at Frankfurt. This threatened directly only the Czechs and the Slovenes – another reason for draping Slav 'folkdom' round the practical political issue. The Slavs of Hungary (Croats, Serbs, and Slovaks) were indifferent to the German menace; the Czechs wished to avoid a conflict with Hungary, yet would not repudiate the Slovaks, who alone could swell their numbers.

The real stumbling-block for a common Slav policy came from the Poles. The Poles of Galicia were indisputably Slavs and indisputably Habsburg subjects; yet Russia was their only enemy, and they welcomed both Greater Germany and Great Hungary. The Poles who were threatened by the Germans were under Prussian rule in Posnania. To exclude them would weaken the struggle against Frankfurt decisively; to include them would trespass beyond the frontiers of the Habsburg Monarchy and so make nonsense of Austroslavism. In fact, the Slav Congress had stumbled on the Polish problem. The Poles of the Austrian Empire would not work with the Czechs or against the Germans; the Poles of Posnania would work against the Germans, but equally emphatically would not work with

Russia. The Czechs insisted that Poles from outside the Austrian Empire should attend the congress only as guests; the Poles would not recognize the frontiers of the Polish partitions, and when the Polish section of the congress met it made the Poles from Posnania full members, one of them, indeed, becoming its chairman.

This intrusion of non-Austrian Slavs had a further embarrassing consequence. No one minded the presence of Serbs from Turkey: the solidarity of the 'master nations' did not yet extend to the Turks. But if the Slav Congress was to include all Slavs it was impossible to exclude the greatest branch of the Slav race, and the revolutionary Bakunin imposed himself upon the congress as the solitary, self-appointed representative of the Russian people. Bakunin had no patience with the cautious Austroslavism of Palacký; he demanded both the destruction of the Habsburg Empire and revolution in Russia. His goal was a federation of free peoples, based on the natural democracy of the Slav peasants. Like later versions of Pan-Slavism, Bakunin's vision rested on the dogma of virtues innate in Slav peoples which would save them from the failings of others.

Pan-Slavism evoked no response from the Slav Congress; indeed, Pan-Slavism had sense only as a translation into racial mysticism of the Byzantine and Orthodox heritage shared by some Slav peoples, and almost all those present at Prague were Western and Roman Catholic. The Slav Congress produced two contradictory programmes. The Poles drafted a manifesto to the peoples of Europe which recognized the existence only of the 'historic nations' – Poland, Germany, Hungary, and Turkey – and politely invited these to treat their minorities better. The Czechs drafted an address to the Austrian Emperor which asked for the remodelling of the Austrian Empire into a federation based on national units. Perhaps the most concrete effect of the congress was its division into three sections – Polish–Ukrainian, Czechoslovak and South Slav – for these anticipated the 'national amalgamations' which served as the basis for pseudo-national states (Poland, Czechoslovakia and Yugoslavia) in 1918.

All these programmes received only preliminary statement. The congress met for the last time on 12 June. Then fighting broke out between the Prague radicals, both Czech and German, and the imperial forces; and on the suppression of the rebellion the congress was dissolved. In its ten days of activity it had stated all the solutions for the problem of central Europe which have been attempted from then until now. The Czechs followed Austroslavism for half a century after 1848; its essential condition, a federation of free nationalities, was granted by the Habsburg emperor only on 16 October 1918, when the empire was already in ruins. The last echo of Austroslavism was heard in the Slovakia of Tiso and the Croatia of Pavelic. The Poles tried to act as partners of Greater Germany and Great Hungary in the days of Colonel Beck, and thought that they had reached their aim when they established a common frontier with Hungary in March 1939 – six months before their destruction. Bakunin's first demand was fulfilled with the dissolution of the Habsburg Monarchy in 1918; failing the establishment of democracy in Russia, the Slavs had to look for support to the Western democracies and suffered ineffaceable disappointment at the time of Munich. Now fear of Germany makes them pretend that Bakunin's second condition has been fulfilled, and the 'democracies of the new type' rest on the double pretence of Russian democracy and Slav solidarity.

1848: Opening of an Era

This was first published as the major part of Alan Taylor's Introduction to The Opening of an Era: 1848. An Historical Symposium, *edited by François Fejtö, with an Introduction by A J P Taylor (London, Allan Wingate, 1948).*

It nearly appeared at the same time as Alan Taylor's rewritten version of The Habsburg Monarchy 1809–1918, *which Hamish Hamilton intended publishing in early 1949. On 1 December 1948 Alan Taylor wrote to Hamish Hamilton in embarrassment about this:*

As a matter of fact, quite to my surprise, there will be a book in the shops on Saturday with my name on the cover. I wrote a 5,000 word introduction for a volume of essays on the revolutions of 1848 which Allan Wingate are bringing out; and they have presented it as though I were sole author. I apologize to you if this is in any way a handicap – as I say my contribution is a small one. It would, I am sure, have been bad to have had two books with my name on them out at once; but by January the Allan Wingate book will act as a form of publicity for the real one – at least I hope so. I stipulated that I could use the introduction after twelve months' delay in a book of collected essays; and it is really a good piece of work.

* * *

Robert Owen, on a visit to Paris, described his economic system as 'the railway which will take mankind to universal happiness'. His phrase crystallized the spirit of the year of revolutions. Movement, and a conviction that Utopia could be reached, were the essence of 1848: underlying these was a faith in the limitless goodness of human nature. The revolutionary cry, 'All change!' sounded across Europe. Hope lit the dawn of a new Europe; and mankind clambered into the trains of political and social upheaval, all of which claimed to be directed to the same terminus – the Kingdom of Heaven on Earth. New faiths, new nations, new classes announced their arrival; each was the confident possessor of an exclusive truth. Before 1848 the rights of individuals and of states were a matter of history and of settled law; the revolutions substituted the rule of abstract principle. Louis Philippe said bitterly of the revolution of 1830 which brought him to the throne: 'What perished in France in 1830 was not respect for a dynasty, but respect for anything.' This was demonstrated anew in France in 1848 and, for the first time, was demonstrated throughout Europe as well. Reason took the place of respect; and self-interest the place of tradition.

Movement was both the cause of the revolutions and their outcome: the revolutions threw down established landmarks that were already ruinous. In the preceding fifty years tumultuous development had taken the place of imperceptible change. There was an unprecedented growth of population, an unprecedented advance in the methods of industry and of transport, and an unprecedented novelty in the world of ideas; the three together composed the background to the revolutions. The old order had assumed stable populations; these ensured stability between classes and stability between states. For half a century before 1848 the increase of population had been gathering strength, and this contributed more than anything else to the illusion of progress. The increase was less in France than elsewhere in Europe; and the wise student of population figures might already guess that France, hitherto the greatest European power and the most revolutionary nation, would soon become the most conservative and the least great of the powers. The universal growth of population had profound consequences. Where the peasant was already free, as in western Germany, the surplus was being pushed into the towns. In the Austrian Empire the peasants could no longer tolerate the burden of feudal dues and of feudal subordination; moreover, with the increasing demand for food, the great landowners could no longer operate their estates by the traditional methods. Both lords and peasants turned against the old order of settled obligations; both demanded freedom of movement and the rule of the market. Almost the first act of the liberal parliament in Hungary was to abolish the old agrarian social order; and the Austrian Constituent Assembly followed suit (its only effective act) on 7 September. The destinies of fifty million people were affected. The more prosperous peasants got the chance of survival; the poorer peasants lost their last traditional protection and were the victims both of the richer peasants and of the capitalistic great estates. The way was clear for the emigration to the towns and overseas which characterized the second half of the century. It was no accident that England and Russia, the only countries of Europe to escape the revolutions, had already found the way of emigration before 1848: the road to Siberia had been open since the beginning of the century, and the emigrant-steamers took the life out of Chartism when they began to sail from Liverpool in 1844. The rest of Europe had lacked the technical and social conditions for mass emigration: peasant emancipation came in 1848, and railways followed. These provided a safety valve which postponed further European explosions until the twentieth century. Modern industrial America, as well as modern industrial Europe, would have been impossible without the revolutions of 1848.

The ideas of 1848 spread later to Russia; and the Russian revolutions of the twentieth century were in the true spirit of 1848. In fact, Russia, missing the disillusionment which followed the failure of 1848, alone retained faith in the revolutionary course. America was already democratic, and therefore for her, though there was no need for revolution, there was no need for disillusionment either. For a generation after 1848, and even longer, America offered to the peoples of Europe the economic and political prizes which failure had denied them in Europe. Still, 1848 left no tradition in either Russia or America. Eighteen forty-nine has some meaning in the history of both countries. For Russia it brought a victorious repression of revolution in Hungary; for America it marked the discovery of gold in

California. To the present day, the one Great Power offers Europe repression, the other material wealth. Neither can offer the liberty of spirit which was the true aim of 1848.

The staggering growth of towns throughout Europe was a consequence of the revolutions. Still, even before 1848, the swelling towns amazed and alarmed contemporaries; and their isolation – urban islands in a rural continent – emphasized their revolutionary character. The conscious revolutions of 1848 were all exclusively urban. 'The German revolution' is a misleading generalization for the Berlin revolution and the Vienna revolution; 'the Italian revolution' still more misleading as a title for the revolutions in Venice, Milan, Florence, Rome, Naples and many more. The contrast was sharpest in France. The Great Revolution of 1789 had been the movement of a people, the revolution of 1848 was a movement of Paris against the rest of the nation. Isolated in place, the revolutions were equally insular in idea: they had no agrarian programme and offered the peasants – troglodytes, in Marx's phrase – nothing but extinction. For the first time news of a revolution passed from one town to another by telegraph; it no longer needed to filter through, and so to affect, the countryside. The revolutionaries travelled by train from one revolution to the next; they had neither eyes nor thoughts for the country through which they passed. The revolutionaries equated revolutions with street-fighting. Their occasional forays into the countryside – from Hecker's raid on Baden in April 1848 to Garibaldi's march across Italy in July 1849 – were the organized hikes of town dwellers.

Even the largest towns lacked industrial development. Labour had arrived before capital was ready for it. Only Belgium had experienced an industrial revolution; and therefore, despite its urban character, enjoyed a unique freedom from revolutionary danger. The revolutions elsewhere were not revolts against the machine; they were demands to be employed by it. The slogan of 'the right to work' was a symbol of immaturity; an industrial proletariat would have demanded the right to work less – as indeed the English working class had already done with success in 1847. 'The right to work' was a protest as much against social inequality as against harsh living conditions. Nevertheless, by formulating this protest in economic terms, it launched the idea that liberty and political equality were negligible, or indeed valueless, in comparison with food and clothing. This idea was not intended by the social revolutionaries of 1848, who took up economic grievances principally in order to add greater force to their political demands. All the same the damage had been done. Continental socialism, which had its origins in 1848, wrote off political democracy as bourgeois and accepted the doctrine that violence and intolerance were a small price to pay for social change. Class war took the place of the struggle for political liberty, and the Rights of Man were a casualty of 'the right to work'.

The announcement of an economic programme was certainly the startling novelty of 1848; nevertheless the revolutions were not simply the product of economic circumstances. These determined the moment of revolution, not that it should occur. The economic upheaval and the upheaval in men's minds were two aspects of the same process. Certainly the age of coal and iron enforced daring political schemes and made them possible; but equally it needed a daring mind to think of the railway and the blast furnace. The great towns of modern Europe could not have been maintained without railways, steam power and a revolution in agriculture; but the movement to the towns depended just as much on the spread of new ideas which prised men away from their traditional beliefs and traditional surroundings. The railways found people ready to move; otherwise they would have run empty. Reason was the great dissolvent force. This made men dissatisfied with their traditional homes and with their traditional place in society just as much as with the traditional methods of production. The radicals of 1848 were the heirs of eighteenth-century enlightenment: sublimely confident in human nature (except that of their fellow revolutionaries), they believed that their only task was to shake off the hold of established beliefs and established institutions. Their common programme was 'to strangle the last king with the bowels of the last priest'. The natural goodness of man would do the rest.

The old order, thus dramatically threatened, claimed to depend on habit, on history and on established rights. No historical conflict is, in fact, fought on these easy terms. The old order was itself more rational and artificial – just as the revolutionaries were more traditional – than either side liked to admit. Revolutionary ideas had affected the upper classes before they spread to the masses; and the impact of the great French Revolution had long shaken the foundations of the European system. Men were argued into conservatism as they were argued into revolution. The kings who were threatened by the movements of 1848 had less than a century of possession behind them, and many more were the creations of Napoleon. Even the house of Habsburg, the only genuine historic dynasty, had acquired a new title and new territories a generation previously and had knocked all life out of historic institutions everywhere in its dominions except in Hungary – and there from lack of strength, not of will. The 'old aristocracy' was a creation of the eighteenth, or occasionally of the seventeenth century. Most of all the territorial settlement of the Congress of Vienna was as artificial as the empire of Napoleon which it replaced. The peace which followed the Napoleonic Wars sprang from exhaustion, not from belief or from content; and the society which perished in 1848 had no moral justification other than the desire of the possessing classes to enjoy their privileges.

The kings, aristocrats and states of the Vienna system had not even given themselves the trouble of being born; they had been conjured up ready-made by conservative theorists. Thus Metternich, to give historic character to the Austrian Empire (which had acquired legal existence only in 1804), proposed to invent for the emperor a traditional ceremony of coronation. Metternich, symbol and chief exponent of conservatism, claimed to be building a dam against revolution. In reality, his effort to set up a universal 'system' of political ideas and institutions was typical of an eighteenth-century doctrinaire. He approached politics in the spirit of Robespierre: the only difference was in his employer. The dissolvent of reason could have been resisted only by communities with a living history; few such existed on the continent of Europe, and these few (Switzerland, Hungary and perhaps the Low Countries) did not accord with Metternich's conservatism. As a result, the system of Metternich was not overthrown in 1848; it collapsed. This collapse astonished contemporaries, other than Metternich himself: he had always appreciated the artificiality of his own system and had never felt the faith which he demanded in others.

In 1848 Europe broke consciously with its past. This was the indelible achievement of the year of revolutions. Yet more than destruction was intended. Bakunin, most extreme representative of the spirit of revolution, once declared that if his plans succeeded he would at once begin to pull down again everything he had ever made; this did not take the zest from a lifetime of planning. The radicals of all schools were as convinced as Metternich of the need for belief; and, unlike Metternich, themselves believed in the systems which they expounded. Their systems, too, were universal and dogmatic. All assumed that reason was adequate as the sole guide in human affairs; and they assumed also that there was no limit to what reason could do. The revolutionaries differed as to the means by which the human race might be made perfect; none disputed that the goal would be attained. The radical systems provided new absolutes for old and gave final answers in politics, in society and in international affairs. The sovereignty of the people overthrew the sovereignty of kings; nations took the place of states; and intellect ousted heredity as the source of authority.

Though the sovereignty of the people had already served as inspiration to the French Revolution of 1789, its operation had been restricted. The distinguishing mark of 1789 had been the confidence that universal principles could be limited in their application and a revolution arrested in its course. This expectation was not proved false until 1848. When all hereditary rights were repudiated, the right of private property had remained inviolate and was indeed reinforced; and the dogma of the sovereignty of the people was used to justify the franchise of the property-owning middle class. In 1848 the term of this compromise expired; and the bourgeoisie, once the leaders of revolution, became the symbol of conservatism. Almost the first act of the victorious revolution in France was to abolish the property qualification and to proclaim universal suffrage. This became everywhere the most concrete expression of the revolutionary programme. Only Hungary, which combined – or perhaps stifled – revolutionary principle with historic institutions, held out against universal suffrage until the twentieth century. The events of 1848 challenged also the economic privilege of the owners of property. The June Days in Paris gave dramatic announcement of the arrival of a new revolutionary class, 'the proletariat'. The June rising was not fought to promote any practical economic change; it was a social war, a slave revolt, and its repudiation of the moral superiority of the bourgeoisie could not be wiped out by all the executions and deportations which followed defeat. Before the June Days private property had been regarded as essential for liberty; after the June Days it became the symbol of oppression, and the capitalist took the place of priest and noble as the object of democratic hostility. Henceforth the bourgeoisie was morally on the defensive, ashamed and anxious. This was true not only of the French bourgeoisie who had genuinely experienced the 'social peril'. The alarm of the June Days spread across Europe; indeed, apprehension increased as the reality of danger became more remote. The middle classes outside France abandoned the revolutionary cause almost before they had taken it up and sought for allies against a proletariat which was still imaginary. Thus, the October Revolution in Vienna, though it had a programme with no social implications, sent the German-Austrian middle classes over to the side of absolutism; and within a few years of 1848 German liberalism came to regard universal suffrage as its mortal enemy. The French bourgeoisie had pride enough to remain radical though they ceased to be revolutionary and adhered to the sovereignty of the people in the sense that they took into partnership the French peasants who had saved them in the June Days. Though universal suffrage, the work of the revolution of 1848, became everywhere a mainstay of conservatism, in France it sustained at least the Third Republic and later, in the Dreyfus case, upheld the Rights of Man. In Germany, however, it was the instrument of Bismarck and in Austria it became in 1907 the last prop of the empire of Francis Joseph.

In the world of nations, too, the revolutions of 1848 ended the compromise which had been the outcome of the revolution of 1789. The French revolutionaries had launched the national principle; they supposed that this would operate to the sole advantage of France and that when all else of the old order was destroyed the predominance of France would remain unchallenged. France liberated other nations as the French bourgeoisie liberated the French people: freed from their hereditary rulers, they were expected to welcome French leadership instead. The empire of Napoleon expressed the French version of the national principle: German, Italian, Polish and even South Slav nationalism were evoked as auxiliary weapons for the French cause. France was the only one who knew how to wield the national appeal, and remained the greatest single power in Europe even after the fall of Napoleon; the other Great Powers of the Continent were states, not nations, and therefore without the strength of popular enthusiasm. Thus the French nation claimed the cultural and political heritage of Louis XIV, despite the guillotining of Louis XVI and the renewed expulsion of the Bourbons in July 1830. This cultural headship was recognized for the last time at the beginning of 1848, when the other nations of Europe waited for the February Revolution in Paris before starting their own. Thereafter it was no longer enough to have taken the trouble to be born French. The laws of inheritance were repudiated between nations as much as between individuals. The lesson was not lost on the French themselves;

henceforth the French nation was as much imperilled as, say, the dynasty of Habsburg by European upheavals, and France – previously the promoter of change – became the principal advocate of conservatism and of the status quo.

In 1848 every nation followed the example set by the French in 1789. Each claimed to be perfect: each, therefore, was entitled to lay down its own limits or, if it preferred, to recognize none. Moreover, each nation asserted a purity and greatness of character which made it an example to Europe and justified its bringing other less noble people under its own rule. Thus, Poland had long announced herself as 'the Christ among the nations', and her liberation was regarded as the first object of the revolutionary cause; this liberation did not, however, extend to the Ukrainians under Polish rule. Similarly Mazzini, despite his denunciations of French arrogance, set up Italy as 'God's word in the midst of the nations'. Rome was to be the capital of a new federation of nations, all duly humble, which were to be cut and shaped to suit Italy's convenience. Kossuth, too, insisted on the unique civilization and political gifts of the Magyars. Though partly Slovak by birth, he denied the existence of a Slovak nation, and, since he could not deny the existence of the Serbs, proposed to root them out with the sword.

Magyar exclusiveness was relatively harmless, except to the subject nations of Hungary. The will to dominate was a more dangerous matter when it was taken up by the Germans, already the most numerous nationality in Europe. The revolutions of 1848 discovered 'the German mission'. This mission was simple: it was, simply, to be German. Europe was corrupt – French sophistication, English materialism, outworn institutions were all to be redeemed by the irruption of the clear-eyed, healthy German barbarian:

> *Und es soll am Deutschen Wesen*
> *Noch einmal die Welt genesen.*

A unique character was found in the German spirit (*Deutscher*

Geist), and for that matter even in German rivers and trees – the one wetter and the other more arboreal than any others. Other nations based their claims on superiority of culture, as in the case of France or Italy, or at any rate on superiority of class – as Polish and Magyar nationalism sprang from their landed nobility. German nationalism was the first to depend solely on language: the future Germany was to extend wherever German was spoken. The *Volksdeutsche* were an invention of 1848. Since Germany had no 'natural frontiers' – or none that gave such an easy excuse for expansion as the Rhine to France or the Alps to Italy – national Germany used a simpler argument and claimed whatever was necessary to her existence. Thus Bohemia, despite its Czech majority, could, according to Engels, 'only exist henceforth as a part of Germany'; and the German liberal spokesman at Frankfurt said of western Poland: 'Our right is that of the stronger, the right of conquest'. This phrase supplied the basic theme of German history, until it turned against Germany a century later.

Resistance to German claims was not delayed until the twentieth century; it was the motive of the Slav Congress which met at Prague on 2 June 1848. The Slav peoples of eastern Europe were individually too small to hold out against German pressure: therefore, improving on the German model which had made language the basis of nationality, they tried to find a bond of alliance in ethnography and philology. The Slav Congress had practical motives of defence against German nationalism and had no time to trouble about the virtues of the Slav character. Still, even at Prague, Bakunin, one of the inventors of Slav solidarity, found in the Slavs 'an amazing freshness and incomparably more natural intelligence and energy than in the Germans'; and he expected them 'to renew the decadent Western world'. The Slavs of the Austrian and Turkish Empires had enough to do renewing themselves and thereafter quarrelling with each other. The only contribution Russia made to the Western world in 1848–9 was to crush the revolution in Hungary. But the spirit of radicalism was not permanently arrested at the Russian frontier; and Pan-Slavism, which evoked little response outside Russia, became the delayed gift of 1848 to the Russian intellectuals. In the twentieth century they escaped from this ethnic intolerance only with the aid of class intolerance, which was the other legacy of 1848 to mankind.

The revolutions of 1848 dispelled the Utopian dreams of the eighteenth-century rationalists. These had supposed that mankind would attain universal happiness if traditional beliefs were abandoned and traditional authorities overthrown. The experiences after 1789 did not destroy this idea. Social concord accompanied the rule of the bourgeoisie, and a true international order was established with the empire of Napoleon; it could plausibly be argued that achievement fell short of the ideal only because success was incomplete. Had the tricolour really 'toured the world', universal happiness could have been expected to follow. In 1848 no bounds were drawn against revolutionary victory: no European country, except Belgium, escaped, and the established system lost its traditional authority for ever. The outcome was conflict, not concord. The June Days announced class war; the record of the German, Italian and Hungarian revolutions announced war between nations. Peaceful agreement and government by consent are possible only on the basis of ideas common to all parties; and these ideas must spring from habit and from history. Once reason is introduced, every man, every class, every nation becomes a law unto itself; and the only right which reason understands is the right of the stronger. Reason formulates universal principles and is therefore intolerant: there can be only one rational society, one rational nation, ultimately one rational man. Decision between rival reasons can be made only by force. This lesson was drawn by the greatest political genius who observed the events of 1848: 'The great questions of our day will not be settled by resolutions and majority votes – that was the mistake of the men of 1848 and 1849 – but by blood and iron.' After 1848, the idea that disputes between classes could be settled by compromise or that discussion was an effective means of international relations was held only in England and America, the two countries which escaped the revolutions.

The liberals, the moderate men, shirked the problem of authority; it was faced by the radicals. They found a substitute for tradition in 'the religion of humanity', just as their nationalism took the place of the decayed loyalty to kings. Above all, they found a substitute for the hereditary governing class in themselves. 'The aristocracy of intellect' had a limitless confidence in its right to govern; for it spoke 'in the name of the people'. The radical leaders nominated themselves to this post: none of the great revolutionaries – not Marx nor Engels, Bakunin nor Blanqui – ever secured election by a democratic constituency, and, for the matter of that, none of them was sure of a majority even among the circle of his close associates. The greatest radical effort in France was the demonstration of 16 March, which demanded that elections to the Constituent Assembly be postponed until the people were fit to exercise the franchise, that is, until they were willing to vote for the radical leaders. Blanqui, when asked how long the postponement should be, answered: 'For some months, or perhaps years.' By democracy the men of 1848 did not mean the rule of the majority; they meant rather the rule of the discontented, a reversal of the previous order of society. The essence of 1848 was belief in movement; therefore only those elements of the population who desired change were democratic. The theoretical justification for this outlook was provided by Marx; it was his great contribution to history. Marx found the motive force of history in economic change; and this force was now impelling mankind from capitalism to socialism. Since movement and democracy were synonymous, only those who desired socialism were 'the people'. Marx could thus eliminate the peasants from his calculations, though they made up the great majority everywhere in Europe; and democracy could be turned into 'the dictatorship of the proletariat'. Marx was a man of the Enlightenment. He held that every man would recognize his own interest and follow it; therefore every proletarian would be a socialist. The proposition could be more usefully reversed: anyone who was not a socialist was not a proletarian. But the dictatorship was not really to be exercised even by those working men who accepted the theories of the learned Dr Marx. The workers were to be led by the communists, 'everywhere the most resolute and progressive element of the working class'. Since the communists in 1848 consisted of Marx and Engels, this was a satisfactory conclusion – and has proved a satisfactory conclusion for communists ever since. The radical theorists were led inevitably from belief in the people to belief in themselves; and so to advocacy of authoritarian government. Marx was more self-satisfied and despotic than Metternich, the other system-maker from the Rhineland.

Yet these resolute and progressive leaders never displayed their talents in a revolution. The original outbreaks had no recognized leaders; and no one knows the names of the leaders of the June Days in Paris or of the October Revolution in Vienna. The name of an individual leader in the rising of 15 May in Paris has been preserved; he is thought to have been a police spy. Only Kossuth and Mazzini experienced the practical tasks of revolutionary government; and the experience of Mazzini was not very serious. For the most part the self-styled spokesmen of the people were always trying to catch up on revolutions which had taken them by surprise, as Marx and Engels were still correcting the proofs of their revolutionary programme, the *Communist Manifesto*, when the first barricades were already built and the first shots were being fired. Bakunin distinguished himself by arriving in time for the Dresden revolution of May 1849. This was an accident – he was leaving Dresden for an imaginary revolution elsewhere and was prevented from reaching the railway station by unexpected barricades.

There would have been no revolutions in 1848 if it had depended on the revolutionary leaders. The revolutions made themselves; and the true heroes of 1848 were the masses. The radical intellectuals had supposed that, once tradition was overthrown, the masses would acknowledge instead the claims of intellect. Nietzsche expressed later this great illusion of 1848:

'Dead are all Gods. Now the superman shall live.' The masses never responded to the ambitions of the intellectuals. Though the masses, too, sought the superman, they sought in him an extension of themselves. The first of these supermen, concentrating the impulses and contradictions of the masses, was Napoleon III. He was a clever French guess at the future, not the real thing; for France remained too conservative in institutions and social structure to experience the full rule of the masses. The real superman of the masses was Hitler, in whom anonymity was personified; or perhaps even more in the enigmatical politburos of the 'new democracies', who have put the superman into commission.

In a deeper sense, the true superman, for whom 1848 prepared the way, has turned out to be the masses themselves. The masses have performed labours greater than those of Hercules and have accomplished miracles more wonderful than those of a divine saviour; more than any individual superman, they have shown themselves to be beyond good and evil. The age which began in 1848 was the age of the masses: the age of mass production, of mass migration and of mass war. In the pursuit of universal happiness everything became universal: universal suffrage, universal education, universal military service, finally universal destruction. The train which Robert Owen signalled has been driven by the masses themselves; the intellectuals have remained passengers, criticizing or – more occasionally – commending the train's progress. The historic task of the intellectuals was to sever mankind from its roots and to launch it on its career of movement. This was the task which was accomplished in 1848.

The Last of Old Europe

Previously published as the Introduction to The Last of Old Europe *(London, Sidgwick and Jackson, 1976).*

*   *   *

The year 1848 was of great moment in European history both
as an end and as a beginning. It was the year of revolutions,
the culmination of the political upheaval that had started with
the French Revolution of 1789. Every country on the continent
of Europe was affected, Belgium less than the rest. Only the two
countries on the fringes of Europe – Russia on the east and
Great Britain across the Channel – were unshaken. In this
Springtime of Nations everything seemed made anew. Absolute
monarchies were challenged. Liberal constitutions were
established. In France universal suffrage had its first triumph.
Recognized nations, such as the German and the Italian, asserted their political rights. Nations hitherto unknown sprang
into existence.

Within a year the revolutionary wave faltered and broke. In
much of Europe the traditional order was restored, seemingly
unchanged or even stronger than before. All that remained to
outward appearance was a fairly liberal constitution in
Piedmont – the Kingdom of Sardinia – a less liberal constitution
in Prussia and a Bonaparte – later to become Napoleon III –
instead of a Bourbon king as a ruler of France. No doubt the
appearance was misleading. The ideas of liberalism and nationalism retained their force and were to achieve many successes in
later years, though by less revolutionary means. But the great
age of revolutions on the French model was over. There was
none of any importance between 1848 and the end of the First
World War except for the belated and comparatively unsuccess-

ful Russian revolution of 1905. Even after the First World War, only the Bolshevik Revolution had any basic significance. After the Second World War there were no spontaneous revolutions at all in Europe except perhaps in Yugoslavia. The shadow of revolution often raised an alarm. It remained a spectre.

Yet 1848 marked much more a beginning than an end. This new revolution was less specific than the political turmoils that had preceded it. It was a change in men's beliefs, in their view of the universe and more prosaically in their way of life. Darwin was to shake men's confidence that they were a unique creation, only a little lower than the angels. Freud was to destroy men's conviction of their own rationality. Scientists ended the reign of Newton's immutable laws and substituted for them the principle of indeterminacy. Men lost their old security. At the same time they were free to believe there was no limit to what they could achieve if they set themselves to it. Men came to see themselves as lords of the universe just when they ceased to be lords of themselves.

The basis for this limitless and indeed grotesque confidence was to be found in British achievements during the preceding hundred years. The Industrial Revolution was Great Britain's individual contribution to civilization, a process that had no precise beginning and in a sense has had no end, but a revolution all the same. For the first time since the invention of the wheel men increased their physical power. Until 1830 motive forces were men themselves, draught animals – horses or oxen – and occasionally wind and water. Suddenly machines driven by coal took the place of men and animals. Men could move faster and further. They could produce more. George Stephenson, inventor of the *Rocket* locomotive, took the place of Rousseau, author of *The Social Contract*, as the exemplar for mankind. Great Britain, not France, became the European ideal, and the City of God was found in Manchester instead of in Rome or Paris. Textiles counted for more than the Rights of Man. Napoleon, the erstwhile conqueror of Europe, was overshadowed by the Napoleons of railway-building and finance.

Until the middle of the nineteenth century Great Britain led and the rest of Europe lagged behind. The Great Exhibition of 1851, the first of its kind, symbolized the future which Great Britain offered to the peoples of Europe and ultimately to the whole world. Many Europeans were eager to follow the British lead and did so in the subsequent half-century. The spread of this new economic order was not even. By the beginning of the twentieth century, Germany surpassed Great Britain as the greatest industrial power in Europe. Meanwhile such areas as the Balkans, southern Spain and southern Italy were hardly affected. For much of the period Russia was a byword for backwardness, yet by the beginning of the twentieth century some of the largest and most advanced industrial establishments were to be found in Russia, and the way was already clear for the developments that have made Soviet Russia the second-greatest industrial power in the world.

Old and new were mixed together, sometimes side by side, sometimes overlapping. If we went back to the Europe of a century ago we should often feel at home. We should know how to buy a railway ticket, how to draw a cheque, how to put on our clothes and in what order. We could read a daily newspaper and send a telegram. On the other hand our driving lessons would not qualify us to drive or ride a horse. Once off the beaten track we should find men still living in primitive straw huts, making their own traditional clothes and sometimes dying of starvation. We should find men who could not read and write and had no idea what state or nation they belonged to. We should find men who were respected for their hereditary rank instead of for their money. We should even find monarchs with absolute power of life and death.

Moreover even in the most revolutionary times many men do not notice what is happening although it is happening to themselves. During the great French Revolution, for instance, a Scotch gardener, employed to tend the palace gardens in Paris, kept a regular diary. He never made any reference to political events except on 10 August 1792, when he noted that crowds had trampled on the flower beds at the Tuileries. This was in fact the armed rising which led to the fall of the French Monarchy. In much the same way there were, throughout the later nineteenth century, village communities following the styles of life they had always followed, while not far away men in cities already possessed many of the advantages which we regard as characteristically modern – electric light, indoor sanitation, telephones, speedy travel.

These sixty years of unprecedented change are more vivid for us than any that went before. Thanks to the invention of photography we can actually see them. Photography was itself a product of the age. Though it did not depend on factories or steam power, it had some connection with science, an essential characteristic of the time. Also, perhaps, it derived partly from the increasing desire for information, a characteristic shown in the wider circulation of newspapers. The photographs of this time were stills in a literal sense. They needed a five-minute exposure and thus were spoilt by any considerable movement. Hence the earlier photographers preferred city streets when they were almost empty. In the same way the human subjects were clearly posed. We should not suppose that they were equally immobile in real life. On the contrary, men were on the move as they had never been before.

Karl Marx was fond of quoting the Greek philosopher Heraclitus: Πάντα ρεῖ, all things change. Change and movement were the dominant features of the age. There were changes in men's minds, changes in their way of life and changes in where they lived. The change in ideas is the one most difficult to illustrate. Photographs show devout congregations attending their village churches as they had always done; other photographs remind us that as many churches were built during the nineteenth century as in the Middle Ages. Nevertheless the proportion of believers steadily decreased, and many of those who still called themselves Christians did not believe in the old fundamental sense. There were fewer who accepted the divine inspiration of the Bible or its literal truth. There were more who believed in progress or in economic law even when they continued to attend church or chapel on a Sunday. The only English census of church attendance was taken in 1851. It revealed that few of the industrial working class ever went to church or chapel.

The change was even more pronounced in political ideas. Despite the failure of the revolutions of 1848, liberalism triumphed everywhere to a greater or lesser degree. In 1871 Germany got unification and universal suffrage. Russia got a sort of constitution in 1906. Austria got universal suffrage in 1907. Even Turkey got a constitution in 1908, though it rarely operated. By the end of the period Monaco was the only European state with an absolute ruler. More fundamental was the decline in the political power of the landowning aristocracy, though not in their wealth. During the revolution of 1848 *robot* – the labour rent paid by the peasants for their holdings – was abolished throughout the Austrian Empire. Serfdom was abolished in Russia in 1861. Peasants were free to leave their holdings for the towns or for countries overseas. In time they began to organize their own peasant parties, as happened sensationally in Ireland. The town workers were more consciously aggressive. The socialist parties that sprang up all over Europe were less significant for their doctrines than for their class consciousness. They were the parties of the industrial workers, as the title of the British Labour Party showed at its clearest.

People were not only changing their ideas. There were also more people. The dynamic rise in population started in Great Britain during the eighteenth century. Now it began to operate all over Europe. Historians are not agreed as to why this happened. Some have pointed to improved medical services, though this is a doubtful factor in the more backward parts of Europe. Better sanitation may have counted, though it sometimes made things worse: water closets increased the incidence of typhoid as long as domestic sewers were allowed to contaminate the supply of drinking water. Some historians have prosaically remarked that people were eating more potatoes – a factor which carried the population of Ireland to the point of catastrophe. The immediate cause of the rise in population was probably a decline in infant mortality, but this itself is still in need of explanation. All we know is that population was increasing at an unprecedented rate. When there was no corresponding increase in resources, famine followed – most notoriously in Ireland in 1846, but also in Spain and southern Italy later.

Throughout most of Europe the increase in food supplies took place. Even where aristocrats retained their great estates, they became agricultural businessmen, as much concerned to raise their rents or farm profits as to preserve their social position. The Hungarian nobility, for instance, continued to display their traditional dress and to pose as the descendants of Arpad and his companions. Nothing seemed more unchanging than life on the *puszta*, the great Hungarian plain. But in fact there were more steam ploughs in Hungary than in any other European country. Thanks to such innovations Europe could for a time still feed its growing populations. Later on food came more and more from overseas. The United States had a revolutionary effect on Europe in many ways. It offered a new home. It represented a democratic ideal. It also supplied wheat to the industrial countries of Europe, and England in particular. By 1914, ninety per cent of British wheat for bread was coming from overseas. The British farmer, when not ruined, preferred the more profitable, though more wasteful, activities of stock raising and dairy farming for the nearby towns.

Towns had existed in Europe since the early Middle Ages and played a more decisive part than their mere size indicated. They were the centres of finance, commerce and culture. Often they were the political capital, which sometimes meant that they were also the residence of the monarch. The largest towns were rarely the centres of industry, which, when they occurred at all, were usually found in the country near a good supply of water. Even the Industrial Revolution created new towns of medium size rather than adding to the great ones. In 1848 only

London and Paris had more than a million inhabitants. By 1880 Berlin had joined them. By 1910 there were five more – Glasgow, Istanbul, Vienna, Moscow and St Petersburg. Only Glasgow and Moscow were not the political capitals, and Moscow had been and was to be again.

Nevertheless towns were the symbols of contemporary civilization as they had rarely been before. This was the age of the bourgeoisie, and bourgeois is merely the French word for a citizen – a town dweller. By 1851 more than half the English population was living in towns. Half a century later the Germans had joined them. Towns absorbed much of the increase in population. This development was aided by the new freedom of movement which in its turn had both political and physical causes. The new political freedom is often overlooked, perhaps because it is inconceivable to the present generation. We pride ourselves on our emancipation from the hindrances to movement which shackled previous generations. But it is now impossible to travel without a passport. In some countries visas – that is, permits to enter – are still required and these are often not given without securing a permit to work. In some countries it is impossible to leave without official permission.

All such restrictions were swept away during the second half of the nineteenth century. The change came with startling suddenness. Before 1848 a passport was required in the Austrian Empire even to go from one town to another, and the first people to disregard this regulation were the deputies elected to the Constituent Assembly at Vienna in the year of revolution. Within a few years all the barriers were down. Passports were abolished except for Russia and Turkey. No permits were needed to leave one country or go to another. By the mid-1870s most European currencies were based on gold and were freely interchangeable. A man living in London could decide at a moment's notice to settle in Vienna or Paris, and he could move himself and his possessions there the same day. Europeans had never enjoyed such freedom and were never to do so again.

This political freedom was of practical use only because of the physical freedom that went with it. Railways were the greatest stroke of emancipation in the history of mankind. Until the middle of the century men could move only as fast as their feet or a horse could carry them. The armies of Napoleon often won victories by their speed, but they went no faster than the Roman legions had done, and most armies went a good deal more slowly. Suddenly men who had moved at three or at best ten miles an hour could go at fifty, and that without any physical effort on their part. By 1848 only Great Britain and Belgium had established their main railway networks. British projectors and British workmen were beginning the creation of railways in France, much to the annoyance of Frenchmen with a vested interest in horse traffic. Fifty years later the European network was complete everywhere except in Russia, and there were more miles of railway than there are now. Geographic obstacles disappeared. The Semmering railway linked Vienna and Trieste in 1854, enabling Trieste to become a great port. The Mont Cenis tunnel through the Alps was opened in 1870, and other Alpine tunnels were soon to follow.

The railways brought unity to Europe despite the political divisions. Trains crossed the frontiers with little formality. The transcontinental expresses provided dining cars and sleeping cars, carrying passengers from one end of Europe to the other in conditions of unparalleled luxury. In 1888 the *Orient Express*, most romantic of all trains, began to run from Calais and Paris to Istanbul. Man seemed to have conquered space. The railway terminus replaced the cathedral as the architectural achievement of the age. St Pancras station in London excelled in its Gothic fantasy. King's Cross, its immediate neighbour, was modelled on the Tsar's riding school at St Petersburg – an indication that railway passengers were now as important as monarchs.

Sea transport took longer to accept the reign of the steam engine. Until the 1860s the clippers were faster than steamships across the Atlantic. Sailing ships handled most of the world's carrying trade until the 1880s and even thereafter retained much of the local traffic. Fishing fleets in local waters still operated under sail, usually without an auxiliary engine. At the time of the Crimean War most of the Royal Navy was still composed of sailing ships, and until the first years of the twentieth century, British warships retained their masts and sails in case their engines broke down.

Nevertheless steam triumphed in the long run and nowhere more decisively than in the crossing of the Atlantic. This was the great field of the emigrant ship, carrying passengers at almost nominal rates and of course under inhuman conditions. Liverpool and Glasgow were the first emigrant ports. Soon they were joined by Hamburg and Bremen. The British were the first to move in large numbers, and the Germans followed. Later in the century the flood of emigrants came from Italy and eastern Europe with Russians last of all. A few emigrated for political reasons – Chartists from England, and German radicals after the revolution of 1848. Most fled from hardship and starvation as the Irish did. Most of them believed they were going to the Promised Land. They were often disappointed.

The European continent was united in less tangible ways. The greatest achievement here was the electric telegraph, which was invented in 1836–7. It was at first used in railway signalling. Soon it became general. There were 2,000 miles of telegraph lines in Europe in 1849, 111,000 twenty years later. England was linked to the continent by submarine cable in the early 1850s; Europe to America in 1865. Six years later cables girdled the globe. Here was an almost incredible advance in communications. From this moment men could know what was happening in any part of the civilized world within a few minutes instead of after days or even months. By means of the electric cable, British troops returning from the Crimea were diverted to India at the time of the Mutiny. It was no accident that Julius Reuter founded his telegraph agency in 1851. News became worldwide. So, too, did prices on the commodity markets of the world. Police and military administration relied on the telegraph. The private citizen was not forgotten. Most telegrams, it seems, were exchanged between relatives.

The improvements in communications brought with them international institutions. Telegrams prompted the International Telegraph Union of 1865. Railways carrying mail prompted the Universal Postal Union in 1875 with international coordination of postal rates, a union that has continued to operate even between belligerent nations. Perhaps the most symbolic institution was the International Meteorological Organization of 1878. Previously countries had used their own meridian. French maps were drawn on the meridian of Paris, Dutch on that of Amsterdam. Now all accepted the meridian of Greenwich, though the Dutch were half-hearted about this until 1940 when they were forced into conformity by their German conquerors. It is a striking tribute to British astronomers and maritime supremacy that everyone in the world now sets his watch by Greenwich Mean Time, suitably adjusted plus or minus so many hours according to his geographical position.

Railways and steamships not only promoted migration across the seas. They also promoted travel from one town to another. Provincial businessmen could go up to London or Vienna for the day. Families scattered over the country could visit each other instead of saying farewell for ever. Schoolboys could go home for the holidays instead of remaining at school for seven unbroken years as my great-grandfather did. Indeed railways produced that characteristic nineteenth-century invention, the holiday. Previously aristocrats and other rich people moved from their town to their country house for the summer, and fashionable people settled at Bath or Baden-Baden for the winter. Most people never moved, though they sometimes took a day off. In the 1930s, I had an elderly neighbour in the Peak District who had been born in the house where he was still living and had never slept away from it for a single night. By then this was unusual. In earlier centuries it had been the common lot.

Now middle-class families went to the seaside or the country for a fortnight's holiday in the summer. Brighton, which had previously been a resort of the fashionable, became the nearest playground for thousands of Londoners. Blackpool and Southport catered for industrial Lancashire. Dieppe took holidaymakers from Paris. Leopold II equipped Ostend with palaces on the scale of Versailles from the profits of the Congo. The Riviera, discovered by Lord Brougham, provided for those rich enough to take a winter holiday as well as one in the summer.

The nineteenth century also discovered the countryside. Perhaps this came from reading Wordsworth's poetry. At any rate the Lake District, North Wales and the Scotch Highlands all had their holidaymakers and their organized tours. River steamers took holidaymakers up the Rhine. Switzerland had the greatest success. It became the playground of Europe. Previously, though people had sometimes taken country walks, no one had thought of climbing mountains. Now this became a widespread enthusiasm among the middle classes. At the end of the century skis were introduced from Norway and improved for sporting purposes, thus making Switzerland as popular in the winter as it had been in the summer. Holidays as pleasure were in fact the most beneficent innovation of the nineteenth century.

There were still blank areas of the world waiting to be explored – Antarctica, nearly all Africa, much of Asia and some remote parts of Europe, especially in the Balkans. The explorer was a characteristic feature of the time, carrying with him mapping equipment, the Bible, gin and European firearms. As Belloc wrote in *The Modern Traveller*: 'We have got the Maxim gun and they have not.' By the end of the period nearly all the unknown world had been penetrated by European transport and ideas, though the Balkans did not become popular tourist resorts until after the Second World War.

To our eyes there was one curious flaw in this story of easier movement. It was easy to move wherever there were railways or steamships. It was still difficult to make shorter journeys – from one village to the next, or even from one railway terminus to another in the great cities. France was the only country covered by a network of narrow-gauge railways, chugging along the country lanes or through the village streets. Everywhere else the horse still reigned for local movement. Visiting any city of the time, we should notice the general grime from steam trains and domestic coal fires. We should be struck even more by the smell of horse dung and the dirt in the streets. Crossing a street was a daring venture, rarely attempted by a lady in a trailing skirt. The street sweeper was a figure as universal as the newspaper vendor.

The great age of the railway was thus paradoxically also the last great age of the horse. Though the stagecoach and the diligence disappeared except in mountainous or backward districts, the horse still provided all local transport. Every big town house had its mews, and every country house its stables. Every great man and every fashionable doctor kept his own carriage. The nineteenth century, putting most things on a cash basis, also produced horse-drawn vehicles for hire, complete with taxi meters. England had its own speciality, the hansom cab, a two-wheeled vehicle with its driver perched at the back and sometimes called the gondola of the streets. Continental cities had four-wheelers: landaus, fiacres or, in honour of the great Queen, victorias. For humbler citizens there were horse-drawn omnibuses and sometimes horse-drawn trams.

Horses also did most of the agricultural work. Oxen drawing the plough could still be seen in Dorset in the 1880s, and a few can still be seen in eastern Europe. At the other end of the scale, the steam plough was an occasional rival to the horse. But the usual rural scene was the ploughman and his horse turning the furrows. The farmer, the country doctor and the country clergyman did their rounds on horseback, though the continental priest was probably too poor to afford one. Fox hunting on horseback flourished in England and Ireland and was imitated by continental aristocrats in France and Hungary who prided themselves, rightly or wrongly, on their resemblance to English milords.

A great improvement in city transport came in 1883 when

Siemens, a German engineer, invented the electric tram. Soon every city in Europe, indeed every city in the world, had its trams. London had its trams. Manchester had its trams. Paris had its trams. So did Moscow, Palermo and even Istanbul. The tram was the first civic blow at the dominance of the horse. London, usually a centre of initiative, was curiously backward. The House of Lords would not allow trams along the Embankment or across the Thames bridges. Hence the City and the West End had to rely on horse-drawn omnibuses until the first decade of the twentieth century. English cities were also the only ones with two-decker trams, perhaps on the omnibus model.

The dominance of the horse was further shaken by the coming of the bicycle. For the first time travellers were not tied to the iron rail. In its early days the bicycle, still rather an uncomfortable vehicle, was quite a fashionable form of travel. Aristocrats going off for the weekend took their bicycles with them and rode on them from the local station to their country house. H G Wells dedicated a whole novel to them, revealingly called *The Wheels of Chance*. The final blow to both horse and railway was at any rate foreshadowed before the outbreak of the First World War. This was the internal combustion engine and its instrument, the automobile or motor car. At first this was used mainly for public transport. The huge private cars or horseless carriages remained a luxury until after the First World War. Rich people went for drives or occasionally for tours. Jack Tanner in Shaw's play *Man and Superman* set out to drive from England to Morocco, though he was trapped by a designing female, Ann Whitefield, in the Spanish Sierra.

Electricity was a great civilizer in other ways. It began to replace gas for street lighting, and the city streets became well lit for the first time. This no doubt helped to reduce the violence which till then had been common. Garrotting had been a more painful form of mugging in the 1860s. Policemen patrolled the poorer quarters of cities in pairs, and there were many city streets where they did not dare to venture at all. Women of the more respectable classes never went out unattended. The violence was not all on one side. Public executions continued in England until the 1860s and in France until the twentieth century.

Recreation was another civilizing force. There had always of course been popular sports – rough games, combats with single stick, cock fighting and bear baiting. Now the crueller sports were made illegal, though this did not always end them. Games with codes of rules flourished, some to play and some to watch. Association football was England's great gift to the world, one that will survive when all other English achievements are forgotten. Lawn tennis, another invention of the elegant English upper classes, also became universal later, and the Scotch made their own contribution with their national game, golf.

The great cities of Europe reached new pinnacles of glory. Resplendent town halls rivalled the railway stations and symbolized bourgeois civilization at its highest. On the Continent they usually followed the Gothic models of the medieval Hôtel de Ville or Rathaus, as in Paris and Vienna. English towns, more eclectic, varied between Gothic and classical, in either case palatial. Every continental city had its great opera house, another symbol of bourgeois triumph. Previously opera had been the entertainment of princely courts. Now bourgeois audiences were accommodated as well. Even London had its opera house at Covent Garden, though no regular opera company. And even Edward VII dragged himself to the annual cycles of Wagner's *Ring*, though he ate and drank during much of the performance.

Continental cities also developed cafés, social centres often of great magnificence. Of course there had been coffee houses for a long time, and the original cafés still flourished in eastern Europe – primitive buildings where the customers sat cross-legged, smoking hookah pipes. The new cafés were different – vast halls glittering with mirrors, each one with its special clientele. Some were for artists, some for politicians, some for writers and some for chess players. Here again England was an exception. There were few great cafés, only the Café Royal, an importation from France as its name and the N (for Napoleon III) on its façade implied. The English social centre was the club, also palatial, and each also with its special membership. There were Reform Clubs for the Liberals and Carlton Clubs for the Conservatives, Athenaeum Clubs for aspiring intellectuals and Crockfords for card players. There were a few continental imitations such as the Jockey Club in Paris. Essentially the club was an English institution.

There was another side to city life. A mile or so away from the grandiose centres people were living in worse conditions than those that they had fled from in their peasant homes. The slum was as universal as the town hall or opera house. The swarm of new arrivals was relegated to decaying houses and worked in sweat shops for starvation wages. Every big city – London, Paris, Vienna and Berlin – had its slum area, breeding disease which often spread to the bourgeois quarters. Poverty in the countryside had its redeeming features. In the cities it had none. Photographs of slum dwellers and especially of slum children are a reminder that this age of bourgeois civilization brought greater prosperity and wealth for a few and greater hardships for the many.

The contrasts between the rich and the poor, between those who had moved with the times and those who had stood still, were greater and more savage than before. Until the nineteenth century even the wealthiest classes, even kings and queens, lived in conditions that we should now find appalling: no sanitation, no pure water, no efficient medical services, hideous discomfort when travelling. Now a few had escaped from these hardships. The rest were still exploited and still suffered. The cleavage was purely of class and historical tradition, not innate. All Europeans were of the same colour – dirty pink or, as it was called, white. Outside the Balkans all except for Jews and a few sceptics were Christian, though divided into three sects – Orthodox, Roman Catholic and Protestant. All observed the same calendar with a variant of twelve days between Orthodox countries and the rest.

Nearly all spoke a form of Indo-European, with the Hungarians, Finns, Basques and Albanians as isolated exceptions. All had the one-man, one-woman family except for those of irregular life.

Yet, as Disraeli wrote and as Karl Marx demonstrated at length, there were Two Nations, which seemed to differ as much as black and white. The cleavage took on many aspects. Despite the industrial boom, only Germany and Great Britain were fully advanced communities where industry predominated. There was a middle zone of France, Italy and Austria-Hungary, where industry and agriculture still balanced. Eastern Europe was barely touched by the new civilization except for the intruding railways. There life went on unchanged as it had done since time immemorial. Centuries seemed to divide the Ringstrasse in Vienna from the Balkan peasant village. Yet they were only a day's train journey away from each other.

The cleavage was not merely geographic. It existed within each country. English agricultural labourers still wore smocks. Peasants everywhere clung to traditional costume not for display but because it was the only possession they had. Such costumes could be seen as much in Dutch villages as in Albania or wildest Spain. If by the typical European we mean the majority of Europeans, then the typical European still lived on the edge of starvation and still worked unlimited hours for inadequate reward. He was illiterate, his mind a jumble of superstition and rural cunning. He never left his village, knew nothing of politics and accepted unquestioningly the religion he was taught by the priest.

One factor pulled town and country, rich and poor, new and old together. Though the industrial system created great things, it had less effect on small ones. The craftsman still held his own. Factories produced cotton or wool cloth. But the shirts, dresses or suits made from them were produced by hand. The village tailor cross-legged with his needle was no different from the smart tailor in Bond Street, except that he received less for his work. Poor people made their clothes at home or adapted the cast-offs of the rich. Shoes were made by hand, and the village cobbler was the local radical in England, though not in the Balkans. Much of the furniture in poorer homes was made by craftsmen and handed down from generation to generation. The survival of the horse demanded a smithy in every village. The horse's harness was the work of craftsmen. Great breweries relied on craftsmen to make the beer barrels. Craftsmen and industrial workers were worlds apart even if they appeared under the same heading in the census returns.

Retail selling was another occupation almost untouched by the new spirit. Many commodities were already traded on a world market, yet when these same commodities finally reached the consumer, this was in a small shop handling only a few goods and probably run by the proprietor and his family. The shopkeeper was a survival from a pre-industrial age of individual trading on a small scale. He was the essential 'little man', sometimes a radical in politics but sometimes enthusiastic for a plebiscitarian dictator such as Napoleon III or, in later days, Hitler. There were street markets in every town and the great fairs still flourished alongside the new international markets of London. There were already a few multiple stores such as Printemps in Paris and Harrods in London. But the village shopkeeper handled more goods everywhere from Great Britain to the Balkans.

The greatest unifying force was also paradoxically the greatest cause of division. This was nationalism, the dominating political feature of the nineteenth century. Previously men had often felt patriotic loyalty towards an existing state. Now they developed national consciousness and national pride. The national idea was a creation of the French Revolution, carried across Europe by the revolutions of 1848. But the greatest missionary of nationalism was the schoolteacher. An illiterate man does not know what nation he belongs to. He can only say, 'I come from here.' Once he can read and write, he uses the national language and soon knows he is doing so. Universal primary education was established in most European countries during the later nineteenth century. The village school became almost as common as the village church, usually cooperating with it, sometimes, especially in France, promoting a rival creed. The education provided was often crude and in eastern Europe far from universal. Nevertheless the decline in illiteracy was as striking as the increase in population.

Higher education also served the cause of nationalism, extolling national traditions as well as spreading the national language. Historians especially were exponents of the national cause. They wrote national histories designed to emphasize the peculiar greatness of their particular nation. German historians played a leading part in the creation of German unity. English historians exalted the British constitution and the British Empire. French historians paraded the achievements of the great revolution and the glory of Napoleon. On a more popular level daily newspapers helped to strengthen national unity. They were a recent invention, symbolizing the triumph of the machine, in their case the steam press. Railways enabled them to cover the country where previously they had been local. By the end of the century Englishmen were reading much the same news each morning. Public opinion in the modern sense had been born.

Education weakened local speech and local loyalties. Sir Robert Peel was the last English prime minister with a local accent (Lancashire), though there were of course prime ministers with a Welsh or Scotch accent in the twentieth century. Frenchmen thought of themselves as French, not as Normans or Provençals. All Germans could speak *hoch Deutsch* (High German) though they retained their provincial speech for family use. Italy is perhaps the most impressive case. Italy had never been a political unit. Speech differed so much from state to state as almost to be different languages. Few Neapolitans felt that they had anything in common with Venetians or Piedmontese. Yet within a comparatively few years Italian nationalism swept all before it. Italy became a rigorously unified state, and all Italians spoke Tuscan.

The most practical and perhaps the most powerful expression of nationalism was the army or as it was often called 'the nation in arms'. The old armies had been composed of long-term conscripts, isolated from the rest of the community. The victories of the short-service Prussian Army in 1866 and 1870 caused a general conversion. All continental countries went over to universal military service for a two- or three-year period. The soldier came from the civilian community, and nearly all males in that community had been soldiers. During their period of service the soldiers wore 'uniform', its very name implying the ironing out of local differences. The process was of course never complete. Crack cavalry regiments, such as the German Death's Head Hussars, wore exotic uniforms that were survivals from a more barbaric age, and in most armies class differences prevented any uniformity between officers and other ranks. Great Britain was a clear exception to the continental pattern, clinging to a professional army and navy until the First World War. Even so, countless music hall songs and Kipling's poetry bear witness that the British Army and the Royal Navy had also become symbols of national pride.

In the early days of nationalism men assumed that it would reinforce the existing great states or create new ones. Great Britain and France would be even greater; a united Germany and a new Italy would join them. Lesser nationalities, when considered at all, were dismissed as picturesque survivals of the same kind as spinning wheels or peasant costume and like them doomed to disappear in the modern industrial age. This view was particularly common among men of radical opinion, impatient with the past. Marx and Engels for instance expected that such 'tribes' as the Czechs or the Croats would simply be eaten up by the German nation. At first this seemed likely to happen. Very few Frenchmen worried in the nineteenth century about the Breton or the Basque problem. Very few Englishmen worried about the Welsh problem and most Englishmen assumed that the Scotch were delighted to have become next door to English people. The English certainly worried about the Irish problem but much more on religious and economic than on national grounds, at any rate until the end of the century. Even so the English had one unique victory. At the beginning of the nineteenth century nearly all native Irishmen spoke their national tongue, Erse. At the end of the nineteenth century, thanks to an intensive system of English education, virtually none did so. There is no other case in Europe of the disappearance of a national language, at any rate since the death of Cornish in the seventeenth century. It was however far from meaning the disappearance of the Irish nation.

National survivals or revivals struck deeper in eastern Europe. The prophecy of Marx and Engels was not fulfilled. Half-forgotten nations became fully conscious and were joined by nations such as the Slovaks who had been forgotten altogether. The Austrian Empire, or Austria-Hungary as it was called after 1867, was the one Great Power that failed to transform itself into a national state, though Hungary claimed to have done so. The Czechs had their own opera house and their own musical composers such as Dvořák and Smetana who, though assertively national, were clearly of European stature. They had their own university as did also the Croats and the Serbs. The Ottoman Empire was an even worse case. Its military rule over Christian Balkan peoples could never take on a Turkish national character. Instead the series of wars culminating in the Balkan Wars of 1912–13 were wars of national liberation.

War in general provided a curious contradiction throughout this period. Many observers believed that Europe had become too civilized to resort to war or, to put it another way, that peace – in this case the advance of industry – had its victories no less renowned than war. Nevertheless the first twenty years of the period, between 1850 and 1870, saw a series of wars: the first, the Crimean War, a confused muddle, and the others wars of national purpose if not of liberation. In 1859 the French and Sardinians ended Austrian predominance in Italy, a process completed in 1866. In 1864 Austria and Prussia acquired Schleswig and Holstein from Denmark in the name of German

nationalism. Finally Prussia united Germany, or most of it, by
defeating Austria in 1866 and France in 1870. Thereafter to
everyone's surprise there were no more serious wars in Europe
for more than a generation except for the Balkan war between
Russia and Turkey in 1877–8. Instead there was the Armed
Peace with every Great Power increasing its military forces,
Austria-Hungary and Italy somewhat ineffectually.

In some ways these forces were modern. Railways for instance
played a decisive part in Prussia's victories. All plans for
mobilization centred on the railways, and generals had to be
expert in railway timetables. The new steel industry supplied
the guns for the armies and the material for the battleships. In
other ways the military forces remained stuck in the past. The
horse was still their only means of transport, with forage for the
horses providing as great a problem as food and munitions for
the men. Tactics on the battlefield were unchanged from the
days of Napoleon: masses of men flung against each other in
ever greater numbers. Uniforms were still gaudy until the British
developed khaki during the Anglo-Boer war. No general ever
consulted a scientist or an industrial leader. For them the
Industrial Revolution had not taken place.

The Armed Peace had great political effects. The military
forces and virtues were still exalted. Monarchs found a new
occupation in symbolizing the nation in arms just when their
political functions were diminishing. Some monarchs still chose
their ministers. Few determined policy. But they concealed this
by parading their military character. European monarchs on
their public appearances always wore military uniform, dressing
up as field marshals, honorary colonels or admirals of the fleet.
This was new. In earlier ages monarchs did not wear military
uniform unless they were actually serving officers. Louis XIV
did not do so. Nor did George IV, earlier the Prince Regent,
despite his claim to have been present at the battle of Waterloo.
The practice was commoner among the German princes and
perhaps became universal in the later nineteenth century
because nearly all monarchs after the fall of Napoleon III were

either Germans, of German descent or married to Germans. Every English sovereign for instance between Queen Anne and George V had a German mother, except of course for Edward VII who had a German father.

The European monarchs had a field day in this period thanks to the railways. They could move about more freely and took advantage of this to meet each other constantly, showing themselves off to their peoples on the way. Germany was their favourite meeting place, partly because of its central position and partly because of the family connections most monarchs had there. The Tsar went there nearly every year. Edward VII passed through Germany and called on his German relatives on his way to Marienbad. France, having become the only republic in Europe in 1871, missed most of these royal visitors except for the unofficial visits of Edward VII to Paris when Prince of Wales. But Russian grand dukes settled on the Riviera with their ballerina mistresses, and Queen Victoria, travelling as the Duchess of Lancaster, often went there in her old age.

The monarchs were often called 'the crowned heads of Europe'. Few of them however actually held a coronation. The smart new ceremony took the form of an oath to the constitution. Franz Joseph managed to be crowned king of Hungary in 1867, but there was no coronation for the recently invented emperor of Austria. Nor was there any coronation ceremony for the German emperor. In England, George IV's was the last full-blown coronation. William IV had a cut-price one, and the example was followed by his successors. Victoria atoned for this by celebrating both her golden and her diamond jubilees. Only the tsars maintained the ancient splendour, and the coronation of Nicholas II was a last blaze of the old Europe, recalling the great days of Byzantium.

Monarchs were symbols of social stability as well as of nationalism. The social peril was still supposed to be great. The one great outbreak of political violence was the Paris Commune of 1871, which was not so much a proletarian or socialist revolution, despite Marx's championing of it, as a spontaneous protest by the Paris poor against defeat and harsh conditions. The Commune was suppressed with great savagery – twenty thousand or more were killed, over ten thousand transported. This was a curious commentary on the claim of the bourgeoisie to be more civilized and tolerant than the absolute monarchs. Despite this most socialist parties, even when theoretically Marxist, lost their revolutionary character and came to believe that the social revolution would be achieved automatically once they had won a majority of votes. The ballot box superseded the barricades.

There were still exiled revolutionaries, now mostly Russian where they had previously been French or Italian. Anarchists were a speciality of the period. They commanded a sizeable following in Italy and Spain. Otherwise they were lone operators, hoping to provoke a social collapse by individual acts of violence, like Conrad's Secret Agent who, however, only caused an explosion by accident. Monarchs were the favourite target of the anarchists and of their Russian counterpart the nihilists. The anarchist bag was considerable: a tsar of Russia, a king of Italy, an Austrian empress and a French president.

There were also immigrants to western Europe of a different political kind. These were the Russian Jews, fleeing from the pogroms and lesser brutalities that tsarist governments sought to maintain themselves by. Vienna and Berlin had their Jewish quarters. In London the Jews took over much of the East End from the earlier slum-dwellers. Russian anti-semitism was of the traditional kind that was as old as Christianity itself. There was also a new political anti-semitism, partly a bastard product of nationalism and partly a product of economic jealousy. There were anti-semitic political parties in Austria and Germany. In France anti-semitism provoked in the Dreyfus case the gravest crisis of the Third Republic. Anti-Jewish riots were not uncommon in English towns and quite common in Welsh ones. Curiously, while poor Jews usually settled in London or Leeds when they could not move on to America, Jewish intellectuals preferred central Europe – Berlin or Vienna – and Germany was generally regarded as giving Jews the warmest welcome. Even in the First World War the British government took up Zionism in order to win over European and American Jews who it was believed would otherwise support Germany.

We know a great deal about the later nineteenth century. There are far more statistics than for any previous age. Indeed reliance on fairly accurate statistics became common for both political and economic purposes. There are far more records, ranging from newspapers to the papers of government departments. There are reports of parliamentary debates, many of them verbatim. There was more serious study of economic and political problems. There were more observers of other countries, studying everything from folklore to contemporary art. Yet virtually all the books and articles written then and most of those written since by historians leave out half the human race. It would almost seem that European men appeared in the world fully grown or were brought into it by the agency of storks. In fact at least half the inhabitants of Europe and probably a little more were women. Neglect of them was evidently a characteristic of the age, and continuance of this neglect indicates that most writers, especially historians, have not outgrown nineteenth-century habits.

Surely women too did not pass through this age of change unaffected. The legal changes are easiest to identify. In many countries there were restrictions on the work women could do in industries and limits on the hours they could work. Mining was often forbidden to them altogether. Women had always taught in the lowest level of primary schools, and now other professions were grudgingly opened to them, beginning with medicine. A few were able to attend universities. There were a few women journalists and even daring women explorers of Asia and Africa. Women gifted enough to become writers, especially novelists, could escape from their inferior position almost completely. No one could suppose that George Sand was unemancipated, and many, including Gladstone, read the works of Mrs Humphrey Ward as though they were a new gospel.

For the great majority of women life was what it had always been: domestic service for either their husbands or for an employer. No man in any class ever did any domestic work of any kind. In Ireland or the Balkans where man, wife and donkey went together to market, the man returned home on the donkey and the wife trudged behind carrying the day's purchases. Even in Great Britain, the most industrialized country, domestic service was still the largest single occupation. Indeed the later nineteenth century was the golden age for the employer of domestic servants. In the seventeenth century Pepys, a top civil servant at the Admiralty, had one resident female servant. His nineteenth-century successor had six. Higher up the social scale noblemen had households of fifty or more. The Earl of Derby for instance had one dining hall for his guests, a second for the fifty upper servants, and a gloomy dungeon for the lowest rank of servants who did all the menial work and waited on the upper servants. A Hungarian count often had a town palace and three or four in the country, each with a staff of eighty.

In well-to-do houses there was usually a housekeeper as intermediary between her employer and the maidservants. In great houses there were separate staircases for the domestic servants who lived in tiny cells under the roof, often with forty of them sharing one cold-water tap. Domestic service was drudgery unaided by modern ingenuity. Coal had to be carried by hand often to the bedrooms as well as to the living rooms. The daily bath, now usual with the upper classes, meant that hot water had to be carried to every bedroom and then carried away. Coal fires involved the daily dusting of rooms, a particularly laborious task thanks to the clutter of bric-à-brac. The domestic servant was a 'slavey', her position redeemed only by the sense of belonging, in however degraded a way, to a community.

In all the welter of modern inventions few benefited women. One was the sewing machine, developed during the 1850s. Often it was the only machine women ever saw, certainly the only one they ever used. In domestic use it was an unmixed blessing. In wider use it added to women's burdens. The song of the shirt was now the song of the sewing machine. In the sweat shops of the city slums women, working sewing machines, were driven harder than before, and their sufferings were one of the scandals of the age.

Perhaps the typewriter should be added to women's blessings, at any rate towards the end of the period. In time it enabled the woman typist to replace the male clerk with his elegant copy hand. But most of this happened only during and after the First World War. The bicycle was a true emancipator. Women as much as men used it from the first and thus acquired a new freedom of movement. The bicycle also helped to stimulate the first step towards more rational women's clothing, in this case bloomers. But the pictures of this period show that women, particularly in the upper classes, took little advantage of their emancipation. Even the suffragettes were attired in the height of fashion, with hobble skirts and picture hats.

The greatest step towards women's emancipation is also the one most difficult to explain or even to document. During the later nineteenth century the birth rate began to decline in most European countries, most markedly in the most advanced. Women were bearing fewer children. We do not know why or how. Was there some rational choice in favour of fewer children? If so, how did it spread across Europe, in villages as much as in towns, in Roman Catholic countries as much as in Protestant ones? Were there more abortions? Were artificial means of birth control used, presumably the sheath? There was a certain amount of illicit contraceptive propaganda, but surely too little to produce such decisive effects. One gets the impression of a vast secret society of women spreading the glad tidings in ways that no historian will ever detect. At any rate it happened. Women were bearing fewer children, one of the greatest revolutions in the story of mankind.

In other ways women were far from emancipation sexually. The principle of one sexual law for men and another for women reached its highest point in the later nineteenth century. Gladstone said that he had known eleven British prime ministers and that seven of them had been adulterers. The twentieth-century figure is much lower. Respectable married women were supposed to have no sexual feelings though plenty of children. As Lord Curzon said, 'Ladies don't move.' Women lower down the social scale were regarded as providing the safety valve for rigid morality higher up. There were probably more prostitutes than ever before though there is no precise means of knowing how many. Every continental town had its brothel which often acted also as social centre and café. In the capitalist order of the day women, too, became a commodity to be freely bought and sold. On the other hand protests against this double system were beginning to grow. The demand for the equality of women did not have to wait for the twentieth century.

Wherever we look there is the same clash between what had been and what was to come. On the whole the principles of change and movement were still winning. Despite all the differences of class, region, occupation and even sex, Europeans were becoming more alike. Trade-union leaders in their group photographs look indistinguishable from employers: the same clothes, the same beards, the same gold watch-chains across their portly stomachs. Girls on the beach at Brighton in the early twentieth century were wearing dresses not all that different from those worn at Ascot. Third-class railway carriages had become not much less comfortable, though sometimes more crowded, than first class. A Bulgarian prime minister looked much like a British prime minister, pursued much the same policies and used much the same political phrases in his speeches. Socialists came together in the Second International and even interfered in each other's domestic affairs, forbidding French socialists for instance to become members of bourgeois governments.

State frontiers seemed to have lost most of their significance. Men crossed them freely and so did ideas. There has never been a time when European culture was so truly one. Tolstoy was the most highly regarded novelist in every European country. Shaw's plays were more widely performed in Germany than in England, and Germans spoke of 'unser Shakespeare' without provoking a smile. Stravinsky's *Rite of Spring* provoked a riot when it was performed in Paris, not however on nationalist grounds. The Hallé Orchestra in Manchester had a German conductor. English artists settled in Etretat, and artists from every country found their home in Paris. Nearly everywhere men could be sure of reasonably fair treatment in courts of law. No one except the Russian Jews was killed for religious reasons. No one was killed for political reasons despite the synthetic outbursts of political rhetoric. There was security at all levels. Men and even women could walk the streets safe from violence and as yet pretty safe from the automobile. Money was safe from fluctuations. Even the poor were becoming less insecure and were protected from the extreme rigours of poverty and unemployment. The wonders of science were spread wide before mankind. It was a golden age or seems so in retrospect.

For this miraculous age of prosperity and security ended abruptly in 1914 with the outbreak of the greatest war ever known. In June 1914 Europe was in a state of profound peace as it had been for forty years past. A month later all the Great Powers of Europe except Italy were at war, and Italy joined in nine months later. Old Europe perished, and much of new Europe perished also. New differences arose, and Europe was not to know unity again.

Crimea: The War That Would Not Boil

First Published in History Today, *February 1951.*

* * *

John Bright, with ponderous Victorian wit, called the Crimean War 'a crime'; most historians have presented it as a bewildering series of diplomatic and military blunders. With the experience of the last few years to enlighten us, we should do better: we know that the diplomatic tangles since 1945, which may seem bewildering to the future historian, conceal the reality of 'the Cold War'. The Crimean War was the Cold War in an earlier phase. Two world systems, mutually uncomprehending, lurched against each other, each convinced of its defensive good faith. The struggle between them was fought in a ragged way at the edges. Both sides shrank from the head-on collision which would have produced a war to remake the world – Russia from lack of strength, the Western powers from lack of conviction. Though the Crimean War seemed indecisive, great decisions followed from it. Without it neither Germany nor Italy could have been united; without it Europe would never have known 'the liberal era', that halcyon age which ended in 1914 and which, for centuries to come, men will regard as 'normal times', just as the barbarians looked back to the peace and security of Augustan Rome.

The Crimean War is often treated in England as a war over the Eastern question, a war to secure the route to India, and thus a rehearsal for Disraeli's 'peace with honour' campaign in 1878. This is to err both in time and place. The war had little or nothing to do with the security of India. The Suez Canal was not built; the overland route catered for a few travellers in a hurry; for that matter Russia's land-route to India was still in the future. The Crimean War was fought for essentially European considerations – against Russia rather than in favour of Turkey. It was fought for the sake of the balance of power and for 'the liberties of Europe'; more positively, it aimed to substitute diplomacy by agreement, the Concert of Europe, for the settlement of affairs at the dictation of a single Great Power. Disraeli was a consistent disciple of Metternich when he criticized the Crimean War and yet opposed Russia in 1878: the Crimean War had general altruistic motives, the crisis of 1878 was caused solely by the defence of imperial interests. In other words, 1878 was a Tory affair; the Crimean War, with all its muddle, sprang from Whig principles, the last fling of a dying party.

British policy in the Near East had not been consistently anti-Russian before the Crimean War, though it became so afterwards. Canning, for instance, cooperated with Russia throughout the Greek war of independence; and though Palmerston thought of working with France against Russia in the Near East in 1833, he ended up by working with Russia against France in 1839 and 1840. Throughout the eighteen-forties, and indeed until the beginning of 1853, British suspicions were turned against France both at Constantinople and in Egypt; and Great Britain and Russia often made common cause in resisting French encroachment. Nor can there be any easy dividing line in their attitude to the Ottoman Empire, as though Russia wanted to break it up and Great Britain wished to preserve it. Both powers found it a convenience; and both powers doubted its capacity to survive. Their difference was in timing, not in judgement of the situation.

The British attitude to Russia was very different when it came to Europe; hence the Crimean War makes sense only with a European background. Ever since 1815 British statesmen had been obsessed with the thought that, if France ceased to dominate Europe, Russia would take her place; as Napoleon had said, in fifty years all Europe would be either republican or Cossack. Hence Castlereagh's rather absurd alliance with France and Austria in January 1815; hence Canning's calling in of a New World to redress the balance of the Old (though the New World did not respond to his invitation); hence Palmerston's welcome to the July Monarchy in France and his Quadruple Alliance with Spain and Portugal as well in 1834. This was one side of British policy: to maintain France as a Great Power and yet to keep her harmless – just strong enough to check Russia's domination without reviving the same taste in herself. The other element in British policy was to develop the independence of central Europe, so that it could hold its own against both Cossacks and republicans without constant alarms or war. This was what was meant by the favourite description of Prussia and Austria as Great Britain's 'natural allies': they were serving the purposes of British policy without any effort on the British side. Curiously enough, Metternich and Palmerston, who were supposed to hate each other so much, were pursuing the same aims and served each other's needs. So long as the 'Metternich system' worked, central Europe was independent of both France and Russia; and the balance of power in Europe freed Great Britain from European commitments.

The revolutions of 1848 ended this finely drawn policy. The fall of Metternich was a disaster to the British position; and it was little consolation to make out that he had fallen because of his refusal to take British advice. The revolutions of 1848 seemed to make France more powerful than before; to weaken Prussia; and to threaten Austria with elimination from the ranks of the Great Powers. Europe would become either republican or Cossack. Though this bitter saying was not at once fulfilled, it seemed at most postponed. On the one side, France emerged from the revolutionary year under the rule of a new Bonaparte, inescapably committed to the overthrow of the treaties of 1815 and almost as much to the restoration of French domination in Europe. On the other, the revolutions in central Europe – in Germany, in Italy and in Hungary – were defeated only with Russian backing; so far as Hungary went, only with Russian military aid. By 1850, Francis Joseph of Austria and Frederick

William IV of Prussia seemed to be Russian dependants, subservient not only from ideological similarity, but from their inability to hold their monarchical power except with Russian support. The Holy Alliance was the Cominform of Kings.

The defeat of the revolutions of 1848 with Russian aid had a profound effect on British public opinion. Before 1848 fear of Russia had been a diplomat's calculation; there had been no 'Russian bogey'. After 1848 British liberals picked up the habit of continental radicals and began to regard Russia as the tyrant of Europe. War against Russia was regarded as the preliminary to any radical success elsewhere. The old diplomatic apprehension of Russia now seemed tepid and half-hearted. In radical circles, for instance, it was common doctrine that Palmerston was in Russian pay; the proof was found in his reluctance to launch the great European 'war of liberation'. This theory can be found worked out in the essays which Karl Marx wrote on *The Eastern Question*; he learnt it from the pro-Turk lunatic, Urquhart. Except among radicals and exiles, fear of France still predominated in England until the spring of 1853. Indeed, belief that the British were more apprehensive about Belgium than about Turkey was one of the factors which led Tsar Nicholas to act so carelessly and so provocatively in May 1853, when the war-crisis first began to stir.

There was, of course, another and more obvious cause of Russian confidence. A coalition ministry had been formed in England at the end of 1852 under Lord Aberdeen; and Aberdeen, though a free-trader, was an old-fashioned Tory. He had no sympathy with radical hostility to Russia; great confidence in the Tsar's good faith; and great distrust of Napoleon III. If Aberdeen had had his way there would have been no Crimean War. Russia would have strengthened her position in Turkey, consolidated her reactionary hold over Europe; and Great Britain would have consoled herself by taking Egypt. This would have been a reasonable, though not an idealistic, solution; hence the later regrets of Lord Salisbury, a reasonable man without ideals, that it was not adopted. It could only have been adopted by a purely Tory cabinet; and from such a cabinet Aberdeen was barred by his free-trade doctrines. Instead, he was saddled with Whig colleagues, Palmerston and Russell, who were both in their way friendly to France and who both, without yet distrusting the Tsar, wished to draw a sharp line against any new Russian advance. Russell had been prime minister; Palmerston was going to be. They were both pretty clear that a firm line against Russia would be a winning card in the game for public favour which they were playing against each other. Here too, if Palmerston and Russell had had their way, there would have been no war. The Tsar would have stepped aside from the Eastern question before his prestige was involved and waited for a more favourable opportunity. Perhaps even, as we go on dreaming nowadays, Russian despotism would have saved everyone the trouble of a war by crumbling from within. It was this mixture of conciliation always too grudging and firmness always too late which, on the British side, produced the Crimean War.

There was, however, another principal in the war, one often forgotten in British and even in Russian accounts. Neither the Tsar nor the British government wanted war; Napoleon III did. Not necessarily the Crimean War as it worked itself out, but a war which would disrupt the existing structure of Europe. Thus Great Britain became involved in war in order to preserve the balance of power and to defend the liberties of Europe; Napoleon III pushed into war in order to overthrow the balance of power and to clear the way for French domination. After all, it is a simple calculation that if the allies of a great war fall out the defeated party will come into his own. In 1853 the calculation was made in Paris; now it is made in every German village. The Crimean War was not a good war from Napoleon III's point of view; a war in Poland, in Italy, or on the Rhine, would have been much better. But it was better than no war at all. On the other hand, Napoleon III had learnt from his uncle's failure – had learnt, that is, in the scrappy, illogical way in which men use the past to prop up their own prejudices. Napoleon III supposed, though wrongly, that his uncle's great mistake had been to quarrel with England; his key to success was therefore to be the British alliance, and the Crimean War was welcome to him in that it gave him this alliance. In the long run, however, Napoleon III did no better with the British alliance than his uncle had done without it – unless it is better to die in Chislehurst than at St Helena.

By the summer of 1853 France, Russia and Great Britain were all tugging themselves into war in their different ways. The Tsar, though with no deep-laid plans for encroaching on Turkey, had grown too confident; regarding Prussia and Austria as his satellites, he supposed that he could display his prestige at Constantinople without risk. When this proved mistaken, he – like the Russians generally when they are challenged – felt genuinely threatened with aggression; and in Russian eyes the Crimean War was a defensive war. The British government, though also without deep-laid plans, would not allow the Tsar's claims and, in their anxiety to win the alliance of France, often acted more firmly than Napoleon III expected or desired. Napoleon, on his side, wanted to shake Russia's prestige and to build up his own; but most of all, he wanted to keep in step with the British, who, with the same motive, constantly quickened the pace until the two fleets tumbled into the Black Sea more to prove mutual good faith and enthusiasm as allies than to oppose Russia. As a matter of fact, when the British and French fleets entered the Black Sea at the end of 1853, the Crimean War, not yet started, had already been won so far as the original causes of war, or excuses for it, were concerned. That is, the Tsar was quite prepared to drop his immediate claims on Turkey, once it became clear that England and France intended to resist them. This did not satisfy the Western allies. With their public opinion roused and their resources mobilized, what they wanted was a decision, not merely the withdrawal of the present Russian demands. The problem of the Crimean War, never solved, lay here. The Russians had dropped their demands because the British and French fleets had entered the Black Sea. How could the renewal of these demands be prevented when the British and French fleets went away again?

The problem had two sides, military and diplomatic. The military problem was, how to get at the Russians, in order to inflict on them the defeat which would make them accept the terms needed for Europe's security? The diplomatic problem was, what were the terms which should be imposed on the Russians when they were defeated? The two problems were mixed up throughout the war. Sometimes the allies tried to devise terms which would make a defeat of the Russians unnecessary; sometimes they dreamt of a defeat so decisive as to spare them the trouble of devising terms. At bottom the problem was insoluble. The Western powers could not alone inflict on Russia a decisive and lasting defeat; nor, even were she defeated, could they devise terms which would ensure against a renewal of her expansion. It would have been a different matter if Austria and Prussia, the states of central Europe, could have been drawn into the war. Hence the real decision of the Crimean War came from the two Germanic powers when they decided to stay out of it. Austria and Prussia were 'the third force'. Their persistence in this line of policy both caused the Crimean War and led to its being indecisive. Until the beginning of 1854 the Tsar had regarded them as reliable satellite states, dependent on his support. As soon, however, as he depended on their support, they ceased to be satellites. He could no longer keep France out of the Near East by a threat from Prussia on the Rhine and from Austria in Italy.

The Western powers imagined that 'the third force' had come over to their side and that a full-scale defeat of Russia was in sight. Certainly a coalition of all the Great Powers of Europe against Russia would have excluded her from Europe, might even have destroyed her as a Great Power. Poland would have been restored, Turkey secured; Louis Napoleon would have become master of Europe. This was an outcome more unwelcome to Prussia and Austria even than Russian domination of Turkey. Whereas the Western powers wanted a decision, the Central powers wanted no decision; and they got their way. Prussia had the great advantage that she was indifferent to the affairs of the Near East, though concerned with the general European balance. Hence her neutrality was genuinely impartial. Her only aim, which seemed craven enough, was to ensure that no fighting took place on Prussian soil. This no doubt benefited Russia and won her gratitude; but since Prussia did not promise anything to the Western powers, she did not disappoint them either. When the war ended, Prussia was not at first invited to the Peace Congress at Paris. This seemed a humiliation; later events showed the enormous gains to be won from keeping out of other people's quarrels. Any contemporary statesman who wishes to reap the advantages of the third course should study the policy of Prussia during the Crimean War.

Austrian policy is equally instructive: it shows the disadvantages of a neutrality which offends both sides. Whereas Prussia was neutral from indifference, Austria was neutral from being too deeply committed. She had her own grounds for opposing Russia. Russia's control of the mouth of the Danube, where her troops had established themselves in 1853, cut one of Austria's main economic arteries with the outer world. Thus the practical aim of Austrian policy was to get Russia out of Romania and to get herself in. But there were complicating factors. If Austria entered the war on the side of the Western powers, she would bear the brunt of the fighting; worse, an allied victory, expelling Russia from Europe, would make Napoleon III supreme and thus clear the way for the national principle. Austria would win Romania at too high a price if she lost her Italian lands, the symbol of her imperial greatness. Yet, apart from her anxiety about Romania, Austria dared not favour Russia nor even keep a resolute neutrality, for fear that Napoleon III would explode Italy against her. As a result Austria followed the worst of all policies. She offended the Tsar by refusing to promise a secure neutrality; she offended the Western powers by refusing to go to war. She pressed her alliance on England and France in order to conciliate them; she failed to operate it and left them more estranged than before. Neutrality, like virtue, has its merits if maintained inviolate; it can also be sold for a high price. The one impossible thing is to be up for auction and to remain virtuous at the same time.

The first stage of the Crimean War was the stage when the Western powers imagined that 'the third force' could be drawn into the war and a real decision thus produced. This stage lasted until the summer of 1854, by which time Prussian neutrality was certain and Austrian belligerence uncertain. The Crimean War, in the strict sense of the term, followed – the war with all its blunders and muddles which perplexed contemporaries and baffled posterity. Yet the confusion had a simple cause – how could the allies get at Russia when the great neutral buffer of central Europe was interposed between them? The allies had hoped that the Russians would obligingly remain in Romania in order that they might be defeated there; instead the Russians withdrew from Romania in July 1854. In their perplexity the allies decided on Sebastopol, the Russian naval base in the Crimea, which was supposed to be vulnerable to an amphibious operation. As a matter of fact, it took nearly a year's fighting and the mobilization of armies on a continental scale for this amphibious operation to succeed.

It takes two to make a war. Russian strength in the Near East lay in her proximity; her strength in the European balance lay in her army. Her naval power in the Black Sea was a secondary affair; and it could always be checked if the British and French fleets, or even the British fleet alone, passed the Straits. If the Russians had abandoned Sebastopol and sealed off the Crimea, the Western allies would have scored a success of prestige; but Russia would have been weaker than before. The allies would have cruised undisturbed in the Black Sea until their position became ridiculous; they would then have retired, and Russia's pressure on Turkey could have been resumed. But autocratic monarchies also have their prestige. The Tsar did not grasp that if the allies failed to defeat him, he had won; whereas, whatever efforts he made at Sebastopol, he could not defeat the allies. Russia's military strength lies in withdrawal; but this has always to be imposed upon her by her enemies, instead of being a conscious choice. Alexander I fought Napoleon at Austerlitz and even wanted to fight on the frontier in 1812; Stalin was only saved from catastrophe on the frontier in 1941 by being caught unprepared. In the Crimean War, the Tsar obligingly provided the maritime powers with the battlefield which they could never have found for themselves. Instead of being withdrawn, the Russian armies in Sebastopol were reinforced; and Russia exhausted herself for the sake of the maritime powers. The allies lamented that they had not taken Sebastopol by a *coup de main* when they landed in 1854; if they had, there would have been no Crimean War and nothing would have been achieved at all. For the essence of war is not to take this point or that, but to destroy, or at least to weaken, the military strength of the enemy. This was accomplished by the year's fighting in front of Sebastopol. The Russian armies were greatly weakened; Russia's military prestige lessened; most of all, Russia's economic resources were intolerably strained. It took Russia a generation to recover from the effort of the Crimean War; and in this generation Europe was remade without Russian interference.

The defeat of the Russian armies, and the weakening of Russian power, were the real result of the Crimean War; but this was a result too vague to satisfy the victorious allies. Their victory had to be translated into a treaty of peace; yet they had no clear idea what this treaty should contain. As on other occasions, the Western powers knew what they were fighting against, not what they were fighting for. They were fighting against Russia; and their real wish was that Russia should cease to exist or – what amounts to the same thing – become a modest and satisfied member of an Anglo-French world. Napoleon III was prepared to accept the logic of this wish. When Sebastopol fell, he proposed to the British government a programme which would sweep Russia from Europe and destroy her as a Great

Power – the programme of full national reconstruction, especially
of Poland, which would incidentally make France supreme
in Europe. The British government had the exactly opposite
aim: they had wished to destroy Russian supremacy in Europe
without putting French supremacy in its place. Yet on the other
hand they were the more eager of the two to continue the war
until a 'decision' had been reached. A characteristic compromise
followed. Each accepted the other's negative: the war was
brought to an end, without any positive war-aims being drawn
up.

This is not to say that the Crimean War accomplished nothing,
or even that the Treaty of Paris contained nothing of moment.
Apart from the weakening of Russian power, which could not
be put into a treaty, the Crimean War had two achievements,
one which lasted for nearly eighty years, the other for fifteen
years. The more permanent outcome, as things go in international affairs, was the independence of Romania, freeing the
mouth of the Danube from either Russian or Austrian control.
The Russian Army had withdrawn in July 1854; the Austrian
Army had taken its place, and the Austrians had hoped to annex
Romania. But they would not pay the French price, which was
to give up Italy; therefore they had to withdraw in their turn,
and Romania became a genuinely independent state, a buffer
between Russian interests and those of central Europe, until the
time of Stalin and Hitler.

The more prized achievement of the Treaty of Paris was the
'neutralization' of the Black Sea. Russia was forbidden to
maintain a fleet in the Black Sea, or to rebuild her naval
arsenals; it is true that the same restrictions were imposed on
Turkey, but since the Turks could maintain a fleet in the Sea of
Marmara they could always dominate the Black Sea in time of
war. The neutralization clauses of the Treaty of Paris were a
rehearsal for the demilitarization of the Rhineland in the Treaty
of Versailles, and equally futile. Either Russia accepted them
because she feared England and France; in that case she would
repudiate them when she ceased to fear England or France.

Alternatively Russia accepted them because she had changed her ways and given up aggression against Turkey; in that case they were unnecessary. The British and French would not keep their fleets in the Black Sea indefinitely; they were not even sure that they would remain indefinitely on good terms. Hence they tried to make the Russians promise that they would continue to behave as though the allied fleets were still in the Black Sea when in fact they had been long withdrawn. A treaty of peace can only define the conditions of the present; it cannot bind the future. This the Russians demonstrated fifteen years later, when they repudiated the Black Sea clauses of the Treaty of Paris. The British doctrine of the sanctity of treaties was upheld only by the pious pretence of a conference in London, at which the powers, to no one's surprise, confirmed what Russia had already done. The neutralization clauses taught a lesson which was ignored in 1919: if you wish to perpetuate a military victory, you must perpetuate the balance of forces which produced that victory.

The Crimean War was, in short, a war that did not come off, a war without a decision. But that was itself the decision. Though Russian strength was not broken, Russian influence in Europe was lessened. Though French prestige was increased, France did not become dominant in Europe. Napoleon III thought he had freed his hands in order to remodel Italy and Germany to his own taste; it turned out that Italy and Germany had freed their own hands to remodel themselves against him. Cavour and Bismarck, not Napoleon III, were the real victors of the Crimean War. If there were a moral to be drawn from the Crimean War which might apply to the present, it would be this: in a war between Russia and the West, it is the powers which keep out who will be the real gainers. Last time it gave Prussia mastery of Germany.

For the British, the Crimean War, though superficially inconclusive, was less of a disappointment than it was to Napoleon III. They had set out to lessen Russian power; and they had succeeded. Later on, they imagined that they had intended to give Turkey the chance of reforming herself; and were correspondingly embittered when no reform followed. Nevertheless, the Crimean War brought real gains to the British. The balance of power in Europe was strengthened, not overthrown; and Great Britain did not need to intervene in a continental war for sixty years thereafter. Two generations of peace are something to be thankful for; it is more than we have had in our lifetime.

John Bright and the Crimean War

This was first given as a lecture at the John Rylands Library, Manchester, and published by the Library in 1954. Alan Taylor wrote of it: 'The lecture was the only one I ever gave with a prepared script. It was an offshoot from The Struggle for Mastery in Europe 1848–1918. *If I were to deliver the lecture again, I should be less critical of John Bright and more critical of British policy.'*

*   *   *

John Bright was the greatest of all parliamentary orators. He had many political successes. Along with Richard Cobden, he conducted the campaign which led to the repeal of the Corn Laws. He did more than any other man to prevent the intervention of this country on the side of the South during the American Civil War, and he headed the reform agitation of 1867 which brought the industrial working class within the pale of the constitution. It was Bright who made possible the Liberal party of Gladstone, Asquith and Lloyd George, and the alliance between middle-class idealism and trade unionism, which he promoted, still lives in the present-day Labour Party. Yet his noblest work, as certainly his greatest speeches, were made in a campaign which failed – a campaign which brought him much unpopularity and led finally to a mental collapse; his opposition to the Crimean War. His attitude caused him to lose his parliamentary seat at Manchester in 1857 and so severed his political connection with this city for ever. Bright blamed the merchant princes of Manchester for his defeat, and it is therefore especially fitting that we should look again at Bright's stand during the Crimean War on a foundation established to commemorate one of the greatest of these merchant princes.

I have personal reasons, too, for this gesture of atonement. At

Bright's old school, where I was educated, there was an annual prize for a Bright oration, and I have heard his great speeches against the Crimean War recited a score of times in the school library which bears his name. I, in revolt as usual against my surroundings, sought only something to Bright's discredit and proposed to offer one of his speeches against the Factory Acts. But these were not included in his collected speeches, and I was not used, as I am now, to going through the columns of old *Hansards*. I therefore remained silent, and it is only now, thirty years later, that I come to repeat the greatest sentences ever uttered in any parliamentary assembly. I am not, however, concerned to defend Bright, much as I now admire him. I have also learnt to admire the diplomatic skill and judgement of 'the aged charlatan', Palmerston. Bright said of him:

I regard him as a man who has experience, but who with experience has not gained wisdom – as a man who has age, but who, with age, has not the gravity of age, and who, now occupying the highest seat of power, has – and I say it with pain – not appeared influenced by a due sense of the responsibility that belongs to that elevated position.

I do not think that any historian who has examined the record of Palmerston's foreign policy would now endorse that judgement, though he would still be struck by Palmerston's jocular self-confidence and even occasionally by his levity. It is my intention – and I can say in all sincerity that I did not know when I started how the conclusion would work out – to examine Bright's criticism of the Crimean War in the light of later events and of the more detailed knowledge which we now possess, rather than to vindicate or condemn him.

When I began this inquiry, I was struck and indeed surprised by the material for my theme. I have some experience of public agitation on issues of foreign policy. I have sat on committees for aid to Spain and Czechoslovakia and for Anglo-Soviet friendship. I can remember vaguely the pacifist movement of the First World War. I expected to find the same hubbub of public meetings, pamphlets, letters to the press, articles in newspapers and periodicals, which serve as the undertone for debates in parliament. Gladstone used all these weapons in his attacks on Disraeli's Eastern policy only twenty years later. Indeed, he did better than we. He used to stick his head out of the railway carriage and address waiting crowds at every station he passed through. Here was Bright engaged in the greatest political conflict of his career, yet he used none of the means that we should think essential. He did not write a pamphlet. He did not address a single letter to the newspapers. He wrote one letter to Absalom Watkin, designed for publication and stating his case against the war, on 29 October 1854, when the war had already been raging for six months. He attended in all three public meetings, over a period of nearly two years, and all in Manchester. They were designed to explain his attitude to his constituents, not to appeal to public opinion. The first, held on 18 December 1854, was not organized by Bright, but to declare against him. Neither he nor his opponents could get a hearing. At the second, on 5 April 1855, he spoke for an hour. The third was held on 28 January 1856, after the peace preliminaries had been signed. Bright, speaking for two hours, defended his past conduct and collapsed at the end. Thus he made one public speech against the war while it was on, and this was to a limited audience.

We have therefore to look solely at Bright's speeches in the House of Commons. And here is another surprising thing. He never spoke against the war before it was declared. Let me refresh your memory with some dates. The diplomatic conflict between Russia and the Western powers, Great Britain and France, began at Constantinople in May 1853. Russian forces occupied the mouth of the Danube in July. The allied fleets passed the Straits in October. They entered the Black Sea in December. Throughout all this time there are only two passing references to the crisis in Bright's diary, one at the end of May, one in July. In October he addressed a conference of the Peace Society, but mainly on generalities with little reference to immediate events. Early in 1854, the crisis grew graver; on 27 March war was declared. Again Bright remained silent. On 15 March he wrote a letter to Lord Aberdeen, the prime minister, not for publication, arguing in favour of peace. His first speech was on 31 March, four days after the declaration of war. It was a speech to clear his conscience, not to change the course of policy. 'I am unwilling to lose this opportunity . . . of clearing myself from any portion of the responsibility which attaches to those who support the policy which the Government has adopted.' At the end, he strikes the same note:

For myself, I do not trouble myself whether my conduct in Parliament is popular or not. I care only that it shall be wise and just as regards the permanent interests of my country, and I despise from the bottom of my heart the man who speaks a word in favour of this war, or of any war which he believes might have been avoided, merely because the press and a portion of the people urge the Government to enter into it.

Bright did not speak again on the war until 22 December 1854. This speech, too, was vindication, not advocacy – vindication this time more of Cobden, who had been attacked by Lord John Russell, than of himself. And there is the same note of clearing his conscience:

Let it not be said that I am alone in my condemnation of this war, and of this incapable and guilty Administration. And, even if I were alone, if mine were a solitary voice, raised amid the din of arms and the clamour of a venal press, I should have the consolation I have tonight – and which I trust will be mine to the last moment of my existence – the priceless consolation that no word of mine has tended to promote the squandering of my country's treasure or the spilling of one single drop of my country's blood.

In February 1855, negotiations for peace – abortive, as it turned out – were opened at Vienna. On 23 February, Bright made a short speech, appealing for an immediate armistice if the negotiations showed promise of success. Though this speech contains his most celebrated oratorical passage – the Angel of Death has been abroad throughout the land – it had a practical aim, and for once Bright addressed both Palmerston and Lord John Russell in conciliatory, friendly terms. Finally, when the negotiations at Vienna had failed, Bright spoke again on 7 June. He argued that the proposed peace terms would have been satisfactory and that there was no purpose in continuing the war. But this time he did not merely protest or clear his conscience. He appealed to the House to revolt against Palmerston's government and against the bellicose press:

If every man in this House, who doubts the policy that is being pursued, would boldly say so in this House and out of it, it would not be in the power of the press to mislead the people as it has done for the last twelve months . . . We are the depositaries of the power and the guardians of the interests of a great nation and of an ancient monarchy. Why should we not fully measure our responsibility? Why should we not disregard the small-minded ambition that struggles for place? and why should we not, by a faithful, just, and earnest policy, restore, as I believe we may, tranquillity to Europe and prosperity to the country so dear to us?

Thus Bright spoke in all only four times on the war in a period of nearly two years. Only his first speech and his letter to Absalom Watkin stated his case against the war at length. Indeed we may say that his reputation as an opponent of the war was gained as much by silent and sustained disapproval as by his speeches. Before I discuss his criticism of the war, I should like to turn aside for a moment to consider why Bright was relatively so inactive – so much more silent, for example, than at the time of the American Civil War a few years later. In part, he felt it hopeless to contend against the war-fever of the press. Cobden felt this even more strongly. He said in 1862:

I was so convinced of the utter uselessness of raising one's voice in opposition to war when it has once begun, that I made up my mind that so long as I was in political life, should a war again break out between England and a Great Power, I would never open my mouth upon the subject from the time the first gun was fired until the peace was made.

This is a surprising tribute to the power of the press, the more surprising when one reflects that the total newspaper-reading public in England did not at that time number 100,000. Perhaps this is itself the explanation. In 1854 Bright sat for a middle-class constituency and thought only of his middle-class voters. His only public speech was an explanation to his constituents, not a general appeal. After 1858, when he sat for Birmingham, he addressed himself to working-class opinion, regardless either of the middle-class voters or the middle-class press. Indeed, it was the Crimean War which helped to set Bright on the democratic path. To adapt George III's remark to William Pitt, it taught him to look elsewhere than the House of Commons, or even the electorate, for the will of the people.

Of course, this was not new to Bright. He was always more of a man of the people than Cobden. Cobden lived in Sussex, a failure as a businessman. Bright never moved from Rochdale, next door to his mill. Their paths diverged after the repeal of the Corn Laws. Free trade had always been an international cause for Cobden – witness his triumphal tour of Europe in 1846 – and he went on to preach international arbitration and disarmament. Bright had been interested in the practical issue of cheap bread, and he turned from free trade to parliamentary reform – a course of which Cobden disapproved. This led Bright largely to ignore foreign affairs. It is no accident that Cobden spoke in the great Don Pacifico debate in 1850 and Bright did not – it was not his subject.

The early radicals thought in terms of criticizing the established government, not of superseding it. Witness again Cobden's remark that he could have had a great career in the United States, but that it was useless for him to harbour ambition in aristocratic England. Bright and Cobden assumed that England was fated to endure aristocratic misrule for many years – Cobden supposed at least during his lifetime. Bright gradually moved to the more constructive position that aristocratic rule could be ended and democracy take its place. His last Crimean War speech contains a first statement of this new attitude. Yet, even now, it was the promise of a political leader of the right views from within the closed circle which gave him greater hope. This leader was Gladstone, after his resignation from Palmerston's government at the beginning of 1855. Here was the first hint of the alliance between Gladstone and Bright which triumphed in 1868 – an alliance in which Gladstone was the statesman and Bright the agitator.

Bright therefore learnt his way slowly in foreign affairs, beginning with a few radical prejudices and gradually examining the practical issues. Observe: I do not say Quaker prejudices. Though Bright spoke often – as anyone would – of the horrors and bloodshed of war, he never used pacifist arguments against it. Indeed, he was not a pacifist. He supported the forcible suppression of the Indian mutiny. He urged the North to continue the American Civil War to decisive victory, when even Cobden favoured compromise. Bright doubted, I think, the relevance of Quakerism to public life. Dr Trevelyan remarks casually that Bright never spoke in Meeting, but draws no moral from it. Perhaps only someone of Quaker stock and upbringing can appreciate its significance. The Society of Friends was still 'quietist', concerned with the inner light, not with social duty, and, in addition, there was a distinction between 'ministers' and other members of the Society which has now almost disappeared. I do not say that Bright ever ceased to regard himself as a full member of the Society; but he thought that, by entering politics, he had made himself the humblest of members and, conversely, he kept Quakerism out of his politics. Or rather, though he kept out Quaker principles, he used Quaker methods. His speeches, for all their oratory, rely on fact and argument as much as on emotional appeal. As Bright said in answer to Palmerston: 'I am not afraid of discussing the war with the noble Lord on his own principles. I understand the Blue Books as well as he' – a claim that was fully justified.

Though Bright did not condemn war from pacifism, he certainly condemned it on grounds of economy. His Crimean War speeches all speak of the disturbance to trade and the increase of taxes. He has often been blamed for this. Tennyson wrote at the time of

> The broad-brimmed hawker of holy things,
> Whose ear is cramm'd with his cotton, and rings
> Even in dreams to the chink of his pence.

I should add, in fairness to Tennyson, that there is much other internal evidence in 'Maud' to suggest that the hero, or narrator, of it was mad. Sir Llewellyn Woodward, who refers to 'the prosy and, at times, repellent religiosity of his letters and diaries', discredits Bright with the comic quotation: 'Our carpet trade grievously injured by war raising the price of tow.' Sir Llewellyn Woodward, I suspect, had heard that Bright was in the cotton trade and did not appreciate that John Bright and Bros manufactured carpets, as they still do. What therefore more natural than that he should make a business note in his private diary? Bright showed during the American Civil War that he could rise above arguments addressed to his economic interests or those of Lancashire. The story of Bright's commercialism, which brings together not only Tennyson and Sir Llewellyn Woodward but such strange companions as Palmerston and Karl Marx, springs largely – as Bright himself said – from the inability to answer his more serious arguments.

In any case, it is well to bear in mind the composition of the House of Commons, in which Bright delivered his speeches. Neither of the two great parties – the Conservatives under Disraeli and the Whigs led, if that is not too dignified a term, by Lord John Russell – had a majority. The balance was held by the Peelites – the remnant of those Conservatives who had followed Peel over free trade in 1846 – and the radicals. These last two had much in common so far as economic doctrine was concerned, despite their difference of social background. The government of Lord Aberdeen, which began the Crimean War, was a coalition of Peelites and Whigs, with one radical member, Molesworth, and possessing radical support. Palmerston's government, which took its place in 1855, was Whig and radical, the Peelites in uneasy and discredited neutrality. To whom then was Bright to appeal, if he was to achieve a practical effect at all? Not to the Conservatives. For, though they claimed to oppose Palmerston, Bright had an incurable distrust of Disraeli. Remember his reply when Disraeli said to him after the 'Angel of Death' speech: 'I would give all I ever had to have made that speech you made just now.' 'Well, you might have made it if you had been honest.' He could not appeal to the Whigs. He regarded Russell and Palmerston as the principal authors of the war and directed his main arguments against the Whig doctrine of the balance of power. Besides, the Whigs had a long record of frivolity and incapacity in regard to finance.

Hence, his practical object was to persuade the Peelites and radicals to take advantage of their balancing position. They could bring the Whigs to heel if they wished to do so. His economic arguments were designed for the Peelites, as were his recollections of Peel himself. 'I recollect when Sir Robert Peel addressed the House on a dispute which threatened hostilities with the United States – I recollect the gravity of his countenance, the solemnity of his tone, his whole demeanour showing that he felt in his soul the responsibility that rested on him.' This appeal certainly had its effect on Gladstone, particularly after his resignation from office in February 1855. But Bright had to appeal especially to the radicals and free-trade liberals – his former allies who had now abandoned their principles of economy for the sake of fighting a war of liberation against Russia. This is an essential point, one lost sight of in later years, when the Eastern question came to be regarded as bound up with the route to India. The route to India had nothing to do with the Crimean War. The Danube, not the

Suez Canal, was the only waterway involved. The Crimean War was fought much more against Russia than in favour of Turkey. And it was fought not only in the name of the balance of power. Russia was regarded as the tyrant of Europe, the main prop of 'the Holy Alliance', and English radicals thought that they were now getting their own back for the Russian intervention which had helped to defeat the revolutions of 1848. The veteran radical, Joseph Hume, who had moved a reduction in the army estimates every year since 1823, voted for the estimates in 1854. There could be no more striking evidence of the radical conversion.

The radical crusading spirit against Russia could be illustrated in a thousand ways. I will limit myself to one quotation from a correspondent of Cobden's:

This, then, is my creed. I look upon Russia as the personification of Despotism – the apostle of Legitimacy. In the present state of Poland and Hungary we see her work ... Such a power can be curbed only by war, and must be so curbed sooner or later, if Europe is to remain free ... If we believe that God wills the liberty and happiness of mankind, how can we doubt that we are doing God's work in fighting for liberty against aggression?

Perhaps I should add that this is a genuine quotation from a letter of November 1855, and is not taken from yesterday's newspaper. Bright's principal arguments were directed against this radical enthusiasm. Why was he not affected by it? It was, I think, a lesson learnt from Cobden. Cobden had always preached non-intervention in European affairs. What is more, he had always looked with a friendly eye on Russian expansion. In a pamphlet which he wrote as early as 1836, he asked: 'Can any one doubt that, if the Government of St Petersburg were transferred to the shores of the Bosphorus, a splendid and substantial European city would, in less than twenty years, spring up in the place of those huts which now constitute the capital of Turkey?' In this pamphlet Cobden even challenged the radical predilection for Poland. Russian rule, he wrote, 'has been followed by an increase in the amount of peace, wealth, liberty, civilization and happiness, enjoyed by the great mass of the people ... The Polish people, though far from prosperous, have enjoyed many benefits by their change of government.'

Bright had not always shared Cobden's view. As a young man, he wrote a poem in favour of Poland – a very bad poem – which he once quoted with startling effect in a parliamentary speech. But he came in time to accept Cobden's belief that free trade would civilize every country, including Russia, and that political freedom would follow of itself. He wrote to Cobden in 1851, at the time of Kossuth's visit to England:

I shall go against any notion of *fighting* for Hungary or any other country ... By perfecting our own institutions, by promoting the intelligence, morality and health of our own country, and by treating all other nations in a just and generous and courteous manner, we shall do more for humanity than by commissioning Palmerston to regenerate Hungary by fleets in the Black Sea and the Baltic.

He struck the same note in April 1854: 'they confound the blowing up of ships and the slaughter of thousands with the cause of freedom, as if there were any connection in matters wholly apart'. This was a clear doctrine of non-intervention, applicable to all wars of intervention anywhere at any time – applicable, for instance, as much to Italy as to the Balkans. But in regard to the Crimean War Bright did not really take a purely neutral attitude. Not only did he think that nothing good could be achieved by a Russian victory over Turkey. He dismissed all claims that the Ottoman Empire had reformed, or was capable of reform, and he referred to 'the natural solution' – 'which is, that the Mahometan power in Europe should eventually succumb to the growing power of the Christian population of the Turkish territories'. Observe that he does not refer to the national conflict between the Balkan peoples and their Ottoman rulers, and indeed he seems to have been unaware at this time that Turkey-in-Europe was inhabited by peoples of different, even conflicting, nationalities. He anticipated the establishment in Constantinople of 'a Christian state'. The Christian population would 'grow more rapidly in numbers, in industry, in wealth, in intelligence, and in political power'. Why did Bright believe this? He knew no more about Turkey than anyone else. No independent reporters had visited Turkey, and Bright took his information on conditions there from the Blue Books. His faith in the Balkan Christians rested solely on dogma – above all, on the dogma that they were more capable of absorbing the lessons of free trade. The dogma was well founded. All the same, there is a striking contrast with the discussions on the Eastern question later in the century – discussions which were based on reliable first-hand information and on awareness of the national issue.

Bright claimed to approach the Crimean War with detachment. In reality he came to it with his mind made up. First he was against the war; then he discovered the arguments to justify his opposition. But this is perhaps to anticipate what should be a conclusion. Let me turn to the arguments which he used. It will, I think, be convenient to put them into two categories, though Bright did not make this logical distinction: arguments against any war over the Eastern question – perhaps even against any war at all – and arguments against this particular war, based on the Blue Books which recounted the diplomatic events of 1853. Incidentally, here is a practical reason why Bright only spoke so late in the day. The first Blue Book was published on 17 March 1854. Bright spoke against the war a fortnight later. He could not have made his case earlier. This speech gives Bright's main arguments against the war, and I shall analyse it in detail.

He begins, quite rightly, with the French demands of 1852 in favour of the Latin Church at Jerusalem. Then, he says, Russia 'required (and this I understand to be the real ground of the quarrel) that Turkey should define by treaty, or convention, or by a simple note, or memorandum, what was conceded, and what were the rights of Russia'. Turkey, he insists, was decaying, and Russia was bound to 'interfere, or have a strong interest, in the internal policy of the Ottoman Empire'. This Russian interference was, of course, the mission of Prince Menshikov to Constantinople. Here Bright made his first substantial point. On 5 May 1853, according to him, Lord Stratford de Redcliffe, British ambassador at Constantinople, insisted that the Turks should refuse the Russian demands. 'He urged upon the Turkish Government the necessity of resistance to any of the demands of Russia, promising the armed assistance of England, whatever consequences might ensue.' He makes the same point in the letter to Absalom Watkin.

But for the English minister at Constantinople and the Cabinet at home the dispute would have settled itself, and the last note of Prince Menshikoff would have been accepted . . . Lord Stratford de Redcliffe held private interviews with the Sultan, insisted on his rejection of all terms of accommodation with Russia, and promised him the armed assistance of England if war should arise.

Here then is the start of Bright's case. The Turks wanted to sign the Menshikov note; the French government did not object; 'it was through the interference of Lord Stratford de Redcliffe – acting, I presume, in accordance with instructions from our Cabinet, and promising the intervention of the fleets – that the rejection of that note was secured'. On the basis of Bright's argument Stratford de Redcliffe has been branded with responsibility for the war from that day to this. But does our later knowledge confirm the accusation? I am afraid it does not. Firstly, there was never a secret interview of 5 May, and Bright himself subsequently dropped the story. Far from encouraging the Turks to resist, Stratford advised them to meet the Russian demands fully over the Holy Places; he took a different line only when Menshikov demanded the recognition of a Russian protectorate over all Orthodox Christians in the Ottoman Empire. The Turks would have resisted this claim with or without Stratford's advice – which was, in any case, directed to compromise, not rejection, and even now he gave them no promise at all of British support. Moreover, Russia's demands were not as innocent as Bright made out. Menshikov wanted to make Russia supreme at Constantinople – 'to end the infernal dictatorship of this Redcliffe' and to put that of Russia in its place. The Russian claims were based on an interpretation of the treaty of Kutchuk Kainardji which the Russian experts themselves knew to be false, and in the following year Tsar Nicholas I admitted that he had not realized what he was doing. 'His conduct in 1853', he said, 'would have been different but for the error into which he had been led.' The Russians were, in fact, demanding a protectorate over Turkey, and the Turks were bound to refuse, if they were to keep their independence at all. Of course, Great Britain could have washed her hands of Turkish independence, but this was not Bright's case at this stage. He claimed that the Russian demands were harmless. Stratford judged better.

At all events, Menshikov failed. Russia broke off relations with Turkey and, in July, occupied the Danubian principalities. Bright called this 'impolitic and immoral' in his letter to Absalom Watkin; he did not condemn it in his parliamentary speeches. The other powers – England, France, Austria, and Prussia – then drew up in August 'the Vienna Note' which they offered as a settlement of the quarrel. It was accepted by the Russians in, says Bright, 'the most frank and unreserved manner'. The Turks had not been shown the note beforehand. When it reached them, they saw at once the interpretation that Russia would place on it and refused it. This certainly reflected sadly on the diplomatic gifts of the negotiators at Vienna. But surely the question is – were the Turks right in their suspicions? Nesselrode, the Russian chancellor, proved that they were. Early in September, he issued an interpretation of the Vienna Note, claiming that it gave to Russia the full protectorate over the Orthodox Christians allegedly stipulated in the treaty of Kutchuk Kainardji. What does Bright say to this? Merely, 'I very much doubt whether Count Nesselrode placed any meaning upon the note which it did not fairly warrant, and it is impossible to say whether he really differed at all from the actual intentions of the four Ambassadors at Vienna.' Again, 'this circular could make no real difference in the note itself'. Now this was being more Russian than the Russians. In October the Tsar met Francis Joseph, Emperor of Austria, at Olomouc – the place which was then called Olmütz. He confessed that Nesselrode had made a 'forced interpretation' and now offered to withdraw it. In other words, the Russians had tried to cheat, and the Turks had caught them out. No one would deduce this from Bright's speech.

The meeting at Olomouc offered the one serious chance of avoiding war. Nicholas I was alarmed and in a conciliatory mood; he withdrew, for the time being, the demands that he had previously made. The British government rejected his offer; they insisted that the Russian troops should be withdrawn from the principalities; and when Turkey declared war independently a couple of weeks later, they allowed themselves to be dragged into war on her side. Bright had a strong case here. He would have said to the Turks: 'If you persist in taking your own course, we cannot be involved in the difficulties to which it may give rise, but must leave you to take the consequences of your own acts.' But he weakens this case irremediably when he says a few sentences previously: 'It is impossible fairly to doubt the sincerity of the desire for peace manifested by the Emperor of Russia.' This is just what it was possible to doubt from the record of the previous months. Desire for peace perhaps; but equally a desire to get his own way at Constantinople even at the risk of war. Bright failed to allow for the suspicions which Russian policy had caused and for the Russian aggressiveness which the hesitation and muddle of British policy encouraged. Indeed, the war would have been avoided if Great Britain had followed the resolute line advocated by Palmerston and Russell – whom Bright blamed for the war. The responsibility for the war lay with the pacific Lord Aberdeen, whom Bright admired,

and Aberdeen later admitted it himself. Like King David, he
refused to rebuild a church on his estates. 'But the word of the
Lord came to me, saying, Thou hast shed blood abundantly
and hast made great war: thou shalt not build an house unto
my name.'

So much for Bright's criticism of the diplomatic background
to the Crimean War. But his criticism did not stop at diplomatic
detail. Indeed, this was not much more than a *tour de force*
designed to show that he could meet ministers on their own
ground. In reality, Bright did not accept this ground. He
rejected the basic assumptions of British diplomacy. The major
part of his speech of 31 March 1854 shows this. He turns from
the Vienna Note and the Olomouc meeting to challenge the
doctrine of the balance of power.

He has great fun quoting the opinions of the great Whigs –
Burke, Fox and Lord Holland – against any idea of supporting
Turkey; opinions that must have much embarrassed Lord John
Russell, the last of the great Whigs, yet an enthusiastic supporter
of the Crimean War. Bright continues: 'If this phrase of the
"balance of power" is to be always an argument for war, the
pretence for war will never be wanting, and peace can never be
secure.' 'This whole notion of the "balance of power" is a
mischievous delusion which has come down to us from past
times; we ought to drive it from our minds, and to consider the
solemn question of peace or war on more clear, more definite,
and on far higher principles than any that are involved in the
phrase the "balance of power".' This last sentence seems to
promise that Bright will at any rate hint at an alternative
foreign policy, but he does not do so. He merely goes on
analysing the excuses for the Crimean War and demolishing
them.

The integrity and independence of the Ottoman Empire? But
Turkey cannot be independent with three foreign armies on her
soil. If the government had wanted to preserve the independence
of Turkey, they would have advised the Turks to accept either
Menshikov's conditions or the Vienna Note. 'I will not insult

you by asking whether, under such circumstances, that "integrity and independence" would not have been a thousand times more secure than it is at this hour?' This was exactly the argument – if you will forgive a contemporary allusion – with which Lord Halifax justified the desertion of Czechoslovakia in 1938: 'I have always felt that to fight a war for one, two, or three years to protect or re-create something that you knew you could not directly protect, and probably could never re-create, did not make sense.'

Next, what about curbing Russian aggression? Bright answers that it cannot be done. 'Russia will be always there – always powerful, always watchful, and actuated by the same motives of ambition, either of influence or of territory, which are supposed to have moved her in past times.' 'It is a delusion to suppose that you can dismember Russia – that you can blot her from the map of Europe – that you can take guarantees from her, as some seem to imagine, as easily as you take bail from an offender, who would otherwise go to prison for three months. England and France cannot do this with a stroke of the pen, and the sword will equally fail if the attempt be made.'

Finally, 'how are the interests of England involved in this question? . . . It is not a question of sympathy with any other State . . . It is not my duty to make this country the knight-errant of the human race, and to take upon herself the protection of the thousand millions of human beings who have been permitted by the Creator of all things to people this planet.' On the other hand, taxes have gone up, trade is injured, thousands of men are being killed. 'My doctrine would have been non-intervention in this case. The danger of the Russian power was a phantom; the necessity of permanently upholding the Mahometan rule in Europe is an absurdity . . . The evils of non-intervention were remote and vague, and could neither be weighed nor described in any accurate terms. The good we can judge something of already, by estimating the cost of a contrary policy.' (These two sentences are from the letter to Absalom Watkin, but they fit in with the argument of Bright's speech.)

Finally, Bright moves on to assert the general merits of non-intervention for this country 'where her interests were not directly and obviously assailed'. If we had adopted non-intervention for the last seventy years:

This country might have been a garden, every dwelling might have been of marble, and every person who treads its soil might have been sufficiently educated. We should indeed have had less of military glory. We might have had neither Trafalgar nor Waterloo; but we should have set the high example of a Christian nation, free in its institutions, courteous and just in its conduct towards all foreign States, and resting its policy on the unchangeable foundations of Christian morality.

Every orator must be forgiven something in his peroration.

The speech of 31 March 1854, which I have analysed at length, gives Bright's considered case against the Crimean War. The two speeches of 22 December 1854 and of 23 February 1855 do not add anything to that case. The one, as I said earlier, was a defence of Cobden; the other urged an armistice during the negotiations at Vienna. We can leave them aside when considering Bright's views. If we were considering his oratory, it would be a different matter; for they contain his most moving and also – a characteristic sometimes forgotten – his most humorous passages. The speech of 7 June 1855, however, raises some new points. In it Bright discusses not the causes of the war, but how it should end. I must turn aside to explain the diplomatic background. In the autumn of 1854 Austria – not herself a combatant, but wooed by the Western allies – drafted 'Four Points' as reasonable terms of peace. These Four Points were accepted by England and France in the hope of drawing Austria into the war; then they were accepted by Russia in the better hope of keeping her out. The four powers met in conference at Vienna in March and April 1855 in order to define the Four Points more closely and to turn them into practical terms. There was no difficulty about three of them.

Russia was to give up her protectorate of the Danubian principalities; the freedom of navigation of the Danube was to be secured; and the Christian populations of the Ottoman Empire were to be put under a general European guarantee, instead of under that of Russia. Incidentally, these three points were already an answer to the assertion that war accomplishes nothing. Russia would never have agreed to them without the Crimean War. I don't venture to determine whether they were worth a war, but that is a different question.

The dispute at Vienna came over Point III. This provided that the Straits Convention of 1841 should be revised 'in the interests of the balance of power'. In other words, Turkey was to be given some sort of security against Russia's naval preponderance in the Black Sea. Lord John Russell, the English representative, and Drouyn de Lhuys, the French representative, went to Vienna with instructions that they could agree to one of two things: either the Russian fleet in the Black Sea should be limited or the Black Sea should be neutralized altogether. Gorchakov, the Russian delegate at Vienna, refused to accept either. Buol, the Austrian foreign minister, then came forward with another proposal: equipoise. The Russians could keep their existing fleet, but, if they increased it, the British and French could send ships into the Black Sea to balance the increase. Neither Russell nor Drouyn was authorized to agree to this scheme, but Drouyn was afraid of missing any chance of peace, and Russell was afraid of getting out of step with Drouyn. Both therefore accepted 'equipoise'. When they returned home, Napoleon III rejected the compromise and the British government followed suit. The peace conference was abandoned, and the war was renewed. This was a bad, muddled piece of diplomacy. It is hardly surprising that Bright saw his chance and took it.

There is much the same pattern as in the earlier speech of 31 March 1854. He begins by meeting ministers on their own ground and attacking their incompetence; gradually he shifts his emphasis and moves over to more general principles. He

asks what the war is about. It is not a war for Poland or for
Hungary or for Italy. It is solely a war – and here he quotes
ministers themselves – for the security of Turkey. Very well
then, we want to reduce Russian preponderance. 'How is that
preponderance to cease?' Bright looks first at the idea of neutral-
izing the Black Sea and dismisses it with vehemence. 'I conceive
that was so monstrous a proposition, in the present condition of
Europe, that I am surprised it should have been entertained for
a moment by any sensible man.' He says much the same of
limiting the Russian fleet. 'If any diplomatist from this country,
under the same circumstances as Russia was placed in, had
consented to terms such as the noble Lord had endeavoured to
force upon Russia – I say, that if he entered the door of this
House, he would be met by one universal shout of execration,
and, as a public man, would be ruined for ever.' Bright has an
alternative: the Straits should be opened to everybody:

Our fleets would visit the Black Sea in the course of the season, and
the Russian Black Sea fleet, if it chose, would visit the Mediterranean.
There would be no sort of pretence for wrangling about the Straits;
and the balance of power – if I may use the term – between the fleets
of Russia, France and England would be probably the best guarantee
that could be offered for the security of Constantinople and Turkey,
so far as they are in danger of aggression either from the Black Sea or
the Mediterranean.

   This is a surprising proposal. I say nothing of the fact that
Russia would have rejected it emphatically, whatever
Gorchakov might hint at Vienna. But Bright, in his eagerness to
discredit imposing any terms on Russia – terms that certainly
could only be imposed after her defeat – is reduced in practice
to the crudest *realpolitik*. He says in effect: no treaty stipulations
are of any value; the only effective course is to maintain a
balance of power, a balance of actual force, by keeping a large
fleet in the eastern Mediterranean. If Palmerston had said this,
what an outcry Bright would have made; what assertions of
Russian good faith; what cries, and justified cries, about the

weight of taxes to maintain such a fleet. It has often been said that non-intervention and splendid isolation are luxuries dependent on naval supremacy; but Bright never came so near admitting it as in this passage. His judgement of fact, however, was not correct. Six months after he made this speech the Russians accepted the neutralization of the Black Sea, which he had dismissed as a monstrous proposition. It is true that they denounced it again fifteen years later when the diplomatic structure of Europe had changed fundamentally. Nevertheless Bright underrated what a power will agree to when it has been defeated.

The rest of Bright's speech moves away from these diplomatic questions. He points to the folly of saying that Austria must be preserved and yet trying to draw her into a war that would exhaust her; he warns against the danger of relying on France as an ally; he denounces the idea of defending the liberties of Europe:

What a notion a man must have of the duties of the . . . people living in these islands if he thinks . . . that the sacred treasure of the bravery, resolution, and unfaltering courage of the people of England is to be squandered in a contest . . . for the preservation of the independence of Germany, and of the integrity, civilization, and something else, of all Europe!

He quotes the things that Palmerston and Russell said against each other in the past. But his greatest emphasis is on the burden of taxation and the crippling effect which this will have in our competition with the United States.

Hon. Members may think this is nothing. They say it is a 'low' view of the case. But these things are the foundation of your national greatness, and of your national duration; and you may be following visionary phantoms in all parts of the world while your own country is becoming rotten within, and calamities may be in store for the monarchy and the nation of which now, it appears, you take no heed.

It may seem a little unfair to end the survey of Bright's speeches on this note, but it is the note on which he himself chose to end and, in the parliamentary circumstances of 1855, perhaps rightly. What are we to say, after this examination, of Bright's attitude towards the Crimean War? We are bound, I am sure, to admire the courage with which Bright expressed his views and still more the brilliance of his performance. If I had merely read to you one of his speeches, instead of trying to analyse them, you would certainly have been swept away and have been convinced, without further argument, that the Crimean War was all that Bright said – unnecessary, unjust, in short a crime. But do we feel the same if we escape from their spell? I have suggested, during the course of this lecture, that Bright was not always sound when he came to the details of diplomacy. It is difficult, when criticizing the government of your own country, not to skate over the faults of other governments, and Bright did not escape this danger. He was harsher towards Stratford de Redcliffe than to Prince Menshikov; professed more faith in the statements of Nesselrode than in those of Palmerston; gave the Russian, but not the British, government the benefit of the doubt. There was certainly much muddle and confusion in the diplomacy of the Crimean War, but, to judge from Bright's speeches, you would imagine that it was all on the British side. This one-sidedness is almost bound to happen in parliamentary speeches. You may achieve some effect by attacking your own government; you will achieve nothing by attacking foreign statesmen. In exactly the same way, Charles James Fox was often more charitable towards Bonaparte than towards William Pitt, and pacifists of the First World War, such as E D Morel, had more sympathy with German than with British imperialism.

One looks in vain in Bright's speeches for any satisfactory explanation of the causes of the Crimean War. He seems to suggest that it was due solely to newspaper agitation and to the irresponsibility of Palmerston and Russell. 'The country has been, I am afraid, the sport of their ancient rivalry; and I should be very sorry if it should be the victim of the policy which they have so long advocated.' Cobden was more cautious. He held that Russia, too, was 'much in the wrong' and therefore kept quiet, washing his hands, as it were, of both sides. Bright often implied that Russian expansion against Turkey was an unexceptionable, even a praiseworthy process. Not always. He said in his first speech: 'If I were a Russian, speaking in a Russian Parliament, I should denounce any aggression upon Turkey, as I now blame the policy of our own Government; and I greatly fear I should find myself in a minority, as I now find myself in a minority on this question.' But is not this justice a little more than even-handed? Does it not imply that to attack Turkey and to defend her are equally reprehensible and provocative? If Russian aggression, though deplorable, is inevitable, then is not resistance to this aggression equally inevitable? Or do we make allowances only one way? In the next Eastern crisis of 1876–8 Gladstone took a clearer and more consistent line. He held that the destruction of the Turkish Empire in Europe was eminently desirable and therefore wished Russia to succeed, preferably in association with England. Though he opposed the actual course of British policy, he offered a positive alternative. Bright's attitude was one of aloof neutrality.

He was not clear about this himself. In a speech to the Peace Society, which he made on 13 October 1853 – before the Crimean War broke out – he attacked the idea of war 'for the miserable, decrepit, moribund Government which is now enthroned, but which cannot long last, in the city of Constantinople'. Surely the logical conclusion from this should have been to cooperate in the Concert of Europe, as Gladstone later advocated. But Bright always denied that he favoured the Russian cause, and in a later speech on foreign policy, which he made on 29 October 1858, preached high-minded isolation. This country should have 'adequate and scientific means of defence'.

But I shall repudiate and denounce the expenditure of every shilling, the engagement of every man, the employment of every ship which has no object but intermeddling in the affairs of other countries.

He refused to admit that an active foreign policy could ever be justified. 'This foreign policy, this regard for "the liberties of Europe", this care at one time for "the Protestant interest", this excessive love for the "balance of power", is neither more nor less than a gigantic system of out-door relief for the aristocracy of Great Britain.' All foreign policy was unnecessary. Instead 'we have the unchangeable and eternal principles of the moral law to guide us, and only so far as we walk by that guidance can we be permanently a great nation, or our people a happy people'.

When Bright said this, he had left Manchester and was already the representative of Birmingham. This was symbolic. Though he seemed discredited while the Crimean War was on, he triumphed afterwards. By 1858 he was back in the House of Commons, and his version of the Crimean War was already being accepted. English people usually think their wars a mistake when they are over and they thought this of the Crimean War sooner than usual. As a matter of fact, it achieved its purpose rather better than most wars. Russia's control of the Danube mouth, which was the largest issue in the war, was recovered only in 1945, and Turkey, whose demise has been so often foretold, possesses Constantinople and the Straits to this day. I do not venture to say whether these achievements are desirable. Bright, however, said that they were impossible. Most Englishmen soon came to agree with him. It is Bright's version of the Crimean War which has triumphed in popular opinion and in the history books. Bright had more success. Once it was agreed that the Crimean War had been a mistake, it was easy to draw the further conclusion that all wars were a mistake. The moral law which Bright invoked turned out to be the doctrine of the man who passed by on the other side. It is no accident that Bright, at the end of his life, had Joseph Chamberlain as his colleague in the representation of Birmingham. There was a continuity of ideas from Bright to Joseph Chamberlain and from Joseph Chamberlain to Neville. The Munich settlement of 1938 was implicit in Bright's opposition to the Crimean War. I am not sure whether this condemns Bright's attitude or justifies Munich.

John Bright: Hero or Humbug?

A review of John Bright *by Keith Robbins* (*London, Routledge, 1979*),
first published in the Observer, *28 January 1979.*

*   *   *

John Bright has been with me for a long time. When I was a
boy at Bootham just a hundred years after he had been, I was
offered him as a hero and thought him an old humbug. Later,
after studying his speeches on the Crimean War I decided that
he was a hero. Now the excellent biography of him by Keith
Robbins, flatteringly dedicated to me, convinces me that I was
right both times: Bright was a hero and there was something of
the humbug in him as well. Henry James characterized him
well:

He gives an impression of sturdy, honest, vigorous, English middle-
class liberalism, accompanied by a certain infusion of genius, which
helps one to understand how his name has become the great rallying-
point of that sentiment.

It gives added piquancy to this impression that it was recorded
when Bright and Henry James were guests of the Earl of
Rosebery at Mentmore – surely an odd place to meet the great
denouncer of 'our effete aristocracy'. Not at all: Bright was
equally at home with the Duke of Argyll at Inveraray, with the
Earl of Aberdeen at Haddo and with the Duke of Devonshire at
Chatsworth.

Bright's great strength was as a speaker at mass meetings,
though also in the House of Commons. His speeches are
incomparable, greater than Gladstone's, greater than Lloyd
George's. They rank with Burke's as the only speeches in English

which can still be read as literature. I rate highest Bright's speech at Birmingham on 29 October 1858, if only because it contains the best survey ever given of British foreign policy from the Glorious Revolution to the middle of the nineteenth century. All Bright's speeches combine wisdom, advocacy and humour. His oratory was purely English: he never studied the Greek and Latin classics and was soaked in the English classics instead.

Bright was carried to the public platform by the campaign against the Corn Laws and was rightly a little jealous when Cobden claimed to have imposed their repeal all on his own. Thereafter Bright outstripped Cobden as a popular leader. His sustained criticism of the diplomacy that preceded the Crimean War, though unsuccessful at the time, triumphed eventually in the long period of Splendid Isolation.

Bright did not carry his Quakerism into public life. He was an isolationist, not a pacifist. He agreed reluctantly with the military suppression of the Indian mutiny; he applauded the victory of the North in the American Civil War. But he was steadfastly against any entanglement in European affairs, even if it was disguised as a crusade for national liberation: 'It is not my duty to make this country the knight-errant of the human race.' He resigned from Gladstone's government in 1882 in protest against the bombardment of Alexandria and the conquest of Egypt – acts as foolish and wicked in their way as the later incursion at Suez. All the same he had some odd ideas about Europe, as when he wrote in 1870:

France is deposed and Germany is exalted, a great gain I think for liberty and for peace. It will be a great gain too for Protestants and the imposture which is still throned on the seven hills will be less able to claim military support.

Bright had one great practical achievement: he did more than anyone else to promote the second Reform Act which established household suffrage, though it is characteristic that he stayed away from the great demonstration in Hyde Park which ended in rioting. His political radicalism had strict limits. He opposed universal suffrage and was even firmer against votes for women: 'men-women are not a pleasant addition to our social arrangements'. He opposed the factory acts or any other interference with 'the natural laws', of which trade unionism was the worst. Thus he wrote of a strike at Preston in 1853:

The battle must be fought out, when combinations are entered into. When once the natural adjustment of wages is departed from, then there remains only to learn who is the strongest.

Twenty years later, during a period of trade depression, he was still saying the same: without trade unions 'the labour markets would have been more steady and the enormous loss caused by strikes would have been avoided'. He also opposed any interference with the sale of alcohol and said of the temperance reformers, 'It is always so when great questions get into the hands of weak people – weak heads are liable to be run away with.'

Bright began well over Ireland. He was among the first to advocate a system of land purchase which would transform Ireland into a community of peasant proprietors and he pushed this cause hard throughout the 1870s. The Home Rule Party, as led by Parnell, forfeited his sympathy by their aggressiveness. Perhaps he resented their interruptions of his speeches. The Parnellites became for him 'rioters' and 'rebels', unfit to rule their own country. Belatedly he discovered, too, the Protestant cause in Ulster. Bright contributed as much as Joseph Chamberlain to the defeat of Gladstone's Home Rule Bill in 1886, a sadly conservative end to a radical's career.

Beneath an appearance of charm and benignity there was a complex character. He had two serious breakdowns which took him out of public life for years at a time. He was also very selfish. He led an active social life in London at the tables of the great. His wife was left in Rochdale for months on end to care for their considerable family. Nor did she accompany him on his excursions to Scotland or abroad. He sometimes gave the impression that he was prouder of his 'magnificent barouche' than of his political achievements. Perhaps he secretly reproached himself. He wrote in 1876, when invited to accept some office in the Society of Friends:

The labours of life have taken me out of the way of service for our little Church. I feel that there is nothing above the humblest office – shall I say that of doorkeeper? which I could properly undertake.

Yes, he certainly was an old humbug. Or so I think until I read again one of his speeches. Then I must acknowledge that he really was a great and noble man.

Ranke : The Dedicated Historian

This essay on Ranke (1795–1886) appeared as 'The Dedicated Historian: Leopold Von Ranke's Correspondence' in The Times Literary Supplement *on 12 May 1950 after the publication of Ranke's* Das Briefwerk, *edited by Walther Peter Fuchs, and* Neue Briefe, *edited by Hans Herzfeld, in Hamburg by the publisher Hoffman and Campe in 1949. Alan Taylor's essay sparked off a controversy in the pages of the* TLS *with letters from, among others, Noël Annan, Pieter Geyl and G P Gooch. Annan argued that Ranke 'was not a positivist but a moderate Hegelian'. Alan Taylor replied, defending the view he expressed in this essay.*

*   *   *

Though standards vary, greatness remains; indeed it is the true mark of greatness that it can survive changing standards. Shakespeare was great to Johnson; great to Coleridge; is great to us. Ranke was a historian of the same grandeur – great to his contemporaries, still great after the passage of a century; if not the greatest of historians, securely within the first half-dozen. Great as a scholar, great as a master of narrative, Ranke has the special claim of having achieved something more than his own work; he founded a school, the school of scientific historians, which has dominated all historical thinking since his time, even when in reaction against it. His wish to present the past 'as it really was' became, in the German phrase, 'a winged word'; one of those pregnant sayings which concentrate the aspirations and outlook of a generation. Indeed the past 'as it really was' can be put with Bismarck's 'blood and iron' as the two most important spiritual legacies left by the Germany of the mid-nineteenth century. A composite picture of the German character would have to include Ranke, just as it would have to include Goethe and Schiller on the one side, Hitler and Himmler on the other. Perhaps Ranke displayed even more clearly than these other representative figures the strength and achievement, also the weakness and the defects, of the German character.

The present revival of Ranke is not simply a publishing accident. The German interest in Ranke is one attempt among many to find normality and self-confidence among their own kind; it is also, however, one attempt among many to evade the responsibilities of the day, as Ranke evaded them, by a sort of political quietism – finding God in history in the hope that He will take the blame for everything that goes wrong. In his life, as in his work, Ranke remains full of lessons for the Germany of the present day and also for the historian in every country.

Ranke has one qualification which he himself regarded as essential for the study of a subject: there is plenty of material. His works stretch at unrivalled length on the shelves; and his life was as interminable as his works. Few historians have matured so young; none other of the first rank has kept going, in full possession of his faculties, until well over ninety. His first published letter is dated 1814, the last 1886. Both show the same gravity and self-confidence. These qualities made Ranke a great historian. He never doubted what he wanted to be and what he wanted to do. Though he was an affectionate son and brother and, late in life, an affectionate husband, he was dedicated to the study and writing of history, accepting without complaint the solitary existence which that involved. He never sought guidance or instruction; when he met other historians, it was to discuss questions of organizing historical studies, not to debate historical problems. He never troubled about criticism, except when this challenged the accuracy of his facts. Facts were his guiding star, one might say his illusion. In a letter to his brother Heinrich in 1831 he wrote:

My basic thought is not to accept either one theory or another, not even the one which lies between them; but to recognize the facts, to master them and display them. The true teaching is in the recognition of events.

Forty years later, facts had become even more sacred. He wrote in 1873:

The historian exists in order to understand the sense of an epoch in and for itself and to make it understood by others. He must keep his eye with all impartiality only on the subject itself and on nothing else. Through everything runs the divine order of things, which certainly cannot be precisely displayed, but is to be felt all the same. The significant individuals have their place in this divine order, which is identical with the succession of epochs; this is how the historian must comprehend them. The historical method, which seeks only the genuine and the true, thus comes into direct contact with the highest questions of the human race.

Yet what were these facts which revealed the divine order of things? Simply the documents which had survived by accident and which jealous archivists allowed him to see. Time and again he wrote to the archivists (or, when these proved stubborn, to their official superiors, even to Metternich) for one more document, one more 'fact', endlessly confident that with this extra 'fact' everything would at last fall into place and the divine purpose be revealed. He supposed that in writing documents men record their motives; he almost assumed that men wrote documents for the benefit of historians. The supreme consequence of Ranke's doctrine was the belief, universal after the first German war, that if the archives were combed through an 'explanation' of our twentieth-century turmoil would be discovered. Nowadays we know better and read diplomatic history for purposes of entertainment. 'Facts' have crumbled along with the Newtonian system of the universe. Ranke would have been bewildered by a judgement essential to modern science: 'The person of the experimenter is himself part of the experiment.' Or, to put it in terms of the historian: 'Impartiality gives a more dangerous bias than any other.'

Though impartiality is impossible, accuracy is a different matter. A historian can copy a document accurately, though he can never give to it a full, final and lasting interpretation. Impartiality would not have carried Ranke so far, if he had not been accurate as well; and maybe he would not have been accurate without his worship of the elusive 'fact'. The present-day historian feels his mouth water as he reads of Ranke's three years in Italy, moving from one archive to another and seeing them opened for historical purposes for the first time. Ranke was then a little over thirty, perhaps the best time for a historian to engage in intensive research: old enough to know what he was doing, young enough to have energy and zest. We smile at the assiduity with which scholars nowadays get their foreign travel at other people's expense – a week at Monte Carlo at the expense of UNESCO, three months in America at the expense of some foundation, a trip round the world at the expense of Andrew Carnegie or Cecil Rhodes. Ranke did far better than his modest successors: he spent three years in Italy at the expense of the Prussian state. No historian without private means has ever had such a stroke of fortune. While in Italy he bought every manuscript and early printed book which might be useful to him for the Royal Library in Berlin; on his return he borrowed them for as long as it suited him – a convenient arrangement. For Ranke, though remote from the world, was not without worldly skill.

It is curious to trace, in his letters, Ranke's growing realization that the historian, especially of modern times, will do well to be on the right side of the authorities. There was no element of dishonesty in this; Ranke had been on the side of authority from the beginning. Though he wrote his letters on a desk that had belonged to Gymnastic-father Jahn [Jahn was leader or 'father' of the Gymnastic Unions (*Turnverein*) which became an expression of student radicalism after the Napoleonic Wars], and had always a touch of German romanticism in his private judgements, Ranke had no sympathy with the political enthusiasms which spluttered among German students after 1815. His religious convictions were deep; among these was a confidence in the divine mission of the monarchical state. He wrote of a speech delivered by Frederick William IV in 1847:

I say definitely that I know nothing since the psalms where the idea of a religious monarchy has been expressed more powerfully and more nobly. It has great passages of historical truth.

Since this religious monarchy was a 'fact', Ranke was never troubled by any conflict between his devotion to 'facts' and his loyalty to the Prussian state. It never occurred to him that he might discover a fact discreditable to the Prussian Monarchy; and sure enough he never did. Each year, in his old age, Ranke would produce a new volume of history 'as it really was'; and each year a copy of the new volume would be sent to William I with an accompanying letter, emphasizing that the volume was devoted to showing the religious mission of the August House.

Thus Ranke escaped from the problems of intellectual integrity which have troubled many academic figures. His nearest contact with it was in 1837, when the famous 'seven of Göttingen' protested against the abolition of the Hanoverian constitution and were deprived of their chairs. Ranke thought their action unnecessary; on the other hand, he refused to accept one of the vacant chairs. It may be wondered whether his refusal would have been so firm if the offer had come from the house of Hohenzollern. This is not to say that Ranke approved of all that happened in Prussia after 1862. His ideal king was Frederick William IV; and though he tried to turn William I into a pillar of European peace, he had difficulty in striking the right note with Bismarck. Ranke distinguished clearly between states and nations; and he regretted Bismarck's association, however equivocal, with German liberalism. He believed that a divine monarchy must keep finance and the army out of parliamentary control. Bismarck had done this in Prussia; but the imperial constitution of 1871 made dangerous concessions to liberalism. It is not surprising that Ranke sought escape from Bismarck's policy by editing the letters of Frederick William IV to Bunsen – editing them, as he explained to William I, with the necessary discretion. Between Ranke and Bismarck there was never more than a watchful, doubting truce

– a conflict of character rather than of fundamental outlook. After all, Bismarck, too, was engaged in preserving the August House (to his own later regret); and Ranke's disciples, though not Ranke himself, had no difficulty in fitting Bismarck into the divine order of things.

Though Ranke did not ignore domestic events either in history or in politics, his consuming interest was in foreign affairs – the domain of history in which the 'fact' is at once most attainable and most elusive. Here, too, he found a divine order, but of a different kind. Within the state the divine order rested on monarchical authority; in the wider community of Europe it was expressed by sovereign states acting to preserve their independence. Not that Ranke was unconscious of the cultural links which held Europe together; after all, he enjoyed a European reputation. He visited Macaulay (though disapproving of the way 'in which he illuminated the present by the past'); he was on intimate terms with Thiers and had an important conversation with him at the height of the Franco-German war; he appreciated Italian art in his rare moments of escape from the archives. But these cultural issues seemed to Ranke to have little to do with politics; or rather, he regarded the conflict of states as an aspect of European culture. Since he accepted the Prussian Army as a special manifestation of divine providence, he found no fault in war as such; he condemned only wars fought to spread 'red republicanism' or to establish the domination of a single power on the Continent – in other words he condemned wars fought against Prussia. For when one comes to look for other monarchies which would display the divine purpose they are difficult to find. Ranke was on friendly terms with King Maximilian of Bavaria and even claimed that Maximilian, who died in 1864, would have prevented the Austro-Prussian War. But this was no more than a gesture of appreciation to a generous patron of history; besides, the divine order in this case had a curious origin, for the Kingdom of Bavaria had been created by Napoleon.

Austria was a different matter. Here, too, was an August

House, of indisputable historical character, and the traditional opponent of revolution. So long as the Habsburg Monarchy cooperated with Prussia, it received Ranke's blessing; when it sought to overthrow the divine balance between the two German powers, Ranke discovered that Roman Catholic powers did not understand the workings of Providence. It was no accident that in the same year, 1865, Ranke on a visit to England observed a revival of intolerant Protestantism and was glad of it; 'for positive religion, which rejects the general flight into a vague liberalism, accords with my own beliefs'. Thus, the war of 1866 appeared to Ranke as a war of Prussian defence, meant to restore a divine balance which Austria had threatened to overthrow. Once Austria returned to cooperation with Prussia, she became again part of the 'God-willed' order. Beyond these two German powers, one so full of defects, the monarchical system seems hardly to have extended. Ranke makes virtually no comment on Russia: only Bismarck understood that German destinies depended on what happened beyond the Vistula. Ranke saw catastrophe to the divine purpose in the French Revolution; though he spoke often of Franco-German cooperation he assumed that this could only follow a repudiation by the French of the revolutionary tradition – a sound judgement, as the story of Vichy shows. He welcomed the war of 1870 as a war both against Jacobinism and against Napoleonic imperialism; it was for him a war of the balance of power, a war of self-defence. This carried him far from the controversies of the nineteenth century. He told Thiers in October 1870: 'The King of Prussia is not fighting any longer against Napoleon, who is a prisoner, nor even against France as such; he is fighting the idea of Louis XIV.' Yet it is difficult to think of any monarchy more divinely appointed than that of the Bourbons. Here again the divine order turns out in practice to mean nothing more than increase of Prussian strength.

Worship of power was the creed which bound Germany together; it is a more repellent creed when decked out with phrases of Christian religion. Ranke's letters are a strange mixture in which love of nature and sincere religious feelings are compounded with sycophancy towards the great and apologies for Prussian power. A reader of them turns almost with relief to those latter-day Germans whose orthodoxy did not shrink from straight brutality and dishonesty. Yet this feeling is as mistaken as the hero-worship of Ranke, traditional in German scholarship. Ranke was by no means a hypocrite. He was a man truly dedicated to his task. In his own words: 'I know that I am born to do what I am now carrying out, that my life has no other purpose. I must go on whether I want to or not.' And again: 'I'm content to know what I live for; my heart leaps with happiness when I foresee the joy that executing an important work will give me; I swear daily to execute it without departing by a hair's-breadth from the truth which I see.'

This dedication was a noble passion. But it rested on the assumption that others were dedicated to public duties as Ranke was dedicated to history. Ranke spoke of historians as priests; he regarded kings as the most sacred of priests. The state could never sin; and if it did, this was not his affair. This was the spirit of the learned classes in Germany which brought Hitler to power. Ranke and his followers were not National Socialists, not even their precursors. They were all dedicated men, simple and pure in their private lives. But they regarded the state, whoever conducted it, as part of the divine order of things; and they felt it their duty to acquiesce in that divine order. They never opposed; they rarely protested. Inevitably, therefore, they usually found themselves apologizing for what the state had done. If Hitler was merely the working-out of historical forces, then how could historians condemn him? Ranke had 'explained' the revocation of the Edict of Nantes; his successors 'explained' the gas-chambers. Nor can the Western world regard Ranke's political quietism with complacence. The English or American scientist who believes that he has discharged his duty to society by working devotedly in his laboratory evades responsibility as Ranke did; and will end in the same service of blind power. It is tempting to believe that government is a special calling and that the calling will always be of God. If history has any lesson it is that men should resist this temptation and should recognize that no member of a community can escape responsibility for its actions. The historian or the scientist does well to lead a dedicated life; yet, however dedicated, he remains primarily a citizen. To turn from political responsibility to dedication is to open the door to tyranny and measureless barbarism.

Cavour and Garibaldi

A review of Cavour and Garibaldi 1860: A Study in Political Conflict *by D Mack Smith (Cambridge University Press, 1954), published in the* New Statesman *on 24 April 1954.*

*   *   *

It used to be the fashion to contrast the unification of Germany and of Italy. In Italy idealism; in Germany *realpolitik*. In Italy the spread of parliamentary liberalism; in Germany the triumph of the Prussian Army. Bismarck appeared always in a general's tunic, ruthless, unscrupulous, a master of force and dishonesty. Cavour was the civilian statesman, relying on parliamentary speeches for his success. The failure of the German radicals was lamented; there were few to regret the failure of Mazzini or Garibaldi. They were impractical dreamers who did not understand the greatness of Cavour; and it was a good thing for Italy when they were shipped off, Garibaldi to Caprera, Mazzini back to exile in London. More recently, Cavour has had a bad press. His private correspondence has been published and his own words have shown him to be much more like Bismarck, much less like Gladstone, than used to be supposed. He wielded the weapons of traditional diplomacy with incomparable skill, but also with incomparable lack of principle; and Metternich turns out to have been his exemplar as well as his enemy.

Cavour did not care much about the unification of Italy, or at any rate ranked it low in his scale of values. Himself with little national feeling, preferring to speak and write in French, his deepest concern was for moderate liberalism. He wanted a free press, free trade, and a parliament based on limited suffrage, first in Piedmont and then perhaps in northern Italy. But he did not regard the unification of the whole peninsula as a noble idea or believe that it would of itself bring about a moral regeneration. He had nothing but contempt for idealists like Mazzini and could have said with Bismarck: 'The great questions of our day will not be settled by speeches and majority resolutions but by blood and iron.' What he lacked in blood and iron he made up for in deceit. The Italian question was for him a problem in European diplomacy, not a matter of national sentiment. He hardly thought about the Italian people except to fear them. His thoughts were concentrated on Napoleon III. And the later observer must confess that the unification of Italy might well have been impossible, unless Napoleon III had been brought in to defeat Austria in 1859. After all, the victory of nationalism was not inevitable. Poland had to wait until the twentieth century, despite a much stronger national sentiment; the Ukraine waits to the present day.

We still need a history of Italian unification from the European angle. Professor Valsecchi of Milan is writing it; but so far he has only got to the early days of the Crimean War. Meanwhile, Mr Mack Smith has given us a new version of the story at a later stage – the stage of 1860, when Lombardy and central Italy had been united to Piedmont, but when the Two Sicilies and the Papal States (to say nothing of Venetia) had still to be liberated. This was the moment of greatest contrast between Cavour's reliance on diplomacy and the faith of the radicals in their own ideals. Cavour still feared the intervention of 'the Holy Alliance', still pinned his calculations to the favour of Napoleon. Garibaldi believed that the entire peninsula could be brought together by a spontaneous outburst of national enthusiasm; and he thought the prize worth any risk. He was determined to act somewhere – against Austria in Venetia, against Rome despite its French garrison, or, when Sicily rebelled, against the Bourbon kingdom of the Two Sicilies. It used to be held that Cavour secretly encouraged Garibaldi and was in alliance with him. The truth is less creditable. He pushed Garibaldi off to Sicily in order to get him out of the way and in the hope that failure would ruin the radicals once and for all.

Instead, Garibaldi succeeded beyond his wildest dreams; and Cavour had to sweep up the pieces of a policy in ruins.

Mr Mack Smith has produced a surprising book to come out of Cambridge. He acknowledges his debt to Professor Butterfield; and one would have expected praise of Cavour and condemnation of Garibaldi from a member of this neo-Machiavellian group. But not at all. With brilliant, though well-founded, perversity, Mr Mack Smith turns things upside down. It is Garibaldi who was the realist, arriving at the right conclusions by instinct, and Cavour who was the dogmatic muddler. Mr Mack Smith is perhaps a little unfair to Cavour. As things turned out, Italy in 1860 was able 'to do it herself', as she had mistakenly boasted she would in 1848; and Europe counted for little. But this could not have been foreseen when the Thousand sailed. Napoleon III still seemed to dominate Europe, his decline lay far in the future; and Cavour was not the only man to fear the might of France. Moreover he was right on one essential point, the question of Rome. Rome dominated the Italian problem; and even Garibaldi went to Sicily principally in order to reach Rome by the back door. Yet the French could be got out of Rome only by diplomacy, not by force; and for the sake of Italy Garibaldi had to fail before he reached Rome, unless the pope had already withdrawn – and the French along with him. Moreover, Mr Mack Smith underrates the danger that Austria, Prussia and Russia would come together in resistance to 'the revolution'. They nearly did when they met at Warsaw in October 1860; and they were prevented more by the diplomacy of Napoleon III (and hence indirectly of Cavour) than by Garibaldi's success in the south.

Still, by and large, the emphasis is put the right way. Cavour was blinded by his rigid hostility towards the radicals. He saw in them only 'the social peril', and was convinced that anarchy must follow their victory. His primary object was that Garibaldi should fail; only in the second place did he want Italy to be united. This view divided him not only from the radicals, but even from his king, Victor Emmanuel, who was ready 'to become simple *monsu Savoia* and clap his hands at Mazzini's success if this sacrifice were necessary for the making of Italy'. Yet Cavour's own policy was more Utopian than that of any radical. He imagined that Italy could be brought into being solely by the moderate liberals – the most useless of all classes in a revolution. Ricasoli's ruthlessness made this policy work in central Italy; but in the south there was nothing between the aristocracy and the masses. The few middle-class lawyers there supported unification only in order to get the courts open again; they would not fight for it, and Garibaldi succeeded by rousing the masses. This was a social revolution against the landowners – a revolution which Garibaldi exploited for the national cause. He had no social programme, despite his emotional sympathy with the peasants and despite Cavour's suspicions; and he allowed them to fall under the rule of a harsher, more rigid Piedmontese bureaucracy without ever understanding how he had betrayed them.

Cavour always suspected Garibaldi; Garibaldi never suspected Cavour. This is the central theme of the whole affair. Of course, Garibaldi disliked Cavour and resented his cession of Nice to Napoleon III; but he thought that, just as he had dropped his republicanism, Cavour would drop his hostility to the radicals for the sake of united Italy. If the radicals united Italy, this would certainly weaken Cavour and perhaps even lead to his fall; but again Garibaldi, being ready to make the greatest personal sacrifices on his side, could not understand that Cavour would not do the same. Cavour, like Bismarck, regarded himself as indispensable; when he proved unyielding on this, everyone had to give way to him in the last resort – and Italy paid the price. Garibaldi put Italy first; Cavour put himself first. Therefore Cavour was bound to win in the end, despite the great advantages which Garibaldi accumulated in Sicily and Naples.

For they were great advantages. The liberation of the Two Sicilies seems easy in retrospect; we almost fail to notice that it needed a leader of genius to accomplish it. European radicalism produced three great dictators – Kossuth in Hungary, Mazzini in Rome, Garibaldi in the Two Sicilies. Garibaldi was the least intellectual of the three, with few ideas and unable to formulate even these clearly. Yet he was easily the most successful. He evoked from the people and even from the politicians a personal devotion almost without parallel in modern history; again and again he chose the right course by instinct; and he showed himself the greatest general that Italy has ever produced. In the late summer of 1860 Sicily was a true radical paradise, radiating the hope – or perhaps the illusion – that every evil legacy of the past had been swept away. Cavour was not the serpent in this garden of Eden; Garibaldi's success had eclipsed him for the time being. The real trouble was that Garibaldi and the people of Sicily were at cross-purposes. They supposed that he had brought them freedom; he looked on Sicily only as the first halt on the road to Rome. Both alike resisted Cavour's plan for an immediate annexation of Sicily to the kingdom of Sardinia. But the Sicilians wanted permanent autonomy for their island; Garibaldi and his radical supporters wished to use Sicily as a base for further successes. Once Garibaldi had crossed to the mainland and carried all before him, he lost interest in Sicily; and it irritated him to have to return in order to settle its internal conflicts. Even in Naples, he listened impatiently to the republican arguments of Mazzini and the federalist schemes of Cataneo. The march on Rome was the only thing that interested him.

The resistance of the Neapolitan Army on the Volturno gave Cavour his chance. He was able to stop Garibaldi just in time. He acted no doubt cynically and basely, discrediting Garibaldi unjustifiably with the king and killing the idealism of the radical movement. But there was something wrong with a radicalism which could think only of further battles. The radicals had an aggressive foreign policy; they improvised casually in home affairs. Mr Mack Smith is inclined to regret that Sicily and even Naples did not survive as autonomous radical states. Was Cavour alone to blame? After all he had only another six months to live; and the radicals had plenty of chance in the future if they could take it. They never made much of it; and Italy has been kept going (so far as it goes at all) by hard-headed officials of Cavour's stamp. Idealists make revolutions; practical men come afterwards and clear up the mess. Garibaldi was luckier than most revolutionary leaders. He remained an idealist to the end of the chapter. If Cavour had not existed, Garibaldi must either have failed or have ended by playing the part of Cavour himself. Perhaps it was Cavour who made the greatest sacrifice after all. Garibaldi returned to Caprera; Cavour remained in power.

Men of 1862

'*The Men of 1862*' *was a series of weekly television lectures broadcast by BBC Television after ten p.m. from 26 May to 1 July 1963. The texts were published in* The Listener *between 6 June and 11 July 1963, but have never since been reprinted.*

The television series was among Alan Taylor's best. He was at the peak of his powers. After the public and academic rows over his Origins of the Second World War *he was especially concerned to make a favourable impact with the lectures.*

Although he wrote to Roger Machell of Hamish Hamilton: '*You will probably think, as I do, that they are too ragged to make into a book', he appears to have been hoping a publisher would take them up, either on their own or with other material. Given that two other books were in the offing –* The First World War: An Illustrated History *(1963) and a collection of essays 'mostly on twentieth-century themes', which was to be published as* Politics in Wartime *(1964) – doing something with these television lectures was not a priority. Later, when his publisher suggested to Taylor that he add them to* Politics in Wartime, *he felt they were unsuitable for that volume. This was perhaps because they covered an earlier period and because he had included essays on the same topics in earlier collections. In these portraits he often drew heavily on his earlier writings. As they stand, these six essays provide Taylor's later assessments of major figures who had much interested him during the first three decades of his academic career.*

Alan Taylor also discussed with the US publisher McGraw-Hill the possibility of publishing '*The Men of 1862*' *along with some other nineteenth-century essays in the USA. He broke off his talks with that firm in favour of having a larger selection of his essays published there. These were selected from his three earlier British collections of essays –* From Napoleon to Stalin *(1950),* Rumours of Wars *(1952) and* Englishmen and Others *(1956) – and published under the title* From Napoleon to Lenin: Historical Essays *as a Harper Torchback in 1966.*

* * *

Napoleon III

In 1862 Europe was stocked with kings and emperors and powerful statesmen; but few people would have disputed that the most important of them, the man who held the future of Europe in his hand, was Napoleon III, emperor of the French. He was a ruler of a special kind: the first who literally owed his power to the people. If by democracy we mean that men choose their rulers, then Napoleon III was the first who had ever been chosen in this strict sense.

In the United States presidents were already chosen by popular election; but before that they were chosen by party. Napoleon III had no party, he was nothing except himself. When people talked about the Bonapartists they did not mean that the followers of Napoleon III had any formed programme or body of ideas, represented anything, had any kind of organization, except as personal backers of Louis Napoleon Bonaparte, who became emperor of the French. His power came to him ten years before, in 1852; or one could go back further, to when he became president of the French Republic in 1848; his power came to him, as it had never come to anyone before, in this direct way. He was the first man to be carried to the top by direct universal suffrage.

If we ask why in 1862 was Napoleon III emperor of the French at all, we can answer: because of his name – he was the nephew of the great Napoleon. That is to say, he was the nephew of the great Napoleon if indeed he was the son of his father, which some historians have doubted. At any rate, in accepted theory he was the nephew of the great Napoleon. He claimed to represent himself a number of Napoleonic ideas, about which he had written a book. But the technical operation was a straight popular election, when for the first time in European history a people, the French people, all enjoyed the right to vote, and Louis Napoleon was carried to the top as president of the French Republic by this process of direct election. And the same had been true about the various stages in which he had stepped to absolute power. There was – and this is rare, certainly unique in the Europe of the time – no intermediary between him and the people. He was not created by party, he was not created by parliament, he and the people were in direct connection. Napoleon III himself put it well when he said: 'Other French governments have ruled with the support of perhaps one million of the educated classes. I have called in the other twenty-nine million.' It was the twenty-nine million – the people, as it were, who were not in politics, not in public life, people who did not write for the newspapers, people who did not take part in political discussions – who made him emperor of the French and to whom he felt in a sense responsible. He existed for the sole purpose of pleasing them.

Many rulers have sought popularity, but this has been in order to carry out the kind of policies they want or because they love power. In a curious way Napoleon III, although ostensibly the most powerful man in Europe, did not love power. That is to say, he did not like doing things. What he liked was the process of getting there. He was one of nature's conspirators: he enjoyed nothing more than to plot. When, as president of the French Republic, working within a constitution, faced with an elected assembly which he had to cooperate with, he planned to become instead dictator, he spent months working out in extreme elaboration the way in which he would seize power. But once the plans for his *coup d'état* were made he hesitated, not I think out of fear but simply because the plans were so beautiful he was no longer interested in operating them.

In the summer of 1851 the plans for the *coup d'état* were ready, and then he delayed again and again. His fellow conspirators who thought they might well be found out and be sent to prison or lose their heads, urged him: 'We must act; we must put these plans into operation.' He would always postpone action for another day. It was only when the assembly itself took the offensive, in trying to deprive him of the control over the soldiers, that he moved into action (and lamented that if only they had kept quiet he would have kept quiet too). It was always someone else who was pushing him forward.

A few years later, in 1865, when he met Bismarck at Biarritz and they talked about plans for the remodelling of Europe, Bismarck threw out the idea that he was aiming to make Prussia the dominant power in Germany. When he discussed how this should be done, Napoleon III said: 'You mustn't make events, you must wait for them to happen.' Napoleon waited, even though he was at the same time given over to construction. He was, though brought into power as the guardian of order, the man who would end the revolution, at the same time the heir of the great French Revolution, anxious indeed to apply its ideas all over Europe. Yet, having built up the ideas, having accumulated policies and indeed openings by which he could operate, he would then put it off: 'You must learn to wait' was his constant slogan. This is a curious thing. One can understand a conservative believing in waiting; Napoleon was by principle and outlook a revolutionary, and yet a procrastinating revolutionary.

There is another perhaps even more striking example: in 1858 he met Cavour, who was then prime minister of Piedmont, at the little watering-place of Plombières, and together they plotted how they would force a war upon Austria, drive the Austrians out of Italy, and create a united Italy. As long as they were engaged in the detailed plans of how the war should be brought about, of how Austria could be manoeuvred into the position of actually starting the war, Napoleon III was satisfied. They had an agreeable secret three days together. But when Napoleon went back to Paris, and Cavour began to put his plans into action, Napoleon III was constantly rebuking him, saying: 'They're admirable plans, and of course a united Italy is what I want, but let's wait a bit longer'; and at the very last minute when Austria was manoeuvred into war and was indeed driven from northern Italy, Napoleon III was grumbling and complaining that Cavour had dragged him along into operating plans which Napoleon III himself had made.

This is part of his mystery. He was – he liked to believe (perhaps it was one of his illusions) – a man of mystery; Bismarck said that he was a sphinx, but a sphinx without a riddle. I would be tempted to say rather that he was a sphinx with too many riddles, who never attempted really to get on to the answers. He loved to think out riddles, he loved to think of the problems of Europe, but when it came to action he procrastinated, and underneath, perhaps, was aware of the deeper difficulties of his position.

Ostensibly he was the most powerful man in Europe. He was – I was going to say dictator of France. By 1860 he had granted a rather thin constitution which meant that there were elections for an assembly; the assembly was allowed to have a certain amount of discussion; but the power, the decision, rested with him, as indeed it was to remain right to the end of the eighteen-sixties. More than this, France appeared to be the most powerful country in Europe. She had behind her the prestige of the Napoleonic Wars, when the great emperor had conquered all Europe as far as Moscow. She was regarded as the driving force, the great progressive nation, the leader, who would gather the other revolutionary ideas and revolutionary countries behind her. It was still believed that she was the greatest military power in Europe: men all spoke with respect of the French Army and feared what it would do. Her population was not quite the greatest in Europe, but it placed her high among the ranks of the Great Powers.

As one can see from what contemporaries said about France, it was feared there would come from her another wave of aggression and Napoleonic domination. In 1865, when Prussia had become more powerful, Palmerston said at the very end of his life:

It's very regrettable that Prussia's become more powerful. Nevertheless, it's better that Prussia should win than France. If there's going to be a conflict between Prussia and France, then it is in British interests that Prussia should come out the victor, because she is the weaker of

the two. And a French domination of Europe would be very dangerous; Prussian domination of Europe won't happen.

Napoleon III sensed that there was much that was illusory in
his position. France, and for that matter Napoleon III himself,
were running on their prestige. The French people had made
big efforts to accomplish great things in the days of Napoleon,
and now the spirit of domination had gone out of them. They
had become basically a conservative, contented people; they
asked for no more; and Napoleon III was strong in talk but less
effective when it came to action. Just before this time, in 1859,
when there had been the war with Austria, the French Army
had won but not in the old decisive way in which the French
armies won in the days of the great revolution and the great
Napoleon. There had been battles of terrible carnage in which
only at the last minute had there been some sort of a decision,
and the experience on the battlefield – not merely the bloodshed
but the difficulties, the risk, the feeling that the French Army
could not carry all before it – had made Napoleon himself
shrink from further wars, though not from further conspiracies.

When the great Napoleon was emperor of the French, this
empire extended right across Europe. Parts of the Adriatic were
included in France itself; so in 1810 it extended as far, say, as
Hamburg. There were dependencies right up to the Russian
frontier: this was a true empire. The French Empire over which
Napoleon III ruled was simply France under another name.
When he made himself emperor of the French, it was simply the
France that there had been before, and in the course of his reign
he added to this empire only Savoy and Nice, on the borders of
Italy, and one small bit of Indo-China. The name was what
Napoleon III had provided, and he inevitably relied more on
conspiracies and manoeuvre than on realities of power. One
could put it in more practical terms. A far-sighted man who
had looked at the figures of French coal and iron production,
which had been the leading figures on the continent of Europe,

and had then looked at what was happening in Prussia, would have realized that in a relatively few years – and it had already happened by 1870 – Prussia was going to be a greater economic power than France; and that some years after that – this was to happen by the end of the century – France would be comparatively backward as an economic power and Prussia would be at the top. Napoleon III was shrewd enough to see this. He had, he believed, one enormous asset – the asset which had brought him to power – that he, unlike the other rulers of Europe, who had only a governmental machine and the support of an aristocracy or governing class, had behind him the people.

This is what had brought him to power in France; this is what made him pursue, as no other ruler did at the time, a creative social policy. He believed also it was his great asset in Europe. He was what I often think is a dangerous thing for a statesman to be – a student of history; and like most of those who study history, he learnt from the mistakes of the past how to make new ones. He studied in particular his uncle's career and drew from it the lesson – mistaken, I think – that the great Napoleon had been brought to the ground when he had roused the opposition of the other peoples of Europe and that, in particular, the French Revolution, by spreading the spirit of nationalism right across Europe, had stirred up other nations to resist French domination. This was the key to Napoleon III's policy. He believed that the new forces were bound to win, and that therefore a man who went with these new forces would win also. The new force in Europe was nationalism: the belief that men should come together in their own states on a national basis. If, therefore, Napoleon III could cooperate in this work of national unification and liberation, the peoples who achieved their national states would be grateful and France would be at the head, as it were, of a new sort of federation – the federation of free nationalities.

He had done this already with Italy. It was largely thanks to Napoleon III that the national kingdom of Italy was made. At the beginning of 1859 Italy was broken up into a half-dozen kingdoms, duchies, and so on. By 1861 the whole of Italy was united as a single national state with the exception of Rome, which was still under the pope, and Venice, which was still under Austria. By the time Napoleon III fell, in 1870, these two had been brought into the Italian kingdom also – Venice because of his assistance, Rome because of his fall. One could say without hesitation that Napoleon III was in the first rank among the makers of Italy; and here was, as he believed, his policy in operation – the new national Italy would look automatically to France as inspiration and example and would follow his leadership.

He was now dreamily moving towards the same sort of policy in Germany. Here, too, was a divided people, split into thirty-five different kingdoms and states, divided particularly between two Great Powers, Prussia and Austria, with, so it seemed, a conflict for primacy coming between them. Napoleon III was well aware that France would gain by this rivalry. He was ready to encourage it but he had a great handicap – it was, indeed, to be part of Bismarck's secret of success – that in the last resort he could not play it even as between Prussia and Austria.

France, after all, greatly benefited from the disunity of Germany. It was because over the Rhine there were these weak kingdoms divided among each other that France was completely secure. A statesman without ideas would have said to himself: 'Let's keep it like that; there's nothing better for the rest of Europe than to have Germany divided. Let's leave well alone.' Napoleon III could not do this: although he often talked about a conservative policy with Austria, though indeed he was to meet Francis Joseph in 1867 and to plan an alliance with him, his principles in the last resort forbade it: this would be going against the great national doctrine. When Bismarck was able to describe how victory for Prussia would not be a victory merely for military might but would be a victory for the German nation, Napoleon found this irresistible.

He did not, as he had done with Italy, want to fling himself into the conflict; he wanted to stay out; and here, again, Bismarck, at any rate later on, produced the great temptation that if Napoleon III simply stood aside, Prussia would win. So here were two great temptations: Napoleon did not need to do anything and, at the same time, he would get what he wanted, a united Germany based on the national principle – a free nation again looking to Paris as the centre and inspiration. This was his great dream for a future Europe. He has been called, I think with some exaggeration, the first visionary of a federal Europe. He sometimes talked in this way: how the rivalry of powers would come to an end, how once every nation was free in its own soil there would grow up a European federation. He was one of the first to say – and it strikes an echo in our own day – that in a Europe of free nations there would grow up a power so strong that it would be independent both of Russia on the one side and of the United States on the other, and that in the twentieth century it would be a European federation created by him which would still make Europe the leading power in the world. He hoped to achieve all these tremendous things under French leadership and yet without doing anything.

Much the same was true inside France. Though Napoleon III depended on popularity, it was a popularity which in many ways he hoped to achieve by doing little. He had a genuine belief in improving the lot of the masses; indeed, his government did more for the ordinary people of France than any government before or since. It was he who introduced social reforms, raised the standards of life of the factory worker, secured the peasant on his land, and thought in terms of the ordinary man. Napoleon also liked show. He recognized that anyone who seeks to be popular must, as it were, make a splash. He said once: 'When a man of my name is in power, he must do great things' – or, at any rate, one might say, appear to be doing them.

Like his uncle, though much more thoroughly, he dreamed of creating a great, impressive, new economic order and, in particular, building a monument which would last – and in this he succeeded. When we look at Europe or at France, we cannot see much that reminds us of Napoleon I; but in the most striking, simple way, you cannot escape Napoleon III. Anyone who visits Paris at the present day sees the city which Napoleon III created. All the old Paris which existed when Napoleon III came to power, the whole medieval structure of the city, has been swept away; all the present shape of Paris was made by Napoleon III, and for that matter, the whole structure of the French railways was made by Napoleon III; the whole pattern, one might say, of French life as it appears to the ordinary person is a creation of the Second Empire.

Napoleon III had enemies in France and he always recognized this: not the revolutionaries of 1848 from whom he had sprung; though the leaders disliked him because he had been more successful than they were. None of these great revolutionaries who talked so much about the people ever managed to get returned for anything – even on to a local council at any sort of election. Napoleon III had had millions of votes, and they were jealous: he had applied the principle more successfully than they had. The people who disliked Napoleon III, who refused to cooperate with him, were what one might call the moderate liberal classes: the men who were interested not in democracy but in constitutionalism, in the process of law – the lawyers, professors, the academic advocates of moderate freedom. They were the men who had been defeated by Napoleon III in 1851; they were the men who later on were to obliterate him from French history. It is a most extraordinary thing, even at the present day, that while most periods of French history are studied intensely and with remarkable scholarship, the Second Empire passes almost unknown. You can find any number of books about the revolution of 1848, about its social work, its democratic work, and so on, and then suddenly it all ends, and the Second Empire is an absolute blank until you get to the end when the academic figures who still had not forgiven Napoleon III can write about his failure and can point to the fact that the Third Republic followed him and this dictator was pushed aside.

It is not only that he did them all out of a job; he destroyed what we might call the system. What the Second Empire lacked was a governing class. There were people who administered for Napoleon III; most of them were scamps, as in a sense Napoleon III was himself. No body of men, I suppose, has ever done better out of governing a country than the associates of Napoleon III. And unlike Napoleon, because they thought it would not last, they built themselves up, they became princes, they acquired vast estates. All of them were incompetent. Napoleon III was tremendously aware of this; not that he was competent himself, but he was competent enough to judge the incompetence of others. In 1870 when, in order, as he supposed, to express the feeling of France, to respond to the cause of popularity, he plunged France into the war against Prussia, he knew that the French Army was in no state for war and that it would be catastrophically defeated. It was; it vanished. Incidentally, the wide boulevards he had made in Paris were planned so that if there were riots the crowds could easily be shot down. But when there were riots there was nobody to shoot the crowds; the Second Empire fell without a conflict of any kind. In 1873 Napoleon III became an exile in England, though he hoped to return. He was operated upon so that he could sit upon a horse again but died under the surgeon's knife. At his funeral, the only Frenchman who came over from France to be with him was a trade unionist.

Francis Joseph, Emperor of Austria

Francis Joseph, the emperor of Austria, was an institution, not a man; a gaunt wooden figure, one feels, who moved by clockwork. He had one of the longest reigns in European history; he came to the throne as a grown man in 1848 and died in November 1916 – and he never missed a day in performing his duties as emperor. You probe behind this and wonder whether there was anything interesting like human feelings or weaknesess – and find nothing.

His wife, the Empress Elizabeth, was said to be one of the most beautiful women in Europe, and he was, no doubt, deeply attached to her, but never for a moment did he contemplate neglecting his imperial position for her sake. She was driven mad with boredom at the Habsburg court and after a few years couldn't stand it. She travelled all over Europe, went to Ireland for the hunting, and was hardly ever in Vienna; no doubt this was deeply upsetting to Francis Joseph, yet he never weakened: there was never a suggestion that the court should be brighter, that they should do something as a distraction. He sacrificed himself to his duty and he expected everyone else to do the same.

He had a mistress, Frau Schratt, who was actually found for him by the Empress Elizabeth but, as far as we can tell, this was a platonic relationship. What Francis Joseph wanted again was a matter of routine – that he could walk across the park every morning, call on Frau Schratt, take a cup of coffee with her, and walk back – and it was, one feels, more the routine, and the few words, no doubt, of relaxed conversation where he escaped just a tiny bit from duty, that mattered. Indeed, later on, he had little feeling for Frau Schratt except a vague sentimental attachment, and he kept up the visits, again from duty. All over the empire, when he was a man in his eighties, people were relieved when they read that 'the Emperor took his usual walk this morning' – they felt that was all right; he's in good health; the empire will stand. The poor old man jogging across the park, creaking and rheumatic, was hardly on a gay, amorous adventure; but he was showing that he was still the man of duty who kept his formal pattern.

He had an extraordinary obtuseness; almost without feelings himself, or, rather, having forced down what feelings he had, he totally disregarded the feelings of others. When he came to the throne in 1848, Hungary was in rebellion. Indeed, shortly after he came to the throne, the Hungarian parliament declared him dethroned and appointed Kossuth as supreme governor. Hungary was reconquered, with Russian assistance and after fierce battles. Some twenty years later in 1867 Francis Joseph made it up with the Hungarians. He restored their liberal constitution; he behaved as a liberal monarch; they had a free parliament and responsible government, and it was obviously necessary for his empire that he should conciliate them and give them the impression that, as king of Hungary, they really mattered to him. He resided for parts of the year in the royal palace at Buda. He restored and decorated it – and with what pictures? With great mural pictures of the battles of 1849, in which his army had conquered the Hungarians. It never occurred to him that this might offend the Hungarians, that they, then the defeated party, now later the victors, would not care to pass through a palace in which there was nothing but pictures of their defeats. One feels this obtuseness going on all through his life. Never, at any moment, did he show any gratitude to the statesmen and politicians who served him. As long as they were necessary he was polite and considerate to them; the moment he felt they had served their term or failed, they were shot out of office without a word of thanks, never seeing him again.

This may seem a hard and unattractive character, but the truth is perhaps rather different. Francis Joseph sacrificed others because he had first sacrificed himself. He represents a supreme example of an idea which has often appeared in European history – the idea of sacrificing individuals to an institution, and in this case a venerable, historic institution – the Habsburg Monarchy. You look at Francis Joseph and ask, as I'm sure he never asked himself, did he like being emperor of Austria, king of Hungary, and all these other things? Did he get any pleasure or pride from it? but you feel – no, there was nothing like this in it. The things he liked doing, if he could ever have conceived of such an idea as liking doing things, were simple: that morning walk in the park, his summer out at Ischl, and the times when he went hunting in leather shorts. This simple life of a humble country gentleman was agreeable to him, but it did not occur to him that he ought to judge it this way; he was the first servant of the monarchy and nothing else.

All his life, even on the day when he was dying in November 1916, he slept on a hard, iron, truckle bed. He got up and washed in cold water early in the morning. By five o'clock he was sitting at his desk, and spent most of his day, when he was not involved in routine and ceremonies, slaving at papers – a pure, narrow functionary. One feels that he had no idea that he ought to lead and inspire his empire: he had simply to serve it.

When he became emperor in 1848, he made his one human remark. The revolutions of 1848 were devastating Europe – the then emperor, Ferdinand (Francis Joseph's uncle), was almost an imbecile, and the moment that Francis Joseph himself came of age, at eighteen, Ferdinand was persuaded to abdicate. In a huggermugger way, in a back room in a provincial castle, Ferdinand signed the deed of abdication, and as Francis Joseph, in his turn, was signing the document which made him emperor, he said 'Farewell youth!' Indeed, it was more than farewell youth – farewell life, farewell individuality, farewell anything except his persistent, endless duty to maintain the institution. The institution was not only the man; it represented a great historic tradition. There is, perhaps, in modern times, nothing more dramatic and striking than the clash between the democratic idea represented by Napoleon III – even though Napoleon III was a despot – on the one side and the idea on the other of the traditional, historic monarchy. If one asks how it was that in the middle of the nineteenth century the great monarchy, the empire of Austria, existed, the answer is simply – history.

Many people had tried to tie it to an idea to give it a significance. Hundreds of years before, it was supposed to stand as the guardian of Europe against the Turks – and twice, in 1529 and 1683, the Turks reached the gates of Vienna and were driven back. There was a time when it was supposed to stand for the counter-reformation and the pushing back of Protestantism in Europe. There was a time – just before Francis Joseph came to the throne, under Metternich – when it was supposed to stand for resistance to the French Revolution, resistance to the modern emancipating ideas; and during the reign of Francis Joseph, many highly intelligent men looked round for another idea. All through the reign of Francis Joseph people were discussing this question. In his very last days, just before the outbreak of the First World War, there is a whole pile of writing depicting wonderful new ideas that the monarchy might stand for: for economic advancement, supporting the lower classes against exploitation; that socialism or at any rate a whole great programme of social reform could come by means of the monarchy; that the monarchy would stand for this wonderful crusade of modern enlightenment.

Essentially, it never stood for any of these things. It existed for its own sake. The Habsburg Monarchy, the empire of Austria, was a collection of great family estates. The reason why the particular states over which Francis Joseph ruled were grouped together under a single head was not because of the will of the people; it was not even often because geography had forced them together; it was because they had been collected by the dynasty in earlier times – a marriage here, a bit of conquest there, a manoeuvre, a swap of territory. In the nineteenth century one of the missions of the Habsburg Monarchy was supposed to be the protection of Italy from French invasion or, for that matter, from liberalism – and Lombardy was one part of the territories of the Habsburg Crown. Until 1859 Francis Joseph possessed among his many other ornaments the Iron Crown of Lombardy, and Milan was one of his capitals. In 1815 there were some embarrassing distant lands along the Rhine which were not wanted, so the monarchy took Lombardy instead. It held Venice – again a swap – not because there was any long-standing tradition of Habsburg influence in the Adriatic, but because the Habsburgs for a long time had ruled in The Netherlands what is nowadays called Belgium – and in 1815 they did not want Belgium back, so they said if we could get rid of Belgium we would like to keep Venice. The monarchy was simply a collection of estates, and Francis Joseph was the man who served this inheritance and hoped to carry it on. His reign marked the final point of the Habsburg Monarchy; the moment at which its existence was basically challenged and two years after his death it fell to pieces.

The reason is simple: until the nineteenth century most states in Europe existed as the personal properties of their rulers. Some of the rulers were kind and considerate men; often they cared for the condition of their subjects just as a man who is keen on fox hunting likes to keep his horses in good condition. But with the French Revolution and with the awakening of ideas which permeated society instead of remaining only with the aristocracy at the top, there comes the feeling, which was spreading all over Europe in the nineteenth century, that states must be at any rate tied up with the will of the people. Only if a state could be associated with a national sentiment did it seem justified, and those states proved strongest in the nineteenth century which were already bound up with a longstanding national feeling.

If we look, for instance, at Great Britain, nobody would say that even in the eighteenth century Britain was merely the property of the house of Hanover; that George III could look out of Windsor and say, 'I own all that and all these people.' He was to the men even of the eighteenth century simply the chief magistrate – one among many political functionaries who were associated with the people: and this had happened in France with the French Revolution – Louis XIV no doubt regarded his people as instruments to his power; Napoleon, though he exploited his people far worse in many ways than Louis XIV did, and certainly caused the death of far more, at the same time felt that he was serving some national idea. It was the misfortune of the Habsburgs that they did not manage to associate themselves with any single national feeling. The great empire which they had collected was not only a ramshackle collection of territories, it was also a ramshackle collection of peoples. There were times – and indeed in the early reign of Francis Joseph this was much discussed – when highly intelligent, skilled politicians played with the idea that the emperor should find some peoples to associate himself with, should take on a national character.

When Francis Joseph came to the throne, his empire already seemed to be dissolving. Hungary had broken away, the German parts were wanting to join a national Germany; Italy was seeking independence – and within a year, relying on the army, all these national movements had been crushed. The institution which Francis Joseph operated in 1849 after his victory, and which remained unchanged for ten years until 1859, was an institution simply of narrow absolutism; he did it all and it had no national character; this was, one might say, a last appearance of the historic, absolute monarchy existing not at all for the sake of the peoples but for the sake of the Habsburgs.

Francis Joseph's grandfather, Emperor Francis I, had once been told of someone that 'he's a good Austrian patriot', and Francis said, 'That's no good; is he a patriot for me?' Between 1849 and 1859 this is the only question: is he a patriot for Francis Joseph? Then, in 1859, came the beginning of the long process of disintegration. There had been the war in Italy in which Napoleon III had come to the assistance of the Italians, when the Austrian armies had been defeated, when some – though not all – of the Italian territories had been lost; and from this moment there begins a strange thing in the life of so rigid a man – a prolonged period of experiment. Francis Joseph himself had no feeling for concession. Left to himself, he would have responded simply by orders. Just as he himself obeyed the orders of the institution, so he expected all others to obey him; but once it was brought home to him that the army on which he based everything had been defeated, he was prepared to make concessions in any direction.

After 1859 came the problem of building up; it came to a climax in 1861 and from then on, throughout the sixties, the future pattern of the Habsburg Monarchy was being shaped. There were two decisions which Francis Joseph had to make. In some way he would have to improve the finances of the empire; and in some way he would have to make the army stronger, and this could only be done by getting rid of some of the discontent and making some people, at any rate, feel that the empire was something for them.

One of these decisions was whether he should keep the empire as a single, centralized force – though giving it a liberal parliament – or whether he should attempt to remodel it into a federation. The other, however, is more fundamental: it explains both the problem and the decision which was then made; it explains most of what came afterwards. If he is going to make concessions, to which group shall he make them? The peoples of the Habsburg Monarchy fell broadly into two sorts of nation: one were what you might call the privileged nations, the nations which had the property, which had the history, which were conscious already of their existence: these were the Germans and the Hungarians. The Germans were the capitalists of the monarchy, the administrators, the bureaucrats. They had, they claimed, the only great language of culture. Their history had never been interfered with, despite the fact that they had never been a united German state; there had been a German history for a thousand years and they, the Germans, regarded themselves as the people of state. The Hungarians, again, had always maintained their history. Hungary had remained a distinct state within the empire. They had maintained their own parliament – and particularly they had maintained their aristocracy. Indeed, in the nineteenth century the Hungarian aristocracy was second only to the British aristocracy in wealth and grandeur and pride.

There was another, numerically greater, body of people in the empire: the people without a history and without power and significance; those who had been pushed down, those who had lost their own natural leaders, who were only just beginning to develop a middle class, who were only just beginning to get wealth. They were mainly composed of peasants recently emancipated from the soil. These were in many ways going to be the people of the future, in the sense that the privileged nationalities represented an idea of power and tradition which was itself being challenged. These other peoples – mainly Slavs, Czechs, Croats, Slovenes, but also Romanians – seemed a long way down, and there were those who said Francis Joseph should, as it were, become – as Napoleon had done in France – the leader of the masses against the few at the top. Much speculation went into this; for a traditional monarch brought up with such a background of duty and rigidity, the idea of turning himself into a peasant emperor and becoming a Napoleon was really inconceivable.

Between 1861 and 1867 Francis Joseph employed many expedients. He played at one time at being the leader not only of the Germans in his empire, but actually of setting himself up as the leader of the German nation. When Bismarck came to power in 1862 it was Prussia which was threatened by the proposed unification of Germany, because it appeared that this unification would be under Austrian leadership and Bismarck was to claim that many of his actions were in self-defence, not at all in aggression against Austria. Francis Joseph also negotiated with the Hungarians, and in 1866, believing that he had quietened Hungary to some extent, he faced the challenge from Prussia and helped to bring on the war of 1866, which led to Austria's defeat.

After this, shaken by a second defeat, his concessions had to be larger, and the great decisive concession which he made in 1867 was to the Hungarians. From that moment, the empire of Austria changed into Austria-Hungary, and it was this institution which, henceforth, he kept alive. He believed that while he had made internal concessions, the things essential to the monarchy were still preserved. These were the existence of Austria-Hungary as a Great Power and, therefore, the maintenance of the Austrian Army as a great army; and in securing these, with the confusions and conflicts of the rest of the reign, he failed. In 1914, when the moment of decision came, when he was asked 'Shall we declare war on Serbia?' he said, 'If it is necessary to preserve the monarchy, yes!'; and the monarchy was then faced with the fact that this great institution, the army, was not strong enough. Two years after Francis Joseph's death, the Habsburg Monarchy fell to pieces primarily because it had been defeated in war. But with the death of Francis Joseph the Austro-Hungarian Empire lost the last great consolidating institution which had held it together.

Lord Palmerston

In 1862 Lord Palmerston still seemed to be the representative Englishman of his age. This in itself tells us a good deal about England and the differences between England and the Continent. Most of the other men I am discussing in this series were kings and emperors. Palmerston was more important than Queen Victoria in determining British policy. Queen Victoria disliked him, deeply regretted having had to make him prime minister, and spent much of her time trying to prevent his carrying out the policies he wanted to carry out. The only alleviating feature in Palmerston, from Queen Victoria's point of view, was that he was less objectionable than Lord Russell, the foreign secretary, once a famous statesman and now, I suppose, mainly remembered as the grandfather of Bertrand Russell.

Palmerston was much older than the other men I have been discussing; he is the only one of them who had been born in the eighteenth century. He was already a junior minister in the time of the Napoleonic Wars, when most of the others had not been born. He had a lifetime of experience, so far as foreign affairs were concerned, and played a much bigger role than any other Englishman of the time. He was largely responsible for creating an independent Belgium, a Belgium guaranteed by the Great Powers. He had conducted great policy in the Near East, and he had been swept to power as prime minister in the Crimean War, as the man who could win the war. In a somewhat unsatisfactory way, he won it.

Unlike other men who have come to power to save the

country and win the war – unlike Lloyd George, unlike Churchill – Palmerston had continued in power afterwards, and there he was apparently unshakeable for his lifetime. He was now nearly eighty: in spirit still juvenile, with enormous energy, capable two years afterwards, in 1864, of making a speech of something like four hours' length in the House of Commons which ran on till the early hours of the morning, and then when he had finished and had won a somewhat precarious majority in the House, of running – at that age – up the steps of the Ladies' Gallery, in order to receive congratulations from Lady Palmerston.

To a superficial glance, also, he still looked a middle-aged man. He dyed his whiskers black, and in earlier life he had been called 'Lord Cupid', not only for his good looks but also for his interest in the things that Cupid was interested in; and he maintained this interest into extreme old age. A man of zest and enthusiasm; a man, also, of very considerable knowledge. No man of his time knew more about foreign affairs; no man had studied them more intently. Palmerston did more than any other Englishman to bring order into the conduct of the Foreign Office.

He had, incidentally, the most beautiful handwriting, and it was his habit to rebuke members of the Foreign Office who did not write as clearly and beautifully as himself. He never bothered to take advice from them: the only comment they ever got was a criticism if their writing was untidy, or if the copy of his draft was not as neatly and accurately made as he required. Underneath, he was an old man, and one is tempted to say he was out of touch with the times. He was more a symbol of British greatness than one who carried it forward. The Great Britain in which he had grown up and come to power had been, so far as foreign affairs were concerned, very much the victor of the Napoleonic Wars; the power which had finally won the battle of Waterloo, and had terminated the whole epic of Napoleonic times by keeping Napoleon a prisoner till he died on St Helena.

Other countries had suffered conquest, and still worried that they might be conquered again. No continental country could look at Napoleon III, for instance, without thinking: maybe another Napoleon will ride in triumph into our capital. No such thought crossed the minds of Englishmen. For them the great Napoleon had been a trouble and involved them in a long war but they had beaten him, and they were confident that they could beat the third Napoleon in the same way.

Not that they were without apprehensions. A few years before, when Napoleon III first came to power, Palmerston had been perhaps the Englishman most friendly to him, and during the Crimean War Palmerston had worked closely with him as Great Britain's ally. The thing which alarmed Palmerston, and in a sense was a symbol of what the greatness of Great Britain was based on, was when in 1857 Napoleon III invited Queen Victoria and Prince Albert to visit him at Cherbourg. Cherbourg had just been created a great naval port, and from this moment there began a shadow over British policy, a shadow small at that time but which was to grow greater and greater as time went on, until in the early twentieth century it overshadowed everything else: the shadow of apprehension that naval power, the security of the seas, might be less easy to keep when steam decided things than in the old days of sail. Palmerston, indeed, with the curious ability which old men often have of jumping to new conclusions, despaired of sea power altogether from the moment that steam came in. He was confident that a French steam navy, based on Cherbourg, would be able to cross overnight and seize the Isle of Wight before the British Navy was aware that anything was happening. This, of course, was an exaggeration: invasions cannot be laid on in this twenty-four-hour way.

One of the products of these apprehensions can still be seen on the south coast; for miles behind Portsmouth there are brick fortifications as there are also in the entrances to the Solent and Spithead, all created during the naval panic of 1860, 1861, 1862. You can see adjacent to one another the great fortress of

Porchester, which the Romans built in order to keep off the first Saxon pirates in the third or fourth century, and the brick fortifications which Palmerston built a hundred years ago to keep off the French; and you can discover also the fortifications put up in the last war, mainly tank obstructions, against the most dangerous threat of invasion which this country had known for a long time.

As a matter of fact, this threat was by no means so great as Palmerston made out. Not only was invasion, even with a steam navy, technically much more difficult than he was inclined to imagine, but politically it was more remote. It is a mistake often made by statesmen when they look at the armaments of other countries to assume that these armaments are directed against them. Napoleon III had no plans for invading England. He had plans to increase the French Navy because when men are in power, particularly men like Napoleon III who wanted to do great things, they think they must have great armaments. Often, for no purpose at all, armaments are pursued as an end in themselves. If the British have a navy, the French must have a navy too! I doubt if there was much more to it than that. In any case, in a few years France had many other things to worry about, and it was not until the twentieth century that the German Navy raised once more the apprehensions that sea power was going to be difficult to maintain.

But this is a curious flash of the future, towards the end of the career of a man who spanned vast areas of the past. Palmerston's approach to foreign affairs was based, as that of all British statesmen was based, on sea power, but in the earlier part of his career he did not draw from this by any means a lesson of isolation. He did not say: since we control the seas, since we are secure with the protection of our great navy, we should not bother about Europe. The Napoleonic Wars, indeed, saw the exact opposite. Great Britain was at war, not always on the Continent but in regard to continental matters, for over twenty years – from 1793 until 1815 with one short break; and thereafter, particularly when Palmerston was in power, British policy played an active part on the Continent.

It was largely British support which enabled the unification of Italy to be carried through. Statesmen all over the Continent, when they wondered, for instance, whether it would be possible to bring the German nation together, immediately considered the role that Great Britain would have to play; and only a few years before, in the Crimean War of 1854 to 1856, Great Britain had taken part in a great war – from her point of view, the only big war between 1815 and 1914.

Palmerston was the man who represented the way in which Great Britain was an active continental power. The strength of Great Britain rested, so far as Europe went, on two things. The first was the navy itself – not merely as an instrument of protection for this country but an instrument also which enabled Great Britain to intervene here and there in Europe where she wanted to do so. The most dramatic illustration of this in our history is the Peninsular campaign during the Napoleonic Wars, when, on the basis of sea power, Great Britain had been able to put an army into Portugal and from Portugal to harass the French in Spain and ultimately, after four years of campaigning, to drive the French from Spain altogether. Here had been a land operation in which the Duke of Wellington had risen to fame, which was yet essentially part of sea power: it was entirely a combination of the British Navy and the British Army working together. In the same way, during the nineteenth century, Great Britain played an important part where sea power seemed to enable her to step on to the Continent and to use what small army she had. It was sending the fleet to Antwerp in 1833 which had given a decisive twist to the Belgian question. Although Great Britain never intervened in Italy, it was the security which the British Fleet in 1860 gave to Garibaldi that enabled him to invade southern Italy and so liberate it; sea power which had again made Great Britain the decisive factor in the unification of Italy; and exactly the same thing applies in regard to Turkey and the Near East; the navy cleared the way for the army which ultimately could be sent to the Crimea.

This was one aspect of Great Britain's European position; the other was the assumption that the European powers were rivals and that Great Britain, because of her detachment, could play one side off against the other and thus promote the interests of smaller countries and ultimately the interests of European security. Palmerston believed in the balance of power but what he meant by this was that the balance between the European countries was constantly precarious, one side being too strong, the other side bobbing up in the air, and that Great Britain kept things steady by balancing between them. The balance of power was not a let-out. It meant you must keep things actively in balance, supporting Napoleon III so long as he was moderate and promoting a liberal course of policy: on the other hand, swinging round against him if he, in his turn, threatened to become too aggressive. You can work this out easily in regard to the Crimean War, which was the big switch for British policy from the idea of stability by supporting Russia, the 'Holy Alliance', to stability by supporting Napoleon III and the 'Liberal Alliance'.

In 1862, Palmerston still supposed that these factors would work and it was for this reason that he was running into failure. Perhaps I ought not to have been talking about Palmerston as the representative Englishman but rather of Richard Cobden, a back-bencher, a man who never held office and yet who, so far as the shaping of British foreign policy went, was going to have a deeper effect, and perhaps one of longer term, than Palmerston had. This deep underlying change was that British opinion was losing interest in the Continent altogether. No doubt, like Palmerston, they wanted to see liberal states all over Europe, but they were coming more and more to think either that liberalism would win by itself or, in any case, that it was the job of the European peoples to do it, that we were not called upon, as John Bright said on one occasion, to be the liberators of Europe.

Moreover, this new school tended to think that if somebody else did it, this meant that the liberation was not successful, that nothing would be achieved, and that war, being the greatest of all evils even if fought in the name of liberty, would do more harm to liberty than standing aside. They held also – and this, I think, is one of the biggest things that happened in British history in the nineteenth century – a different view of the balance of power. They did not think, like Palmerston, that it was something unstable which had to be balanced; they assumed that it was there. Cobden and most of his followers certainly held this view, and most held that the European powers balanced each other out and that whatever happened, if one power won wars and another power lost wars, it would not basically make any difference: countries would still remain independent countries; and, more than that, Europe would never be brought together, as it had been in Napoleonic times under a single ruler, in such a way as to endanger this country. Cobden, indeed, looking back, argued, as Charles Fox had done, that even French predominance on the Continent would not be a danger to this country, that nobody wanted to invade us. Cobden said of the idea of the balance of power that it was a vast chimera, and that the best thing for this country would be to have no foreign policy at all: in other words, turn your back on Europe, the Europeans can arrange their own affairs.

This change of attitude had taken place imperceptibly. In the Crimean War Cobden and his associate John Bright had been utterly rejected; in the general election of 1857 they both lost their seats, but they were back now and they counted; and when, soon after this, Great Britain was faced by Bismarck with a problem of what to do, these factors came into operation. Great Britain was the first country which experienced Bismarck's impact. In 1864 Prussia and Austria invaded what was then more or less the southern part of Denmark – the two Duchies of Schleswig and Holstein. Denmark had been guaranteed by this country. More than that, it was regarded as important for this country that Denmark, a friendly but small power, should control the entrance to the Baltic, and when the thing started there was a good deal of talk by Palmerston himself that anyone who tampered with Denmark would find that it was not with Denmark alone that he had to do; but, as the thing developed, as the Prussian and Austrian armies went on, the Danes were inevitably defeated and it turned out that Great Britain could do nothing.

In the first place, supposing she had a navy; supposing even she sent it to Danish waters, what could she do? The British Army was certainly not on a scale which enabled it to face the Prussian and Austrian armies combined, and, incidentally, most of the British Army was at this time locked up in Canada, where it was supposed that the United States – though in the midst of the Civil War – were about to invade and seize Canada for themselves. So that from the point of view of material there was nothing to operate on, and in the second place there were no allies. The suspicions which Palmerston had of Napoleon, the fear of the French Navy, made him think that it would be worse for Great Britain to win a war in alliance with Napoleon than, as it were, to lose a war or to run away from a war because you could not have the support of Napoleon.

Looking back with later knowledge, we may say that Palmerston was lucky. The French Army was not the great army which people imagined, and a few years later it was to suffer disastrous defeat at the hands of the Prussian Army, so that maybe if Great Britain and France as allies had tried to intervene in 1864 they would have been defeated; or, rather, the French would mainly have been defeated; Great Britain would have been in a more embarrassing position than before. However, the strongest reason why Great Britain did not intervene to aid Denmark is that British opinion no longer wanted it, that the English people did not want to be a European power. They did not think that Europe mattered. The man who determined foreign policy in 1864 was no longer Palmerston, no longer Russell, it was without the slightest doubt Richard Cobden, with Bright supporting him and the great bulk of the Liberal Party in the House of Commons agreeing with him.

Among Russell's papers at the Record Office there is a little scrap of paper from the cabinet meeting of 25 June 1864. Russell had wanted to send the fleet and on this scrap of paper are written various suggested resolutions for the cabinet. It was no good; Russell closed it up, put it away in his file and there it still is – and from the point of view of British policy it is one of the most significant documents in our history, because from that day on for forty years, except under Disraeli in 1878, British governments did not contemplate, however remotely, interfering in continental affairs. June 25 1864 ended a whole period when Great Britain had been shaping Europe, and it is the moment when the British said: we are finished with Europe. We shall rely on our sea power, on the specific nature of other countries, on the fact that European countries balance each other out, and we shall leave Europe to get on as best it can. Forty years, I said: as a matter of fact, it was just over that. June 25 1864 begins British detachment from continental affairs from the military point of view. Plenty of diplomacy went on – and 31 January 1906 begins a new period of involvement when a British government, or rather a British foreign secretary and prime minister, without telling their colleagues, decided to have military conversations with France, preparing for intervention in the next war against Germany. But for a whole generation and more the thing was over, and when it came back, it came back in a different form.

Palmerston maybe had outlived the circumstances in which he could be great. It would be wrong to say that this discouraged him: he was always cheerful in adversity. For one thing, he shifted off on to Russell all the responsibility for the failure and the responsibility even for the talk about sending fleets. He took also the view – one held, I suppose, by most Englishmen (very important indeed for Bismarck's success) – that if there was going to be a conflict between France and Germany, and he expected one, it was in British interests that Germany should win. He thought that the Prussian Army would be defeated; he still thought the French Army much the greatest; but he hoped that Prussia would win because he thought that France was too powerful, and also more likely to cut across Great Britain's imperial interests; whereas Prussia, a more or less land-locked country, even when it became national Germany, would be sensible, free-trade, engaged in economic activities all over the world but never a rival to this country, and never, for that matter, likely to dominate Europe. In the long run, this judgement was somewhat mistaken. Nevertheless, it was representative of the times. Palmerston showed, one might say, even at the very end of his life, an ability to keep up with events, to judge in a reasonably fresh way, because although his opinion that Germany was no danger and that France was a great danger became ultimately out of date, it was not out of date in the eighteen-sixties, and the experience of the later part of the nineteenth century justified, on the whole, the view that Germany was a stable and pacific power.

It is curious that the man who had been first defeated or checked by Bismarck was also the man who was sensible enough to appreciate that Bismarck's success would be to his own advantage; and, more than this, could judge – this is not a bad thing for a statesman – in terms that were right even for thirty or forty years ahead. All statesmen, of course, judge wrongly if they judge all that far ahead – but Palmerston remained, to the day of his death, confident, cheerful, and still believing that he could run things better than anybody else, still believing that he could go on – and indeed everyone admitted it. Palmerston lasted until he dropped – and he dropped. He died literally in twenty-four hours: he caught cold riding on a horse out to Harrow, came back, died. It is ironical that this man who was the symbol of British involvement in the Continent should have ended with Great Britain completely withdrawn from European affairs.

Alexander II, Tsar of Russia

Unlike most rulers, Tsar Alexander II was a good man. I do not mean that he had a tremendous sense of duty or industry; he spent far less time at his desk working on papers than, say,

Emperor Francis Joseph of Austria. I certainly do not mean that he was in the ordinary sense a moral man: on the contrary he is one of the few rulers who actually installed a second family in his palace when his first and official wife was still alive. It is true that he married this second wife on the death of his first, and was devoted to the second family, but it is an unusual thing to have two families living in the same palace. In this way, people shook their heads and regarded him as more immoral than, say, Napoleon III, who had a great many connections but did not install them in the palace.

Alexander II really wanted to do good to his people. He did not merely think of them as instruments for his power, as Francis Joseph did. He was not interested in popularity, and, indeed, he was very unpopular most of his life. He had a deep duty – 'these are my people and I want to do good for them'. I can hardly think of a ruler who spent more of his life worrying about how he could make things better for the people over whom he ruled. He was not much good at his job; he was an ineffective good man, which makes him even more attractive. He spent most of his time as a ruler in bewilderment. In theory, he was the most powerful man in Europe, if not in the world.

Every other monarch in Europe by this time had some kind of restraint, had to operate some imitation of a constitution, to observe standards of law and to conform to practices which had been built up by his predecessors. The tsars remained as they had always been, despots in the strict sense of the term. They inherited the term indeed from the emperors of the eastern Roman Empire; they claimed in many ways to be the heirs of this eastern Roman Empire which had perished in 1453. They were far more than Louis XIV had been or the great Napoleon. They were the state. Without the tsars, the state could not exist. Alexander II was theoretically a despot, and yet he tried to use for good this enormous power which he was supposed to possess. He found himself – and I suspect that he was by no means the last Russian ruler who found himself in this position – in conflict, as it were, with a sort of feather bed. To be a despot where you are pushing against a great mass of custom and obstinacy and futility is a hard job, and it broke him. Often he would despair.

The thing which dominated his life was the appalling condition of the Russian people and, particularly, the Russian peasantry: the state of serfdom, the degradation of the common mass of people, so that they were a sort of human cattle attached to the land. This had been the common thing in the European Middle Ages, and the history of modern Europe in a large part turns on the way in which this degrading human condition was brought to an end, sometimes by means of liberation, as in the French Revolution. In this country the solution was rather different. We got rid of serfdom by the simple way of getting rid of the serfs. We cleared the land. The agricultural labourers did not suddenly become free human beings; they were just pushed off elsewhere. But whereas others had got rid of it, serfdom not only remained in Russia, it had become much worse. Russia was, strangely enough, one of the last countries to adopt this system. In the sixteenth century the Russian peasants were free men, and Russia was actually imitating this terrible system when others were breaking free from it. The most brutalizing point of serfdom was in the eighteenth century, when in Europe as a whole it was crumbling; and in the mid-nineteenth century there were still tens of millions of Russian people who were sold along with the estates. They were treated simply as objects of property. There was even a movement to create industrial serfs as well.

Nobody can pretend that this is a good way of running agriculture, still less of running factories, and Alexander's father, who was much more hard-hearted than he was, had often dreamt of getting rid of serfdom, but he had done little about it. From the time when Alexander came to the throne in harsh circumstances, in February 1855, he had made this idea of getting rid of serfdom the key-point of his policy. But unlike some of the German rulers he was not personally a bureaucrat. He set up a committee and in no time at all this first committee was captured by those who believed in serfdom. After three years of work, the committee submitted a long report in which certain laws were put forward which would have left serfdom as it was before. So Alexander set up a second committee and it was not until 1861, when he had been on the throne for six years, that the great edict of emancipation was passed.

It would be foolish to pretend that the edict of emancipation, which ended serfdom in Russia, brought with it a great era of liberty and emancipation and made the Russian people suddenly not only free but prosperous. The Russian peasants remained living under harsh conditions. One could even go further and say that even the revolution of 1917 did little to improve their conditions. Yet, with all its failures, the edict of emancipation was one of the great acts of the nineteenth century – and Alexander, with all his weakness, deserves to be remembered. He made a larger change in Russian history than anyone between Peter the Great and Lenin – and he made the kindest and most generous change that there has ever been in Russian history. Two great emancipations took place in the world more or less at the same time – Alexander's edict of emancipation of 1861 which ended serfdom in Russia and President Lincoln's freeing of the slaves in 1863, which, again, did not achieve all it was meant to do because the coloured people of the United States have not stepped into the position of complete equality which freedom implies. Yet these were both notable edicts of freedom.

Alexander was not a great man. The edict emancipating the serfs was one of the big moments of history but the way in which it was done did not turn Alexander into a great man. It in some ways seems to me much more touching to be an ordinary feeble man and yet do one of the great things in history – which is what Alexander did; it is something for which he deserves to be remembered. He did it in a bewildered, puzzled way, without understanding quite how it should be done or what the details should be, but it is one of the few acts of genuine, uncalculating goodness which the nineteenth century can show. Then, within a few years, there came the movement of those who wanted Russia to become not merely a country where there were no longer serfs, but a constitutional country, a country which was sharing in the liberal developments in the rest of Europe. This made Alexander as unpopular as his predecessors had been.

This was the burden of being a despot who did not want to be a despot, the burden of running a great state when he would much rather that others would have run it if only they had done it in an enlightened way. This was not the only burden which Alexander II carried. He was the first Russian ruler for a long time who had to carry the burden of inferiority with the rest of Europe. In his reign there began a long period in which Russia as a Great Power felt that she was not being treated on an equality with the others and in which there was built up a long tradition of resentment and suspicion against the rest of Europe.

From the middle of the eighteenth century, or indeed a little earlier, from the time of Peter the Great, Russia had stepped right on to the European stage as a Great Power, and if one goes back a hundred years before Alexander II, to the time of the Seven Years War, nobody at that time thought that Russia was different from other European countries: indeed, they thought Russia was pretty formidable. Russia was certainly more formidable an enemy for Frederick the Great than either Austria or France, and in the negotiations of the time Russia played a full part as a European power. In the Napoleonic Wars only Russia and England escaped being conquered by Napoleon and forced within the Napoleonic Empire. The existing European order, the balance of power which held France in check and also, of course, the monarchical order, all rested on Russian strength. When monarchs were in trouble they knew that Russia would come and help them out. Russia was really the shaping force over much of Europe; it was only in Great Britain and France that Russian power was checked at all. When Francis Joseph came to the throne in 1848 and was faced with a great rebellion in Hungary which the whole powers of the Austrian Empire could not subdue, he appealed for aid to Nicholas I and, in no time at all, a Russian army came in and subdued the Hungarian revolution. It was in 1849 that the Russian troops first, as it were, got the experience of crushing a Hungarian revolution – this time for the benefit of the monarchical order in Europe – and then, five years later, there came the Crimean War.

By a series of terrible miscalculations, Russia got involved in war with the Western powers and was defeated by them. In the middle of the war, in 1855, Nicholas died and Alexander II came to the throne. Within a year he had to make a peace of defeat, and with this Peace of Paris in 1856 Russia was really excluded from Europe, treated as almost a second-rate power. This begins a long period of Russian history: it runs from the end of the Crimean War in 1856 until the meeting at Potsdam in 1945, when Russia appeared as a victor – though, even then, a bit doubtful whether she was going to be treated on a basis of complete equality by the other victors, and particularly by the United States; and this long background begins with Alexander II. He was the first Russian ruler who felt 'the others are against me; the others have done me down'.

Over and over again – and it explains much that happened in central Europe at this time – when Russia was faced with a problem in regard to the policies of central Europe or in regard to relations with France and with Great Britain, the only answer which Alexander II could give was 'I want to break the ring which was formed against me at the time of the Crimean War.' It was one of the secrets of Bismarck's success. Within nine years he was able to defy all the powers of Europe and to unite Germany. Russia under Alexander II had lost interest in Europe and was simply saying: if we can get rid of what was done in the Crimean War, if we can break up the European coalition against us, we can weaken France, weaken Austria, make England isolated, and we do not care what happens in Germany. It is a fantastic and fascinating story of an obsession, and it dominated Alexander.

In the course of the nineteenth century men – writers, intellectuals – invented, I was going to say, the idea of Slav solidarity: that Russia should be the leader of the Slav countries and that Russia should seek to promote their cause and to protect them and to free them from the rule of the Turks. Nicholas I had not cared much for this idea. Alexander II did. As Slav feeling grew in Russia, he felt himself drawn into it, and when, in 1876, the Slav people of the Balkans – the Bulgarians – were being massacred by the Turks, not only was Russian feeling stirred up, but Alexander's own feeling was stirred up. He did not want a war; he knew that again Russia would probably make a mess of it; but he went back to Moscow in 1877 and announced: 'We must feel a solidarity with the suffering Balkan peoples.' As a result of this, he was plunged into a Balkan war; he did make rather a mess of it, and Russia was again humiliated at the Congress of Berlin. But all the same, Alexander II is remembered in Bulgaria today as the tsar liberator, the man who is responsible for the fact that there are national states in eastern Europe at the present time.

He would have liked, even, to liberate the Poles, but again it went wrong with him. As soon as he did anything to give the Poles a better life they began to quarrel, and Alexander is remembered instead as the man who crushed the second Polish rising, the man who established a Russian tyranny over Poland which was to last until 1914. At the end of his life Alexander wanted to carry this process of liberation further. He wanted also to make Russia look like a civilized country. He wanted Russia to have a constitution. One of the first things he said was: 'In my reign, Russia will cease to be a backward country' – and he meant by this that Russia would acquire some of the liberal institutions which existed everywhere else in Europe. The truth is they were not there and that the only thing which was really there was the will of the tsar. With Alexander, this was more than usually lacking, and there was no reason why there should be a generous response on the part of those who wanted Russia to be liberal. They were not to know that

Alexander had good intentions, and even if he had good intentions this did not interest them: they wanted something serious to happen; nothing was happening.

It is, indeed, in the reign of Alexander II that the revolutionary organizations were founded which, later on, were to bring the old Russia down and in which the revolutionary spirit was established. It is a strange but, of course, not unusual thing that it is in the reign of the well-intentioned that revolutions start. Alexander was, I would say, the best-intentioned of rulers and, therefore, one is not surprised that it is really in his reign that the revolutionary organizations begin. His father was a straight, narrow tyrant who really devoted his energies to nothing else than to keeping the people down. He was known as the gendarme of Europe – and in his time there were very few stirrings.

In Alexander's time everything went soft and easy, and the men who ought to have been working together, Alexander and the reformers, pulling the people into life, found that they were working against each other and that all the energies and activities of the revolutionaries were directed not towards creating a free, public life, but against Alexander: he became the most endangered of monarchs. Tsars had, on the whole, a dangerous time; Alexander's grandfather was murdered and his father practically committed suicide, but Alexander was the only one of them who was killed in the streets – and this out of kindness of heart because when a bomb blew up under his carriage he could have escaped, but he stopped the carriage to find out what had happened to those who had been injured. This gave the assassins a second – this time a successful – opportunity to kill him.

Karl Marx

Karl Marx looks as though he has got in almost by mistake among all these kings and emperors and great rulers. In 1862 Marx was an exile, living in humble circumstances in London, in considerable financial trouble. He had kept himself for some years by making contributions to American newspapers, writing up in a rather dramatic way what was happening in Europe, announcing that a new revolution was coming. When the American Civil War started there was not a great demand for dramatic news from Europe – they had much more dramatic news in their own country – and Marx lost his job. He was in hard circumstances: isolated, hardly knowing anybody in London, certainly not counting much on the continent of Europe – not counting in history in 1862. Yet he was in some ways the most important, the most dynamic and significant figure of those I have been discussing.

It would be wrong to say that Marx is here because he represented revolution. He represented this and much more. Somebody has to come in among the great outstanding figures of a hundred years ago to represent revolution. All the events of a hundred years ago – indeed, for quite a long time thereafter – were operated under the shadow of the revolutions of 1848. This was the great dividing line of the century, so far as Europe goes. It means less to us because all we had in 1848 was the big Chartist demonstration on 10 April on Kennington Common, which is now devoted to the more useful purpose of cricket. It is the Surrey cricket ground. Kennington Common saw the last great revolutionary demonstration in this country: the last time when it appeared that the masses would rise and would tear down the existing system, and all it ended in was a sort of picnic, with the revolutionaries collecting indeed on Kennington Common, and then pulling out their hampers and having an agreeable lunch of meat pies and beer and being persuaded to go home.

But on the continent of Europe the revolutions of 1848 had indeed threatened to tear everything to pieces; and of those I have been discussing Napoleon III owed his throne to the revolution; Francis Joseph had been brought to the throne when the whole of the Austrian Empire was torn apart by revolution; Alexander II, who was to be killed by a revolutionary, was thinking all his political life in terms of the shadow of revolution. These monarchs, although they looked so grand, apart perhaps from the rulers of this country, were by no means so secure as they appeared. They were harassed by assassinations, by fears that new popular movements would arise, by the problem of facing the great new problem of the nineteenth century, that for the first time in the history of mankind history had stopped being the story of a few people at the top. This is the major thing that happened in the nineteenth century: it started with the French Revolution and has gone on until our own day. Before the French Revolution it really is true that what we call history is the story of what is happening to just a few people at the top; and the masses of people have no more history than if they were cattle. The fundamental transformation of the destinies of mankind that started with the fall of the Bastille, was carried through to the nineteenth century, and has delivered us into what we are at the present day, is that the masses of mankind have ceased to be cattle. They are often block-headed in other ways, as we all are, but they are not cattle any more; and the significant moment for Europe as a whole was that they were not cattle in 1848.

If you had asked men of 1862 who was the revolutionary, not many would have picked on Marx. They would have picked men who had been important in 1848: Mazzini, for instance, was a much more significant figure in 1848. Mazzini represented the spirit of 1848, the belief in Utopia, in man's goodness; the belief that by a simple operation, by a declaration of liberty, by an emotional appeal to the nation, mankind all over Europe would step forth into a life of happiness, and the problems of ordinary human existence could be answered. Mazzini, as a matter of fact, was a finished force. Though he was still around as a writer he meant nothing.

Many people would have picked the man who was a glamorous revolutionary figure in 1862, Garibaldi, the redshirt, who by his own inspiration had completed the liberation of Italy. When bits of Italy had been freed from the Austrians, but most of it was still a disunited country, Garibaldi with his 1,000 had gone to Sicily – an enterprise, in its way, as great as the invasion of Sicily by General Eisenhower. But General Eisenhower and the British and American armies had two great empires behind them, and a gigantic organization; Garibaldi invaded Sicily with one little ship and 1,000 men. He conquered it, he conquered Naples, he swept through Italy. General Garibaldi, without any doubt, was in the romantic sense the greatest of the revolutionaries; and a very attractive man, too – a man of simple belief in humanity.

In 1864, when he came to this country, he received, I suppose, the most enthusiastic reception which any foreigner has ever received, except possibly President Woodrow Wilson at the end of the First World War. You can still find – if you are interested in such things – oaks planted in 1864 by the hero of liberty, General Garibaldi; and you can be sure that if these are on some estate it shows that the landowner there was himself a fine radical and regarded General Garibaldi as the hero of liberty.

Yet he, too, was finished: there was nothing that he represented thereafter. This liberation of Italy was a fine and inspiring thing, but what did it end up in? Redshirts in 1860 – Blackshirts in 1922. Garibaldi, a fine theatrical figure and a hero of liberty in 1860 – Mussolini, the same sort of figure, same sort of posturing: not much really to choose between them; the thing ran thin.

The significance of Marx is that he was more than a figure of melodrama. In 1848 he played a very modest role. He was a journalist. Just before the outbreak of the revolutions of 1848 he and his friend Engels wrote a programme for a society of German tailors and shoemakers in Brussels. There were only about twenty of them altogether, and he drafted, as people did in those days, a universal programme for the twenty. A few hundred copies were printed just when the revolutions of 1848 broke out. I would guess that in the course of 1848, out of the hundreds of thousands of people who took part in the revolutions, who went to the barricades, not more than one in 100,000 read this little programme. It was called the *Communist Manifesto*, and it was in ideas, though not in influence, the most significant thing that had happened in the revolutions of 1848. When the revolutions of 1848 failed, Marx came as an exile to this country: there was no other free country at this time. Imagine England being regarded as a free country! It was a strange time.

In those days anybody who wanted to come to a free country was actually allowed to come – they took freedom seriously. Marx expected a new revolution, but nothing happened. In 1857, when there was indeed another economic crisis, more unemployment, Marx said 'This is it.' Nothing happened. And by 1862 he was in a gloomy mood: financially in difficulties, with not much prospect, as he believed, of another economic upheaval. Still interested, still fascinated, but mainly driven back into long-term speculation. The revolutionary work which Marx accomplished was not carried out by means of secret conspiracies. Unlike most revolutionaries of the eighteen-sixties or seventies, Marx never constructed what was called in those days an 'infernal machine' – I suppose what we should call bombs. Nowadays though, it is not revolutionary to make infernal machines; the better scientist you are the more infernal the machine you make. But in those days it was revolutionary. The only infernal machine Marx made was an idea; and he made it not by going out into the streets and agitating but by settling down and working day after day in the library of the British Museum. He is indeed the only man who has changed the whole destiny of the human race simply by sitting in the British Museum.

You may say that Lenin did it later, but this is not so; Lenin did not get anything out of the British Museum, he went there to read out of interest. It was not the operation of what happened in the British Museum that made things different for him; but with Marx it was. It was these ten or fifteen years which he spent in the British Museum which enabled him to recast the picture of man's place in society and to discover far more explosive power than was ever to be found by grubbing around in cellars and scratching out saltpetre, which is the way that revolutionaries usually operated.

Marx's discovery – his theory or instrument – looks like many discoveries, which, once they have been made, are simple. They tell me that most of the things that modern scientists do are really quite simple: that after they have done it, people have looked back and said 'Why didn't we think of that before?' I cannot understand them, but the younger generation say there is no problem here, the theories of Einstein are child's play, anyone who tried to look at the universe without an Einstein approach now would really be as block-headed as the flat-earth man. With Marx it is much the same. Once you get hold of this device it seems so obvious; and has indeed seemed obvious to many people thereafter. Marx started by being a revolutionary. Long before he applied serious analysis and looked round for what was happening in the world, he was against it. He was revolutionary in the way that Mazzini was, or Garibaldi, or Orsini, who had tried to blow up Napoleon III by an infernal machine; he was by background, by origin, a radical, he was *against*. Why people should become radicals and revolutionaries by emotional feeling I do not know. Other historians have spent a long time puzzling over this. It puzzles me the other way round: why people are not all revolutionaries: why they are not all carrying the torch aflame to set the whole system alight. At any rate, right or wrong, Marx started as a revolutionary; he thought that revolution to blow up existing society was a good thing. And he looked around at what had happened in 1848, at the discontents: men wanted the vote, they wanted universal suffrage, they wanted to be recognized as equal citizens; they resented the fact that some people had rank and some people had not.

Then – and this is the new trick he played – Marx said the people who were most discontented and the people whose discontent took the strongest form were the working class: the people who were experiencing the hardships of factory life. With other people, that is to say with people who were reasonably off, tolerably educated, comfortable, the discontent, the radicalism, is something in the head. For instance, Marx wrote a series of articles denouncing Lord Palmerston as the specific wicked aristocrat. This is something in the head! Marx had never seen Lord Palmerston, he was not really any worse off because of Lord Palmerston's existence; he had a mere intellectual dislike: 'I do not like the thought that that frivolous old man is running the destinies of the British Empire and determining the destinies of Europe.'

But when we go to the working class – to the industrial worker – their discontent is not in the head; it is in day-to-day conditions. They are discontented because their wages are not enough, because they have to work too long hours, because their living conditions are bad, because of the way in which their children are treated, because the whole atmosphere of the towns in which they live is revolting. And the discontent they have is a stronger and deeper discontent, and one which is more persistent. There were many people in the beginning of the revolutions of 1848 in France, in Italy, in Germany, in Austria, in Hungary, who had appeared on the streets and manned the barricades, because they had discontent in the head. And how long did they stay on the barricades? They stayed for a day – a couple of days – and then they went back to their more comfortable life. But the working class of 1848, the men who had suffered not only terrible unemployment in the winter of 1847–48 but also grave starvation, had gone on demonstrating, agitating, being discontented and being ready to fight on the barricades for much longer.

Marx drew from this a simple and, as it seemed at the time, an obvious conclusion: that if you want to change, funda- mentally, the whole structure of society, if you want to get rid of this wonderful hierarchy of kings and emperors and lords and ladies, and to have instead a society which will consider the needs of everybody – in other words if you want a democratic society – the driving force for this will come from the working class, from those who have practical material grounds for discontent. Marx did not say anyone who is poor has the sort of discontent which makes him into the right kind of revolutionary; he thought only industrial workers, only those who come together in political groupings and particularly in trade unions are those who can really lead a democratic community. Marx had experienced the revolutions of 1848, and it had turned out one of the bitter lessons of 1848 that unorganized discontent gets you nowhere: or, rather, it gets you into a position where you can be dispersed, if not destroyed, by an organized force. The only organized force which could be set against the organized force of the state seemed to be that of the working class. Not just crowds of starving people: the people who starved worst just before 1848 were the Irish; two million of them died; but they also resisted the least. When one of the landowners appeared on the terrace of his house, 200 of his tenants were there, and one of them called out 'On your knees – perhaps he'll give us bread.' That is all the starving can do.

But the organized working class were the ones that Marx believed in; with this wonderful new discovery he was able to turn round to the revolutionaries and say: 'You want a new revolution, you want to create democracy; you can only do this on a class basis; it is only by an organized class as pugnacious and aggressive and, if you like, grasping as the upper classes have been that you will beat them.'

Apparently this policy worked: the combination of the two things – discontent leads to revolution, the working classes are the most discontented, they are therefore the reliable revolutionary force. In 1862 Marx counted for nothing: hardly anybody had heard of him. Two years later there was a big international gathering in London, representatives came from France, from Germany, from Belgium, from Switzerland; they came to demonstrate in favour of Poland, which at this time was being again oppressed by the Russian tsar, Alexander II. But when they were there they said they would like to set up an international organization of a revolutionary kind. Marx provided the basis: not, he said, just an organization of revolutionaries; let this be what he called 'the international working men's association'. One of the decisive moments of history was when – again in London – the International Working Men's Association was set up. The British trade unions provided most of the money (they were the only ones who had any). But there were also trade-union and socialist representatives from other countries, and the ideas were provided by Marx.

This was Marx's period of triumph, the period when he stepped on to the public stage; just when others also were having their successes, when Bismarck was pushing forward, Marx too was being transformed from a mere theorist and speculator into a popular, significant figure. Between 1864 and 1871 the Workers' International became accepted as an effective thing. I do not say that it was very effective; when the rulers of Europe trembled at the name of the International, as Marx boasted, they were trembling largely at something imaginary. But this was a new twist to the whole political set-up; that where previously men had thought simply in terms of conservative or radical, or had thought in national terms, here was a new idea, the idea of a revolutionary international class. The working class – what Marx called the 'proletariat' – would represent the future and would go driving forward.

In the eighteen-sixties, when Marx was writing his work of theoretic economics called *Capital*, he picked up the idea of evolution, the idea that history is on the move: exactly at the same time that Darwin was applying it to animals and to ordinary life, Marx picked it up as a social idea. Society, he said, is on the move: just as the ichthyosaurus and diplodocus get outworn and are pushed aside by higher forms of life, so existing forms of society will be pushed aside; the capitalist and the aristocrat will become outmoded in their turn, and will be replaced by a higher form of life: the really enlightened discontented force which was also a constructive force, the proletariat. In this final revolution a thin layer of the minority would be replaced by the majority. This is why Marx, in holding himself to be a democrat, also invented the phrase 'the dictatorship of the proletariat' because he said the dictatorship of the proletariat would be the dictatorship of the majority, meaning the industrial working classes over the corrupt property-owning minority.

There are many other assumptions which Marx made. He assumed for instance that industry would become worldwide, that in every country the factory workers would be the overwhelming majority. He assumed that as industry developed the factory worker would become the characteristic figure, where maybe the machine and very few workers associated with it is becoming the characteristic figure. But there are refinements: the mighty weapon which made Marx confident, and which also made even the most powerful men of the time tremble, was the belief that he had the future on his side and that the proletariat, because they were discontented, would carry through a triumphant revolution.

Why did it not happen? This, although it is looking forward into the future, is a fascinating point; and I think the answer is the very calculation Marx made, that the discontents of the proletariat were practical discontents. When these practical discontents were redressed, then their desire for a revolution vanished. If you want to see the explanation, go to Maitland Park Villas, which is where Marx was living at this time in the eighteen-sixties. His comfortable bourgeois house has vanished: it has been replaced by luxurious flats – far more luxurious than the greatest aristocrat of the time could have imagined a hundred years ago – for the oppressed proletariat.

Bismarck

At the end of the nineteenth century Germany was a greater industrial power than Britain. In fact, she transcended all the powers of Europe, and was runner-up to the United States. It would be impossible to understand Bismarck's career and

Bismarck's success without appreciating the things that were happening in Germany. Nevertheless, Bismarck was the man who realized that they were happening, and it was Bismarck who transformed the map of Europe, the structure of Europe, the outlook of Europe, and, I am inclined to think, also the social character of Europe.

It is probably true that if there had not been Bismarck there would have been somebody else; but it happened to be Bismarck. Compared with the other men I have discussed in this series, compared with Marx for instance, with his highly distinguished academic training and sophisticated upbringing in the Rhineland; compared with Napoleon III with his appreciation, so he supposed, of the modern forces in Europe and his understanding of the career of his great uncle Napoleon I; compared even with Francis Joseph, who despite being a wooden-headed character had in him all the traditions of the Habsburgs – Bismarck was a little man from nowhere. In physique he was a big man, but he belonged to what we should call modest gentry. He had a humble upbringing, living on a farm, doing plenty of the farm work himself; he did not have a particularly distinguished career at the university. There was another extraordinary thing about him: until he became prime minister, almost dictator of Prussia, he had never held any political office. He had held bits of diplomatic office. Where did he get his vision, his grasp of what was going on in the world? Did he read lots of books about economics, did he read John Stuart Mill, did he read de Tocqueville on sociology, did he even read the writings of Marx? It would not seem so. He liked the novels of Sir Walter Scott and Dumas. Strange things, these, to produce the greatest political insight of the nineteenth century.

A few years before, in the revolutions of 1848, he was a violent reactionary; he thought the masses should be shot down, that one should return to extreme conservatism – or so he said. No great statesman, I think, has been more solitary. He lived to be eighty-three, and in all this long life he had hardly a friend, and the friends he had were outsiders like himself – none from his own class of Prussian gentry, or, later on, of German nobility; among other German statesmen, no friends at all. He never visited other great houses. Think of Gladstone: there was not a moment during the long summer holidays when Gladstone was not clocking in at one aristocratic house or the other. Bismarck hated other people's houses; they did not give him enough to eat and drink, for one thing. It was only in his own house that he could get those enormous whole hams on the sideboard, and bottles of champagne before dinner just because he was thirsty, and the bottle or two of brandy afterwards, and the eight or ten Havana cigars which he smoked in the course of the afternoon or evening. His only real friend was an American whom he met when he was a university student, Motley, the author of *The Rise of the Dutch Republic*, who was at one time American ambassador in Germany and other places. But he did not care for his own people. He loved his wife, though he did not regard her in any sense as his intellectual equal. He was devoted also to his children. At the end of his life, when people said to him 'What is the greatest thing that has happened to you?' and they expected him to say 'I've unified Germany, I've been made a prince, I've been made a great statesman', he replied 'That God did not take any of my children away from me.' In a curious way he spent his entire life in enormous public affairs, and the only thing that mattered to him was his devotion to his sons, whom he tried to fiddle into high public office – not altogether successfully.

Bismarck seems to have grasped what was going on in the world by solitary meditation – plodding along in those plains of north Germany, observing the birds and the trees, brooding a great deal (he was a tremendous brooder). His ideas came to him at night, other things came to him at night too – the intensity of personal feeling. When he was particularly brisk he used to come down rubbing his hands and say: 'I've spent the whole night hating.'

He complained that he slept badly, like most people who

have managed to sleep, say, eight hours out of the ten that they are in bed. It used to annoy him very much that the king of Prussia, William I, later the German emperor, also complained of sleeping badly. When Bismarck was in a mood to arrive with his master and say 'I've had a very bad night,' William himself would start 'I've had a very bad night.' Bismarck constantly complained about this. He said it showed the king was a very unfeeling man. 'Monarchs', he said, 'are not like human beings: there are three sorts of people, there are white people and black people and monarchs' – the implication being that monarchs are the most awful of the lot, absolutely hard-hearted. 'I cannot be the servant of princes,' he said, though he also said he was a tremendous monarchist, saving his monarch's throne, and so on. I do not think he really bothered much about this.

Bismarck's most marked distinguishing characteristic, I think, is this. He was by inclination and upbringing a conservative; he belonged to the existing society; but no one else in his community, perhaps no one else in Europe, had the penetration to see that this society could not stay still, that the structure of Europe – in which Germany counted for little and the princes counted for everything and the power of the new capitalist middle class counted for nothing – would not last. Bismarck's main distinguishing feature was that he went along with the forces of change in order to keep them in hand. Most moderate men are soft: it is the radicals, the revolutionaries, who are hard and ruthless. Bismarck was that extraordinary thing, a hard moderate. He was utterly ruthless and cynical in the methods which he employed; and he employed them for the most cautious and limited aims.

He was quite capable of planning wars – a great deal more capable, incidentally, than Hitler. Hitler thought it would be a fine thing to have wars; he did not plan them. Bismarck planned wars but they were little wars; and from the moment that he had got his war, he was thinking how he could stop it, with limited cautious aims. Usually, if you are wicked enough to plan wars – Bismarck was, like all other statesmen, a very wicked man – you do it on a big scale. But with Bismarck you get the impression he was out to make Prussia somewhat more secure. He realized, indeed he said, that unless Prussia became greater she would become less. From the moment he became minister president of Prussia in September 1862 he knew that Prussia's position was precarious: that Napoleon III was planning to remodel the whole of Europe, that Francis Joseph in Austria wanted to establish Austria as the dominant German power, and that Prussia was likely to have a rough time unless she looked after herself. Bismarck played things wonderfully: he separated France and Austria, he built up a situation in which he could present Austria with a war and yet France would approve of this war and be glad that Prussia had won it. The Prussian Army won the war in 1866 in seven weeks. The moment the war had started, Bismarck was already planning to end it on extremely moderate terms; all he wanted was that Prussia should win, that the Austrians should recognize they had been defeated and would no longer seek to rival Prussian leadership in Germany: no indemnity, no surrender of territory, no resentments thereafter, just the victory.

Once this had been done, he made Prussia the leading state in north Germany, established a North German Federation in 1867, and then again manoeuvred things. One of the things one never knows about Bismarck, and perhaps one should not ask, is, did he plan a war with France? I would be inclined to say, of the war with Austria in 1866, that he more or less laid it on. He put things in such a position that they could hardly happen otherwise. The Austrians helped; it always takes two to make a war, a thing which people often forget nowadays when they talk about war guilt. Big powers can attack little powers; but among great powers it takes two to make a war.

Did Bismarck plan a war with France in 1870 in the same way? Did he say 'It is necessary to have a war in order to unify Germany'? I am inclined to think he did not plan it: that, rather, he set up his position by which Germany was going to get stronger and more secure, and he hoped this would happen without a war. There was a long time when people thought he had laid a deliberate trap for the French in 1870, when he ran a Hohenzollern candidate for the throne of Spain. He did run this Hohenzollern candidate; but I do not think, and for once I have the impression that most historians have come round to agree with me, that he ran it in order to land the French in a war. He ran it for quite different reasons.

Whatever happened, he got his war of 1870 – a war which ended that French domination of Europe that had existed for nearly 300 years: it was the end of France as the leading power in Europe. And here again Bismarck ended it in moderation – not as much moderation maybe as he would have liked. This time he had to demand some French territory, Alsace and Lorraine; and whether he did this as reluctantly as he sometimes made out, it is difficult to say. Later on, he said what a mistake it had been, that it had been imposed on him by the generals: he was wonderful at blaming other people. Maybe he also was a bit carried away by excitement. He claimed an indemnity, and people have shaken their heads thereafter and said what an appalling indemnity, what a Prussian brutal thing, it was. It was, in proportion to population, exactly the indemnity which Napoleon I had claimed of Prussia in the year 1807. But we in this country can read English, we can read French – but we do not read German. Therefore anything that happens to France is an injustice, but anything that happens to the Germans is all right. Everybody has forgotten the indemnity which Napoleon I imposed on Prussia; everybody remembers the indemnity which Bismarck imposed on the French.

At any rate, there it was: Germany was a great power in Europe. But there is another equally important side to Bismarck's work: he made Germany inside. He came to power in 1862 because the king of Prussia was in terrible trouble with his parliament; it looked as if he was going to abdicate, or that if he did not he might have his head cut off. Bismarck certainly saved the Prussian Monarchy. He carried on the conflict with parliament until later on the parliament compromised and gave way. What many overlook is that he also saved the Prussian parliament, that when the king's advisers said 'Let's shut parliament down altogether', Bismarck kept the constitution going. He lives in history for a phrase he admitted himself was an indiscretion, when he said in October 1862: 'The great decisions of our day will not be made by paper resolutions and the decisions of majorities – that was the mistake of 1848 [the time of the revolution] – they will be made by blood and iron.' Actually he said 'iron and blood' and for some reason the words got turned round in all the books. People said what a wicked thing it was to say; but isn't it a fact that all the great decisions in international affairs are made on the basis of power? When Bismarck said 'iron and blood' he did not mean by this simply killing people, he meant iron, industrial strength; blood – hard work, and the drive of nations. Isn't this what all international decisions are made about? Has any important decision ever been made by paper resolutions and the votes of majorities? Bismarck put it in a provocative form, instead of wrapping it up. But the other side of him is that, having said this apparently appalling thing, he used blood and iron to shape the destinies of mankind in a most moderate and modest way. He could, with his grasp of a European situation, with the backing of the German Army, maybe have conquered all Europe for Germany. It was the last thing he wanted to do: always he wanted to stop and be moderate.

Look at his extraordinary social work. Bismarck, more than anyone else – more than these British statesmen who are often extolled for this purpose, more perhaps even than Lloyd George – was the man who defeated Marx. Bismarck understood about Marx. One of Bismarck's confidential secretaries – a man called Bucher – had been a revolutionary associate of Marx, and indeed at one time, in 1867, Bismarck invited Marx to join the German propaganda service. Nowadays Marx would have taken the job – the more revolutionary you are as a writer the more eager you are for official commissions; but in those days people had consciences of a sort, and maybe the pay was not good enough in any case. At any rate, Bismarck understood the Marxist analysis. He understood the whole way in which Marx had imagined there was going to be revolution, and it was Bismarck, I think, who first in Europe grasped the answer to Marx and his revolutionary forecasts. Bismarck said: 'What do the masses want? Do they want – as even Marx imagined – recognition as men? Do they want to become full citizens? Do they want to feel that they are the real equals of Prince Bismarck? Or do they want security? Do they want tolerable economic conditions?'

In Bismarck's view security would destroy the revolutionary feeling of the masses. This, after all, is the great Marxist issue, the issue which Marx had raised already in the eighteen-sixties and seventies and which was to be raised again and again in the twentieth century. We know that the masses in many parts of the world are revolutionary, but why? Is it because they do not like masters at all? Or are they revolutionary because their conditions are bad? Bismarck gave the answer which came characteristically to him: 'Give them security and they'll be quite content with their existing masters.' Bismarck invented the whole system of giving people security; he invented insurance against ill-health, against sickness, against unemployment, against old age. He provided the German masses with a system which was called state socialism. Indeed, it is this Bismarck system of state socialism which has spread all over Europe, and has made the masses of the people contented as long as they have employment and good pay, with the security of their cards, duly stamped by the employer, by the state, and so on, and they know that they can look forward to a reasonably secure old age. The revolutionary zest has gone out of things. As between Marx and Bismarck, I think Bismarck won, and even present-day Marxists, in a way, confess that he won, because what they say is: one of these days the masses will find that, despite this wonderful card they have got with all their stamps, they are hungry and unemployed and then they will again become discontented. This is the message that is still delivered from Moscow; the message which Marx began to sketch out 100 years ago.

There are few people who say: 'Even if people are contented they still don't want a boss, they still don't want a master.' And it was Bismarck who broke this idea that most people would like to be free. He was a bit cynical about people; maybe he was a bit cynical about himself. Within him there were strange uncertainties. He was neurotic, he always blamed other people for things that went wrong. When he got upset it was always the fault of his enemies. When his cheeks swelled up he used to say: 'That's because people upset me in the parliamentary debates.' As a matter of fact it was because he had toothache, and when he had his tooth taken out there was no more swelling of cheeks, but also there were no more good political effects. He could not stand up on the tribune and say: 'Look what you've done to me. Look at this agony you've caused me.' With all his faults, I feel he was an attractive and fascinating character. But he had this common German characteristic – he always blamed other people. He took credit for his achievements, and they were great; but for anything that went wrong, it was somebody else who did it. He was always, indeed, parading his grievances, and the longer he had successes, the greater he became, the more he paraded his grievances. If he is still a puzzle to you, he is a puzzle to me; and he was very much a puzzle to himself.

Bismarck and Europe

A J P Taylor's books of essays (1950–80) consisted of essays all of which had been previously published except for this one, which first appeared in print in Rumours of Wars *(London, Hamish Hamilton, 1952). Probably it was written in 1951 and is an offshoot from his volume in the Oxford History of Europe:* The Struggle for Mastery in Europe: 1848–1918 *(Oxford University Press, 1954).*

* * *

Legends of Bismarck sprawl over the history of the later nineteenth century. First, the contemporary legend – the Bismarck who produced calculated effects on diplomats and politicians, wore military uniform and revealed only late in life that he had done it in order to save the wear-and-tear on his more expensive civilian clothes. Then the legend of German historians who saw in Bismarck the maker of German unity and for whom he could do nothing wrong or even mistaken. And, the reverse of this, the legend primarily of French historians, though often accepted in England too, for whom Bismarck could do nothing right – the man who planned the downfall of France as a Great Power and was responsible for three invasions of 'the national territory'. More recently there has grown up a version, to which I myself have contributed a little, of Bismarck as the thwarted conservative, exponent of the doctrine of 'the lesser evil', of whom one might say that everything he did he did unwillingly and only because anyone else could have done more of it. Though his political offspring were illegitimate, they were 'only little ones'. The study of Bismarck has become a modern scholasticism, each act and each saying combed over and elaborated on as though it were Holy Writ or one of those few documents which, surviving by chance, give medieval historians the illusion that they are engaged in a more scientific discipline than ours.

I have recently been fortunate enough to start examining Bismarck's diplomacy all over again. It would be foolish to pretend that it is possible to shut out of mind the versions of those who have gone before – Sybel and Ollivier, Friedjung and Matter, Grant Robertson and Marcks, Eyck and Srbik. But all of them had some political axe to grind; they were all concerned to show that he had failed or, more rarely, succeeded. I have clean hands. I really do not care – though this may sound untrue – I do not care about the Germans any more one way or the other. I am prepared to believe that Europe is finished; and I am only curious to know what happened to Europe in the second half of the nineteenth century without worrying any more about the outcome. So much of the diplomatic record has now been published that it is possible to write the story virtually from the archives, at any rate so far as Austria, France and Prussia are concerned. Some details of British diplomacy could, no doubt, be added from further study of the archives, though I do not think they would be details of much moment. Russian policy is admittedly still obscure; and a documentary study of this between 1863 and 1871 would be one of the most welcome tasks which a Soviet scholar might perform. But even here the broad outline is clearer than it was a few years ago. I would add two points of caution or of apology. First, I am only concerned to look again at Bismarck's diplomacy, not at his work in Germany. I am convinced that his decisive achievement was in domestic politics and that the Bismarckian compromise or contradiction within Germany – it comes to much the same thing – is what mattered most in European history. Second, there can be no doubt that Bismarck was a great man. He ran down his predecessors and exaggerated his own achievements; he made more mistakes than he or his admirers would admit; he knocked sometimes at the wrong door and more often at doors that were already open. All the same, it is impossible to read his most casual utterance without feeling that here was someone outsize. It would be a waste of time to try to prove anything else; and equally unnecessary to be reiterating how great he was.

It is a great mistake to begin the story of German unification with Bismarck's accession to power in 1862, or even to treat the events of 1848 as a preliminary without relevance. Everything, including Bismarck's own work, springs from the revolutionary year. It is now widely held that France or Russia or both of them would have forbidden national unification in 1848. There seems little evidence of this. The French radicals supposed that national Germany would be their ally in liberating Poland; and though Bastide, foreign minister from May until December 1848, saw no reason to encourage a national Germany, his only approach to Russia was made to deter the Tsar from reviving the policy of the Holy Alliance. The Tsar's policy in 1848 was simple: he was determined not to move his armies beyond Russia's frontiers. Hence, he refused to intervene even in Schleswig-Holstein, though an important Russian interest – free passage of the Sound – was at stake there. In fact the only power who threatened action over the Elbe duchies was England, the power which otherwise favoured German unification. This is what Palmerston meant by his complaint against 'the parcel of children' at Frankfurt. The German liberals, he thought, ought to be creating 'a natural ally' for Great Britain on the Continent instead of threatening the security of the Baltic. In any case, whatever the attitude of France and Russia to a hypothetical liberal Germany, neither of them made any objection to the consolidation of north Germany under Prussia. The Erfurt union, which made Prussia supreme north of the Main, was carried through without objection from either Russia or France. It is true that the Tsar's object in intervening in Hungary was, in part, to restore a balance in central Europe between Prussia and Austria; but he held, as the French did, that this balance was improved rather than the reverse by the strengthening of Prussia in northern Germany.

Russia followed the same policy in the crisis of 1850 which

ended with the agreement of Olomouc. Certainly the Tsar wished to prevent a war between Prussia and Austria; but he wanted a settlement without either victors or vanquished. His real aim was to consolidate both Prussia and Austria as a neutral conservative buffer between Russia and western Europe. Hence he declared that he would support whichever was attacked; though, in fact, at the crisis Russia promised Austria only moral support. It was not danger from Russia which led the Prussians to give way; nor, for that matter, was it military weakness. Prince William was confident that Prussia could win; and this opinion was shared by the Russian generals who had seen Austrian troops in action in Hungary. Paskievich, the Russian commander-in-chief, even believed that Prussia would be a match for Russia and Austria combined. Prussia's real weakness was that both Frederick William IV and his conservative ministers regarded war with Austria as 'wicked'. They gave way more from conviction than from fear; and after 1850, as before it, Prussia was committed to the policy of reconciling hegemony north of the Main and partnership with Austria. This was also Russia's policy, as was shown in the spring of 1851, when the Tsar forbade Schwarzenberg's programme of uniting Germany under Austria – the empire of seventy millions.

Though Bismarck welcomed the settlement of Olomouc, no one has contributed more to the version that Prussia thereafter became subservient to Austria. This version cannot be sustained. There was perhaps subservience when Manteuffel, the Prussian foreign minister, made a defensive alliance with Austria for three years in 1851. This certainly implied a Prussian guarantee for Austria's possessions in Italy, which she steadily refused thereafter; but it also barred the way against what seemed more likely in 1851 – an Austrian alliance with Napoleonic imperialism. At any rate, there was no subservience in the alliance when it was renewed on 20 April 1854. Though it, too, seemed to serve an Austrian purpose – by guaranteeing the Danubian principalities (later called Romania) against Russia – this was in reality only the bait by which Austria was held from making an alliance with England and France. If Austria had joined the Western powers in war against Russia, Prussia could not have stayed out. Whichever side she joined, she would have had to bear the main brunt of a war fought probably on her own soil – a war from which she could not possibly have gained and in which she might well have lost her Polish lands. As it was, Prussia performed the great service to Russia of keeping Austria neutral at no cost to herself; and, by advocating neutrality at the Diet, won the leadership of the German states as well. Yet this was the time when Bismarck denounced the incompetence of his official superiors. He opposed the alliance with Austria. At the beginning of the war he would seem to have favoured supporting Russia; at the end of it he preached, in one of his most famous compositions, that Prussia should make a third in the coming partnership between Russia and France. His own action in 1879 is the best comment on this policy. As imperial chancellor, Bismarck judged Manteuffel to have been right and himself wrong; but he took care not to say so.

Bismarck overrated all along the dynamism of the Franco-Russian Entente. He thought that Napoleon III and Alexander II were set on remaking the map of Europe, both east and west, in the immediate future and that Prussia must hasten to play the jackal with them if she were not to be left out of things. Official Prussian policy, whether under Frederick William IV and Manteuffel or under the Prince Regent and the despised Schleinitz, stuck to its old line: support for Austria once she had recognized Prussian hegemony north of the Main. This policy came within sight of success in the Italian war of 1859. If Napoleon had insisted on his original aim of liberating Venetia as well as Lombardy, even more if Alexander II had taken the opportunity to reopen the Eastern question – in fact, if France and Russia had been as dynamic as Bismarck supposed – Austria would have had to pay Prussia's price. As it was, she lost Lombardy and thus ended the war without Prussia's help. The real turning-point came in the following year, 1860. In

July, Schleinitz and Rechberg, the Austrian foreign minister, met at Teplitz and agreed on a defensive alliance between their two countries – an alliance which Bismarck himself quoted as a precedent in 1879. The awkward question of Prussian hegemony north of the Main was postponed to a military convention that was to be negotiated subsequently. All this was a preliminary to a meeting of the two German rulers with the Tsar at Warsaw in September. They believed that Alexander II had taken fright at Napoleon's revolutionary policy and would now urge joint resistance in Italy. When it came to the point Alexander II could not give up his hopes for revising the settlement of 1856 in the Near East with French help and therefore would do nothing against Italy, Napoleon's satellite. The Holy Alliance turned out to be a mirage; and the Prussians were quick to draw the lesson. They screwed up their terms in the military discussions with Austria; and when these broke down, the alliance vanished with them. If there was a decisive moment in the relations between Prussia and Austria, it was in April 1861, and not after Bismarck became prime minister.

Bismarck's predecessors perhaps had different allies in mind. Schleinitz counted on the 'liberal' alliance with England, so far as he counted on anything at all. This policy was ruined by the American Civil War, which locked up British military resources in Canada. Moreover, the British were increasingly aware that their navy was out of date. These factors, rather than any ideological swing towards isolationism, made Great Britain ineffective during Europe's years of destiny. Bernstorff who followed Schleinitz looked instead to France; his object was to replace Russia as France's continental ally. When Bismarck arrived in October 1862, he certainly meant to play the role of a Prussian Cavour; but with this difference from Cavour (as from Bernstorff) that he intended to cooperate with Russia as well as with France – a partnership therefore that would be anti-British as well as anti-Austrian. In fact he missed the bus (if there was ever one to catch). He assumed that the Franco-Russian Entente was solid; instead it collapsed before he had been in office six months. Almost his first act was to ask in Paris what the French attitude would be 'if things hot up in Germany'. He was too late. Drouyn de Lhuys, enemy of Russia and advocate of alliance with Austria, had just returned to the Quai d'Orsay. Bismarck's query was brushed aside. Three months later the Polish revolt blew the Franco-Russian Entente sky-high. Years afterwards Bismarck built up the story that he had pulled off a great stroke of policy by supporting the Russians in Poland and therefore winning their gratitude. This is untrue. The Russians thought they could deal with the Poles alone and much resented Prussian patronage. Moreover Bismarck's step ensured that, if it came to war over Poland, Prussia would have to fight for the sake of Russia's Polish lands; and he had to beg to be excused from the alliance with Russia within six weeks of making it. Even as it was, the quarrel over Poland was disastrous for Prussia. The great hope of Prussian policy had been that the French threat to Venetia and Russian threats in the Near East would so embarrass Austria as to make her surrender the hegemony of northern Germany to Prussia without a war. This hope was now ruined. The Franco-Russian Entente had never been a threat to Prussia; rather it gave her security. The entente was directed against Austria; and France would not endanger it by seeking gains on the Rhine. The French threat there, if it ever existed, was created by the estrangement between France and Russia, not by their entente. No doubt Russia was now prepared to tolerate a Prussian war against France; but so she always had been, and this was a very different thing from active support – that the Russians never offered.

The truth is that, once the Franco-Russian Entente broke down, Prussia was forced back to friendship with Austria as her only means of security. Here again Bismarck later created a myth – the story that the Schleswig-Holstein affair was a trap for Austria from the beginning. I think rather that, as so often, Bismarck, always impulsive and always exaggeratedly nervous of the aggressive designs of others, rushed himself into a commitment and then had to exercise all his great genius in order to get out of a tangle of his own making. For there is the fact. In January 1864 he made an alliance with Austria which did not include the recognition of Prussian hegemony north of the Main on which his predecessors had always insisted. His motive was fear, not gain; fear that, as in 1848, Prussia would be pushed forward in Schleswig by German feeling and then have to face a coalition of the powers, reinforced this time by Austria. The Conference of London which tried to settle the Schleswig question showed that these fears were exaggerated. The Russian government was estranged from the Western powers both by the Crimean War and, more recently, by the Polish affair. Besides, the Russians did not object to Prussia's gaining control of the Sound so long as she did not do it on a basis of nationalist enthusiasm. They objected much more to Austria's getting a foothold there and would have preferred an isolated Prussian action. Thus, curiously enough, the partnership with Austria – which Bismarck had insisted on as essential – was the one thing that worried the Russians and made them hostile. Still they did not mean to act in 1864 – as, for that matter, they had refused anything but moral reproofs in regard to Schleswig in both 1848 and 1850. The real opposition in the previous crises had come from England; and the British – estranged from Russia by the Crimean War, suspicious of Napoleon III as a result of his annexation of Savoy, and with their forces tied in Canada – had no means of action. It is inconceivable that there could ever have been an Anglo-Austrian alliance to check Prussia in Schleswig; and, short of this, there was nothing the British could do. They twice took soundings for French support, in February and again in June. Both met with the same response. Napoleon would not act against the 'national' principle; Drouyn, who hated nationalism in general and Prussia in particular, demanded concrete gains on the Rhine – a prospect more unwelcome to the British than the Danish loss of the duchies.

The three non-German powers were in fact far more suspicious of each other than concerned about what might happen in Germany. The only thing that alarmed them was Prussia's alliance with Austria – Bismarck's own doing. Had he acted alone against Denmark, he would have had the approval of all the powers except Austria; but he would have had to act on a liberal basis. Prussia's foreign danger, in short, was increased, if not created, by Bismarck's conflict with the liberals. He made the Austrian alliance, not to trick Austria, but to save himself. This is, I think, the answer to the disputed question whether Bismarck was ever sincere in his conservative partnership with Austria. He was a man of extremes. He could conceive a full return to the system of Metternich; hence in August 1864 he pressed on Austria not only a Prussian guarantee of Venetia, but a campaign for the recovery of Lombardy. He could also conceive of a 'revolutionary' alliance with France, by which Prussia expelled Austria from Germany north of the Main while France gained land on the Rhine. What he never foresaw was the moderate outcome – neither reactionary nor revolutionary – for which he has been so much praised. Moderation is said to be the most difficult of policies; it was certainly difficult for Bismarck.

I make no doubt that the offer of an alliance which he made to Austria in August 1864 was genuine. It seemed to him 'in the logic of the situation'. If Prussia was not to follow a revolutionary course, she must follow a reactionary one. Once more he asked less than his predecessors. In his exaggerated fear of French aggression, he offered Austria alliance against France without demanding Prussian hegemony north of the Main. William I, not Bismarck, insisted on this condition; and the Austrians thought Prussia so dependent on their support that they named Silesia as their price. The deadlock drove Bismarck off on the alternative 'revolutionary' course. He screwed up tension against Austria; and in May 1865 spoke openly of his policy as 'war against Austria in alliance with France'. A new compromise followed in August 1865, the Treaty of Gastein. This compromise came mainly from the side of the Austrians; and Bismarck accepted it merely because it was offered. But he was also bewildered by the failure of his 'revolutionary' policy to explode. When he approached the French for an alliance, they refused to display territorial ambitions. Napoleon went ostentatiously into the country; and left policy to be defined by Drouyn the conservative.

In October 1865, Bismarck visited Napoleon at Biarritz in order to clear up the mystery of French policy. It is often said that he tricked Napoleon by vague talk of future French gains in Germany. This is not so. It is true that the two rogues discussed 'advantages which might offer themselves unsought', advantages, of course, in Germany: but this was a casual theme. Napoleon's overriding interest was Venetia; he was determined to complete the work of 1859 and not leave to his son 'a volcano for a throne'. His price was Venetia; and Bismarck paid it. He promised that he would not guarantee Venetia to Austria; and in return Napoleon promised that he would not make an alliance with Austria against Prussia – 'he would not go and stand beside a target'. This was the essential bargain of Biarritz: Venetia for Italy, and French neutrality in a war between Prussia and Austria. Bismarck gave the bargain a positive shape when he concluded his alliance with Italy in April 1866; this assured Napoleon that he would get what he wanted, and Bismarck was able to wage a limited war against Austria. Napoleon, not Bismarck, made the moderate programme possible and enabled Prussia to win hegemony north of the Main without a general European upheaval. To the very last Bismarck could not believe in his own success. In May 1866 he offered the Austrians peace if they would share the military headship of Germany. The Austrians would have agreed if they could have had in exchange a Prussian guarantee of Venetia; this, owing to his bargain with Napoleon, was the one thing that Bismarck could not give. Venetia compelled Bismarck to go to war. It also compelled Napoleon to favour war – it was the factor which wrecked his proposal for a European Congress. Most paradoxically of all, it even led the Austrians to want war. By May 1866 they had come to believe that the only way out of their difficulties was to surrender Venetia and gain Silesia in exchange. This would win Napoleon as an ally against both Prussia and Russia; it would free their southern frontier; and it would restore their prestige in Germany. But it was only possible by means of war against Prussia. Therefore, in the last resort, it was the Austrians who were eager to bring the war on. It is a curious fact that every European war between 1815 and 1914 was exploded by the power standing on the defensive: England and France insisted on the Crimean War; Austria on the wars of 1859, 1866, and 1914; and France on the war of 1870. It is also a curiosity how little military considerations weighed in the decision to provoke war or to avoid it. Thus, the Prussians accepted the compromise of August 1865, although they were confident of victory. There is little foundation for the later story that they put off war until they could clinch their military superiority by making an alliance with Italy. And this alliance, when it was made in April 1866, was concluded for its political effect on Napoleon, rather than to divide the Austrian armies – this again was an advantage which the Prussians only discovered after it happened. On the other side, the Austrians provoked war in June 1866 not because their military position had improved, but because it had got worse; they could bear the tension no longer. Finally, the French decision not to intervene after the Prussian victory at Sadova sprang purely from considerations of policy; the question whether the French Army was capable of intervention was hardly raised. I am not sure whether any conclusion can be drawn from this odd ignoring of the basic facts.

There is another oddity. The war between Austria and Prussia had been on the horizon for sixteen years. Yet it had great difficulty in getting itself declared. Austria tried to provoke Bismarck by placing the question of the duchies before the Diet on 1 June. Bismarck retaliated by occupying Holstein. He hoped that the Austrian troops there would resist, but they got away before he could catch them. On 14 June the Austrian motion for federal mobilization against Prussia was carried in the Diet. Prussia declared the confederation at an end; and on 15 June invaded Saxony. On 21 June, when Prussian troops reached the Austrian frontier, the crown prince, who was in command, merely notified the nearest Austrian officer that 'a state of war' existed. That was all. The Italians did a little better. La Marmora sent a declaration of war to Albrecht, the Austrian commander-in-chief, before taking the offensive. Both Italy and Prussia were committed to programmes which could not be justified in international law, and were bound to appear as aggressors if they put their claims on paper. They would, in fact, have been hard put to it to start the war if Austria had not done the job for them.

The war of 1866 was not the revolutionary war which had been preached by Bismarck until his visit to Biarritz; it was the moderate war as always envisaged by the Prussian statesmen whom Bismarck had despised. It is often regarded as something of a miracle that Bismarck carried it through without intervention from either France or Russia; but in truth neither of them had any objection to a Prussian hegemony in northern Germany which is all that was accomplished. The Russians, in any case, were in no state to intervene. For fifteen years after the Crimean War they almost ceased to be a military power so far as Europe was concerned. Between 1856 and 1863 the annual call-up for the army was not enforced: and the Polish revolt in 1863, itself caused by an attempted call-up, further delayed their recovery. They owed their security during this period of neglect to the Prussian buffer; and were therefore glad to see it strengthened. No doubt they would have expostulated if Bismarck had annexed the states of southern Germany or dismembered the Austrian Empire, but this was never on the programme. His moderation against Austria in 1866 has been much vaunted. Yet even he put up his terms. He excluded Austria from Germany, instead of dividing it with her at the Main. The king and the generals, who grumbled at his moderation, merely wanted some satisfactions of prestige – annexation of some Austrian territory in Silesia or a victory-march through Vienna.

They certainly had no thought of destroying the Habsburg Empire. Nor is it true that Austria was reconciled by Bismarck's moderation. The Austrians had burnt their fingers in 1866 and meant to take fewer risks next time; but they still hoped for a next time. The war of 1866 was a milestone, not a turning-point, in Austro-Prussian relations.

The real turning point, for all Europe, was, no doubt, that France did not intervene; but even the dramatic nature of this has been exaggerated owing to the fact that history has been written by those who opposed or regretted the decision, while Napoleon, the man who made it, remained silent. He had made up his mind all along; he was on the side of 'the revolution', on the side, that is, of Prussia in Germany, as he had been on the side of Sardinia in Italy. There was no real crisis of decision in Paris between 4 July and 10 July. It was simply that Napoleon, having deceived his ministers from the first, had now to override them. He thought – and perhaps rightly – that the European situation had changed in his favour; Prussia stronger than before and therefore less dependent on Russia; Austria excluded from Germany and therefore freer to balance Russia in the Near East; Italy contented with the acquisition of Venetia; and southern Germany 'internationally independent'. Even if he had known of the Prussian treaties of alliance with the southern states, he would have regarded this as an improvement on the German confederation. Then southern Germany had been guaranteed by both Prussia and Austria; now by Prussia alone, and with her Napoleon had no quarrel. Indeed he took Bismarck's breath away by insisting on Prussia's annexing the whole of north Germany – a victory for the revolution over moderation.

In the summer of 1866 Napoleon supposed that he had at last achieved the revolutionary coalition with Prussia and Italy; and he meant to complete it by resurrecting his entente with Russia. He was of course misled by the analogy with Italy. He supposed that, since the Italians continued to need protection against Austria, Prussia needed it also; and his half-hearted demands for compensation, which culminated in the attempted annexation of Luxembourg in March 1867, were all designed to make an alliance with Prussia acceptable to French public opinion. It is common to speak of these negotiations, and especially the Luxembourg affair, as a trap which Bismarck laid for the French. If it was a trap, why did he not spring it? The truth is simpler. The affair was not of Bismarck's seeking; it was thrust on him by the French and, though no doubt he had to consider German feeling, he would have welcomed an alliance with France, if Russia had been included in it. There, it seems to me, is the real explanation. The key to European diplomacy between 1866 and 1870 is to be found in the Near East, and not on the Rhine or even in Poland. So long as Russia and France were at loggerheads in the Near East, Bismarck could not let Luxembourg go to France without implicitly taking her side against Russia. But equally he refused a Russian offer to keep Austria neutral, because this also involved paying a price in the Near East. In April 1867 at the height of the Luxembourg crisis, he first suggested the solution that was his ultimate favourite: the revival of the Holy Alliance. It was contemptuously refused by both the other parties. Austria would not join without concessions in Germany, Russia would not guarantee the integrity of Austria nor allow her gains in the Balkans. The Eastern question dictated a peaceful outcome of the Luxembourg affair. France would not allow Russia a free hand against Turkey; Prussia would not allow her a free hand against Austria. Therefore both botched up the Luxembourg question as best they could. The great turning-point had been reached without design and before anyone noticed it. Both French and German public opinion had taken a hand in diplomacy; and henceforth they were not to be reconciled – perhaps not even to the present day.

There is not much to be said of Bismarck's diplomacy between 1867 and 1870. As always when the Near East took the centre of the stage, he had none except to keep out of the way; or, at most, to act as honest broker when the conflicts of the other powers threatened to involve Prussia. When the Franco-Russian Entente seemed to be working in the Near East during the autumn of 1867, he played in with it; and, with Italy joining in too, this was the last display of the 'revolutionary coalition'. Bismarck backed out of the Near East as soon as the entente broke down, so as not to be left alone on the Russian side. In March 1868, he refused a direct Russian demand for an alliance against Austria-Hungary, though 'of course neither power could afford to allow the destruction of the other'. In the autumn of 1868 he used the Hohenzollern family influence to damp down irredentist agitation in Romania, so as to avoid having to choose between Russia and Austria-Hungary; and in 1869 he helped Russia and France to wind up the Cretan affair. He never took seriously the talk of an alliance between Austria-Hungary and France; it was, he said, 'conjectural rubbish', as indeed it turned out to be. He calculated quite rightly that the Habsburg government would never dare to offend Hungarian and Austrian-German feeling by supporting French interference in southern Germany; and equally that Napoleon would not break with Russia for the sake of Austria-Hungary. This disposes of the defence put up for Bismarck by some of his admirers that he had to provoke war against France in order to anticipate either an Austro-French or a Franco-Russian agreement. There was never any serious chance of the first; and the second offered Prussia advantages, not dangers.

There is a simpler defence of Bismarck's policy in 1870, that is, if he needs one: he did not provoke the war at all, except in the narrowest sense of exploding it at the last moment. Later on, when the war had become a national legend, Bismarck tried to take the credit for it; but it was unearned. Of course the Hohenzollern candidature for the throne of Spain was of his making. Its object was to act as a check on France, not to provoke her into war. His encouragement of or indifference towards the Spanish affair varied inversely with the Franco-Russian Entente. When France and Russia were on good terms, this gave Prussia security, both against Austria-Hungary and

against being involved in an eastern war; whenever they quarrelled, he looked round for other means of distracting French
attention from the Rhine. He first took up the Hohenzollern
candidature in February 1869, when Russia and France were in
dispute over Crete. He dropped it as soon as they settled the
question; and left it alone so long as their entente seemed within
sight of renewal. He revived it once more, in the spring of 1870,
when the Franco-Russian approach broke down. But the
Hohenzollern candidature was primarily not a move in foreign
policy at all. Bismarck's overriding concern was with southern
Germany; and a Hohenzollern on the Spanish throne – like the
project of declaring William I German emperor which he aired
at the same time – was designed to raise Prussian prestige south
of the Main. In June 1870 Alexander II met Bismarck and
William I at Ems – one of the many legendary meetings at
which a war was supposed to have been plotted. In fact war
against France was never mentioned. Bismarck expressed disapproval of Habsburg policy in the Near East; and he tried to
persuade the Tsar that the South German princes would make
a better bargain with William I than if they waited to be swept
away by a more democratic wave in favour of his liberal
successor. There could hardly be clearer evidence that Bismarck
was not expecting the Franco-Prussian war at that time.

Of the actual war-crisis in July 1870 two things seem to me
clear beyond all doubt, if one can escape from the layers of
myth and prejudice. First, no one could have expected it to
explode in the way that it did. According to all rational calculation, Leopold of Hohenzollern ought to have been on the throne
of Spain before the French, or anyone else, knew what was
happening. The actual leakage was due to the blunder of a
cipher clerk in the German legation at Madrid – an unpredictable event. Second, no one could have expected the French to
turn the crisis into a war. Bismarck thought the affair would
end in a humiliation for Prussia. That is why he stayed in the
country and left William I to do the negotiating. The course of
events was a setback for Bismarck, though he quickly made the

best of things. So far as he had a settled policy, it was to incorporate southern Germany with Russian and even French approval – a decisive stroke against Austria and back to the dynamic coalition with France and Russia that he had always favoured. After all, he believed, rightly, that the empire was the form of French government most favourable to Prussian interests; and he went on trying to restore Napoleon III even at the beginning of 1871. He had sometimes thought that a French revolution would lead to war; it was quite against his intentions that war led to a French revolution.

It is a further myth that Bismarck's diplomacy secured the neutrality of Russia and Austria-Hungary. Neither power ever had any intention or inclination to go to war. Bismarck made no promises to the Russians of support in the Near East; and they made no promises to him. The Russians did not mobilize any troops in Galicia – they had, in fact, none to mobilize. They did not threaten Austria-Hungary. They promised the Austrians to stay neutral, if Austria-Hungary did the same; but in view of their military weakness, they would have stayed neutral in any case. For that matter, they did not believe that their interests would be injured by a French victory over Prussia – nor by a Prussian victory over France. The Austrians remained neutral solely from consideration of their own interests also. Beust wished to mobilize in order to intervene after the decisive battle had been fought; and, since he expected France to win that battle, his intention was to protect southern Germany against her. Andrássy, too, favoured mobilization; only he insisted on a declaration of neutrality so that, after the French victory which he also expected, both France and Prussia could be persuaded to join a crusade against Russia. This was as crazy as most of Andrássy's schemes. Gorchakov, the Russian chancellor, passed the correct verdict on the French dreams for an Austrian alliance when he said: 'Russia did not paralyse a support which had no chance of being realized.' Neither Russia nor Austria-Hungary cared which way the war went in western Europe. So far as there was any element of calculation in their policy, it was simply that, once France was out of the way, Germany would no longer be able to follow a neutral line in the Near East – the only topic that interested them.

From Bismarck's point of view, the war of 1870 was a senseless affair; and he admitted as much in his many later apologies to the French. So far as he had any responsibility for it (and he did not have much), this sprang from his desire to weaken German liberalism by making France the national enemy instead of Russia. Whatever the responsibilities, the consequences of dividing Germany with Austria and of quarrelling with France were all that Bismarck had foreseen in his days at Frankfurt. Vienna took Berlin prisoner. In the Crimean War Prussian statesmen had worked to prevent Austria's going to the assistance of the Western powers; in the Bulgarian crisis of 1887 Bismarck had to implore the British to go to the assistance of Austria-Hungary; and a generation later his successors had to go to her assistance themselves. In 1879 Bismarck, and none other, tied 'the trim Prussian frigate to the worm-eaten Austrian galleon' – tied them together for good, although the galleon was now more worm-eaten by a generation. Was this really a triumph for his diplomacy?

To my mind, the younger Bismarck was the greater one – the Bismarck who modelled himself on Cavour rather than the Bismarck who modelled himself on Metternich, the 'mad Junker' rather than the sane one. He saw clearly that a national reconstruction of central Europe in cooperation with Russia and France was the wisest course for Prussia. But, when it came to the point, he himself prevented this. He overrated, no doubt, Russian and French dynamism; and when this failed swung away on the opposite tack. But his rejection of his own earlier policy had a deeper cause. The national principle in Europe only made sense on a liberal basis, as Cavour appreciated. Both Bismarck and Napoleon III hated the liberalism which was essential to the success of their foreign policy. Napoleon pretended to accept it; Bismarck hardly troubled to make the pretence. Germany and France could not work together except on a liberal basis; hence Napoleon III and Bismarck between them ensured that they would not work together at all. Everything sprang from this failure. Without French cooperation, Germany could not risk a national remaking of eastern Europe by Russia; therefore she had to prop up Austria-Hungary. The diplomacy of Bismarck's later years was simply an elaborate jugglery to conceal the fact that he had abandoned his earlier visions and had been forced to repeat, or even to outdo, the mistakes of his predecessors. It is curious, and more than a coincidence, that in the very weeks when Bismarck was founding his so-called 'League of Peace' by means of the Austro-German alliance, Gladstone was formulating his principles of international cooperation in the Midlothian campaign. Nor is it, I think, an accident that in every subsequent world conflict, Bismarck's heirs, the boasted *Realpolitikers*, have always been defeated by the heirs of Gladstone, those who hope to make the world anew. Once Bismarck had been one of these. He set out to remake central Europe. Instead he tied himself to the Habsburgs, and, like everyone who follows this path, ended up by believing that peace could be kept by tricks.

Marx's Better Half

Given Alan Taylor's family and then university connections with Manchester it is not surprising that he was much interested in Friedrich Engels (1820–95) and in particular his book The Condition of the Working Class in England *(1845). In 1974 he had praised Steven Marcus's* Engels, Manchester and the Working Class *(London, Weidenfeld and Nicolson, 1974) as 'a remarkable work of literary criticism with history brought in by a side wind', though then observing that the author was 'less convincing when he writes of Engels as a man'. On that occasion Alan Taylor gave the verdict: 'It is hardly an exaggeration to say that Marxism was born in the slums of Manchester . . . What he [Engels] saw provided Marx with the material that consolidated his theories.' This essay appeared in the* Observer *on 25 April 1976, as a review of W O Henderson's* The Life of Friedrich Engels, *2 volumes (London, Frank Cass, 1976).*

*   *   *

The original name of the firm was Marx and Engels: Socialism, Wholesale, Retail and for Export. Later, when new partners joined (Marxist-Leninism, Marxist-Leninist-Stalinism, Trotsky-ism) Engels disappeared from the letter-heading. Now Yugoslavia is the only communist country I know where the portrait of Engels is displayed alongside that of Marx in town halls and government offices. Books on Marxism, when they mention Engels at all, present him only as Marx's loyal disciple, whose principal contribution was to provide Marx with money.

Engels deserves more extended treatment. Though he had talent where Marx had genius – Huxley to Marx's Darwin – he often formulated Marxist concepts clearly before Marx did. His *Communist Catechism*, for instance, with its twenty-five points is dull reading compared to the *Communist Manifesto*, but all the ideas of the *Manifesto* are already in it.

In some ways, too, Engels was the more interesting character. Marx was a staid bourgeois apart from his ideas. Engels, despite being a prosperous cotton merchant, tried to formulate a lifestyle appropriate to a socialist. He lived happily for many years with an Irish factory-girl, Mary Burns, and, after her death, with her sister Lizzie whom he married only the day before she died. Jenny Marx, Marx's aristocratic wife, would not tolerate either of these women in her presence, and Marx conformed to the ban.

Dr Henderson has at last presented Engels as an independent figure. His book is very much a DIY biography. The evidence, largely from the Marx–Engels correspondence, is exhaustively marshalled. Few conclusions are drawn and there is none of the psychological penetration shown in the exciting book on Engels and Manchester by Steven Marcus. On the relations between Engels and his father, Henderson is content to quote the father's complaint, 'It is a heavy cross to bear that I have a son at home who is like a scabby sheep in the flock.' Marcus shows that the father helped the publication of *The Condition of the Working Class in England in 1844* and later welcomed the son as a partner despite his revolutionary activities.

The Condition of the Working Class in England in 1844 was indeed the beginning of Marxism, far more so than Marx's cantankerous philosophizing of the same period. Engels discovered the class war in industry between capitalists and proletarians and foretold that this could end only with the victory of socialism. Marx snatched at the idea and made it the foundation of his system. In 1845 Marx went to Manchester with Engels for four days, most of them spent in Chetham's Library. He went again for a single afternoon in 1865. These were the only occasions when Marx actually set eyes on the Lancashire cotton industry. Engels lived amongst it for twenty years.

The failure of the revolutions of 1848 pushed Engels back into a business career. An even stronger motive was Marx's constant need for money. Marx was a true Micawber who thought that the world owed him a living. Engels provided the answer. He kept Marx for over thirty years and on no mean scale. As Henderson points out, when Marx praised the Paris Commune for fixing the top salary of public officials at £240 a year, this was a great deal less than Engels paid Marx. He also bequeathed most of his fortune, some £30,000, to Marx's daughters or their descendants. Engels performed further services. He allowed Marx to father on him the illegitimate son of the Marx's housekeeper, Helene Demuth, and returned the boy to the true father, Karl Marx, only on his deathbed.

Engels's greatest service to Marx was in the realm of ideas. He turned Marx's brilliant insights into orderly exposition. Most of the precise statements of Marxism as a system derive from Engels. He often provided essential information. Marx, not surprisingly, had no idea how banking and finance worked in practice; Engels told him. Marx was a disorderly scholar, forever turning aside from his central theme to run after attractive irrelevancies. The first volume of *Capital* was published only after many years of exhortation by Engels and then in an incomplete form. Marx did not complete the other two volumes at all. When Engels tried to make something of them, he found only a chaos of detached scraps, some in English, some in French, some in German. Engels wrote most of the newspaper articles with which Marx supplemented his income, though Marx sometimes livened them up. When the first volume of *Capital* appeared, Engels wrote many reviews in German periodicals under different names and in different styles. His devotion never wearied.

Engels had also a remarkable life of his own. He kept two establishments in Manchester: bachelor's lodgings where he entertained his rich friends and a suburban house with Mary Burns where he entertained fellow socialists. He acquired a considerable reputation as a writer on military affairs, not always getting things right. Though he was wrong in expecting an Austrian victory in 1866, he correctly divined Moltke's strategy in 1870.

Engels remained very much of a German despite his fifty

years in England. He was chairman of the Schiller Anstalt in Manchester and a founder of the Hallé Orchestra. During the Franco-Prussian war he raised money to provide relief for the German wounded and did not raise any money for the French. His views on the Slavs were indistinguishable from those of Hitler. He wrote in 1849:

The universal war which is coming will crush the Slav alliance and will wipe out completely those obstinate peoples so that their very name will be forgotten . . . The next world war will wipe out not only reactionary classes and dynasties but it will also destroy those utterly reactionary races . . . And that will be a real step forward.

While in Manchester, Engels went out two days a week with the Cheshire Hunt, claiming that this was good training for the cavalry general of a future revolutionary war. In London he acquired a large house in Regent's Park Road and often ascended Primrose Hill, surveying London with a strategist's eye. After Lizzie Burns's death and Marx's, Helene Demuth kept house for him, a curious arrangement, and after her death Kautsky's divorced wife, which was also odd. Engels was now The General, acknowledged high priest of Marxism. He lived long enough to see the foundation of the Second International and addressed its Zürich conference of 1893, ending with the words, 'Long live the international proletariat!'

Marx and Engels in their deaths were characteristically divided. Marx had a conventional funeral and was buried beside his wife in Highgate Cemetery. Engels was cremated and his ashes were scattered in the sea off Beachy Head. The German Social Democrats claimed to be his ideological heirs. Henderson takes a different view. The biography of Engels ends with a sentence describing Lenin as 'the greatest of his disciples, the leader of the great revolution that Engels did not live to see'. So perhaps the firm should really be called Engels-Leninism after all.

The Paris Commune

This essay was published as 'A Shattered Utopia' in the Observer *on 30 May 1971, reviewing three books published to mark the centenary of the Commune: Stewart Edwards,* The Paris Commune 1871 *(London, Eyre and Spottiswoode, 1971); Frank Jellinck,* The Paris Commune *of 1871 (London, Gollancz, 1937 and 1971); and Alistair Horne,* The Terrible Year: The Paris Commune 1871 *(London, Macmillan, 1971). Alan Taylor had reviewed Jellinck's book somewhat less enthusiastically in 1937. Then he judged the book to be 'free from contemporary passions' but 'shaky' on general history and neglectful of the less dramatic political developments. As for the Commune he stated that it sprang from the traditions of 1789 but 'drew its inspiration quite as much from patriotic indignation at a shameful peace as from enthusiasm for the International'.*

* * *

Most centenaries are drab affairs. Forgotten episodes are piously exhumed and then reburied after a few speeches. When German statesmen met recently in Berlin to commemorate the founding of the German Empire on 18 January 1871, they agreed courageously that this was no longer something to be proud of.

One centenary retains its glory. The Paris Commune was established on 18 March 1871. It endured until 25 May and was then crushed in blood. Karl Marx wrote its epitaph:

Working-men's Paris, with its Commune, will be for ever celebrated as the glorious harbinger of a new society. Its martyrs are enshrined in the great heart of the working class. Its exterminators history has already nailed to that eternal pillory from which all the prayers of their priests will not avail to redeem them.

Staid historians have repeatedly demolished the 'myth' of the Commune which, they allege, Marx manufactured. The Commune, they insist, was not a proletarian movement. It did not seek to establish socialism. Its motive is to be found in patriotic indignation against defeat in the Franco-Prussian War or in federalist dislike of the bureaucratic state. Maybe it was merely a product of the muddle and hardship which followed the war. Such historians are best answered by Dufaure, the French minister of justice, whose repression of the Commune established a record of infamy: 'No, gentlemen, it was not a communalist, a municipal movement; it was in its ideals, its ideas and its actions the most radical revolution ever undertaken!' The Communards, though not factory workers, were proletarians in the original sense. They were the eternally oppressed, and they aspired, however clumsily, to found a society where the tyranny of the few over the many should cease for evermore. Marx said rightly that the Communards were 'storming heaven'. In the Red Square Lenin's body is wrapped in a flag of the Commune, and when three Soviet cosmonauts first broke into space they carried with them a Communard ribbon. We can say more truthfully of the Paris Commune what Charles James Fox said of the fall of the Bastille: 'How much the greatest event since the beginning of the world and how much the best.'

The Commune is fortunate in the books that have been timed to mark its centenary. Alistair Horne achieved distinction six years ago with an account of the siege of Paris and its aftermath, the Commune. He has now concentrated on the Commune, drawing on many contemporary accounts and providing also 250 vivid illustrations. His own narrative is straightforward and relies largely on the illustrations to tell the story. His last words on the Communards are taken from Renoir who narrowly escaped death at their hands: 'They were madmen, but they had in them that little flame which never dies.'

Frank Jellinck's book was first published in 1937 and has become a classic. In some ways it is still the best book on the Commune, if only for its vivid sympathy. Jellinck is one who might well have manned a barricade. It has defects as Jellinck points out in his introduction. His account of the Communard leaders is too systematic, sorting them into political loyalties which were not so precise. As he remarks also, his book was written before the experience of the Spanish Civil War – its closest parallel. All the same, the book combines accuracy and excitement.

The truly new book by Stewart Edwards is more academic in tone though not in sympathy. Despite some excellent French work recently, it is, I think, the most thoroughly satisfactory history of the Commune in any language. Perhaps it has rather too much about the Prussian siege of Paris, which prepared the way for the Commune. But this emphasis can be defended. The Commune illustrates the general principle that a revolution occurs not simply as a result of material suffering, but when a regime is discredited by incompetence and failure. This is what happened in 1871. The workers of Paris – and despite some historians, most of the Communards were workers – recognized that the governing classes had failed. They moved reluctantly into the empty place. The Commune illustrates another principle: a revolution cannot operate without leaders, and the revolutionaries turn to whoever has established some sort of reputation. The leaders of the Commune were a strange collection: old-style Jacobins, Proudhonists, followers of Blanqui, members of Marx's International. The Jacobins wanted 'to make terror the order of the day'. The followers of Blanqui were at a loss without their leader who was already in prison. Some of the military commanders wanted to introduce strict discipline; others believed in the irresistible force of a chaotic onslaught.

For much of the time the Commune behaved as though it were already victorious. Stewart Edwards devotes a whole chapter to its social reforms and another to the festivals which made Communard Paris gay until the attack of the regular army. Here is the sharpest principle of all. The Left preach class war; the Right practise it. The Commune killed a few hostages during its death-throes. The republican government of Thiers killed 25,000 Parisians. When in November 1917 a working class again rose in revolt, it found in Lenin and Trotsky leaders who carried the revolution to victory. Now the Commune seems the nobler event. Stewart Edwards concludes with this tribute:

The Commune was a truly revolutionary event, the breakthrough into a new realm where what seemed barely to be possible becomes, however fleetingly, actual, thereby revealing all other forms as condemned.

Dizzy

First published in the New Statesman, *22 January 1955.*

*   *   *

The somewhat inadequate excuse for the essay was 'Tradition and Change', nine lectures delivered to a summer school at Oxford by leading Conservatives and published by the Conservative Central Office.

'I am their leader; I must follow them.' This, we suppose, is the essence of leadership in a democratic community. The members of a party, or the rank and file of a trade union, express their wishes, and it is the duty of the leader to translate these wishes, prejudices or ambitions into action. We interpret the past in the same spirit. History is no longer the record of the achievements of extraordinary men. Our historians accumulate the biographical details of a thousand forgotten figures, and the great men, if brought in at all, merely provide decorative symbols for the prevailing outlook. Napoleon becomes a shorthand sign for the profiteers of the French Revolution; Hitler for the German capitalists or for the German middle classes who have lost their savings; even that erratic genius Winston Churchill is made to appear somehow as 'old England'. Prime ministers were once little less than gods, shaping the destinies of the country by their individual genius. Now they are lay figures, their sole function to wear the appropriate period clothes. The two Pitts represent aggressive commercial imperialism; Palmerston a declining Whig aristocracy; Gladstone the free-trade manufacturers. Lloyd George speaks for those who made money out of the First World War, and Baldwin for those who lost it.

Of course, there is some truth in this way of looking at things. A public man who cared only for outworn causes would no more command a following than a writer who used classical Latin in an age of vernacular literature would sell his books. Yet reality has a perverse way of going against the pattern that it ought to follow. The leader strays wildly from the class that he is supposed to symbolize and bears little resemblance to a composite picture of his followers. The millions of members of the Labour Party, if superimposed one upon another, would never turn into a portrait of Ramsay MacDonald – or even of Clement Attlee. The shrewd operator of symbols could never divine that 'the gentlemen of England' were led by one who was unmistakably the son of a Lancashire mill-owner, or the radical Nonconformists by a High Churchman of classical education, whose devotion to the traditional institutions of the country was dwarfed only by his absorption in the writings of the Early Fathers. Indeed, the greatest failures as leaders are those who best reflect their followers. Charles James Fox had Brooks's written all over him; Lord John Russell really belonged to a great Revolution family; and Neville Chamberlain had in fact been 'not a bad Lord Mayor of Birmingham in a lean year'.

Great political leaders are much more than symbols. They are individuals, capturing a cause for their own purpose and giving it an unexpected twist. This is tiresome for the historian, but – to adapt a phrase of Trotsky's – he who wants a quiet mind should choose some other study than that of history. Systems, patterns, faiths are an attempt to impose an artificial simplification on the infinite variety of the past. The historian remains sceptical of them all and can derive only malicious amusement from the efforts of present-day politicians to enlist their great predecessors in contemporary disputes. What would Oliver Cromwell have said about the nationalization of steel? He would have been even more tongue-tied than was usually the case with him. Benjamin Disraeli would hardly have expressed himself on 'Tradition and Change' as did the nine Conservatives who evoked his shade at Oxford. Indeed he would not have chosen such a fatuous, banal subject. But, once landed with it, he would have said something provocative and no doubt wrongheaded. The Oxford lectures specialize in the balanced platitude – the conservatism which Disraeli defined as 'Tory men and Whig measures'. Highest award must go, of course, to Mr R A Butler, who described class privileges as 'the richness of developed differences'. But the others qualify, too. Mr T E Utley, concealing the poverty of his thought by the incoherence of his style; Professor Hugh Sellon, ending his survey of foreign policy with the question, 'Are the old principles still a sufficient guide in the new world in which we live?' and answering plaintively, 'I do not know'; Mr Angus Maude voicing his confidence in 'the instincts of our people' – every lecture is excessively pleasurable and only 3*d*. each into the bargain.

Disraeli deserves to be lectured about. He was the oddest great man in our public life by a long chalk. Nothing connected him with the Tory Party of the early nineteenth century – nothing, that is, except his calculation that its leadership would be easier to attain than that of the Whigs. He owned no land; he was not English in blood; he was lucky to be even a nominal member of the Anglican Church. In temperament he was even less conservative than in origin. He had a flighty mind which drifted from smart triviality to adolescent day-dreaming and back again. He held nothing sacred except perhaps some Hebrew phrases vaguely remembered. He despised the members of the aristocracy even more than he disliked the poor. He did not even enjoy power when he achieved it. It was not merely that, in his own phrase, 'it came too late'. Power was too practical an affair to interest him. He relished the trappings of power, not the reality – the drama of great debates, the high-sounding titles, his name echoing through history. Yet in appearance he was least conservative of all. Thick black ringlets, fancy waistcoats, powder and scent were not the marks of a gentleman or even of a politician and his affected voice – half-drawl, half-lisp – completed the foreign impression. Disraeli increased the obstacles in his path for the pleasure of overcoming them.

He was first and last a great actor, watching his own performance and that of others with ironic detachment. He cared for causes only as a means of combat. Having ousted Peel from the leadership of the Conservative Party by defending the Corn Laws, he cheerfully proposed the next year that Protection should be dropped, and he did nothing to aid agriculture when the great depression hit it at the end of the eighteen-seventies. He attacked Palmerston's irresponsible support of Turkey during the Crimean War, yet repeated this support even more irresponsibly twenty years later. He foresaw the independence of the wretched colonies – 'a millstone round our necks' – and welcomed this dissolution of the British Empire. A few years later he claimed a great stroke by making Queen Victoria Empress of India – the biggest piece of tushery even in his career. *Sybil* is supposed to contain a profound social analysis. In fact, it says no more than that the rich are very rich and the poor very poor – by no means a new discovery. His own social policy, when he came to power, turned out to be nothing more startling than municipal washhouses. He took one step of real importance when he placed the trade unions above the law, but this was a matter of electoral calculation, not of social justice. His only genuine emotion in politics sprang from personal dislike – of Peel in his early career, of Gladstone even more strongly towards the end. What these two men had in common was a readiness to put their convictions above their ambition – the worst of offences in Disraeli's eyes.

In his novels Disraeli invented an interpretation of political history which is sometimes still taken seriously and was repeated in the twentieth century by our only anti-semitic writer, Hilaire Belloc. This was the myth of the Venetian oligarchy which was supposed to have taken the Crown prisoner at the time of the Glorious Revolution and from which the Crown should rescue itself by an alliance with the people. This myth had no glimmer of truth. Though eighteenth-century England had indeed a rich and powerful aristocracy, the Crown was always the head of the executive and the ministers were its servants. The Whigs certainly talked of 'forcing the closet', but they never succeeded in doing so effectively until after the great Reform Bill and then only for a decade. The Crown was still of great weight in politics at the time of the Crimean War. By a wild irony, it was Disraeli himself who finally excluded the Crown from politics and turned it into a decorative figurehead. When he introduced household suffrage in 1867 in order to dish the Whigs, he made mass parties inevitable, and these could not be swayed, as the old aristocratic politicians had been, by personal loyalty to the Crown. Disraeli disguised this, perhaps even to himself, by the flattery which he gave to Queen Victoria, as to many other distinguished ladies, but this was play-acting, not politics.

The two-party system does not figure much in Disraeli's writings, but it was the real basis of his political life and his legacy to posterity. The Whigs had had a theory of party conflict, but they regarded this as a conflict between the party of the Crown and the party of the people, by which, of course, they meant themselves. Even when Peel recognized after the Reform Act that the Crown could not sustain a party of its own and therefore built up the Conservative Party, he did not acknowledge any loyalty, as leader, to his own followers and said firmly in 1846: 'I am not under any obligation to any man or to any body of men.' This was his unforgivable sin in Disraeli's eyes. Disraeli hounded Peel out of the party leadership and seized the vacant place. He was the first politician to put loyalty to party above loyalty to country, and his example has been universally admired, though not always followed. Disraeli riveted on our political life the conception that politics consist entirely in two parties fighting for office. These two parties were to represent not programmes but interests. What interests Disraeli did not much mind. Sometimes he talked of the Conservative Party as 'the landed interest'; sometimes he appealed to all who had 'a stake in the country'; in practice his party was an alliance between the City and the mob. None of this mattered. The important thing was the struggle for power – a tradition which the Conservative Party has faithfully observed to this day. It is true also to Disraeli's tradition in not knowing what to do with power when it has got it. To catch the other side bathing and make off with their clothes is still its only resource.

One can understand how Disraeli achieved the leadership of the party by offering the prospect of unremitting combat. The field always prefers a huntsman who halloos them on. But Disraeli knew better tricks. His novels, his speeches, his casual remarks, all held out the promise of a mystery which he never revealed, which was not in fact there to reveal. He, not Napoleon III, was the true sphinx without a secret. Or, rather, his secret was the absence of moral earnestness. A rarefied mountain-air becomes intolerable in time, and the holidaymaker is glad to escape to Monte Carlo. So it was with the Victorians. No age has been more high-minded, and the strain often became unendurable. Gladstone was the Victorian conscience; Disraeli the release from it.

The GOM

Alan Taylor did not write much about William Ewart Gladstone (1809–98). He often appears to have been a little puzzled by him. On another occasion he observed: 'No doubt a great man, but a very strange one.' This essay on the Grand Old Man was published in the New Statesman *on 9 October 1954, as a review of Sir Philip Magnus's* Gladstone *(London, John Murray, 1954), which was for a long time the best available short biography of Gladstone.*

*   *   *

In 1928 Gladstone's son Herbert noted:

Luminous and interesting as are Lord Morley's pages, they do not present, for those who did not know Mr Gladstone, a true and complete view of his personality . . . while the tendency of the modern writers is to seek the truth about great men from the habits and affairs of their private life, Mr Gladstone seems to be excluded from this process.

Sir Philip Magnus has now filled this gap with a biography which is a model of unassuming scholarship and understanding. He has mastered the vast accumulation of Gladstone's papers, more voluminous – as he remarks – than those of any former prime minister; and he has painted a personal picture of Gladstone which is completely satisfactory and will stand the test of time. Sir Philip is a modest author. He rarely thrusts himself between reader and subject, and he throws away his best lines like an actor in modern drawing-room comedy. The best stories are slipped in without preparation or underlining. It would have been easy to make fun of Gladstone. Sir Philip Magnus has resisted the temptation. He leaves Gladstone to make fun of himself.

Gladstone was an extraordinary personality. He was a human volcano; but what made him so terrifying and impressive, as Sir Philip points out, was that the volcano was always under control. Gladstone could turn it on and off at will; or rather he would direct its force solely towards the subject which dominated his mind at the moment. He discovered Ireland in 1845: 'Ireland! Ireland! That cloud in the West! That coming storm! That minister of God's retribution upon cruel, inveterate and but half-atoned injustice!' Yet thereafter he forgot Ireland for more than twenty years and took the question up again only when it served to sweep the Liberal Party into office. This is what Gladstone meant by the sense of timing on which he prided himself, what others called his opportunism or even his hypocrisy. There was no sense in a volcanic eruption unless it achieved some purpose; but we do not expect sense in an eruption. In Gladstone's private life the eruptions were less controlled. He lived at an intensity which would soon have exhausted any lesser man; and it is amazing that it did not exhaust those who lived with him. As a young man he could not meet a girl without writing her a long involved proposal of marriage immediately afterwards; and when he had achieved a singularly happy marriage, an obscure mission drove him to the redemption of prostitutes. In 1878 he recorded his wish: 'when God calls me, He may call me speedily. To die in Church appears to be a great euthanasia, but not at a time to disturb worshippers.' Even in this solemn moment, Gladstone did not forget his sense of timing.

It is a commonplace that Gladstone was a Christian states-man. In this he was not alone. What made him unique in British politics was his resolve to serve God's purpose and his ruthlessness in doing this once the purpose had become clear to him. This made him a bad colleague or leader. His intense personal vision led him to ignore others and to push them out of the way. The only parallel is with Bismarck – a comparison which both men would have disliked. There was the same sense of vocation, the same grumbling at having to accomplish it, and

– as a consequence – the same belief that only Gladstone or Bismarck knew how to accomplish it. We can understand the Christian purpose in the advocacy of Balkan or Irish freedom. But Gladstone felt it just as strongly when he preached public economy or free trade. Whatever he did, including even the conquest of Egypt, was a holy cause; and it is difficult to resist the feeling that Gladstone was on God's side because God had so arranged things as always to be on Gladstone's.

Sir Philip Magnus has penetrated to the heart of Gladstone's personality. We are made to understand everything about him – his relations with his family; his aloofness towards his colleagues; his failure to get on with Queen Victoria. The book is less successful when it comes to politics; and this is a serious defect. Sir Philip is fascinated by Gladstone as a man; he gives the impression of being less interested in him as a politician. This will not do. However extraordinary Gladstone's personality was, we should not bother much about him if he had not also been the greatest Liberal of the nineteenth century. The little slips – such as making Bismarck conquer Schleswig and Holstein in February 1864, or describing Alexandria as a British base in 1878 – are of no importance. But we are not given the full significance of Gladstone as a democratic leader. Sir Philip does not admire 'the people's William'. He does not believe that the masses are more enlightened than the classes. Gladstone did. He may have been mistaken in this, and he certainly regretted it. But only those who share this belief can admire Gladstone wholeheartedly. It was his vital legacy to the twentieth century. He came to have faith in the people; and they responded by being worthy of this faith. Gladstone has had bad luck in his biographers from the political point of view. Harcourt said to Morley: 'You cannot write about his religion; you do not sympathize with it. You cannot write about his fiscal policy; you do not understand it. You cannot write about Ireland; you know too much about it.' Sir Philip Magnus will be highly praised for depicting Gladstone as an extraordinary man; and he will deserve every word of the praise. But in his hundreds of

quotations he has missed one out. Gladstone said to Morley at
the end of his life: 'I was brought up to hate and fear liberty. I
came to love it. That is the secret of my whole career.'

Parnell : The Uncrowned King

First published in the New Statesman *on 3 June 1977, this is a review of* Charles Stewart Parnell *by F S L Lyons (London, Collins, 1977) and* The English Face of Irish Nationalism: Parnellite Involvement in British Politics, 1880–86 *by Alan O'Day (Dublin, Gill and Macmillan, 1977).*

*   *   *

Charles Stewart Parnell is one of the most interesting characters in modern history. He is interesting politically. More than any other man he gave Ireland the sense of being an independent nation. As Gladstone said, he did for home rule what Cobden had done for free trade: 'he set the argument on its feet'. Parnell is also interesting personally: a Protestant landowner who became the most powerful leader Ireland has known and a successful statesman who threw everything away for the love of a woman. There can never be too many books about him.

Leland Lyons, now Provost of Trinity College, Dublin, tells Parnell's story with incomparable scholarship and literary grace. This is a classic biography which will be read as long as anyone cares about Irish history or for that matter about history at all. It is a biography in the strict sense. Parnell always occupies the centre of the stage and even the greatest figures such as Gladstone never steal the limelight from him. The decisive events are treated only in so far as they concern Parnell. Thus in 1886, when he had almost carried home rule to victory, his hopes were ruined by Chamberlain's revolt and the defeat of the Home Rule Bill in the House of Commons. Lyons passes over the debates with hardly any mention. Again the Special Commission of 1889 which restored Parnell's fame yields little drama. Of course we get Pigott and his 'hesitency' – 'with a small h, Mr Pigott, a small h'. But essentially all that matters to Lyons is that Parnell won.

More remarkable still, though Lyons shows how Parnell built up his mastery over the Irish Nationalist Party, he does not discuss the character of that party in any detail. This is where O'Day comes in. Lyons's book is about Parnell without the Parnellites; O'Day's is about the Parnellites without Parnell. O'Day is analytical where Lyons is biographical, and by this approach he lays his finger on one decisive weakness in Parnell's position. Parnell wanted the Irish party to be strictly independent, manoeuvring between the British parties without committing itself to either of them. But most of the Parnellites had little to distinguish them from British Liberals. They had the same Liberal outlook. The most prominent of them lived in England and followed careers there in journalism or at the bar. Even in the days of their parliamentary obstruction they served loyally on parliamentary committees. They were members of London clubs, one of them even a member of the Savile, which was alleged to be almost as good as being a member of the Athenaeum. How could such men wage a political war for Irish independence? As O'Day rightly remarks, the Home Rule Bill would merely have transferred some power from the British ruling class to the moderate representatives of the Catholic Irish nation. The son of a once-famous home-ruler said to me: 'We would have run Ireland for you if you had let us.'

The truth is that the Irish MPs were always threatening to bolt, and the O'Shea divorce case gave them their opportunity. Until then they were whipped into line by Parnell's will. All of them trembled before him. Parnell could be a delightful dinner companion, gentle, amusing and sympathetic. But at the first hint of opposition his 'Red Indian' eyes flashed fire. Parnell had virtually no experience of politics before he began his abrupt rise to the top. He was unshakeably convinced that he was a man born to rule. He had one particular asset which is often unnoticed. He was an Englishman in background and upbringing with all the arrogance of an imperial race. All Irishmen are in the last resort soft. Parnell's will made them seem hard. He took his ascendancy for granted. He kept aloof from his followers and in his later years hardly attended the House of Commons. Lyons thinks he had lost interest. Surely it was rather that, like Napoleon, he had become too confident of his despotic power, particularly of course when he took up with Katharine O'Shea.

Parnell had other gifts beyond mere will-power. Though not a great orator in the nineteenth-century style, he captivated mass audiences by his uncompromising determination and the impression he gave of extremism. Behind the scenes he was a negotiator of the first rank who knew how to take every advantage. He was a match even for Gladstone, the most ingenious negotiator of the age. He was more than a match for the Irish Nationalists who turned against him. No man ever 'bested' Parnell. It was circumstances that brought him down.

Conor Cruise O'Brien argued some twenty years ago that Parnell's aims were essentially constitutional and the argument has been generally accepted. Ireland should receive dominion status and would then cooperate with Great Britain as an equal. Certainly Parnell tamed the men of violence as firmly as he dominated the parliamentarians. Certainly he rejected the idea of a revolutionary war on the practical grounds that Ireland was not big enough to run away in – an argument where Sinn Fein was to prove him wrong. But his rejection of extremism and violence was one of expediency. His aim was an uncompromising independence, not a legislative adjustment of Irish administration. 'No man can set bounds to the march of a nation.' This was Parnell's basic principle.

Parnell was ingenious but in some ways he was outwitted by British politicians, especially by Gladstone. Parnell rose high with the backing of Irish agrarian discontent. Gladstone quieted the discontent by his Land Act of 1881. Again Parnell secured a commanding position in parliament by bargaining with both Liberals and Conservatives over home rule. Gladstone took the home-rulers prisoner when he produced his own Home Rule Bill. Parnell still tried to keep free and maybe even welcomed the O'Shea divorce case for this reason. The other home-rulers never escaped. They were shackled to the Liberal Party for the rest of their existence.

Parnell's relations with Katharine O'Shea were to cause his downfall. The story is still full of mysteries and always will be. We know why Parnell allowed the affair to drift on unacknowledged; he and Katharine O'Shea were waiting for the money she would inherit when her rich aunt died. For the same reason O'Shea made no fuss. But there is much more that needs explanation. Why did Parnell remain friendly with O'Shea when he was already Katharine O'Shea's lover? Even stranger, why did O'Shea remain friendly with him? The friendship was not merely personal. O'Shea was Parnell's political adviser and his intermediary with Gladstone and Chamberlain. Parnell must surely have known that O'Shea was an unreliable negotiator, evading the decisive issues and promising more than he could perform. Why did Parnell use him in this way? And why did Gladstone and Chamberlain, shrewd men and experienced politicians, accept O'Shea at his face value? Surely they could see that he was a light-hearted, garrulous rogue. Perhaps there was more to O'Shea than comes out in the accounts. O'Shea himself aspired to become Irish secretary. Was this pure fantasy? Or did others take him seriously? The answers are beyond conjecture.

Lyons makes somewhat heavy weather over Parnell's love affair, producing psychological explanations that Parnell wanted a home and domesticity. In fact when a man is in love, he is in love and that is all there is to it. Parnell, in his usual arrogant way, was careless over the practical side of the affair. He seems to have thought that he could justify his position, if challenged, by proving that O'Shea had condoned the affair. Apparently it never crossed his mind until too late that such proof, though certainly forthcoming, would bar the way to a divorce and to what he wanted: Katharine O'Shea as his legitimate wife and their children acknowledged as his. His last stroke of ingenuity was to assert that Gladstone was seeking to dictate who should lead the Irish party. Even Parnell's most devoted followers could hardly have believed this but it inspired his last and most romantic fight. Though Parnell did not achieve home rule he made Ireland a nation. He was the uncrowned king of Ireland. He was also Katharine O'Shea's King and she was his Queenie. He did not found a dynasty. His only grandson became an officer in the British Army and died in India of enteric fever in 1934. As Leland Lyons concludes: 'The line of direct descent from Parnell therefore ends in a cemetery at Lahore.'

Lord Salisbury : Last Tory and First Unionist

Perhaps, as initially a diplomatic historian, Alan Taylor was happier dealing with such figures as Canning, Palmerston and Salisbury than Gladstone or Disraeli. This essay was published in the Manchester Guardian *on 22 August 1953 on the fiftieth anniversary of Lord Salisbury's death. Six years earlier, when assessing Salisbury, Alan Taylor had seen such a study as 'a serious attempt to understand Victorian conservatism at its moment of transition'.*

* * *

Lord Salisbury, the great Conservative statesman, died on 22 August 1903. He had been three times prime minister – in 1885, from 1886 to 1892, and from 1895 to 1902. No other man has held the office for so long since the Reform Bill of 1832, and only Walpole, the younger Pitt, and Lord Liverpool outstripped him before it. For most of the time he was also foreign secretary – a combination never attempted again except by Ramsay MacDonald for a few months in 1924; and he held these seals longer than anyone except Palmerston. Success seemed to mark his long record. England enjoyed a security unique in her history; and the empire reached the height of its greatness. He took over from Beaconsfield a crumbling Conservative Party, and he transformed it into the Unionist Party, which has been in power (either alone or in coalition) for forty-six of the sixty-eight years since 1885. Yet it is unlikely that Salisbury, at the end of his life, regarded his achievement with much satisfaction or looked with much hope towards the future.

He cared most for foreign policy and conducted it with unparalleled freedom. There was no prime minister to interfere with him, except between 1878 and 1880; he was removed from the criticism of the House of Commons; and he possessed the full confidence of the ageing queen. He even evaded the scrutiny of the Foreign Office staff by conducting much of his diplomacy through private letters to ambassadors. Only Metternich and Bismarck can be set beside him for their mastery and system in diplomatic performance. Like them he practised *Realpolitik*. He would not use British power for moral crusades, in spite of his private feelings of indignation; and he never judged foreign countries according to their form of government. He thought only in terms of the Great Powers and believed that it was the fate of decaying countries, especially outside Europe, to be partitioned among the strong. He envisaged the partition of the Ottoman Empire; and looked forward also to the partition of Morocco, Persia, and China. As he once said to the German ambassador: 'We have a good appetite. Let us share.'

The European balance of power was the main instrument of his policy and of his success. The agreements which he made in 1887 with Austria-Hungary and Italy were the nearest that this country ever came until the present day to an alliance in peacetime. But he always disliked the dependence on the Central powers, and especially on Germany, which these agreements involved; and he worked steadily towards a settlement of differences with our two imperial rivals, France and Russia. The entente with France, which was already in train at the time of his death, and that with Russia, which followed in 1907, were the outcome of this policy. His most concrete achievement was the consolidation of British power in Egypt and the reconquest of the Sudan. Cutting through the legal tangles which he had inherited from Gladstone's government, he challenged France at Fashoda and asserted in the Nile Valley the right of the stronger 'because it is the simplest and most effective'.

This appeal to material strength was characteristic. Salisbury was an imperialist of the old school, concerned with naval power and strategic bases. The Naval Defence Act of 1889 and the naval programmes of his later government made the British Navy more supreme than it had ever been; and the 'splendid isolation' which he is supposed to have favoured at the end of his life rested on this supremacy. Egypt and the Suez Canal meant much to him; the markets of China a certain amount. For the new fields of capital investment he cared not at all. He regarded the white man's burden with scepticism, particularly when it brought fabulous dividends and a Kaffir boom. He disliked Rhodes and Chamberlain, and had none of the connections with the Chartered Companies which marked Liberal imperialists, such as Rosebery. He loathed the Boer War, though he bore the final responsibility for it. But he could not escape his capitalist allies. Money had become the most effective form of power; and Salisbury, thinking only in terms of power, had to become its instrument.

As with the empire, so with the Unionist Party. When Salisbury entered politics Toryism still meant the Church and the squire. These were the causes for which he cared himself. He and Gladstone were the only prime ministers for whom devotion to the Church of England was more than a phrase; and he carried his hostility to democracy so far that he resigned in protest when Disraeli gave household suffrage to the towns in 1867. The Unionist Party was indifferent to the Church and exploited universal suffrage; it rested on the City and the urban masses. Salisbury made his peace with the Conservative working man. He was one of the greatest orators at mass meetings, and his governments had a better record than the Liberals in practical measures of social reform. He found it harder to swallow the financial magnates, and his final resignation in 1902 is said to have been caused by Edward VII's desire to ennoble a wealthy grocer who was one of his friends. Yet Sir Thomas Lipton was more typical than Lord Salisbury of England in the Edwardian decade.

Salisbury cannot rank among the greatest prime ministers, in spite of his gifts. He was inclined to let his colleagues go their own way, so long as they would leave him alone in foreign policy. If things went wrong he would shrug his shoulders and feel free of blame. He had indeed little interest in his colleagues nor personal contact with them. He was by nature aloof and coldly intellectual, finding emotional outlet only in the warmth of his family circle, which was ideally happy. Perhaps for this reason he was too ready to give high office to his sons and nephews, and his last cabinet was appropriately known as the Hotel Cecil.

In party politics, as in international relations, power was his only concern; and he deliberately heightened the tension of party conflict. In 1885 he destroyed the chance of an agreed settlement of the Irish question in order to score a party advantage, and he thought that Peel should have shown similar intransigence against the Reform Bill of 1832. When it was urged that this would have brought England to the brink of civil war, he answered: 'I see no harm in that.' The experiment was tried after his death, with the assistance of his own sons. Salisbury's bitterness against home rule in Gladstone's time was the example which inspired the Unionist Party in the Ulster rebellion of 1914.

English politics flourish on compromise and generous emotion, though these are perhaps the bane of our foreign policy. Salisbury was too detached and clear-headed to fit comfortably into the warm English haze. The cynic does best to comment on events, not try to make them. Once drawn into practical affairs, his distrust of idealism leaves him defenceless against baser forces. So it was with Salisbury. No man had a purer private character; few statesmen have had worse associates. He treated power as the only reality, and it turned to dust and ashes. Kipling's 'Recessional', written in 1897, passed judgement on Salisbury and his achievement. It was Salisbury's supreme tragedy that he himself endorsed that judgement.

John Morley: Intellectual in Politics

John Morley (1838–1923) was a potential successor to Gladstone as leader of the Liberal Party and was a senior cabinet minister in the last Liberal governments of 1905 to 1915 until he resigned in the summer of 1914 over Britain's entry into the First World War. As 'the last of the great, the true, Liberals' (as the journalist Henry Massingham described him), he was a political figure who interested Alan Taylor. This essay was published in the Observer *on 12 January 1969 as a review of D A Hamer's* John Morley *(Oxford University Press, 1968).*

*   *   *

Political theorists and historians are often tempted to dabble in the practical side of politics. They rarely succeed. Macaulay and Lecky would not be remembered for their political activities if they had not been considerable historians. Gibbon would not be remembered at all. Burke ruined the party for which he gave up mankind. In France de Tocqueville did not make a good foreign minister. Cobden, of course, was pre-eminent both as a political thinker and as a practical politician, but then he was always clear that his thinking had a practical purpose. Otherwise one must look far to find a theorist who rose as high in the political world as John Morley. He is among other things the only editor of a daily newspaper who became a senior cabinet minister.

Morley was not a profound thinker in either politics or ethics, and his works of political biography have lost what merit they once possessed. Even his *Life of Gladstone* has now few readers. Perhaps the comparative slightness of his thought propelled him towards the world of action. Nevertheless he was unmistakably both an intellectual and a practical politician. As such, his career has great fascination for anyone who has tried to combine the two roles, and the ingenious may detect parallels with Dick Crossman – or even with his Tory counterpart, Enoch Powell. There is the same zest to run after new ideas, even to run them to death, and the same belief that a theoretical concept will provide tactical guidance.

The combination of thought and action is the theme of Mr Hamer's remarkable book, firmly based on Morley's published writing and private correspondence. Morley began as an agnostic. He had lost his old faith, longed for a new one, and never found it. He could not accept an arbitrary new system and dismissed the positivist followers of Comte as 'Catholics without Christianity'. Failing a system, he sought a substitute in some 'single great question' – a topic on which men could unite for political action. It did not much matter what the topic was, so long as it conformed to Liberal principle. The important thing was that Liberals should promote it to the exclusion of all else. His first great question when he turned to practical politics was disestablishment, and this brought him into alliance with Joseph Chamberlain. Morley grew disillusioned on two counts. The nonconformists backed disestablishment for selfish sectarian reasons, and Chamberlain was more interested in power than in principles.

Morley condemned Chamberlain's 'want of wisdom and self-control'. Chamberlain dismissed Morley as 'dreadfully timid'. Morley said of himself: 'I am a cautious Whig by temperament. I am a sound Liberal by training, and I am a thorough Radical by observation and experience.' He found a more secure intellectual cause in home rule and a more sympathetic leader in Gladstone. Home rule stamped Morley's life. It had the particular merit in his eyes that for English people it was a purely unselfish cause. They were doing good to others, not for themselves. Moreover, as long as the Liberal Party concentrated on home rule, it was safe from 'the strong socialist doctrine I hate'. Characteristically Morley jeopardized his political career, to say nothing of home rule, by opposing the eight-hour day, simply because he thought that it was theoretically wrong.

When home rule ceased to provide a rallying cry, Morley took up anti-imperialism. His speech against the Boer War is among the noblest utterances in the English language. Yet, having delivered it, Morley withdrew to his study and nearly abandoned politics altogether. When he returned it was ironically as secretary for India, when he displayed few qualities of liberalism or generous imagination. He bestirred himself at last to oppose British entry into the First World War and was proud to repeat Pericles' boast: 'No Athenian by my means was ever made to put on the apparel of mourning.'

His opposition to the war had the curiously theoretical and even wrongheaded basis that Germany was civilized and Russia was not. The preponderance of Russia 'must follow from a successful war'. Would that not be 'a greater menace to Europe than any Germany could offer'? Morley knew nothing of either country. His judgements about them were made up after solitary brooding or reading a few books.

So it was with all Morley's ideas and policies. They were intellectual constructions, not irresistible impulses. Thought was the only emotion he knew and, as with all intellectuals, he doubted even when he thought. Others dismissed this as fear. Lloyd George said: 'Morley is a funk.' This was untrue. No man was braver than Morley in fighting against what he believed to be wrong. His difficulty was that he lacked the same conviction when it came to deciding what was right.

Other intellectuals in politics may draw a moral, at once consoling and restrictive. Their achievement is to oppose, not to lead. Victor Hugo put it more simply: 'Je suis *contre*.' As most things done in the political world are wrong and few right, there remains plenty of opportunity for intellectuals.

Keir Hardie : Labour's Moses

This essay was published as 'Labour's Moses' in the Observer *on 23 March 1975, as a review of Kenneth O Morgan's* Keir Hardie: Radical and Socialist *(London, Weidenfeld and Nicolson, 1975).*

*   *   *

When Keir Hardie died, one journalist wrote: 'The member for Humanity has resigned his seat,' and another: 'He was at once the Joshua and the Moses of the Labour movement.' Sylvia Pankhurst, his one-time mistress, described him as 'the greatest human being of our time'.

Not all socialists were so ecstatic. Engels called him 'an over-cunning Scot whose demagogic artfulness one cannot trust'. For Lenin, 'Hardie's outlook was contemptible, the very epitome of "opportunism".' However, as Kenneth Morgan remarks, 'to many British radicals, Hardie's opportunism amounted to simple commonsense'. One thing is certain: Keir Hardie created the British Labour Party and determined its character – an alliance between trade unions and political radicals, with a leaven of well-meaning careerists.

So far as Hardie is remembered at all, it is as a simple Scotch miner who went to the House of Commons in a cloth cap. This legendary picture is quite wrong. Hardie was far from simple: he was a highly complex romantic. He usually wore a deerstalker and later a slouch hat bought in Philadelphia. After his early years, he had few political links with Scotland, though he always retained a home there. He sat in parliament first for West Ham and then for Merthyr Tydfil, and his nationalism became as much Welsh as Scottish.

His socialism derived more from Carlyle and Ruskin than from Marx. Indeed the only quotation he ever made from Marx was 'Workers of the world, unite!' Socialism, though pre-eminent, was not his only cause. He championed Indian national-ism and international peace, playing a leading part in the Second International. At one moment he threatened to resign from the Labour Party for the sake of women's suffrage. His idealism did not prevent his being a supreme tactician, an opportunist of the highest rank. He preached and created an independent party for the working class. But he was equally insistent that this party must cooperate with the Liberals and welcome middle-class radicals as members.

Keir Hardie has had to wait long for a good biography. It seems almost unfair that Kenneth Morgan, having just written the first good, if short, biography of Lloyd George, should now produce one equally good on Keir Hardie. If he goes on like this, he will put the rest of us out of business. Morgan's book is deeply sympathetic, impeccably scholarly and beautifully writ-ten. It brings out the complexity of Hardie's character and the full range of his interests. Hardie is brought back to life: an inspired orator, an impeccable idealist, and often intensely exasperating.

Hardie was that rare thing: a good man. Though he made many mistakes, he never championed a wrong cause. He told the Scottish miners: 'Drink less, read more and think more.' His greatest commitment was to the unemployed. Here he saw the overriding social evil that condemned capitalism. His socialism was crude. Though he fought the class war, he imagined that it could be won without bloodshed or violence. In time capitalists, too, would see the evil of their way of life. He had some odd quirks, apart from his romantic style of dress which earned him the name of Queer Hardie. He dabbled in Spiritualism and even consulted the spirits as to whether he should vote for the Home Rule Bill of 1893. (The spirits advised him to do so.) Adoration did not come amiss to him. He wrote from India with some complacency:

I honestly believe that I am being worshipped in certain quarters and have been twice decorated with flowers taken from the Temples, an honour reserved for the holiest people . . . It appears that in two of the famine districts rain fell after my visit and *I get the credit.*

When his anti-war meetings were broken up in the early days of the First World War Hardie said: 'I now understand the sufferings of Christ at Gethsemane.'

No doubt Hardie was a difficult colleague. A G Gardiner said after his death that he was the one man in the Parliamentary Labour Party who was unqualified to lead it, and Hardie himself confessed as much by leading it for only a single year. John Burns said that Hardie 'would be known as the leader who never won a strike, organized a union, governed a parish, or passed a Bill'. This, too, was true though John Burns, with his unproductive record, was not the man to say it. Hardie's only practical experience in administration was a brief, and unsuccessful, membership of the Auchinleck school board in the early 1880s. He was incompetent in the conduct of his own finances and those of the *Labour Leader.* He often exasperated even his warmest admirers. All the same his creation of the Labour Party was a miracle of strategy and patience. The political independence of the working class was his guiding star, and he never lost sight of it.

Hardie had unshakeable faith in the ordinary man. This romantic view, now, of course, preposterously old-fashioned, gave Hardie the sincerity and passion which made him the greatest socialist speaker of his generation. Ernie Bevin complained of Hardie and his like that 'they let their bleeding 'earts run away with their bloody 'eads'. It would not come amiss if some members of the 1975 Labour Party merited this rebuke.

The Second International

First published in the New Statesman and Nation, *14 April 1956, as a review of* The Second International *(London, Macmillan, 1956), volume III of G D H Cole's* A History of Socialist Thought.

*   *   *

The nineteenth century travelled hopefully. We have arrived. Everyone is prosperous, secure: television sets and second-hand cars firmly embedded as a cost-of-living. The will of the people prevails at every general election – a will no doubt accurately expressed in a precise balance between two equally ineffective parties. Keynesian principles guard us against every economic ill; and now the hydrogen bomb, it is said, guards us against war. We are in the earthly Paradise. The only price we have paid is to cease to believe in it. Progress has been the great casualty of our age. There is no longer a MacDonald to hold out the prospect of 'up and up and up and on and on and on'. There would be no audience even if a new MacDonald appeared. To recapture the belief in progress we must return to the twenty-five years before the First World War, years in which European civilization reached its zenith. These years were exactly spanned by the Second International, the subject of the third volume in G D H Cole's *History of Socialist Thought*. Its thousand pages present a theme now remote and unsympathetic – futile debates, empty phrases, barren and impotent leaders. Yet there was in it deep tragedy – the tragedy of disappointed hope and the greater tragedy of hope fulfilled.

In Cole's earlier volumes there were few socialists but much thinking. In the present volume there is a great socialist movement and virtually no thought. Take away Rosa Luxemburg, and everyone – reformist or revolutionary, Fabian or Bolshevik

– scrabbled over phrases, while throwing his real energy into winning votes or enlisting members. All were convinced that the victory of socialism was inevitable and that it would be achieved in a democratic way. The German revisionists and English Fabians indeed held that the victory would be imperceptible: there would be no precise moment at which capitalism ended and socialism began. The orthodox continued to believe in 'the revolution'. There would be at some point a jerk, a change of gear, when the socialist commonwealth could be acclaimed. But for them, too, the revolution was simply part of an inevitable process; in democratic countries it would be little more than the appearance of a socialist majority in parliament. Even in countries not yet democratic – Germany in particular – the revolution would be political, not economic: the Social Democrats would insist on a change in the constitution once they got a majority, and thereafter socialism would flow inevitably on. Kautsky, the high priest of Marxism, postulated in *The Way to Power* that the secret of success lay in doing nothing: the longer the Social Democrats sat tight and allowed their supporters to accumulate, the greater and more irresistible would be their triumph when it came.

The greatest handicap of the Social Democrats was their adherence to the Marxist scriptures. Their adherence was selective. They suppressed or ignored Marx's advocacy of violent revolution; and therefore clung the more obstinately to his economic analysis. This was not surprising. Marx saw more deeply than any previous observer; but he drew from the Lancashire textile industry generalizations of worldwide application. The capitalists would grow fewer and richer; the workers poorer and more numerous. In the end there would be nothing in between. Hence the working-class party would inevitably become 'the democracy' by the mere passage of time. The prophecy worked satisfactorily until just before the First World War. Then the German Social Democrats realized that their rate of increase was grinding to a stop, as that of the British Labour Party has now done. The insoluble dilemma was

approaching; do we abandon socialism or democracy? The
Bolsheviks, never having enjoyed democracy, were to choose
socialism; others, doubtful in any case about socialism, preferred
to wait for the majority that never came.

This was not the only gap in Marx's teaching. He had always
promised to provide the equation demonstrating the collapse of
capitalism; but he never found it and for this reason left the
second volume of *Capital* unfinished. He had nothing to say
about the peasants except that they must be destroyed. Later
socialists have improved on this only by proposing (as Lenin
did) that the peasants should be gulled until the moment for
their destruction arrived. Again Marx had no answer to the
national question except that it did not exist: 'The workers have
no country.' The German leaders of the Second International
interpreted this to mean that, since they had achieved their
national freedom, the other peoples of central Europe should be
delighted to become Germans also. When this bargain failed to
attract, the 'Austro-Marxists' of Vienna invented the legend of
the Habsburg Monarchy as a great free-trade area, an International in miniature; and their example has been loyally
followed by socialist enthusiasts for the British Commonwealth
in our own day. The Second International was a combine of
master-nations, secure in their own rights and bewildered by
the claims of others. Even more striking, the International was a
purely European affair with a solitary Japanese representing
nobody. The few socialist parties outside Europe were the work
of immigrants and usually faded away with the second generation. Professor Cole includes a chapter on China for the sake of
Sun Yat Sen. It is modelled on Johnson's chapter on snakes in
Iceland: there was no socialism in China. In this the International reflected the universal assumption of the time. Europe
was civilization; therefore no socialist movement could flourish
outside it.

The Second International carried belief in progress to its
highest point. Progress was both the inspiration of social
democracy and its ruin. Marx shared with Samuel Smiles the

belief that if men pursued their material betterment persistently enough Utopia would arrive. The only difference was that Marx preached this doctrine to the working class instead of to the entrepreneurs. But the principle was the same: demand higher wages, shorter hours, and International Socialism will be here in no time. The Social Democrats discovered to their confusion that the workers, having secured high wages and shorter hours, now demanded wages still higher and hours still shorter, and that socialism was further off than ever. This outcome affected the Social Democrats themselves. Once the German Social Democrats had built up a gigantic party-machine for class war, they shrank from using it for this or any other purpose. The party bosses came to regard themselves as the purpose of the party machine long before the Russian Communists made the same discovery. Ebert, Viktor Adler, or Arthur Henderson might well have said: 'We are all Stalinists nowadays.'

The same law operated between nations. The peoples of Europe had once been oppressed. By the end of the nineteenth century they were living on the plunder of the rest of the world as they still do. The more hard-headed Social Democrats proposed that the workers should enter into a junior partnership with their own capitalists for the exploitation of others – a line taken by some German Social Democrats during the First World War and by Ernest Bevin in England after the Second. Most socialists shrank from the cynicism, but they were not altogether at a loss. The Fabians, in particular, were delighted to demonstrate that the exploited peoples were being plundered for their own good. They differed from their rulers only in holding that the powers should not run into conflict as to which should shoulder the greatest share of 'the white man's burden'. The international 'consortium' was a happy invention before the First World War; the international 'mandate' an even happier one after it. The Second International held fast to its high principle: fair shares, at any rate for the Big Brothers.

Imperialism landed the Social Democrats in the problem of

war, much to their surprise. Marx had given them no warning. He had blamed capitalism for being too pacific, not too warlike. The capitalists of Cobden's day had refused to fight the great war of liberation against Russia which Marx passionately advocated. Even now the Social Democrats went on dreaming that the magnates of finance would pull off a great merger at the last moment. Still they tried to discharge their responsibility. The Second International discussed the problem of war again and again. It laid down a simple truth: the workers could prevent war if they wished to do so. But suppose they did not wish to prevent war, what then? Viktor Adler gave the answer in 1914 when he supported Austria-Hungary's attack on Serbia the moment that the crowds in the streets of Vienna demonstrated in its favour. It is often said that the world war ruined international socialism. A more careful reading of the record shows that it was the other way round. The Second International was already torn wide apart before the crisis of 1914. If it had possessed the unity and strength even of ten years before, the outbreak of war would have been impossible. Success ruined the Social Democrats. They thought that it was essential to be on the winning side; for, by definition, progress means simply the side that wins. Things are much easier now that progress has come to an end. Who cares about success? Right is still right though the heavens fall. And, by the way, the ones who stuck to their hopeless principles got success as an unlooked-for bonus. Lenin achieved supreme power; the German Social Democrats never got anywhere. The more ruthless, extreme, and uncompromising your politics, the greater will be your reward in this world as well as in the next. A most consoling conclusion, though not perhaps for the Rt. Hon. Hugh Gaitskell.

The Vienna of Schnitzler

Alan Taylor's essay provides a rich portrait of the last period of imperial Vienna, the Vienna of the elderly Emperor Francis Joseph and of the youth of the writer Arthur Schnitzler (1862–1931). Alan Taylor had enjoyed his two years in Vienna from 1928 to 1930, learning to ride and to skate and in his final year holding a season ticket for the Vienna Philharmonic. Later, in Manchester, he had also been fascinated by Lewis Namier's recollections of pre-war and immediately post-war Vienna and Austria. His research in Vienna had covered an earlier period but with The Habsburg Monarchy *he had dealt with the late imperial period. Hence in writing this essay, as a foreword to Arthur Schnitzler's* My Youth in Vienna, *translated by Catherine Hutter (London, Weidenfeld and Nicolson, 1971), Alan Taylor was returning to one of his earlier major specialist areas. As for Schnitzler, Alan Taylor had begun reading his work as a nineteen-year-old undergraduate, starting with his* Dr Graesler *(the 1923 English translation of Schnitzler's 1917 novella).*

*   *   *

Es gibt nur a' Kaiserstadt,
Es gibt nur a' Wien.

There's only one imperial city,
There's only one Vienna.

So went one of the sentimental songs that the Viennese sang on their evening excursions as they drank the fresh heuriger wine. The sentiment was sober truth or very near it. Petersburg was an imperial creation. Byzantium was not much of a place until the Roman emperors set up there. Peking has the grandest claim of all. But these cities were far away. Vienna was in the heart of Europe. It had been a Roman settlement. It occupied a strategic position on the Danube. But it counted in the world solely because the Habsburgs lived there, and the Habsburgs counted because from the early sixteenth century they were Holy Roman emperors. They took a more modest title as emperors of Austria only at the beginning of the nineteenth century when the Holy Roman Empire ceased to exist.

Vienna was not the capital of the Holy Roman Empire. That empire had no capital. Vienna was simply the emperors' residence. Not the capital of a country before it became the centre of an empire, it was thus unlike London or Paris which had been the capitals of England and France before they became the centres of the British and French empires. Until the Habsburgs arrived, Vienna was merely the principal town of Lower Austria, on an equal footing with Linz, the principal town of Upper Austria, and without the Habsburgs it would have remained another Linz – a situation to which Hitler wished to degrade it. Only the Habsburgs made it great. The emperors lived in the Hofburg in the heart of the old city. In the eighteenth century Maria Theresa added a suburban palace at Schoenbrunn. From Vienna the Habsburgs ruled two empires: one, the Holy Roman Empire – a dying and ineffective relic; the other, a vast conglomeration of family estates – the Germanic Alpine provinces, Bohemia, Hungary, Croatia, Lombardy, and many added fragments.

This second empire, unnamed until 1804, gave Vienna its character. Though the inhabitants were mostly Germans, they spoke a German of their own and knew little of the Germany beyond the imperial frontiers, an ignorance which the *Pfiff-Chinesers* (spluttering Chinese) returned. Even at the present day, Germans know little of Austrian history, a subject rarely studied in German universities. The Viennese contributed comparatively little to their city's greatness. The burgomaster was an imperial official, not the spokesman of a proud independent middle class. The estates of Lower Austria were a feudal survival. There was no imperial parliament until 1848, the revolutionary year, and no regular parliament until 1867. The nobility from all the Habsburg lands had their town houses in Vienna in order to be near the emperor. The great offices of government were there with the Imperial Chancellery at their head. Even the aristocracy made no political contribution of their own. They were content to sustain Viennese culture. The musicians, Haydn, Mozart, Beethoven and Schubert, who made Vienna famous, were all dependent on aristocratic patrons.

Vienna remained small in size and population until after the Napoleonic Wars. Even in 1848 it still fitted into its medieval walls with a few aristocratic palaces just beyond them and some ribbon-building on the road out to Schoenbrunn. Thereafter it grew tumultuously, and most of it was as much a new town as Manchester or Birmingham. New Vienna, too, was a product of the industrial revolution. The railways, planned by the imperial government, ensured that Vienna became the centre of the empire as it had not been before. Vienna was the great railway junction for Prague, Budapest, Cracow and Trieste. Through trains ran from Vienna to Milan, Paris and Rome. Soon the Orient line ran to Constantinople.

With the railways came finance. Though there had been Rothschilds in Vienna from Metternich's time, the Viennese banks flourished when railways opened the empire to them. They became financiers not only of the empire but of much of the Balkans also. Vienna was not an important industrial centre. But Viennese money fed the industries of Bohemia and Styria, just as the money of London, also not an industrial town, fed the industries of the Midlands and the North.

The revolution and the railways brought another element to Vienna: the Jews. During the later Middle Ages, the Jews had been gradually driven out of western Europe, particularly out of the Rhineland. They found tolerance and refuge in Poland, where they lived until the eighteenth century, still using their medieval Rhenish dialect, Yiddish. Then Poland was partitioned. Galicia passed to the Habsburgs. The revolution of 1848 ended the restriction on Jews. They, too, were free to move, and Vienna was the goal of the more ambitious. The

Schnitzler family were one among many. These new arrivals had nothing in common with old aristocratic Vienna, nor with the incoming stream of working-class people. The most successful went into finance. Many of the others provided Vienna with its professional classes and intellectual life.

Thus late in the nineteenth century, when Arthur Schnitzler grew up, there were two Viennas living side by side and not taking much notice of each other. Old Vienna went on much as before. Emperor Francis Joseph lived at Schoenbrunn and used the Hofburg for official business. The aristocrats still lived in their town houses. There was now a parliament and a ministry supposedly responsible to it. There were glittering ceremonies, an apparently great army, and an ever-increasing civil service, with Francis Joseph as the chief and most industrious bureaucrat.

The city walls were destroyed in 1855, after an attempt to assassinate Francis Joseph while he was taking a walk along them. They were replaced by the Ring – a wide boulevard, designed partly to facilitate the dispersal of crowds by grapeshot fire. New Vienna grew up beyond the Ring. For the first time Vienna had a flourishing professional and intellectual life. Its newspapers, particularly the *Neue Freie Presse*, gained a European reputation. The bourse was of European significance, and the great crash on it in 1873 shook every European market. The university, too, came alive. Now its medical school achieved European pre-eminence, and the Vienna school of history soon lagged not far behind.

The awakening in art and literature was even more striking. In the early nineteenth century Vienna had no art except the Biedermeir style and no writer except the poet Grillparzer. New Vienna was a great artistic centre. Hans Makart, though conventional, could be set alongside Landseer or Millais. The Ring was resplendent with great buildings: imperial classical in the parliament house, the Opera and the Burgtheater, Gothic revival in the Votivkirche and the Town Hall. Later Otto Wagner, an outstanding master in art nouveau, provided Vienna with more than forty great buildings and also adorned the stations of the city railway. One modern department store on the Mariahilferstrasse so shocked Francis Joseph that he resolved never to use that route on his way to Schoenbrunn.

Music still came first, but it was now music for a large middle-class audience rather than for aristocratic patrons. Though the Opera and the Burgtheater were theoretically imperial institutions, they catered mainly to middle-class audiences; Francis Joseph took no interest in them except to get acting parts for his mistress, Katherina Schratt. The opening of a large concert hall, the Musikvereinsaal, was even more significant. Here the famous Vienna Philharmonic Orchestra gave its concerts at eleven o'clock on Sunday mornings – not a time of day favoured by the aristocracy. Musical Vienna was not content to live on its classics, great as these were. In opera, Richard Strauss went on where Wagner had left off. Mahler, great conductor and great composer, both completed the old school and began a new one. After him Schoenberg, Webern, and Berg created a new world of music which owed little to the major and minor diatonic scale. The revolutionary music of the twentieth century stems largely from Vienna.

Vienna of the late nineteenth century was an exciting creative city. Quite apart from the new movements in art and music, Freud was working out a new approach to psychology that would rock the foundations of established morality. Brentano was clearing the way for a new school of philosophy. Boehm-Bawerk and others were equally pioneering in political economics. Austrian sociologists were the first to study scientifically the particularly Austrian problem of nationality. Wits were quicker in Vienna than in Germany, ideas more novel, and spirits less restricted.

What old and new Vienna had in common was that they were Austrian, not German. Old Vienna was aristocratic and cosmopolitan. Most of the new Viennese came from the non-German lands of the monarchy and were at best Germans by adoption. When they travelled, it was to the Salzkammergut, the holiday resort which they created, or to Switzerland and northern Italy. If Vienna had a foreign affiliation, it was with Paris, not with Berlin, Frankfurt or Dresden. Vienna was a German-speaking Paris with even larger cafés and an even gayer life. The Viennese and the Parisians both relied on coffee as their social drink. The Germans drank beer. Viennese German was packed with French words and phrases. The fiacres rolled through the Prater as they did through the Bois. *The Merry Widow*, that Viennese masterpiece, though ostensibly set in Paris, really describes life in Vienna, at any rate on one frivolous level.

Young Schnitzler belonged to this frivolous life and was later to immortalize it in his writings. He was the spoiled son of a wealthy Jewish doctor, and played at being an army officer, though aware of his uneasy standing. He did not need to wait for the permissive society. To judge from his own account, he was rarely without a steady bed-companion, to use the contemporary phrase. These relationships were something of a Viennese specialty. Sentiment had to come into them as well as bed. Love affairs were as light as most Viennese emotions. The male partner was always aware that the affair would end and was usually relieved when it did. There was one difference between then and now. Schnitzler did not find his bed-companions in his own class. They were barmaids, shopgirls, dressmakers, amateurs who were readily available. Schnitzler had his own phrase for them – *das süsse Mädel* (the sweet girl), meaning one who enjoyed being seduced. For Schnitzler and his friends, women were to be grateful for whatever men offered them. Ultimately the men would settle down and become patriarchs, tyrannizing over their wives and children. Freud assumed too readily that all men were like the Viennese.

Schnitzler had artistic interests and literary ambitions which he later fulfilled. He showed no interest in politics, assuming, as many Viennese did, that these could be safely left to the emperor. One political issue broke into his life and ultimately disrupted Vienna as a centre of civilization. This issue was nationality, a loyalty creed. Nationality spelt doom for Vienna, the city with no national loyalty. It spelt doom for the Jews of Vienna, who wished only to be Austrians. Their first impulse was to become Germans as many non-Jewish Austrians did. Heinrich Friedjung, the great historian, was one of the founders of the German Nationalist Party. Theodor Herzl was one of its prominent supporters. Both were Jews. To their dismay they were rebuffed by their own creation. Anti-semitism became an essential part of German nationalism. Friedjung retreated into Austrian imperialism. Herzl, unable to share in German nationalism, turned to Jewish nationalism and founded Zionism. In this sense Zionism was a compensation for the denied German nationalism or an alternative version of it.

Vienna had always been expecting the end from the start of its greatness – doom from the Turks, doom from the French Revolution. This time the expectation was justified. Nationalism disrupted the Habsburg Monarchy. Vienna became the inflated capital of a small Alpine country. Even this was not the end. German nationalism triumphed twenty years after the other nationalisms had done. In 1938 Austria was incorporated in Germany. There was no place for the Jews. They were persecuted, driven out, or murdered. After the Second World War Austria was made an independent state once more. Vienna still had great buildings and a great orchestra. It prospered as an open door between eastern and western Europe. But the life had gone. Vienna is a city living on its past. Schnitzler's autobiography describes the last years when Vienna was still living in the present.

York

This essay appeared as 'The City of York' in the Guardian *on 12 January 1962 as a review of P M Tillott's* The City of York *(Oxford University Press, 1961), in the* Victoria History of the Counties of England.

* * *

A sense of the past can flourish in unlikely places. J Horace Round, for instance, cultivated his at Brighton. But I can hardly believe that the past would have gripped me if I had not spent five years at school in York. Bootham School possesses the oldest school natural history society in the country; and in this society all history was natural. 'Archaeology' – the collecting of ancient buildings – was as respectable as the collecting of stones or butterflies. I spent much of my five years examining the parish churches; speculating on life in York from the Romans until the present day; and recording the results in notebooks, which I destroyed only last year. As an added element of pleasure, the city within the walls was theoretically out of bounds after two o'clock in the afternoon. My first act as a prefect was to give myself leave to enter the city at any time of day; and, by adding to this permanent exemption from compulsory games, I saw a good deal of York thereafter. I know little of the city on the west bank, though it is within the walls; and tell prospective visitors that it contains little of interest except a Saxon tower and some wonderful glass. I expect this is wrong. At any rate, York on the east bank alone offers a procession of history which, for me, has never been rivalled elsewhere.

The remarkable thing about York is its dual character: a museum and yet not a museum piece. It has a Roman tower; a cathedral and a castle; an eighteenth-century assembly room;

and a magnificent nineteenth-century Railway Hotel. Its circumvallation is almost intact. Four bars stand their full height, one of them with a barbican. York has a bit of almost everything except that it is rather weak on the seventeenth century, a time distinguished in York by destruction, not by building. Constantine the Great was here, and also George Fox; Alcuin, and also Feargus O'Connor. Many kings have resided in York, of whom George Hudson, the railway king, was the last. Yet, with all this turmoil of history, York does not feel antiquated. Much of it is squalid, or was when I knew it, in the ordinary nineteenth-century style; the alleyways full of slovenly Irish children. Seebohm Rowntree did not need to move from home when he studied poverty at the end of Queen Victoria's reign; it was there on his doorstep. The city has now brightened itself up, and has taken to being proud of itself. The corporation did not much deserve praise in the past. They would have obliterated most of York's history if their money had run to it. Even the offer of Sir Walter Scott to walk from Edinburgh to York did not deter them from demolishing the barbican at Micklegate. Though York has not been threatened with ruin since the time of the Danes, it has also escaped large-scale industry even to our own day: no woollen factories, no automobile industry, only the cocoa works. Even the railway, though a considerable junction, has been absorbed into the historic city, and has enhanced it. I would sacrifice some of the less distinguished churches rather than the Station Hotel.

Historical imagination can people the buildings of the past, but research does it better and more correctly. I have been carried into a magic world by reading the volume on York in the *Victoria History of the Counties of England*, which has just come out. This is not a book for the casual visitor in either size or treatment. To appreciate it properly, the reader must know York well or be prepared to settle there for a month or so; he will reap a rich reward. Medieval York had a special character. Not only was it the seat of an archbishop and for most of the Middle Ages a fairly prosperous centre of trade. It was the great

outpost of royal power in the north, and often more. During the
long wars with Scotland it came near to being the national
capital. The law courts were often moved here; parliaments
assembled, though the history unfortunately does not say where
they met. The sun of the royal presence warmed the citizens of
York, and rewarded them with increasing privileges. Alone of
northern cities, York escaped provincialism. It was so independent and so treasured that Henry VII forgave its loyalty to the
Yorkist cause and to Richard III. In the sixteenth century the
Council of the North gave York another stretch of importance,
but also of stagnation. It was easier to take the advantages of
being a political centre than to run after the new wealth of the
Tudor age.

The civil wars of the seventeenth century and the decline of
the monarchy brought York down from its high estate. No king
visited York between Charles I and George V. In the eighteenth
century the city had to make do with the Duke of Cumberland
and the Prince of Wales (later George IV), each of whom
received a 100-guinea gold box. Perhaps as a result Charles
James Fox also received a gold box (though only of 50 guineas)
'for upholding the principles of the Glorious Revolution'.
Nevertheless York looked up in Georgian times. In 1763 it
claimed to be 'the capital city of the northern parts of England
and a place of great resort and much frequented by persons of
distinction and fortune'. The second part of the claim was truer
than the first. The landed aristocracy of Yorkshire turned York
for a time into their meeting place and set up town houses there
(one of them became the nucleus of Bootham school). The
Marquis of Rockingham, wealthy if not great, acquired York as
his pocket borough. An odd fact I learnt from the history was
the existence in York at this time of a boarding school for
Roman Catholic young ladies. The original of Dr Slop was a
citizen of York, and, it seems, a more distinguished one than
Sterne made out. Quakers, too, have a long background in
York. They could almost claim it as their peculiar city, though
their meeting-house is not one of its architectural treasures.

York had another run of dull times in the nineteenth century apart from the railway. By escaping the factories, it escaped much of the prosperity also. A hundred years ago, it must have looked most like a cathedral town with little else to keep it going. It ceased to be a regional capital; its corporation was unenterprising when not corrupt; its death rate was consistently above the national average. The cocoa works brought more to York than prosperity; they brought reform and improved standards. Now York is to attain the added dignity, if that be the right word, of a university. I expect that the university will be too enlightened to have much time for history. Everything no doubt will be mixed up together in the modern style – a bit of this, a bit of that, and the students crying out at the end: 'Come over to Macedonia and help us.' If any victim escapes from this pursuit of universal knowledge and grasps at something solid, he will be in the right place. York is a city where you cannot help studying history even at the expense of civics.

Manchester

This is drawn from a television programme, Fabric of an Age. On the Rise of Manchester, *first shown on* BBC 2 *on 16 September 1976. The programme won the Manchester Society of Architects' Award for Architectural Initiative, 1976. It was published in* The Listener *on 16 September 1976, as 'Made in Manchester'.*

* * *

There was a time when Manchester was the centre of a new civilization. It was here in Manchester that the Industrial Revolution was invented. What made Manchester unique was industry. Of course, there had been industrial towns before, but a town devoted entirely to industry, a town given over to factories and machines – Manchester was the first. It was a pattern which was to spread different industries across Europe. The industry which created Manchester was the cotton industry. Wherever you looked in those days, you would see the great factory chimneys and the filthy smoke belching out. They came from all over Europe to see it. Engels came, Carlyle came, de Tocqueville came, because it envisaged an entirely new way of life in which people are absolutely submerged in the pursuit of industrial wealth. Manchester was to be the characteristic, the dominant city of this new capitalistic civilization which was to spread first across England, then across Europe, finally across the world, in the nineteenth century. For a little while, Manchester was a sort of Athens or Rome, and men were to speak in awed tones of the Manchester School, the Manchester outlook or what the Germans called the *Manchestertum.* 'Made in Manchester' in a sense symbolized the nineteenth-century British Empire.

In the eighteenth century, Manchester was a flourishing trading town, dominated by its large collegiate church. It had been a market town since the end of the Middle Ages, and it was a centre for all the trading activities of south-eastern Lancashire and Cheshire. In the early eighteenth century, there came the great change when cotton arrived from across the Atlantic – it was much easier to deliver into the Lancashire ports of the west coast – and soon Lancashire switched from wool to cotton.

The textile trade was still a home industry – there were no factories, and the spinning and weaving were done in the homes of cottagers – often out in the countryside. Weaving was carried out in a shed at the back of a house, or in an upstairs attic room.

The invention of the flying shuttle had almost doubled the output of the weaver. This put pressure on the spinner, who was still spinning yarn on an old-fashioned spinning-wheel. There was always a competition between the spinner and the weaver.

At this stage, the spinner could not provide enough yarn for the weaver, and so the need arose to speed up the spinning process. The great inventions in spinning were all very simple mechanical ones. Hargreaves's spinning-jenny used a wheel on its side, and was able to drive first eight, then up to 120 spindles. Then came Arkwright's water frame, and, finally, Crompton's mule, which could spin a very fine yarn, and was to provide the basic method of spinning in Britain for the next 120 years. The jenny and the mule, even though they were still operated by human force, produced a great deal more yarn than the weaver could handle, so then it was the weaver who became the privileged one. The most backward industry, because it can keep its prices up, is always the most profitable, and so, for the last decade of the eighteenth century and the first twenty or thirty years of the nineteenth century, the handloom weavers were perhaps the most privileged section of the British working class.

It was the human being who turned the spinning-wheel, it was the human being who worked the handloom with pedals, so that, though there was machinery, there was nothing to drive it other than the spinner or the weaver. The Industrial Revolution, put briefly, was the arrival of force. Power to drive the mules, power to drive the looms: this was the decisive thing which led to the real burgeoning of the cotton industry. Water was the first source of power; instead of hundreds of machines in separate houses, they could be grouped together in one large building – the factory. And so began the reign of King Coal and King Cotton – and a very dirty reign it was to be.

Steam power was the real driving force of the Industrial Revolution: driving force not only because it provided far greater power than had ever been known before to drive hundreds of machines, but because it drove men as well. The essential thing about steam power is that it was either on or off, and, when it was on, men had to work to its rhythm. Steam power first compelled men to be punctual – one of the greatest revolutions in the history of mankind; to be punctual not only to the hour or day, but to the minute. The old handloom weaver had to work very hard – perhaps harder than the man looking after a power loom. But he could work when he liked, he could turn off, he could go to the garden for half an hour, as long as he was doing his job. But with steam, the factory dominated, and it was this revolution which was first examined in detail by observers in Manchester in the early nineteenth century when they saw, for the first time, this incredible cleavage between – I was going to say men who were still human beings because they were the bosses, because they could decide, because they could turn the machine on and off, and men who were no longer individuals, but were slaves of the machine; this was the new society which Manchester invented.

Factories were then new, and the horror which people sometimes felt about them was partly because of their very existence, which was inevitable, and partly because of the evils associated with the factory system when it first grew up. The expansion of Manchester, of the factories, of the people, was absolutely breathtaking. The population went up from under 100,000 to 300,000 within a relatively short space of time. The twenty years after the Napoleonic Wars transformed Manchester from a modest market town into a metropolis. Observers came from all over Europe to look at the cotton industry and to see how the factories dominated Manchester. De Tocqueville wrote:

From this foul drain, the greatest stream of human industry flows out to fertilize the whole world. From this filthy sewer, gold flows. Here humanity attains its most complete development, and its most brutish; here civilization works its miracles and civilized man is turned back almost into a savage.

One observer who came to Manchester in the early 1840s was the German, Friedrich Engels. He came as a visitor, and then as a cotton merchant for twenty years. Engels wrote *The Condition of the Working Class in England*, and it remains the most powerful, though not always the most accurate, description of Manchester in the early days of the Industrial Revolution. In these appalling living conditions, it is not surprising that there was profound, though ill-organized, discontent. In the towns around Manchester there was the machine wrecking which was called Luddism. In 1817, the Blanketeers, who were an early form of hunger-marchers, set off on an abortive march to London, and the greatest demonstration of all was planned for 16 August 1819. This was the demonstration which gathered from all over Lancashire and the surrounding cotton towns in St Peter's Fields, and which came to be called the massacre of Peterloo. Eleven people were killed, one of them, incidentally, an ancestor of mine, and that is something to be proud of. But, in the end, this massacre destroyed the old social order.

Ultimately, it was one of the victories of the people of England, and now the spot where Orator Hunt addressed, or was about to address, the assembled crowd before he was arrested, the hustings, is buried under the Free Trade Hall. Though it stands on the site of Peterloo, the Free Trade Hall represents the great middle-class movement for free trade.

It is a unique public building. So far as I can think, it is the only one not dedicated to a saint, not named after some great local dignitary, but dedicated to a proposition – the proposition of free trade, which Manchester was to spread throughout England. The free-trade movement had its origins in the campaigning against the Corn Laws. The object of the Corn Laws was simply to keep up the price of corn to benefit the landed aristocracy. In seeking their repeal, the Anti-Corn Law League aimed not just to reduce the price of bread, but to substitute the rule of merchants and millowners for that of landowners. The Free Trade Hall was built to commemorate the repeal of the Corn Laws in 1847. It marked the emancipation of Manchester from London, and its establishment as a different authority – the Manchester School – which was to dominate British politics for many years to come. Indeed, one could say that Manchester had become the new capital of the new England; but in order to hold her position, she had had to take the lead all the time.

In the 1830s, when canals, rivers and roads were no longer adequate, Manchester took the leading part in one of the country's greatest innovations. The Liverpool and Manchester Railway was the first passenger railway ever opened. As the railways spread, the landscape of Manchester itself changed. The mills dwindled – they moved out into other towns. Manchester itself became the great collecting and exporting centre. All the cotton goods made in Lancashire came to Manchester. In order to accommodate them, vast warehouses were built in a ring around the city centre. So Manchester changed from being a factory city to being a city of warehouses.

There was a very great flow of Germans into Manchester in the early nineteenth century, fairly rich Germans, merchant Germans who provided a powerful element of culture. It was Germans who founded the Hallé Orchestra. Sir Charles Hallé himself, of course, was a German by origin. They founded the Schiller Anstalt, which was a great cultural organization in the beginning of the nineteenth century. In fact, you could really say that the Germans of Manchester were the German liberals who had failed in Germany itself, but who succeeded here in England and did so much to help Manchester liberalism to have its special character; one was Friedrich Engels. Engels was accepted by most people simply as a cotton merchant, but he was also a journalist, a writer of economic tracts, and he spent a good deal of his time at Chetham's Library gathering material for his researches.

Engels's book *The Condition of the Working Class in England in 1844* was based on personal experiences of going about Manchester, experiences which other people like Carlyle had, but a great deal of it was based on research. In fact, I was almost going to say it is a dishonest book, because a lot of what he describes as happening in 1844 goes back to an account he picked up of Manchester in 1818. So that it was deliberately a work of propaganda, and when the book was finished and was out in Germany – it didn't come out in English, I may say, until the 1880s – Marx, Engels's friend, came up to Manchester. He came here for four days, and these four days were the only time that Marx ever saw English capitalism in action, and it is fair to say also that he saw it in very curious surroundings: most of what he saw was Chetham's Library.

Ironically perhaps, in 1844, when Engels was describing Manchester, it was really the beginning of the age of reform, when conditions were enormously improved; and ten years later, by the mid-1850s, Manchester was by no means as filthy and by no means as neglected as it had been. Twenty years later, Manchester could be regarded, though still dirty, as being an enlightened, modern city, and it was then that men set out to create a monument of the first rank to rival the Gothic cathedrals.

The greatest Gothic building of the nineteenth century calls itself a humble town hall, but it is not at all humble. Nor is it just a town hall; it is a palace, something like the Palace of the Doges in Venice. And it is a shrine – not a shrine dedicated to some religious saint, but a shrine dedicated to the cotton industry and to the cotton trade of which Manchester was the centre. It is a shrine in which everything breathes cotton. Bees of industry on the floor, cotton flowers on the ceiling and hanks of cotton round the sides.

In the great days of cotton, Manchester set an example to the world. Manchester had the greatest, and, indeed, the only, permanent orchestra in England, the Hallé. By the 1890s, Manchester had the outstanding liberal newspaper, the *Manchester Guardian*. The high point of all was reached with the opening of the Manchester Ship Canal. This was a great event in the history of Manchester; ocean-going ships could now come up to Manchester.

It is said that the cotton industry produced enough textile goods for the home market before breakfast, and the rest of the day was producing for export. The greatest quantity of cotton goods ever exported from this country came early in 1914. Then came the First World War. The cotton industry was artificially restricted. Inevitably, the markets which Lancashire relied on were lost. India began to manufacture her own textiles and, still more alarming for the future, Japan with her advanced machinery took Lancashire's place. Nobody grasped this at the time. When the war was over, people thought there would be a new boom. In 1919, more mills were built in Oldham than ever before in the history of the town. Many of them were never completed and even many of those which were completed were not used as cotton mills. In 1921, the boom burst, broke for ever. Broadly, one can say that the great textile industry which had made Manchester a metropolis and a symbol of civilization dwindled away, and from the end of 1921 was never to see a real recovery. How ironic, therefore, that the opening of the Royal Cotton Exchange with its great trading floor should coincide so precisely with what we now see was the end of the civilization which the exchange represented.

Ten years later, in the early 1930s, when I came to Manchester as a university lecturer, there was still plenty of old Manchester to be seen. The market-place was absolutely unchanged from the days of the Young Pretender. Cotton was still a dominant industry in Manchester. When you arrived, you thought of it as a great cotton town. Horse-drawn drays carried bales of cotton through the streets. The warehouses were still all cotton warehouses. The Royal Exchange still functioned, if only on a rather diminished scale. And Manchester was a great city. Now it has all gone. Manchester is a bright, clean city. The warehouses have either been pulled down, or been given over to other uses. The few factory chimneys stand up like Egyptian obelisks, as much out of place as Cleopatra's Needle on the Embankment in London. The *Manchester Guardian* itself has disappeared, and its place has been taken only by an anonymous *Guardian* which is published in London. Certainly, Manchester is an enlightened place. It is a much cleaner place than it used to be. It has far more open spaces, some of them attractive, many of them simply where slums have been pulled down and not been replaced. But nobody any longer says, 'what Manchester thinks today, England thinks tomorrow'. The Manchester School has done its work and has vanished.

Edge of Britain: A Lancashire Journey

In June 1980 Alan and Eva Taylor revisited the Lancashire towns of his childhood and youth for four half-hour programmes broadcast by Granada Television on Thursday evenings between 18 September and 9 October 1980. These programmes were well received. The Times's critic Peter Davalle commented when they were shown again as an edited one-hour programme on 21 January 1981: 'He makes a matter-of-fact guide; quietly affectionate about the old things and not a bit sentimental, as Betjeman would probably have been.'

In his autobiography Alan Taylor recalled the month he spent making these programmes as one of the most enjoyable of his life. He would have been tempted to make a similar series but felt that nowhere else was as suitable. He declined Vienna on the grounds that 'my memories are fifty years out of date and not very vivid even at the time'.

These pieces on his tour of the Lancashire coast first appeared in the Spectator, 20 September–11 October 1980.

*   *   *

A Southport Childhood

Southport is a special place in many ways with nothing more extraordinary than its beginnings. Although it came into existence less than 200 years ago, its origins are as legendary as those of Troy. In 1795 there was no such place, no name, no idea that there could be such a place. Within ten years, perhaps within five years, the name had come into existence. Southport existed and began to expand from that moment. What seemed to have happened was this – that in the late eighteenth century a certain number of people used to come down here into the dunes. Just over the dunes was what was then sea, but is now very very dry sand and there were a few bathing huts. The parish centre at that time was Churchtown, which is much further up the coast. And at Churchtown there was an inkeeper called William Sutton who set up a little drinking booth here to which he gave the grandiloquent title of 'The South Port Hotel'. It wasn't a hotel, nor was there a port. There never had been. The name was an invention of William Sutton and in later years his claims became more and more grandiose until he was finally to receive the dignified title of the Old Duke. For fifty years he maintained the claim that he had been the father of Southport. Perhaps not the father, but certainly in my opinion the godfather.

After the legendary story of William Sutton the prosaic truth about Southport is that it was the creation of the local landlords. By the 1820s Lord Street, which had originally been a stretch of sand beside the sea, had become an elegant centre and was referred to elsewhere as the distinctive feature of Southport. And then something even more surprising followed: in the 1860s the whole of Lord Street was brought under a system of arcades. Each arcade was the creation, in theory, of a separate shopkeeper, but it built up into a unique feature. For a long time people said that this was imitated from Haussmann's boulevards in Paris. But more recently it has been confirmed that in fact all the arcades were up ten years before Haussmann made a single arcade in Paris. The most ingenious suggestion is that they were imitated from somewhere in the New World – from Boston or even New York, but this again sounds very speculative. I think the explanation, as with everything that happened from Sutton almost to the present day, is a run of anonymous luck. Some force beyond that of anything that we can name was working to ensure that Southport retained this unique elegance.

Southport got a head start on all the other watering places of the Lancashire coast. These couldn't really get going until the railways were opened. Southport, however, had a first chance twenty years before them, because of the supply of visitors who came on the Leeds and Liverpool Canal. This had been opened at the beginning of the century. The canal brought visitors from Liverpool, from Manchester, from Wigan. The barges came often carrying a hundred visitors at a time. They landed here on the wharf and then the coaches took them into Southport. As a result, by the middle of the 1820s Southport was often having 20,000 visitors a year, and it established clearly its primacy among Lancashire resorts.

Lord Street is among my earliest memories. Looking back I have the most vivid picture not only of my mother, but of the society that she frequented, dressed to the height of Edwardian fashion. They wore enormous picture hats held on by hatpins, dresses down to the ground, heavily corseted and, I believe, with a modesty vest over the cleavage. These ladies looked like ships in full sail, with the same sort of majesty as the Royal Navy possessed. I remember my mother used to take a cup of tea with her fashionable friends in a Lord Street resort known as Thom's Japanese Tea House, a place which I came to loathe and longed to escape from. One of the few minor pleasures that my father and I enjoyed if we escaped from Thom's café was Pleasureland, which in those days had lots of animated penny-in-the-slot machines. Now only a few rather inferior ones have survived – all the rest are gone – the greatest victim I think of metrication. If only we'd thought of that at the time, I think we could have prevented it and perhaps kept ourselves out of the Common Market into the bargain.

The town hall is associated with my earliest political experience though hardly with my political memory. In those days long general elections ran on for some weeks, and the results came out on different days. It was very exciting and dramatic – there was nothing like radio, and therefore the results were flashed across the front of the town hall. In 1906 my mother attended regularly night after night to watch what was the greatest of Liberal victories. As Hilaire Belloc said,

> The accursed power which stands on privilege
> (And goes with women and champagne and bridge)

Broke – and democracy resumed her reign
(Which goes with bridge and women and champagne).

I was present with my mother, but in fact hardly in a position to observe what was going on – she was six months pregnant. It was only three months later that I was born – not, I may say, in Southport at all, but in Birkdale, where I spent the first seven years of my life.

I've always thought I was born in Birkdale and physically that is true, but which is the Birkdale I'm talking about? When I was born, in 1906, Birkdale was an independent urban district council technically in the registration district of Ormskirk so that to my great surprise my birth certificate said that I was born in Ormskirk. In the year 1912, after a passionate political campaign, Birkdale amalgamated with Southport. What was passionate about it I don't know but I know that all the radicals were greatly in favour of the amalgamation, including my father (it was his first political triumph that Birkdale became part of Southport). So now I was born in Southport, and for a long time I used to write in my passport loyally 'birthplace Southport, Lancashire'. But what's happened to me now? Southport isn't in Lancashire any more; it's in this extraordinary place called Merseyside. But Southport geographically is not on Merseyside; it's on Ribble-side. So what am I to put? Am I to say I was born in Ormskirk, or that I was born on Ribble-side? And the most outrageous thing is that what the bureaucrats of Whitehall have done is to say that I wasn't born in Lancashire. But they are wrong. I was. I was born in Birkdale, Lancashire, and that's what I stick to.

I used to walk to school in the gutter so as not to have to mix with the other children on the pavement. The little school was kept by the Misses Filmer. The remarkable thing about them is that they were actually born in Birkdale – the only other people who lived in Birkdale that I knew had been born there. Otherwise the school left little mark on me. I remember that I had to sit at the back of the class and read books because all the other children were being taught to read. The other thing that I remember is that this enlightened school decided that every child should have a glass of milk at eleven o'clock and each child was charged a penny for his glass of milk. I didn't like milk, so I was given a glass of water, but it was felt to be inegalitarian if I got free water while they paid one penny for the milk, so I paid a penny for water out of the tap. I felt that something was wrong, but once egalitarians get going you never know what damage they can do.

I was a little boy in a very political household. My father called himself a young Liberal, though he wasn't a bit like the young Liberals of nowadays. My mother, I think, felt embarrassed that she wasn't a suffragette, and her embarrassment took the form of being very hostile to the suffragettes, whereas my father, who was always tolerant, thought that if women wanted to be suffragettes they were entitled to be. And he had a bedtime story which was one of my favourites called 'Chuck her down'. This was a story about Churchill's visit to Southport in 1909. There were always suffragette disturbances at big Liberal meetings, particularly at Churchill's. He exasperated them more than anyone else, particularly because he was himself in favour of votes for women. The problem was such that you had to have a hand-picked audience, and my father would begin the story by saying how the Liberal agent said, 'I personally guarantee every woman in the audience. Every one of them has been checked. There'll be no trouble.' Churchill had only just begun to speak when from the little loft of the hall there was a woman's cry of 'Votes for women'. This was a suffragette who had concealed herself in the attic two or three days before and now was in an invulnerable position. She couldn't be reached without breaking a great number of doors because she'd locked them all. The whole audience rose and shouted: 'Chuck her down, chuck her down.' Churchill tried to quieten them and said: 'If you don't take any notice of her and let her call out "Votes for women" as much as she likes, she won't disturb the meeting.' 'Chuck her down, chuck her down.' By that time, I was ready to go to sleep.

I in fact encountered a politician for the first time at the January 1910 general election. This was an election fought partly, though only partly, on the Liberal idea for the taxation of land values. The Tories claimed that the valuation put on the land by the Liberals was much too high and that the taxation they'd have to pay was therefore much too heavy. The Liberal candidate was Baron de Forest, the heir of Baron de Hirsch who had built the Orient Line, and himself one of the richest men in Europe. When this Tory complaint was made, Baron de Forest issued a statement that he had deposited his cheque for three million pounds in the local bank and was prepared the following morning to buy all the land of Southport at the valuation the Liberals had put upon it. Not a single Tory accepted the offer. Their complaint that the valuation was too high was not heard again. I actually shook hands with Baron de Forest. I vaguely remember an impressive tall man in a continental greatcoat going right down to his ankles, and an Austrian moustache.

When Southport started, the sea came up to Lord Street and then disappeared again. Now it's vanished totally out of sight. The pier had to be built a mile long and at the end, with luck, you could sometimes see the sea in the distance. There always seemed to be enough high water for the achievements of Professor Powsey. I've known many professors in my time, but never one who fascinated me as Professor Powsey did. He was a professor of deep-sea diving, Bert Powsey by name. He started diving as a boy of eighteen and went on until he was seventy-five. His most sensational dive, which I witnessed, was the dive when he tied both his hands to his sides, tied his legs together, then plunged in and emerged safe and sound with all his ropes loosened. The climax at the end of the whole show, as I remember, was the bicycle dive, an expedition which he conducted down a steep board into the sea with the bicycle set alight and blazing around him. We shall never see the likes of Professor Powsey again.

The Boarding House Culture

The remarkable thing about Blackpool from the first is that it was the creation of its own people. All the various companies, who launched piers or theatres or whatever it might be, were local companies with local investors. When the first railway was created, there was a wide street leading down from the station to the promenade, and this gave a wonderful opportunity for the North Pier, the first of Blackpool's piers which, as it were, caught the arriving travellers, excursionists. The North Pier regarded itself from the first as the elegant pier. One reason for this was that, during the American Civil War and the cotton famine, only well-to-do people could afford to come to Blackpool. They came to the North Pier, and the tone there was restrained, almost with a touch of Southport's dignity. But now the North Pier, like the other Blackpool piers, has no such pretensions.

The Tower Ballroom, for example, represents the great principle of Blackpool carried to its highest point – luxury for the millions. This is, I suppose, the most luxurious, lavish, the most brilliantly adorned ballroom in the world and yet it is not in a king's palace. It is a ballroom available to everybody. The Blackpool Ballroom – opened incidentally in 1894 – represents the triumph of democracy, no class distinctions, no privileges to anybody, everybody sharing the glories of luxury. Blackpool Tower is also a product of the 1890s. Towers were very much in fashion then. I suppose they were all inspired by the Eiffel Tower, which had been built a little earlier in Paris. Blackpool had a tower, New Brighton had a tower, Morecambe had a tower – the only one that has survived, very characteristically, is Blackpool's, which shows not only an obstinacy but I think a conservatism in its entertainments. The Tower justifies itself, however, because the view of the sea and the sand from it is very striking indeed. If you look landside, what you see in all directions are boarding houses.

The boarding house is the quintessential Blackpool institution.

When boarding houses started in the eighteenth century, Blackpool hardly existed. Yet even as early as 1760, Mrs Whiteside opened what is alleged to have been the first boarding house in Blackpool. Now, while other resorts have rather retreated from the boarding house pattern, Blackpool is completely dominated by it. Along the promenade every single house is either a boarding house or, as it is sometimes more grandiloquently called, a private hotel. I observe also that nearly every boarding house now has a little advertisement, 'Private Car Park Available'. The boarding house habitués of fifty years ago would have been astonished to know that their successors each arrived in not only a private car, but probably quite a big private car.

The boarding house is a communal institution. Very often whole groups of friends join in the same boarding house. You might find a whole street of boarding houses occupied by people from the same town, so that they could take with them not only their own outlook and atmosphere, but their actual friends and surroundings. The boarding house is the most homely and welcoming method of accommodating people in a strange place. Immediately they feel at home, and the guests probably get quite as substantial and healthy a meal as those who go to great hotels. Boarding houses, more than anything else, keep Blackpool going. And one should add that running a boarding house is by no means unprofitable.

Who would have imagined that the Blackpool Pleasure Beach would have a masterpiece of thirties architecture like the splendid Casino by the now-forgotten Joseph Emberton? It must be nearly seventy years since I came to the Pleasure Beach for the first time. It represented one of my earliest childhood dreams. Even then it was quite sophisticated. But you could see clearly, and you can still see, how it had grown out of the primitive fairs. The same idea of the shock and the thrill – the excitement of movement, of being swung to and fro. When I came, the Hiram Maxim flying boats had just taken, as it were, to the air. They are still going.

The Pleasure Beach was conceived by an individual – it is not any work of the Corporation. In fact, in the early days there was jealousy between the Corporation and the Pleasure Beach, but perhaps not now. It is also characteristic of Blackpool that the Pleasure Beach is still the property of the grandchildren of its founder. Its detachment from Blackpool is much less than it was. One feels now, in fact, that it is becoming almost a civilized part of Blackpool. It was wilder once. When I visited it, there were still a few gypsies around and fortune-tellers. Now it is immensely sophisticated, and yet the underlying attitude, the underlying criterion, remains the same. It is a work of popular taste – and anyone who thinks popular taste bears any resemblance to good taste should come to Blackpool, and particularly to the Pleasure Beach, where he will be disillusioned.

Trams have been for more than 100 years one of the secrets of Blackpool's success. The first trams were introduced in 1870. These were horse trams. But, by the 1880s, they were running electric trams, though with an underground conduit at that time which proved very difficult because of the inrush of sea and sand; and then they went over to the overhead wire. One historian has suggested that the turning-point of Blackpool's whole success was the introduction of the Sunday tram in 1896. This however was not regarded with favour by everyone. One clergyman wrote: 'Compared to Blackpool, Paris is sweet and Sodom was paradise.' However, the trams continued to run on Sunday, and to give a great deal of innocent pleasure. Blackpool does not mind being out of fashion if it is successful, and the tram is obviously the most agreeable and attractive way in which to travel along the promenade. The whole essence of the tramway system of Blackpool was to preserve the Golden Mile, as it was called, so that it would always be easy of access. This means that the trams always move quickly, that there is no problem with congestion – and for that matter no complaints from the motorists about the difficulty with the tramlines.

One of the worst things that ever happened in Great Britain

was the wilful destruction of the great tramway systems – except in enlightened Blackpool which gives you not only trams, but open-decked trams at that. Apart from the pleasurable ride, you get, free, the wonderful seaside air. And along the route there are entertaining views of the visitors enjoying themselves on Blackpool's unrivalled beaches. You can travel in style *and* comfort all the way to the tram terminus just up the coast at Fleetwood.

Fleetwood itself, however, is a monument of grandeur un-achieved. More than any other Lancashire coastal resort it was the creation of a single man – Sir Peter Hesketh Fleetwood, the local lord of the manor, who gave everything to Fleetwood, including its name. Before his time, there were only a few fishermen's huts. He conceived an ambition that Fleetwood should become, as it was called, 'the gateway to the North'. In those days, just after the railways had begun, it was supposed that it would never be possible to get locomotives over Shap Fell, and therefore Sir Peter Hesketh Fleetwood conceived the idea that trains should come up to Fleetwood. The passengers would disembark and be entertained at the elegant North Euston Hotel.

There they would be refreshed (before making the sea journey to Scotland) in that sumptuous creation of the great architect Decimus Burton. The North Euston Hotel was built by private enterprise and it is still privately owned. That perhaps has ensured its survival, and indeed restoration. It had the great good fortune not to fall into the hands of British Rail.

British Rail usually hate architecture. You have only to consider what happened to Euston Station in London. 'The gateway to the North' itself – the arch at Euston – was wilfully destroyed for a traffic plan which never materialized, so that its site is empty to this day. British Rail actually refused to allow the stones of the arch to be numbered, so they could never be put up again. In Fleetwood, they have destroyed the 'North Euston Station'. But they have allowed the North Euston Hotel to survive, and this makes Fleetwood a great curiosity. But its period of ambition did not last for very long. The high-water mark, the climax of it, was the time when Queen Victoria and Prince Albert came on their return journey from Scotland. They landed and, after being richly entertained, proceeded on to London. But soon after this came disaster. It was discovered that it was possible after all for trains to cross the heights of Shap Fell, and Fleetwood lost its key position in the railway system of the country.

In Blackpool itself, another restoration – the Victorian Grand Theatre – awaits its second grand opening. In 1894 there was a great event in Blackpool – the Grand Theatre opened with Wilson Barrett in *Hamlet*. He said that more tears were shed on that day than on any other day in the history of the theatre, not only of this theatre but of any theatre. The Grand Theatre represents a high-water mark of Victorian theatre building – it whispers the last enchantments of the high renaissance.

In September 1939 two events of some significance happened. One was the outbreak of what is sometimes called the Second World War, though I do not date it from September 1939 any more. The other was a wonderful opening at the Grand Theatre of *The Importance of Being Earnest* with John Gielgud, Edith Evans and Margaret Rutherford. Of the two, I think that the second is probably more significant. In the Second World War again, the theatre became the refuge from London of all the actors and plays: all the London theatres were closing. It had a wonderful record – particularly, of course, because Blackpool was full of soldiers, and particularly airmen, who provided magnificent audiences. After the Second World War, it fell on evil days. It was closed; it was threatened with destruction; and, when restored, it was used as a bingo hall. But now there is wonderful news about the Grand Theatre. The theatre is likely to be rescued from its present activities as a bingo hall. In the spring it is going to reopen as what it was in the earlier part of the twentieth century – a theatre of the first rank. It is wonderful for once to be able to tell a story which has a happy ending.

If you were asked what are the unusual things, the specialities of Blackpool, you would draw up a long list in answer. On serious reflection, I think the most remarkable things in Blackpool are the illuminations – remarkable because they are the speciality of Blackpool and because they carry what we call tourism to its highest point. The illuminations technically started just before the First World War. But it was not until the middle of the 1920s that they really began, and then their first year was interrupted: after the General Strike, they were accused of wasting coal – the kind of thing that people say nowadays when they want to suppress any joyous activity. But the illuminations came into their own after the end of the General Strike. They were sensational during the 1930s, and resumed again in the 1950s; and they are now infinitely more elaborate than they have ever been. Their purpose is simply to win people to Blackpool. They are a wonderful bargain. I am told that this year, 1980, they will cost the corporation £800,000. For this relatively modest sum, the illuminations will attract eight million people, who between them will spend fifty million pounds within the environs of Blackpool.

And there is a new feature this year which is very delightful: enormously inflated saucy postcards. Not *very* saucy, medium saucy. They would not have attracted the attention of the magistrates, even in the days when they used to send the purveyors of saucy postcards to prison. But they are saucy all right. They show nice fat ladies and somewhat rapacious thin men. And I still recognize some of the jokes which appealed to me during my youth.

When one looks at Blackpool and reflects upon its enormous activity, some of it in a way very inartistic – though not the piers, the piers are a beautiful creation of fantasy – it becomes quite clear that the entire population is concerned to make money out of the visitors. It puts me in mind of Dr Johnson's remark: 'No man is more innocently employed than when making money.'

Across the Morecambe Sands

Morecambe began as a little fishing village called Poulton-le-Sands which still remains embedded in Morecambe, as a little fishing village. Poulton-le-Sands, or Morecambe has made at least two distinctive contributions to our life. One was the first fishing cooperative. The fish used to go bad before it reached the Manchester market and, as long ago as 1919, the Morecambe cooperative was founded. It still continues as Morecambe Trawlers Ltd which sounds impressive but in fact comprises only ten families. The other thing Morecambe invented, one might say, made one of the great contributions to modern British civilization – potted shrimps. I have always been addicted to this most agreeable Morecambe export.

Morecambe is the most recently born of the Lancashire coastal resorts and the one most deliberately created by a railway company. The story of Morecambe is fascinating as part of the conflict between two great companies: the Midland Railway – which, as the name implies, covered the rather unsatisfactory middle area of England – and the London North Western, at one time the biggest railway in the world, which covered the entire west coast. There was nowhere, it seemed, where the Midland Railway could break into LNW territory, but north of Lancaster there was a great gap so that deliberately, in the 1860s, the Midland created a major through line from Bradford to Morecambe.

It was a very easy journey, and for the first time Yorkshire holidaymakers could reach a sea coast which had, in summer, a reasonably warm sea. Scarborough is a very attractive resort but the sea there is cold all the year round. The Irish Sea is warmer. So important was this that the Midland Railway ran the daily Residential Line, a special service for businessmen, locally known as the 'Rezzie'. It is alleged that the train contained a barber's shop, so that any businessman who had overslept could have a shave or his hair cut on the way to Bradford. Morecambe should never have taken the place of

Poulton-le-Sands; instead it should have become Bradford-on-Sea.

The Lancashire coastal towns do not have much to show in the way of distinguished modern architecture. The exception came in 1933 with the opening of the Midland Hotel in Morecambe which was regarded at the time as one of the great architectural achievements of the decade. The situation of the hotel is still striking. The architect, Oliver Hill, had a gift for making his buildings follow the lie of the land, and here the hotel follows the curve of the bay. Today, however, the Midland Hotel is, I think, not so much a monument to modern architecture as to the dislike of modern architecture and modern art which has been a characteristic of the 1970s. During the war the hotel was pressed into service as an RAF hospital. The mosaic floors were judged to be too impractical, so they were covered up and the hotel's fittings were dispersed. A highly valued relief by Eric Gill was more recently removed and was the outstanding feature of the Thirties Exhibition in London not long ago. Nearly everything that made this hotel distinguished in the 1930s has been either altered or destroyed or so diminished as not to count any more.

The early Irish missionaries who built St Patrick's Chapel on the cliffs at Heysham Head knew the meaning of danger. And now there is danger to be found at Heysham once again. This is a nuclear power station designed for peaceful purposes. There is a great deal of controversy about it, and I find it difficult to make up my mind. With regard to nuclear weapons, I never had the slightest doubt. I recognized at the very beginning that not only were they indescribably wicked, but they were indescribably dangerous and vastly increased the threat to the security of our island and our future. So I had no hesitation in taking part in the Campaign for Nuclear Disarmament between 1958 and 1962. Nobody took any notice of us, and the campaign ran down. I am glad to see it is starting again, and unless it succeeds, the dangers to this island will increase. But nuclear power for peaceful purposes – for the provision of electricity for the home and for industry – is a different matter. Nuclear power stations certainly provide a substitute for coal and oil-powered stations. But, on the other hand, there are potential dangers too. A mistake at a conventional station does little damage, except in the immediate neighbourhood. On the other hand, a miscalculation at a place like Heysham could lead to the poisoning of the atmosphere, with casualties on an enormous scale.

North of Morecambe there begin the sands. There used to be a regular road across the sands, which reduced the distance quite by half – to about twenty miles instead of thirty-five to forty. In the Middle Ages it was already being developed, and the Prior of Cartmel had the formal right to nominate the official chief sand pilot, who worked out the tracks across the endlessly changing, dangerous estuary. By the eighteenth century regular coaches ran across the sands. Wordsworth described crossing the sands in order to go on to Hawkshead. The great risk for coaches was being blown over. But most of the casualties were over-confident people, like half-drunken farmers, who thought they knew the way across the sands, but could easily misjudge the tides.

With the coming of the railways, however, the journey across the sands became just an occasional adventure. But the importance of the sands, of course, is that it divided the northern part of Lancashire – it was called Lancashire North of the Sands – from the rest. And yet Lancashire North of the Sands had an unmistakably Lancashire character. Nobody who knows this area can possibly doubt that Cartmel, Furness, Hawkshead are Lancashire places. It is terrible to think that now, again, because of a bureaucratic whim, Lancashire North of the Sands, Lancashire for 800 years, has been deprived of this distinction of being part of Lancashire, and has been amalgamated with a shapeless Cumbria.

Preston Revisited

The Ribble, although it comes all the way down from north Lancashire, is very much Preston's river. Preston is obviously not a seaside resort, but I think it holds the whole of the Lancashire coast together – from Southport, which is on one side of the estuary of the Ribble, up to Blackpool and Fleetwood, which are on the other side, and stretching further up into north Lancashire. Preston, after all, is the only significant town and the centre of communications.

In 1648, the Scottish Army, which was then in alliance with the Royalist forces against the Parliamentarians, decided to march down the west coast. They got as far as Preston and stopped the night there. Cromwell was over in Yorkshire, and the conventional thing for him to have done would have been to go south and block their further advance. Instead he daringly decided to come up behind them, and he harried them down all the way from Preston to Wigan. It was a decisive event. It led to the breach between the army and Charles I, and to his execution the following year. In 1715, another Jacobite army came down from Scotland in the name of the Old Pretender, James Edward, and got as far as Preston. They were expecting English Jacobites to join them, and virtually none did. That was the last large-scale engagement on English soil.

Preston is as significant in my mind for Lancashire cheeses as it is for the cotton mills. But the cotton mills mean a lot to me too. My father owned a cotton mill here – a very small one called Oxhey. Both my father's and my mother's families lived in Preston. They thought of themselves very much as Prestonians. I did not so much, because I was not born here. I was thirteen when I came to live in Preston and I only lived here until I was twenty. But still I have an association with it. And I have an association particularly with the historic side of Preston. Preston is one of the new towns in Lancashire which has a really long history and has counted over the centuries.

It was in Preston, for example, that Richard Arkwright developed the water frame for spinning which was the first step towards the mechanized cotton industry as it was developed later in the eighteenth century. He had trouble with the citizens, who were rather sceptical about his inventions and indeed accused him even of witchcraft. But one can say that from here began not only the cotton trade, but also the factory system. Arkwright's house is the oldest in Preston. After his departure, it became first the Arkwright Arms, then a temperance home. Finally it was threatened with complete dilapidation, but it is now being restored, and will become a lasting symbol of the connection between Richard Arkwright and the town.

In the eighteenth and early nineteenth centuries, Preston was the social centre of Lancashire. Many of the Catholic squires, who had been Jacobites and owned the hinterland of the coast, had their legal advisers here. Much of the dealing that led to the development of Southport, Lytham, Blackpool and Fleetwood must have been done in Winckley Square, the social centre of the town.

For over a century the leading Tories in Preston were the Stanleys, the Earls of Derby, who were the outstanding Protestant nobility of the eighteenth century. The centre of Conservative influence – their symbol was the fighting cock – was the Bull and Royal Hotel. There is a painting showing the Tory candidate in the 1862 election celebrating his victory. There is an interesting little point about this.

Though 1862 was thirty years after the great Reform Act of 1832, the electorate was considerably smaller in 1862 than it had been then. In those days, under a system unique to Preston, the vote went to what was called 'the inhabitants at large'. In other words, anyone who lived in a little house, cottage, room, anything, before the election, had the vote. And the population had risen in the early nineteenth century nearly to 10,000. At any rate, the Stanley candidate was not feeling cheerful in December 1830, when he appeared here, because the usual principle was that one member of parliament was run by the Stanleys, the house of Derby, and the other member was run by the Corporation. This saved vast expense. In one area, I believe, a man spent £11,000 for the purpose of buying votes. The sensational thing about this by-election of December 1830 was that Orator Hunt, the hero – or victim – of Peterloo eleven

years before, was the radical candidate. He had tried previously
and been defeated, but this time to general excitement he got
in. He won over 3,000 votes. Every single one of the Preston
electors who had voted for Orator Hunt got a medal. It is not
very striking or significant, but among those who got the medal
was my own great-grandfather, John Thompson, who
endangered his trading position by voting radical. And the
election of Orator Hunt contributed a great deal to the passing
of the great Reform Bill.

In the eighteenth century, Preston was indisputably the social
centre of Lancashire. Liverpool was dominated by its merchant
class. Manchester had hardly got moving at all. But Preston was
already a considerable place of considerable culture. At the Bull
and Royal Hotel, the great balls must have taken place. But it
cannot all have been really elegant, because out of a window
the Earl of Derby could look down at the fighting in the cock
pit and could no doubt shout his bets to the bookies. In the year
of Orator Hunt's victory over the Stanleys, the last cock pit was
closed. The Stanleys, for so long the dominant influence in
Preston life, began to withdraw from the town.

Preston has been for centuries also a great market town. In
my younger days, the distinguishing feature was the cheese
market – where whole rows of great Lancashire cheeses were
exposed for sale. You walked down the rows, carrying a sixpence
– that now forgotten coin – and with the sixpence you dug out
bits of the cheeses and tasted them until you found the one that
you really liked. For many years I used to patronize Livesey
and Toulmin's magnificent cheese shop. It has now, I think,
disappeared. But the name of one earlier Livesey still lives in
Preston records. Joseph Livesey was a cheese-factor in the 1830s
– a man of enormous energy, wishing to raise the standard of
life, the amenities, for the working class. And it was he who,
along with six others, first took the pledge of total abstinence
from liquor. They became known as the Seven Men of Preston.
But the distinguishing feature of the Seven Men of Preston is
that they stood not only for temperance, but also for complete

abstinence. It is alleged that one of them, being afflicted with a stammer, when asked whether he was simply for temperance replied: 'No, I'm for t-total abstinence.' Hence the expression 'teetotal', although I fear that the story is a myth.

Preston has a charter which dates back more than 800 years. It has also an elaborate system of guilds which celebrate their existence, with much civic pomp, every twenty years. My great-uncle, Alderman William Thompson, who had a very long beard, walked in the guild processions of 1862. I myself, as a young man, attended the Preston Guilds of 1922, and so did my father. He, however, had a misfortune. As he went, in all his civic glory, to join the procession, he passed by the rows of spectators, who in those days used to come and watch in wagonettes or charabancs, which were the height of a double-decker bus. Just as he passed one of these enormous structures, a substantial lady fainted, and fell upon him. As a result, my father had to go to hospital, and miss most of the celebrations of the guilds.

But although these guilds were a symbol of class collaboration, of social unity, it would be a mistake to claim that Preston has always enjoyed social collaboration of that kind. The great strikes of 1853 added to our language three words much in use nowadays – 'blackleg', 'scab' and 'lockout'.

And then there was the General Strike of 1926, though that was by no means 'general'. I was personally affected. I was at Oxford at that time. Most of the undergraduates went off to do what was called 'national work', which in other words was strike-breaking. I was anxious to support the strike and went to the dean, the disciplinary officer of my college, and asked for leave. And he said, in a very grudging way: 'Other young men have gone down to do their duty, I suppose you can have leave to go down and do what you think is yours.'

So off I went to Preston. And when I came here, I felt very foolish. After all, the strike was complete. 'Everything stopped' was the slogan. All the trains were stopped, all the buses were stopped, all the trams were stopped, everything stopped. What could one do to help? The chaps did not need any help. The lads were perfectly capable of looking after a strike on their own. And I said to my father, in great embarrassment: 'What on earth have I come here for? There's nothing I can do.' So he laughed and he said: 'You're quite mistaken. You and I are the only two people in the Labour movement in Preston who can drive a car. I'm busy driving my car. You take the second car, go down to the strike committee, offer yourself as a chauffeur and you'll be driving a car hard for many days.' And sure enough I did, morning to night. I drove trade union secretaries, took round money, took round newspapers, all kinds of things. And it really is a striking contrast to realize that, at that time, the whole trade union movement functioned without using cars for, say, the ordinary administrative work of trade union officials. At the end of ten days I remember my father coming home, looking broken and ill and saying: 'The strike's over. We've been betrayed by our leaders.' Whether true or not, historians have debated ever since.

Preston has always been remarkable for the considerable element of Roman Catholics in its population. This is a relic of the Jacobite times, when the old religion and the old outlook stayed on in north Lancashire when it was sinking elsewhere. Then it was reinforced in the nineteenth century by Irish immigration. But whatever the reasons, Catholicism has played a considerable part in Preston's life, and it has contributed to one of the most remarkable parish churches of the whole area – and indeed of Lancashire. This is St Walburge's. The remarkable thing in the first place is that the architect, Joseph Aloysius Hansom, also invented the Hansom Cab. It has the third-highest spire in England – the highest is at Salisbury.

But Preston's fate has been a sad one. It was in the Middle Ages, even in the seventeenth century, one of the most distinguished and interesting of Lancashire's towns. It suffered some devastation during the Jacobite risings and the civil wars. But what really ruined Preston was its period of prosperity, which was brought to it by the cotton trade. You can see the mills which now, compared to the modern buildings, are of course works of great architectural distinction. But in the middle of the nineteenth century the burghers were so proud of their wealth that they destroyed their city, and substituted what appeared to be a characterless nineteenth-century town. But this was not the end. It was only the beginning. After the Second World War in particular, this nineteenth-century Victorian town had acquired a character. This has been absolutely destroyed. When I look at Preston now, it seems to me simply a combination of characterless towns, imposed by architects who had no idea how people should live. And, of course, it suffers from one-way traffic schemes, experiments of all kinds, which make it impossible to have any movement of civilization. Wherever I look, I can see cars – but not a single pedestrian. Now, when I survey the two haunts of my youth – Southport and Preston – I am astonished, full of admiration, for the way in which Southport has maintained its character, and horrified by the ruthless way in which Preston has destroyed what character remained to it.

Index